RESEARCH GUIDE TO ANDEAN HISTORY

RESEARCH GUIDE TO ANDEAN HISTORY
BOLIVIA, CHILE, ECUADOR, and PERU

Contributing Editors
Judith R. and Peter J. Bakewell: *Bolivia*
William F. Sater: *Chile*
Jaime E. Rodríguez O.: *Ecuador*
Leon G. Campbell: *Peru*

Coordinating Editor
John J. TePaske

Duke University Press
Durham, N.C.   1981

© 1981, Duke University Press
Printed in the United States of America

Library of Congress Cataloging in Publication Data
Main entry under title:

Research guide to Andean history.

　　Includes index.
　　1. Bolivia--History--Archival resources.
2. Chile--History--Archival resources. 3. Ecuador
--History--Archival resources. 4. Peru--History--
Archival resources. I. Bakewell, Judith R.
II. TePaske, John Jay.
Z1656.R47 [F3321]　　　980　　　80-29365
ISBN 0-8223-0450-3

To the Archivists and Librarians of
Bolivia, Ecuador, Chile, and Peru

Contents

Preface   xi

BOLIVIA

Preámbulo *Judith R. and Peter J. Bakewell*   2

The Archivo Histórico Municipal de Cochabamba *Brooke Larson*   5

El Archivo de la Universidad Mayor de San Andrés (Cota-Cota) *Alberto Crespo Rodas*   8

El Archivo del Ministerio de Relaciones Exteriores y Culto *Juan Siles Guevara*   15

El Archivo Mariscal Santa Cruz *Phillip Parkerson*   19

El Archivo Metropolitano de la Catedral y El Archivo de la Curia Arzobispal, Arquidiócesis de La Paz *María Eugenia de Siles*   21

Los Archivos de Oruro *Peter J. Bakewell*   28

El Archivo Histórico de Potosí *Mario Chacón Torres*   30

Los Archivos de Santa Cruz *Hernando Sanabria Fernández*   37

Los Archivos de Sucre *Judith R. and Peter J. Bakewell*   45

Los Archivos de Tarija *Peter J. and Judith R. Bakewell*   50

CHILE

Introduction *William F. Sater*   53

The Political History of Colonial Chile *Jacques A. Barbier*   59

Archives and Their Usage: Economic History in Colonial Chile *Marcello Carmagnani*   67

Archival Resources for Chilean Economic History, 1800-1850 *S. F. Edwards*   73

Sources for the Study of Chilean Political History, 1810-1850 *Patricio Estellé*   84

Chilean Economic Development, 1850-1900: A Primary Source Guide *Robert Oppenheimer*   88

Notarial and Judicial Archives as Sources for Nineteenth-Century Chilean Economic History *Thomas F. O'Brien, Jr.*   96

The Study of Chilean Political History, 1850-1925: An Introduction to Sources *Arturo Valenzuela*   98

Chilean Political History Since 1925 *Paul W. Drake*   108

Sources for the Study of Chilean Labor History *Brian Loveman* 118

Civil-Military Relations in Chile *Frederick M. Nunn* 128

ECUADOR

Introduction *Jaime E. Rodríguez O.* 136

Comments on the Historiography of Ecuador's Pre-Independence Period *Adám Szaszdi* 138

Research in the National Period *Jaime E. Rodríguez O.* 146

The Libraries and Archives of Quito *Linda A. Rodríguez* 151

The Archivo Nacional de Historia *Juan Freile-Granizo* 164

The Archivo Nacional de Relaciones Exteriores del Ecuador and the Biblioteca General del Ministerio de Relaciones Exteriores *Joedd Price* 170

The Military Archives of Ecuador *Luis A. Rodríguez S.* 172

The Archives and Libraries of Cuenca *Michael T. Hamerly* 175

The Archives and Libraries of Guayaquil *Julio Estrada-Ycaza* 182

The Provincial Archives and Libraries of Ecuador *Rosemary D. F. Bromley* 197

PERU

Introduction *Leon G. Campbell* 206

Resources for the Study of Colonial Peru *John R. Fisher* 212

Research on Peruvian History: Independence and the Early Republic (1780-1870) *Paul B. Ganster* 224

Research on Peruvian History: 1870-1930 *Jesús Chavarría* 235

Sources for the Study of Twentieth-Century Peruvian Social and Political History *Peter F. Klarén* 243

Research on the Modern Peruvian Military: A Selective Guide *Daniel M. Masterson* 253

Ethnohistory *John V. Murra* 256

Indian Historiography in Republican Peru *Thomas M. Davies, Jr.* 264

Sources for the Study of Peruvian Hacienda History *Susan Ramírez Horton* 273

The Notarial Archives: Facts Behind the Fad *Elinor C. Burkett* 284

El Archivo General de la Nación *Guillermo Durand Flórez* 300

El Archivo del Fuero Agrario *Vincent G. Peloso* 306

The Archives of Cuzco *Donald L. Gibbs* 308

Los Archivos de Trujillo *Hernán Horna* 313

The Archivo Arzobispal of Trujillo *Paul B. Ganster* 316

Resources for the Study of Arequipa *Fernando A. Ponce* 325

The Genealogical Society of Utah (Church of Latter-Day Saints): A
   Research Resource for Andean History *Paul B. Ganster*   330

The Principal Archives and Libraries of Peru: Useful Names and Addresses
   Tita Monzón de Davies   332

Index   335

Preface

In 1970 Andean history in the United States received new impetus from the formation of the Andean Studies Committee, a regional sub-group of the Conference on Latin American History (CLAH). Created to encourage research and scholarly interchange among historians of Bolivia, Chile, Ecuador, and Peru, the Committee has convened annually since 1970 at the meetings of the American Historical Association to discuss current research, new and forthcoming dissertations in Andean history, and matters of common interest to Andeanists. This volume is a project growing out of the activities of that group.

This *Guide* has been in the making for eight years. Preliminary discussions early in 1973 resulted in the appointment of the coordinating and contributing editors of this volume: John J. TePaske as coordinating editor and Judith R. and Peter J. Bakewell, William F. Sater, Jaime Rodríguez O., and Leon G. Campbell as contributing editors for Bolivia, Chile, Ecuador, and Peru respectively. Personally acquainted with the archives and the principal authorities on both the repositories and history of their respective countries, the five contributing editors became responsible for organizing and soliciting contributions for the four sections of the *Guide*. Their choice depended in part upon their ability to persuade or cajole those with archival, methodological, or historiographical expertise to contribute, in part upon the research needs and facilities of each country, and in part upon the development of the historical discipline within each nation. Most of the essays in this volume were written in the mid-1970s, but, as might be expected of an anthology of over fifty articles, some were completed more promptly than others. Then, once the manuscript was finally assembled, editing and publishing delays occurred. Thus, some articles may not be as current as either the editors or the contributors would like. Names of archival directors, archival locations, telephone numbers, and other such detailed information may have changed. Archives may have acquired new documents; additional guides, calendars, and catalogues may have been developed; and fundamental new monographs may have appeared. These may not always be incorporated into the essays in this volume. Still, the editors have made every effort to bring the *Guide* up-to-date and believe strongly that it constitutes a lasting contribution to Andean history and Andean historiography.

Each contributing editor was responsible for developing his own framework and organization. In their individual introductions to each section the editors discuss the rationale for this organization, the contents of their section, and also both the gaps and the lacunae which did *not* get proper attention. These observations need not be repeated here. For the working historian, the practical value of the *Guide* will be immediately obvious: the descriptions of archival organization and archival holdings, a great many described in detail for the first time; listings of fresh topics for innovative research; practical suggestions for getting the most from one's research time in the field; names, addresses, and telephone numbers of archives, archivists, and local bibliophiles; and reviews of special topics in Bolivian, Chilean, Ecuadorian, and Peruvian historiography. But because this volume is a working *Guide* of a practical, utilitarian sort and because most specialists using it will have a specific national or research focus, they may well miss articles more general in scope of importance to *all* Andeanists. Every Latin American historian, for example, should read Elinor Burkett's article on the notarial archives of Arequipa. This is the best, most detailed description anywhere of the types of materials to be found in notarial archives, the possible approaches to these documents, and the pitfalls to be encountered in their use. The essays by Marcello Carmagnani on Chilean colonial economic history and Susan Ramírez-Horton on Peruvian hacienda history also deserve mention because their methodologies and approaches can be applied to other Andean and Latin American situations. The same is true of Rosemary Bromley's piece on the provincial and local archives of Ecuador. Although of practical value in its own right, her description of the vicissitudes and rewards awaiting the indefatigable bibliophile--in the best and worst conditions--is again applicable virtually anywhere in Hispanic America. Lastly, no reader should deny himself the pleasure of reading Hernando Sanabria Fernández's essay on the ruination

of documents in the Bolivian jungle at the hands of climate, bugs, and
people. The tactile quality of his narrative, its ironic twists, and
sense of timing make his article on the repositories of Santa Cruz as
significant for its grace, style, and humor as for its contribution to
our knowledge of Bolivian archives.

The five contributing editors have made special acknowledgements in the
individual introductions to each section; so have many of the contributors.
Still, deep appreciation should once again be expressed to those archivists, historians, and bibliophiles who made this volume possible. Contributions came from three continents and seven countries, demonstrating
that there can be a true community of scholars which transcends national
boundaries. A tribute should also be paid to those archivists and historians, living and dead, on whose work these essays were based. To
Duke University Press, with its long-standing commitment to publication
of works in Latin American history, we express our gratitude. More
particularly, we wish to thank John Menapace whose technical expertise
and aesthetic eye helped at every stage in the publication process. Most
of all, the editors are deeply indebted to Dorothy Sapp, who labored
unstintingly in the preparation of this volume, a monumental and painstaking task. Finally the editors hope that the *Guide* will prove useful
to the historian in the field--both novice and experienced--and that it
will stimulate groundbreaking new research on the history of Bolivia,
Chile, Ecuador, and Peru. The essays in this book make it abundantly
clear that there is a great deal to be done.

                                                    John J. TePaske
                                                    Duke University

BOLIVIA

Preámbulo
Judith R. and Peter J. Bakewell

Sin tener la menor intención de menospreciar los informes que los amigos y colegas bolivianos han contribuído a este capítulo, reconocemos que la descripción de los archivos de Bolivia aquí presentada no es sino una primera visión de la riqueza documental que ofrece este país al investigador--visión que habrá que amplificar y completar. Ha sido nuestro propósito indicar lo que podría encontrarse en los repositorios bolivianos: la tarea de presentar un inventario completo del contenido de cada archivo ha quedado fuera de nuestro alcance. Hemos visitado la mayoría de los archivos mencionados aquí, pero con fines específicos de investigación. Ya habíamos salido de Bolivia cuando se nos encargó la compilación de este capítulo. No nos ha sido posible regresar desde Europa para completar el trabajo en la forma detallada que se podría desear. Nos damos cuenta, sobre todo, de la escasez de referencias a colecciones privadas en las páginas que siguen. No se debe creer que no existan. Igualmente, habrá más documentación de los siglos XIX y XX de la que aparece aquí.

Hemos adoptado un sencillo ordenamiento geográfico: los archivos, ciudad por ciudad. El estado de avance de la historiografía de Bolivia no permite un enfoque sintético--por ejemplo, "fuentes para la historia social." El contenido--la existencia siquiera--de los archivos no se conoce suficientemente.

Los archivos de Bolivia han tenido muchos enemigos--en el oriente, el clima y los insectos tropicales; en todas partes, la inestabilidad política y la indiferencia oficial. Si todavía quedan buenos y copiosos archivos en las regiones históricamente más significativas del país--los valles altos y el altiplano--ello se debe a dos causas: a un ambiente seco y frío; y más aun, a los esfuerzos de un reducido número de estudiosos, dedicados a la conservación del patrimonio histórico de su país. Tales son los que han aportado los informes que comprende este capítulo.

En la lista falta un nombre célebre, el de Armando Alba. Con su fallecimiento lamentado a fines de 1974 perdió Bolivia una gran figura de su cultura moderna, y la Casa Nacional de la Moneda en Potosí, su administrador y, en efecto, el creador de su museo y de su archivo actual. En Mario Chacón Torres tiene don Armando un sucesor hábil y más que digno.

Hay buenas posibilidades de que el presente capítulo pronto esté superado como guía de los archivos bolivianos. Ya en 1971 existía el proyecto, ideado por el Dr. Gunnar Mendoza L., Director del Archivo y Biblioteca Nacional en Sucre, de realizar una encuesta sobre los fondos archivísticos del país. Se enviaron cuestionarios a todas partes--a los archivos y museos ya establecidos, a las instituciones del gobierno, a las instituciones privadas, a toda clase de institución eclesiástica. Un alto percentaje de los cuestionarios fueron devueltos al Dr. Mendoza, quien los pone a la disposición de los investigadores serios. Los datos que continene son de calidad variable--pero son datos que antes se ignoraban absolutamente. Los resultados de esta encuesta habían de presentarse en un congreso sobre archivos bolivianos proyectado para octubre de 1971. Por razones políticas no se verificó el congreso. Sin embargo, es de esperarse que el Dr. Mendoza siga con el proyecto y que dentro de pocos años los investigadores puedan contar con el inventario promenorizado de una larga serie de archivos.

En Bolivia visitamos muchos archivos que administran autoridades universitarias o municipales. En un solo caso se nos negó la entrada por razones burocráticas. Sin embargo, aconsejamos a los investigadores extranjeros que anuncien de antemano su llegada a cualquier archivo, escribiendo a la autoridad pertinente con varias semanas de anticipación. Harían bien los investigadores, igualmente, de llevar consigo cartas generales de presentación de su institución de origen, o de conseguir tales cartas de sus representantes diplomáticos y culturales en La Paz. Jamás sobran referencias de esta clase.

Deseamos reconocer nuestra deuda a la obra pionera del Padre Lino Gómez Canedo, *Los archivos de la historia de América*, 2 vols. (México, D.F.: Instituto Panamericano de Geografía e Historia, 1961).

ALGUNAS DIRECCIONES UTILES

ARCHIVOS DE LA PAZ

D. Juan Siles Guevara
Director de Documentación
Archivo del Ministerio de RR EE y Culto
Casilla 3887
La Paz

Dr. Alberto Crespo Rodas
Casilla 517
La Paz

ARCHIVOS DE COCHABAMBA

D. Adolfo de Morales
Lista de Correos
Cochabamba

ARCHIVOS DE SANTA CRUZ

Dr. Hernando Sanabria Fernández
Biblioteca Central
Universidad 'Gabriel René Moreno'
Casilla 702
Santa Cruz

ARCHIVOS DE POTOSI

D. Mario Chacón Torres
Director del Archivo
Casa Nacional de la Moneda
Casilla 39
Potosí

ARCHIVOS DE SUCRE

Dr. Gunnar Mendoza L.
Director
Archivo y Biblioteca Nacional de Bolivia
Casilla 338
Sucre

The Archivo Histórico Municipal de Cochabamba
Brooke Larson

In a time when local social and economic history is increasingly studied, provincial archives in the Andean countries are being newly explored and indeed discovered. One such archive only recently opened to the public is the Archivo Histórico Municipal de Cochabamba (AHMC). Although Padre Lino Gómez Canedo listed it among Bolivian archives, *Los archivos*, 1:506-507, it has remained inaccessible for over the past decade. When the Archive was finally opened in 1974, no one knew its holdings. The documents are still uncatalogued, and most have yet to be seen by researchers. But that should not inhibit the historian. Wading through over 100 *legajos*, I found fascinating material. A brief overview of the sources I discovered will hopefully encourage future historical research not only in the AHMC but in similar provincial archives as well.

The Archive is housed in the Palacio de la Cultura in Cochabamba. The *legajos* are stored in locked bookshelves in an office which is officially the municipal archive, but which actually has been taken over by the city planning commission. The *sala de investigadores* is tentatively on the fifth floor of the Palacio. Permission to use the Archive is gained from the Director de Extensión Cultural in the same building. The director is a political appointee and may change at any moment, but (s)he is the key person who controls access to the Archive. As in most provincial archives, the researcher should allow a margin of time for the sometimes arduous task of gaining entry. Once permission has been granted to use the documents, the problem becomes one of finding the relevant material. There is still no trained archivist in the AHMC, and locating the necessary sources is a question of patient exploration rather than formal request.

There are two types of sources in the AHMC: local litigation and notarial books. The *pleitos* are unbound documents, sometimes petitions, often *expedientes*, bundled together in no chronological or thematic order.

The date of the manuscript which happens to be lying on top is noted on the outside of the *legajo*, along with the *legajo's* number. Thus, by requesting a *legajo* number which is dated, say, 1750, one finds only the first manuscript to be of that year, and the underlying documents may range over three or four centuries. It is often the case, however, that many manuscripts of the same century as the first are bundled together. The notarial books, on the other hand, are bound and much easier to locate. They are listed according to the notary and their year(s). Although they are not shelved chronologically, they can be quickly located from the Archive's inventory.

The holdings of the AHMC are extensive. There are approximately 600 *legajos* and notary books, spanning a period from about 1550 until the end of the nineteenth century. The documents concerning Cochabamba's foundation (which is a touchy subject, as local opinion continues to debate whether 1571 or 1574 was the official date) are inaccessible thus far, but loose manuscripts from the sixteenth century abound.[1] Most sixteenth-and early seventeenth-century documents I saw pertained to Mizque, which was a separate *corregimiento* from Oropesa (the early Spanish colonial name for Cochabamba). If the Archive is organized some day, these manuscripts should probably compose a separate manuscript collection to supplement the large Mizque collection for the late colonial period housed in the Archivo Nacional in Sucre.[2] The great majority of litigation and notarial books, however, date from the eighteenth and nineteenth centuries.

Although local publicity has recently underlined the importance of the municipal archive, it still stands on sandy ground. A new mayor, for example, could spell disaster for all the attempts to keep the Archive operating. There is an effort underway, however, to have a trained

---

1. The minutes of the Cabildo of Cochabamba are not found in the AHMC. If these are still extant, they should repose in the Alcaldía Municipal. Also to be found in the Palacio de la Cultura is a collection of printed books from the seventeenth and eighteenth centuries, numbering close to 1,000 volumes.

2. The Mizque documents could constitute a third section of the AHMC. In all, they consist of 590 volumes and *legajos*: forty-one from the sixteenth century, 120 from the seventeenth, 173 from the eighteenth, and 256 from the nineteenth. This material is neither organized nor catalogued.

historian appointed as the Archive's director and the AHMC, itself, transferred to the local university, where its fate would not depend upon political maneuverings. Until that is accomplished, the researcher must arm him/herself with a half-dozen appropriate letters and, above all, perseverance. The effort, though, is well worth it. Only through painstaking research in the local archives of Andean America will the historian begin to explore all the avenues to social and economic history which have been opened by the myriad of data found in litigation and notarial sources.

---

3. Cochabamba possesses ecclesiastical archives, but the documents of the Convento de Santa Clara have been lost in a fire. It is believed that the archive of the Franciscans contains useful historical materials, but at present it is not open to the public. The Dominican archive, accessible to researchers, also houses manuscripts of historical interest. For further information on the archives of Cochabamba, see Juan Siles Guevara, "Dos archivos históricos bolivianos poco conocidos: Oruro y Cochabamba," *Anuario de estudios americanos* 26 (1969):35-39 and Adolfo de Morales, "El Archivo Histórico de Cochabamba," *Presencia*, La Paz, December 1, 1974. Señor Morales also has an excellent knowledge of the kinds of materials housed in the AHMC. (PJB)

El Archivo de la Universidad Mayor de San Andrés (Cota-Cota)
Alberto Crespo Rodas

Aunque todavía está lejano el día en muchos países en que no se oigan historias aleccionadoras sobre la suerte de papeles del pasado con interés histórico, vale la pena referir brevemente las circunstancias en que se creó el Archivo de la Universidad Mayor de San Andrés (Cota-Cota), diferente del de la Biblioteca Central.

En 1971, por un azar, el autor de esta nota, se enteró de que la Corte Superior del Distrito Judicial de La Paz, se proponía vender su archivo a una fábrica de cartones, habiéndose llegado a convenir el precio por kilogramo de papel. Trasmitida la información a las autoridades de la Universidad, se detuvo la realización del tal propósito y se consiguió el traspaso de esa documentación, cuyo papel más antiguo es el Registro de Escrituras Notariales de La Paz, de 1593.[1] Firmado un convenio entre la Universidad y la Corte, se amplió el traspaso de todo el archivo hasta el año de 1900. Ese hecho colocó a la Universidad ante la responsabilidad de crear un archivo, destinándose para ese objeto un local provisional que posee en la región de Cota Cota, a aproximadamente 12 kilómetros de la ciudad, a donde fueron trasladados los fondos cedidos.

Lo ocurrido sugirió a las autoridades de la Universidad obtener del estado la cesión de los archivos de las entidades de gobierno, y para eso se tramitó un decreto supremo que autorizaba a tales entidades traspasar a la Universidad sus archivos. Se trataba en realidad de una empresa de emergencia que había que realizarla de immediato para salvar de la destrucción la documentación oficial, que en ninguna de las oficinas se hallaba adecuadamente preservada. El decreto fué dictado en junio de

---

1. Mr. E. William Jowdy informa que en esta colección de escrituras notariales figuran registros de 1585 en adelante; siguiendo la serie, aunque con lagunas, hasta fines de la época colonial. Los últimos años del siglo XVI así como las primeras décadas del siglo XVII se encuentran bien representados en esta serie. (PJB)

1971. Establece la entrega con treinta años de retroactividad con las excepciones de los Ministerios de Relaciones Exteriores, Interior, y Defensa Nacional.

Posteriormente, se retiraron los archivos del Ministerio de Finanzas, de la Prefectura del Departamento de La Paz, Notarías Públicas y parte de la Corporación Boliviana de Fomento.

MINISTERIO DE HACIENDA

El Archivo del Ministerio de Hacienda (de Finanzas, según una denominación posterior y que prevalece en la actualidad), traspasado en 1971, está integrado por libros (empastados) de comprobantes pagados en su gran mayoría, correspondencia, cuentas personales, de militares y civiles, poderes. Llegan a la cantidad de 3,600 libros, que comprenden los años 1931 a 1963.

PREFECTURA DEL DEPARTAMENTO

Documentos incorporados al Archivo de la Universidad en 1972 y compuesto por los siguientes libros:

Registro de libros de tierras comunarias, 36 libros, 1881-1889.
Libros de minutas de tierras comunarias, 12 libros, 1881-1899.
Registro de minutas con el estado, 11 libros, 1881-1899.
Registro de contratos con el estado, 16 libros, 1881-1899.
Registro de escrituras, 12 libros, 1844-1870.
Padrones de naturales y revisitas de diferentes provincias del departamento de La Paz en la época republicana, 51 libros.
Libros manual, diario, mayor, auxiliar, de recibos y comprobantes desde 1825 a 1897.
Libros de oficios de 1879 a 1899.
Libros de "Documentos" de 1825 a 1861.
Manuscritos sueltos, en su mayor parte de tierras de comunidades y de tierras de 1600 a 1900, en 240 cajas.

TRIBUNALES

Compuesta por expedientes de juicios civiles y criminales de los juzgados y la corte de distrito de La Paz de 1600 a 1951, total, 1,800 cajas.

NOTARIAS

Diferentes notarías de la ciudad, 64 libros, 1851-1900.

ARCHIVO EN LA BIBLIOTECA CENTRAL DE LA UNIVERSIDAD

José Rosendo Gutiérrez, un hombre que dividió su tiempo y sus actividades entre la política y los trabajos históricos y bibliográficos, durante la segunda mitad del siglo pasado, además de una rica biblioteca

personal que abarca toda la producción boliviana hasta el año de su
muerte, se ocupó de reunir una documentación manuscrita y original de
excepcional valor. Ambos repositorios hoy se hallan en la Biblioteca
Central de la Universidad Mayor de San Andrés de La Paz.

El mencionado Archivo se halla registrado, pieza por pieza, bajo el
nombre de "Catálogo cronológico de documentos manuscritos," hecho en
dos copias a máquina y empastado. Consta de 2,342 piezas, aunque es
casi seguro que Gutiérrez tuvo a su disposición una cantidad mayor de
documentos. Consignado en el "Catálogo" es el "Primer libro de actas
capitulares del Cabildo de la ciudad de La Paz, desde 1548 a 1562
(el libro original existe en el Museo Británico de Londres). Copia por
José Rosendo Gutiérrez, 73 fs., La Paz, 1873."

Para atenerse a la división tradicional *Colonia-República*, la primera
época abarca 197 documentos y la segunda el resto.

Colonia

Aunque, según parecería, los documentos no han sido elegidos por
Gutiérrez al azar, no se descubre en ellos series orgánicas o siste-
máticas. Existen, de distintas épocas, y tomando en cuenta el mayor
número de los documentos, papeles sobre "Remates de especies pagados como
tributos," "Cuentas de las cajas reales de La Paz," "Cuentas de repartimientos," varios libros copiadores de "Reales cédulas y provisiones,"
"Libros de padrones" especialmente de la provincia de Pacajes (Guaqui,
Tiwanaku).[2]

Una buena parte de los documentos correspondientes a esta época
(89 a 155) se relacionan casi en su totalidad con las sublevaciones
indígenas dirigidas en 1780 y 1781 en el Cuzco y en La Paz, respectiva-
mente, por los caudillos Túpac Amaru II y Túpac Catari. El primero de
ellos es el "Diario de la sublevación de 1780, escrita por orden del
comandante general don Sebastián de Segurola, desde el primer cero puesto
por el insurgente caudillo Julián (Túpac) Catari, sacristán de Calamarca,
a quien lo tenían por rey todos los alzados. Copia en papel corriente
35 fs." Están también los diarios o informes escritos sobre el cerco de

---

2. Según Mr. Jowdy, los más antiguos de los manuscritos a que se hace
referencia en este párrafo remontan a mediados del siglo XVI. Hay remates
de tributos, por ejemplo, de 1558; y cuentas de la real caja de La Paz de
1583. Las series son en general esporádicas. (PJB)

La Paz por Sebastián de Segurola, comandante militar de la ciudad, el coronel José Reseguín, Francisco Tadeo Diez de Medina, Matías Borda. Hay también una buena cantidad de papeles que permiten apreciar las consecuencias que para el tesoro de la ciudad tuvo el levantamiento: recibos de víveres, sueldos para la tropa, gastos para la defensa, donativos hechos por los habitantes. Los documentos con relación a ese suceso llegan, cuando menos, hasta 1785.

Gutiérrez puso también particular interés en reunir documentación referente a la revolución producida en la ciudad de La Paz en el año de 1809 y otros sucesos de los que la ciudad fue posteriormente escenario en la lucha contra el poder español. En realidad, en esta parte, la documentación es más de tipo político que económico; proporcionalmente, el número de libros de cajas reales decrece.

República

Desde el punto de vista de un interés que sale del marco de la historia boliviana, la documentación más nutrida corresponde a la administración del presidente Antonio José de Sucre (1825-1828) y la del general Andrés de Santa Cruz (1829-1838). Aproximadamente la administración Sucre está representada por unos 220 documentos y la de Santa Cruz por 130.

Es imposible dar en los límites de esta nota una información esclarecedora sobre estos documentos, porque se trata de material muy disperso, que van desde una foja hasta un expediente, o el copiador de correspondencia de muchas páginas con comunicaciones tanto de tipo privado como oficial, aunque prevalecen en número estas últimas.

Aunque es difícil tener una idea de la manera cómo José Rosendo Gutiérrez halló tiempo para un trabajo tan arduo, existen en el Archivo dejado por él, varias copias de "manuscritos para la historia nacional 1670-1882," bajo cuyo título los agrupó. Se trata de copias a mano en cuadernos hechas personalmente por Gutiérrez, de acuerdo a una obvia semejanza grafológica. Va desde el Discurso sobre la mita de Potosí, por Vitorián de Villaba, o extractos de la Crónica de San Antonio de los Charcas, de Mendoza, o documentos relativos al establecimiento de Fuente Borbón en la margen derecha del río Paraguay (1792), en 71 fs., o los "Versos de autor incógnito que circulaban manuscritos en La Paz, durante la revolución de 1809." En todo caso, una descripción viable de estos manuscritos es prácticamente imposible.

Fuera del catálogo ya mencionado de la Biblioteca Central de la Universidad Mayor de San Andrés, en el mes de abril de 1974, se hallaron, confundidos con el material de depósito de esta Biblioteca, una cantidad de manuscritos, dispuesto sin ningún orden y cuyo contenido se ignoraba hasta entonces.

Una vez que se procedió a la ordenación de dichos manuscritos que representaban unos 12 metros lineales, se vió que se trataba en su mayor parte de registros de escrituras de la ciudad de La Paz, entre los años 1652 y 1802, pero con muchos años intermedios de los que no existía ningún papel. Tambien se encontraron papeles sueltos, de los siglos XVII y XVIII, referentes a la Orden de los Jesuitas, hacienda, algunos padrones, y tabacos.

Actualmente, estos papeles se hallan preliminarmente ordenados en forma cronológica y colocados en cajas de cartón y continúan en la Biblioteca Central, accesibles al público, aunque no figuran todavía en ninguna lista o índice.

Tanto el Archivo Histórico (Cota-Cota) como la documentación de la Biblioteca Central se hallan en cómodo acceso al público. El horario de atención en Cota Cota es de 10.00 a 17.00 horas ininterrumpidamente. El de la Biblioteca Central de hrs. 9:00 a 12:00 y de 14:00 a 21:00.

MUSEO "CASA DE MURILLO"

En el Museo "Casa de Murillo" (Calle Jaén 790) y que lleva ese nombre por Pedro Domingo Murillo, el principal dirigente de la revolución producida en la ciudad de La Paz contra el sistema español el 16 de julio de 1809, se encuentra una parte de los registros de escribanos de La Paz compuestos por 38 libros. El más antiguo data de 1598 y el más reciente de 1718. Al siglo XVI corresponde un volumen; al siglo XVII, 15 libros; y los restantes al siglo XVIII.

Este archivo es de libre acceso al público.

El Museo, instalado en todo el edificio de la época de la colonia, contiene varias salas con muebles de ese período y una interesante colección de cuadros de ese mismo lapso. Además conserva una colección muy rica de 87 libros impresos de los siglos mencionados. La mayor parte son de carácter religioso.

UN CUADRO GENERAL DE OTROS ARCHIVOS

La situación de los archivos públicos de Bolivia debe ser considerada bajo un antecedente histórico. Hasta 1900 la sede del gobierno nacional era la ciudad de Sucre, capital de la República, y por lo tanto era allí donde se centralizaban los archivos. A partir de ese año, el gobierno se trasladó a la ciudad de La Paz; naturalmente, desde entonces, la documentación central se fue produciendo en La Paz y casi nunca fue enviada para su conservación al Archivo Nacional de Sucre.

El Archivo Histórico a cargo de la Universidad de La Paz fue creado por una coyuntura que se explica líneas arriba, ante la inminencia de la destrucción de valiosas series documentales. Ese hecho no significa un desconocimiento de las atribuciones del Archivo Nacional de Sucre, y la Universidad de La Paz es consciente de esa circunstancia. Cabe expresar en forma muy clara que la Universidad de La Paz procurará crear las condiciones de carácter económico que permitan el traslado de la documentación--de tipo nacional--que hoy tiene en custodia, el Archivo Nacional de Sucre.

Mientras tanto, las autoridades de la Universidad han comprobado que el Archivo del Ministerio de Educación solamente conserva la documentación de unos ocho años atrás. Funcionarios del Ministerio explicaron ese vacío diciendo que los papeles "habían desaparecido durante un disturbio político," pero no dieron mayores precisiones.

El Archivo del Ministerio de Salud Pública comprende únicamente los últimos años, habiendo desaparecido el resto en una asonada política, realmente ocurrida en 1964.

El Archivo de la Corporación Minera de Bolivia (COMIBOL) integrado en gran parte por la documentación de las empresas mineras privadas que fueron nacionalizadas en 1952, se halla en un depósito o galpón en El Alto de La Paz, en condiciones muy precarias de conservación.

INFORMES SUPLEMENTARIOS

Los siguientes datos sueltos pueden interesar a los investigadores. La Biblioteca Municipal 'Mariscal Andrés Santa Cruz,' de La Paz, conserva una colección de periódicos bolivianos. En la United States Records Office, Suitland, Maryland, EUA, se guardan en gran parte los materiales provenientes de la Agencia Estadounidense para el Desarrollo Internacional (U.S. Agency for International Development) de La Paz. La mayoría de estos documentos serán destruidos dentro de 25 años, por no ser clasificados como papeles del Departamento de Estado. El Profesor James Wilkie, Universidad de California, Los Angeles, EUA, subraya la importancia de este material en una carta al compilador de este capítulo de 22 de abril de 1974.

El Profesor Wilkie informa igualmente que posee transcripciones de conversaciones que han mantenido él y su esposa, la Sra. Edna Monzón de Wilkie, con varias personas de relieve en la vida boliviana, sobre el tema de la historia nacional después de la Guerra del Chaco. Las personas de que se trata son: Augusto Cuadros Sánchez, Joaquín Espada, José Felman Velarde, Walter Guevara Arce, Enrique Hertzog, Edwin y Lydia Möller, Hugo Roberts Barragán, Carlos Serrate Reich, David Toro, Víctor Paz Estenssoro. Comprende la entrevista con éste unas 900 páginas, y se espera que se publicará dentro de algunos años. (PJB)

El Archivo del Ministerio de Relaciones Exteriores y Culto
Juan Siles Guevara

El Archivo del Ministerio de Relaciones Exteriores y Culto es el repositorio documental más importante que mantiene el estado en la ciudad de La Paz. Es casi tan antiguo como el funcionamiento del Ministerio de Relaciones Exteriores y Culto como organismo independiente, pues fue creado en 1886 contando, inicialmente, con un solo funcionario.

En la actualidad alberga unos 9,000 volúmenes de documentación, que encierran alrededor de un millón de documentos y unos 5,000,000 de páginas. La documentación conservada abarca documentos desde 1525 hasta 1973. 162 volúmenes corresponden a la documentación del siglo XIX, y los restantes a documentación del siglo XX. El total de la documentación abarca 590 metros lineales de estantería.

El Archivo está organizado en siete secciones: I. Documentos Diplomáticos. II. Documentos Consulares. III. Documentos de Relaciones de la Cancillería con Otras Entidades. IV. Documentos Administrativos Internos. V. Documentos Históricos y de Límites. VI. Telegramas y Cables. VII. Mapoteca.

Para dar una idea de la riqueza de la documentación conservada en el Archivo de Relaciones Exteriores, haremos una descripción algo más detallada del material de sus siete secciones.

La sección Documentos Diplomáticos comprende ocho subsecciones: 1) Correspondencia recibida y enviada por las legaciones y embajadas de Bolivia; 2) Correspondencia de las legaciones y embajadas extranjeras en Bolivia; 3) Instrucciones; 4) Cartas autógrafas; 5) Documentación interna de las misiones bolivianas; 6) Tratados y convenios; 7) Documentación de organismos internacionales; 8) Documentación de misiones especiales. La sección tiene papeles desde 1826 y es la más voluminosa de todo el Archivo, comprendiendo 4,197 volúmenes de documentación correspondientes a las legaciones y embajadas de Bolivia en las siguientes capitales americanas: Buenos Aires (1847-1973), Río de Janeiro (1834-1973), Santiago de Chile

(1830-1962), Bogotá (1920-1973), La Habana (1943-1962), San José (1960-1962), Guatemala (1952-1973), Santo Domingo (1964-1965), Tegucigalpa (1963-1964), San Salvador (1963-1964), Quito (1843-1973), Washington (1867-1973), México (1929-1973), Asunción (1879-1973), Panamá (1959-1967), Lima (1830-1973), Montevideo (1881-1973), Caracas (1895-1973). Además conserva la documentación referente a los siguientes países europeos: Alemania (1910-1973), Bélgica (1913-1952), Checoslovaquia (1936-1963), España (1846-1973), Francia (1865-1973), Gran Bretaña (1897-1973), Hungría (1970-1973), Santa Sede (1897-1973), Suiza (1928-1973), Yugoslavia (1961-1973); y en los siguientes países afroasiáticos: China (1948-1973), Egipto (1961-1967), India (1963-1964), Israel (1965-1973), y Japón (1918-1973).

La documentación de las legaciones y embajadas extranjeras en Bolivia arranca desde 1826 y, en líneas generales, corresponde a los mismos países apuntados anteriormente. En cuanto a la subsección "Instrucciones," ellas arrancan desde 1899 y las "Cartas Autógrafas" desde 1826. La documentación directa recibida de cancillerías extranjeras data desde 1829, y la documentación referente a "Misiones Especiales" a partir de 1864. La documentación interna de las misiones diplomáticas bolivianas en el exterior, lamentablemente, es bastante incompleta, y tiene numerosas lagunas y comprende solo a algunos países. En el caso de la Argentina es continua desde 1879 a 1946; la del Brasil es continua desde 1908 a 1945; de Chile de 1885 a 1955; en el caso de Ecuador, con lagunas, de 1894 a 1940; la de los Estados Unidos, con lagunas de 1900-1931 y de 1956-1964; la de Paraguay, muy incompleta, sólo se conserva la de 1907 y 1921; la del Perú es continua de 1868 a 1960; la del Uruguay de 1879 a 1942;y, finalmente, la de Inglaterra de 1897 a 1936. Por su parte, la documentación referente a tratados, bilaterales y multilaterales firmados por Bolivia, data desde 1847, y la de organismos internacionales (Liga de las Naciones, Naciones Unidas, OEA) desde 1920.

La documentación consular comprende los papeles de: 1) Consulados de Bolivia en el exterior; 2) Consulados extranjeros en Bolivia; 3) Documentación interna de los consulados de Bolivia. Tal documentación está compuesta por 1,222 volúmenes y arranca desde 1830 la correspondencia recibida, y desde 1842 la expedida. Inicialmente Bolivia no alcanzaba a contar con lo consulados en el exterior. El número de consulados a ido en aumento constantemente hasta alcanzar en la actualidad a 192, de todos los cuales el Archivo conserva papeles.

Los Documentos de las Relaciones de la Cancillería con Otras Entidades Oficiales y Privadas alcanzan a 1,797 volúmenes, arrancando desde 1857 la correspondencia recibida, y desde 1865 la expedida. En esta sección se conservan los documentos de relaciones entre la cancillería y el poder ejecutivo (presidencia de la república, ministerios, prefecturas, delegaciones nacionales, etc.). Asimismo, documentación de las relaciones con otros poderes (poder legislativo, poder judicial, contraloría, ejército, e iglesia), finalmente de las relaciones de la cancillería con otras instituciones y particulares (bancos, municipalidades, universidades, y varios).

Por su parte la Documentación Administrativa Interna de la Cancillería comprende 99 volúmenes y arranca desde 1890. Esta documentación está compuesta por: 1) Decretos y resoluciones; 2) Informes y proyectos; 3) Ordenes de pago; 4) Solicitudes y órdenes de servicio; 5) Circulares informativas; 6) Nombramientos; 7) Inventarios; 8) Pasaportes; 9) Documentación de protocolo.

Otra sección de importancia es la de Documentos Históricos y de Límites, que se ha ido acumulando desde fines del siglo pasado, en base a lo conseguido por las misiones bolivianas enviadas a archivos europeos y americanos en busca de documentos probatorios de los derechos de Bolivia a los territorios disputados con sus vecinos. De este modo, se ha logrado reunir una rica cantera de copias de documentos que arrancan desde las expediciones de Pizarro y Almagro al Mar del Sur (1525). Una de las series más interesantes de la sección está compuesta por el cedulario de la Audiencia de Charcas (1563-1745), y otra, por documentos referentes a los Chiriguanos, a las misiones de Ocopa, Maynas, Apolobamba, Guamanga. También es interesante la documentación referente a las antiguas gobernaciones de Santa Cruz, Mojos, y Chiquitos, y al distrito de la Audiencia de Charcas. La documentación reunida en copias de esta sección proviene, fundamentalmente, del Archivo de Indias de Sevilla, del Archivo de Simancas, del Archivo del Vaticano, del Archivo Nacional de Sucre, del Nacional Argentino, y del Nacional del Perú. De modo tal que cualquier punto de los antecedentes sobre los derechos territoriales de Bolivia a sus antiguos territorios, tiene algún apoyo documental en esta sección del Archivo que comprende, también, toda la documentación de trabajos de campo referentes a comisiones de límites en sus 676 volúmenes.

La sección Telegramas y Cables comprende 1,146 volúmenes y arranca desde 1882. Finalmente, la Mapoteca comprende unos 2,000 mapas referentes, fundamentalmente, a las zonas limítrofes de Bolivia, mapas que arrancan desde el siglo XVI.

A partir de 1971 el Archivo del Ministerio de Relaciones Exteriores es una sección del Departamento de Documentación de la Cancillería y Cuenta, además del Director del Departamento, con un Jefe de Archivo, un oficial, y un conserje. Todo su material, de más de 25 años de antigüedad, está a disposición de la consulta de investigadores y estudiosos, para los cuales se cuenta con una sala de consultas, a índices más detallados de sus existencias documentales, que son básicas para cualquier estudio serio que se emprenda sobre la historia diplomática o internacional de Bolivia.

El Archivo Mariscal Santa Cruz
Phillip Parkerson

Posiblemente el más importante archivo privado en Bolivia es el Archivo Mariscal Santa Cruz, que se encuentra en la ciudad de La Paz. Esta colección de los papeles personales de Andrés Santa Cruz Calahumana, presidente de Bolivia y creador de la Confederación Perú-Boliviana, pertenece a la familia Santa Cruz. Ahora esta en posesión del Ing. Andrés de Santa Cruz García, biznieto del Mariscal, que reside en La Paz. Dos miembros de la familia son responsables de la recolección y preservación de estos valiosos documentos. Oscar de Santa Cruz comenzó el trabajo de reunir los papeles de su padre, tarea que continuó el Ingeniero Andrés de Santa Cruz Schuhkrafft, que es el responsable de tan excelente organización del Archivo.

El Archivo Mariscal Santa Cruz, que contiene más de 8,000 documentos, representando una medida lineal de cerca de 1.80 metros, consiste principalmente de cartas dirigidas al President Santa Cruz, pero hay un número considerable de cartas escritas por el mismo. El resto, algunos originales, mientras la mayoría son copias o borradores. El Archivo también contiene muchos originales de documentos oficiales y añadido a todo esto una pequeña pero rica colección de periódicos. También hay una bastante grande colección de libros que en su mayoría contienen trabajos sobre Santa Cruz y su período.

La colección de manuscritos cubre los primeros sesenta años del siglo XIX. Sin embargo, la gran mayoría del material pertenece al período de 1829-1839, años en los que Santa Cruz sirvió como Presidente de Bolivia y Supremo Protector de la Confederación. Entre esas cartas, uno encuentra correspondencia con los que eran las más importantes figuras de la historia de Sud América a principios del período de la independencia. Por esto, es fácil ver que mientras que el Archivo es especialmente importante para la historia del Perú y Bolivia, tiene también algún valor para la historia del resto del continente, particularmente Argentina, Chile, y Ecuador.

El Archivo está organizado de modo que es muy fácil usar el material. Esta dividido en dos partes--cartas de Santa Cruz y cartas a él. Ambas secciones estan arregladas cronológicamente y luego alfabéticamente. Andrés de Santa Cruz Schuhkrafft ha preparado unos excelentes índices cronológicos y onomásticos que hace que uno localice un específico documento con un mínimo de esfuerzo y tiempo.

El Archivo Mariscal Santa Cruz es un archivo privado y, por eso, presenta muchas dificultades en términos de accesibilidad que son características de todas las colecciones privadas. Sin embargo, con un poco de diplomacia, persistencia, y paciencia un investigador puede conseguir acceso a este valioso material.

El Archivo Metropolitano de la Catedral y El Archivo de la Curia Arzobispal, Arquidiócesis de La Paz
María Eugenia de Siles

Las regiones de Charcas fueron atendidas religiosamente en las primeras décadas de la colonización española por el Obispado de La Plata, creado en 1552. Con el crecimiento de La Paz, ciudad fundada en 1548, se constituyó una vicaría con las parroquias de La Paz, Larecaja, Omasuyos, Pacajes, Sicasica, y Yungas. Al mismo tiempo se creaba otra en Puno, para la atención de Chucuito, quedando ambas vicarías bajo la jurisdicción del Obispado de Charcas con sede en la ciudad de La Plata.

En 1605, dada la excesiva extensión de este obispado, se crearon dos más, desembrándosele al primero regiones muy amplias; fueron éstos La Paz y Santa Cruz. Una cédula real de 1607 confirmó estas creaciones. En 1609, el Presidente de la Audiencia de Charcas fijó los límites del Obispado de La Paz, asignándole el mismo territorio de la gobernación, salvo algunas parroquias que se adjudicaron al Obispado de La Plata en el Alto Perú, y agregándole además parroquias del Bajo Perú, como fueron Paucarcolla, San Francisco de la Puna, Guancané, Vilque, Moho, Puno, Coata, Chucuito, Zepita, Juli, Pomata, y otras, que después de la independencia fueron agregadas al Perú por el Libertador Bolívar. El primer obispo en La Paz fué el religioso dominico Domingo Valderrama Centeno, criollo de Quito que ya había sido Arzobispo de Santo Domingo.

El Obispado de La Paz sólo ascendió en 1943 a la categoría de arzobispado, elevándose su catedral a la dignidad metropolitana. El primer arzobispo fué Abel Antezana.

El campo de la historia eclesiástica boliviana no ha sido incursionado con mucha profundidad, aún cuando se hayan escrito estudios fragmentarios sobre instituciones, personajes, o acontecimientos aislados. El canónigo Felipe López Menéndez, en un intento muy loable, ha elaborado dos trabajos, uno sobre la historia del Arzobispado de la Paz y otro sobre la historia eclesiástica de Bolivia, pero a pesar de ello, está por hacerse todavía una historia moderna, escrita a la luz del estudio minuscioso de la documentación existente y que siga las normas con que se realizan estas investigaciones actualmente.

En cuanto a la documentación eclesiástica del Arzobispado de La Paz, es evidente que se han perdido fondos importantísimos. Faltan los documentos de los primeros años del Obispado. Gran número de libros parroquiales fueron quemados y saqueados durante los levantamientos de 1780 y 81. Muchos documentos desaparecieron en la época de la independencia, destruidos por el deán Guillermo Zárate ante la aproximación de las fuerzas patriotas. Otros se perdieron, como lo señala López Menéndez, al trasladarse la sede episcopal paceña a Puno desde 1811 a 1815.

En cuanto a la documentación actualmente existente, se encuentran algunas piezas de este fondo en los archivos parroquiales y en los conventos de las diversas órdenes religiosas, pero las partes más importantes y las mejor cuidadas están en el Archivo Metropolitano de la Catedral y en el Archivo de la Curia Arzobispal, donde pueden encontrarse piezas de incalculable valor, no sólo para confeccionar una historia de la iglesia sino también para esclarecer la historia civil de importantes períodos, tanto coloniales como republicanos.

ARCHIVO METROPOLITANO DE LA CATEDRAL

Constituye este fondo un conjunto bastante cuidado. Los folios y documentos han sido ordenados cronológicamente y empastados, por lo que se conservan en buen estado y a salvo de la humedad y la polilla. Tal labor se debe al canónigo Teodosio Sáenz. Existe además un índice bastante detallado de los diversos libros, confeccionado por los canónigos Roberto Corrales y Felipe López Menéndez.

Dicho fondo está constituido básicamente por el Archivo Capitular, que consta de 213 libros catalogados y 11 sin catalogar. Los catalogados abarcan los años transcurridos entre 1613 y 1936. (En realidad, son 212, porque hay un error de inscripción en el número 200.) Los 11 sin catalogar llegan hasta 1959. De los 213, corresponden 146 a la época colonial, 20 al período de la independencia, y 46 al republicano. Entre los de la época colonial, 24 son del siglo XVII y 88 del siglo XVIII. El contenido de los diversos libros no varía mucho a lo largo de los siglos, tomando modalidades algo diferentes sólo con la expulsión de los jesuitas, las rebeliones de 1781, y, en la época republicana, en los momentos de la organización de la nación y de la toma de medidas secularizadoras por parte del estado. Por lo general la documentación se refiere a concursos de curatos, certificados de ordenaciones, pesquisas, edictos, visitas pastorales, juicios del Tribunal del Santo Oficio, juicios civiles y criminales, juicios de nulidad de matrimonios, cuestiones de indios mitayos y yanaconas, roles de canónigos, y descripciones de curatos de la diócesis.

Fuera del fondo capitular hay cuatro libros sobre la construcción de la catedral; 1 sobre fábrica de diversas iglesias; 1 sobre sentencias de matrimonios, y varios copiadores de cartas del siglo XX.

ARCHIVO DE LA CURIA ARZOBISPAL

Comprende este Archivo series más variadas que las de la catedral. Los documentos están también en buen estado, guardados en armarios cerrados y organizados en libros empastados o en paquetes. Los distintos rubros están organizados cronológicamente, pero su ordenación es más descuidada que la de la catedral, posiblemente porque fueron agregándose documentos traídos de diversas partes de la diócesis, cuando ya se habían empastado los anteriores. La clasificación y ordenación de este Archivo se debe al canónigo Teodosio Sáenz y sobretodo a la labor de Monseñor Exequiel Beltrán, que trabajó en él hasta su muerte, ocurrida en 1973.

En este Archivo encontramos las siguientes series:

Juzgado Episcopal

Comprende 124 libros catalogados cronológicamente y que contienen la labor desempeñada por cada obispo, sus visitas parroquiales y provinciales, y los juicios civiles y criminales que se producen durante el ejercicio de sus respectivos episcopados. Se inician en 1610, correspondiendo 13 libros al siglo XVII. En ellos está documentada la labor de 10 obispos; el primero es Domingo Valderrama y Centeno y el último Bernardo Carrasco de Saavedra. 39 libros corresponden al siglo XVIII; 11 de éstos pertenecen a la época de Francisco Gregorio de Campos y van desde 1765 a 1790. 62 libros pertenecen al siglo XIX, correspondiendo sobretodo a los obispados de Mariano Fernández de Córdoba--21 libros (1849-1868)--y de Juan de Dios Bosque--13 libros (1874-1890). Al siglo XX pertenecen 10 libros que llegan hasta 1923.

Pliegos Notables

Contiene esta serie 11 libros que van desde 1619 a 1960. Están ordenados cronológicamente, pero sin continuidad absoluta. El mayor número de ellos--6 libros--corresponden al siglo XIX. Los documentos del siglo XVII son escasos, siendo el más importante uno del Príncipe de Esquilache sobre composición y amparo de una hacienda en Coroico. Los documentos contenidos en esta sección son bulas, rescriptos, empadronamientos, anexiones de estancias, fundaciones, diezmos y veintenas, autos sobre conducta de sacerdotes, sobre administración de sacramentos, sobre inmunidad eclesiástica, encíclicas, cartas apostólicas, referencias a decretos republicanos, juicios civiles y criminales, herencias, expedientes de concursos, misiones pontificias, inventarios, peticiones al congreso por medidas tomadas sobre libertad religiosa.

Bienes Eclesiásticos

Esta serie está constituida por 6 paquetes que contienen documentos ordenados por jurisdicciones parroquiales, tanto de la ciudad de La Paz, como de toda la diócesis. Se refieren a bienes territoriales de haciendas, fundos, y sitios.

Documentos Rezagados

Comprende esta colección 21 paquetes que abarcan el mismo tipo de documentos mencionados en los otros rubros y que posiblemente fueron llegando al arzobispado con posterioridad a las primeras ordenaciones. Están organizados cronológicamente y comprenden papeles que van desde 1634 a 1969, correspondiendo el mayor número de 10 paquetes al siglo XIX, 2 al siglo XVIII, y 2 al siglo XVII.

Partidas Bautismales

Comprende 119 libros pertenecientes a las parroquias de Carabuco, Lambate, Santa Bárbara, Ambaná, Aygachi, Palca, Timusi, Escoma, San Andrés de Machaca, Jesús de Machaca, Cohoni, Italaque, Pucarani, Zongo, Mocomoco, Ayata, Chanca, Collana, Mecapaca, Challana, y parroquias sin detalle.

Tarabuco, Timusi, y Aygachi ostentan el mayor número de libros, 25 las dos primeras y 16 la última. Los más antiguos son los de San Andrés de Machaca, 1587 a 1708; Jesús de Machaca, iniciados en 1666, y Carabuco en 1695. Partidas del siglo XVIII existen además en las parroquias de Santa Bárbara, Ambaná, Palca, Cohoni, Pucarni, y Zongo. Las demás son sólo de los siglos XIX y XX.

Partidas de Matrimonio

Compuesta de 44 libros de las parroquias de Carabuco, Lambate, Santa Bárbara, Aygachi, Palca, Huarina, Andrés de Machaca, Cohoni, Chanca, Zongo, Mocomoco, Collana, Collocollo, Challana, Tiquina, Obrajes, y Mecapaca. Las partidas van desde 1600 a 1950. Las más antiguas son las de San Andrés de Machaca de 1600 a 1707. Partidas del siglo XVIII sólo existen en las parroquias de Carabuco, Lambate, Santa Bárbara, Palca, Huarina, Zongo, y Obrajes. Hay pocas del siglo XIX correspondiendo la mayor parte al siglo XX.

Partidas de Obitos

Componen la serie 37 libros de las parroquias de Carabuco, Lambate, Santa Bárbara, Ambaná, Aygachi, Timusi, Cohoni, Pucarani, Zongo, Chanca, Mecapaca, y Collana. Abarcan desde 1710 a 1939. Las más antiguas son del siglo XVIII y pertenecen a Carabuco, 1733; Santa Bárbara, 1783; Cohoni, 1787; Zongo, 1710. La mayor parte de los libros pertenecen a los siglos XIX y XX.

Copiadores de Oficios

Hay en esta serie 18 libros que abarcan los años de 1899 a 1920.

Copiadores de Autos

Son 3 libros que van desde 1877 a 1919.

Copiadores de Autos y Oficios

Integrada por 62 libros con documentos que van desde 1920 a 1960.

Vicarías y Parroquiados

En esta serie, que se inicia con a) 34 libros sobre vicarías y parroquiados, 1831 a 1902; existen además, b) 77 libros sobre registros oficiales de comunicaciones, dispensas, obras de templos, tesoro eclesiástico, cartas, delegaciones apostólicas, cabildo eclesiástico, seminarios conciliares, monasterios, oficios ministeriales, prefecturas y subprefecturas, expedientes litararios y de órdenes, cuadros estadísticos, asociaciones pías, municipios, corregimientos, y juzgados. Abarcan estos libros los años que van desde 1828 a 1912; y c) 118 libros sobre gobierno y vicaría de los obispos que gobernaron a la iglesia de La Paz entre 1912 y 1961.

Pliegos Matrimoniales

Incluye 68 libros que van desde los años 1861 a 1955 y 35 paquetes con documentos de 1710 a 1938.

Procesos de Nulidad de Matrimonios

Contiene 5 paquetes con documentos de 1675 a 1960.

Procesos de Divorcios

Con 10 paquetes que abarcan los años que van desde 1647 a 1926.

Fábrica de Iglesias

Comprende esta serie 24 paquetes con documentos referentes a las iglesias de Coripata, Aygachi, Achacachi, Palca, Challana, Copacabana, Viacha, Santiago de Huata, Cementerio, Cohoni, Chirca, Guaycho, Taraco, Zongo, Mecapaca, Escoma, Calacoto, Mocomoco, Ayata, Ancoraimes, Aucapata, Guaqui, Laja, Achocalla, Ocabaya, Chulumani, Copacabana, Jesús de Machaca, Chuma, Seminario, Catedral, Irupana, Lambate, Ambaná, San Andrés de Machaca, Tiahuanaco, Carabuco, y Yanacachi.

Fundación de Capellanías

20 paquetes componen esta serie, que abarca los años de 1647 a 1840.

Existe también en al Archivo del Arzobispado un conjunto de libros y paquetes, que no alcanzan a constituir series ni fondos. Son estos los siguientes:

- 1 paquete con registros de escrituras, minutas, e inventarios, 1675-1950.
- 4 libros con protocolos de escrituras notariales, 1811-1858.
- 1 paquete con testamentos, 1673-1756.
- 5 paquetes con expedientes de sagradas órdenes, 1600-1900.
- 1 paquete con inventarios de bienes de las parroquias de Zongo, Copacabana, Carabuco, Tiquina, y Mecapaca.
- 1 paquete con documentos de los obispos Armentia, Baldivia, y Babia.
- 1 paquete sobre el II Congreso Eucarístico Nacional de 1939.
- 1 paquete sobre el Congreso Mariano de 1948.
- 1 paquete con colección de conferencias morales y cruzada pro indio.
- 8 libros sobre visitas pastorales, circulares a las parroquias, exploración y consentimiento de noviciados, providencias, autos y sentencias de notarías, exámenes de curatos, 1835-1908.
- 1 libro copiador de cartas, 1899-1915.
- 1 libro de planillas de pagos, 1911-1913.
- 1 paquete de documentos rezagados de diferentes obispos, 1926-1969.
- 1 paquete de partidas y pruebas supletorias, 1906-1935.

Todos los documentos arriba descritos corresponden a fondos relacionados con la historia eclesiástica de La Paz. Sin embargo, existen otros expedientes completamente ajenos a este ramo cuya procedencia se ignora. Esos documentos fueron ordenados y catalogados por un equipo de estudiantes de historia de la Facultad de Humanidades de la Universidad Mayor de San Andrés.

Se trata de un conjunto de 777 expedientes de juicios civiles y criminales, escrituras de compra venta, autos, solicitudes, despachos, sumarios, testamentos, e inventarios. La mayor parte pertenece al siglo XIX (734 documentos), distribuyéndose el resto entre los siglos XVII y XVIII.[1]

---

1. Para ampliar este informe de la Sra María Eugenia de Siles sobre los archivos de la arquidiócesis de La Paz, se pueden citar tres archivos mencionados por el P. L. Gómez Canedo, *Los archivos,* 1:503-505. Son el archivo de la Recoleta Franciscana, el del Convento de San Francisco, y el del Monasterio de Concepcionistas.

El primero, según el P. L. Gómez Canedo, posee fondos provenientes principalmente del siglo XIX. Lo más valioso, todo de dicho siglo, serían varios libros manuscritos referentes a las misiones del Colegio de Moquegua en los territorios de La Paz y del Cuzco; relatos, diarios, y memorias de misioneros; y documentos relativos al santuario de Copacabana.

El archivo del Convento de San Francisco 'conserva sólo algunos libros y escrituras,' entre los que señala el P. L. Gómez Canedo un 'Libro de tomas de hábito y profesiones,' que abarca los años 1803-86. En la biblioteca del convento se conservan libros impresos, incluso textos de sermones del siglo XVII y dos tratados teológicos del mismo siglo.

El archivo del Monasterio de Concepcionistas posee un archivo pequeño, en que se guardan, entre otras cosas, varios manuscritos relativos a la fundación del monasterio, evento que ocurrió en 1670. (PJB)

Los Archivos de Oruro
Peter J. Bakewell

La ciudad de Oruro cuenta con fondos manuscritos de gran valor, que hasta el momento (1974) quedan casi sin utilizar. Los documentos se encuentran en distintos lugares, no existiendo, por desgracia, ningún local especial dedicado a su conservación. Los repositorios, y los materiales contenidos en ellos, son éstos:

BANCO CENTRAL DE BOLIVIA, SUCURSAL DE ORURO

Esta colección es bastante completa, con 7 tomos de libros del Cabildo de Oruro. La Profesora June Nash (The City College, City University of New York, Nueva York, EUA), en una carta dirigida al autor de esta nota, indica que en el Banco Central se preservan fuentes que remontan a la fundación de Oruro en 1607. Parecería que se refiere no sólo a los libros de Cabildo sino a otros manuscritos de índole económica.

BIBLIOTECA MUNICIPAL

Esta colección comprende restos del archivo de la real caja de Oruro con libros de 1611 en adelante, aunque la serie no es nada continua. Hay libros de cuentas de la caja hasta 1825--30 correspondientes al siglo XVII; 40 al siglo XVIII; y 50 al siglo XIX. Son, por ejemplo, libros reales del contador o del tesorero; libros manuales de cuentas; libros especiales y sueltos de ciertos ramos de la real hacienda (santa cruzada, media anata, quintos, azogues, alcabalas, etc.) Hay uno que otro libro de la real caja de la provincia de los Carangas incluso de la segunda mitad del siglo XVII.

CORTE DE JUSTICIA

Aquí se encuentra lo que es, con toda probabilidad, el fondo de manuscritos más importante para la historia colonial de Oruro--a saber, una serie de escrituras notariales que va desde 1607 hasta principios del siglo XIX. Esta serie comprende los protocolos de una sola escribanía; y es notablemente densa para los 20 primeros años de la existencia de

Oruro. Judith R. Bakewell y el autor, estando en Oruro a comienzos de 1973, colocaron en orden cronológico los legajos relativos al siglo XVII, faltándoles tiempo para completar esta ordenación. El archivo de la Corte de Justicia conserva también una serie de pleitos, que empieza en la colonia y llega al presente. La serie, menos la sección que se utiliza actualmente, está desordenada. El archivo carece de inventarios o catálogos.

---

1. La mayoría de los datos presentados aquí se han sacado del artículo del Sr. Juan Siles Guevara, "Dos archivos históricos bolivianos poco conocidos: Oruro y Cochabamba," *Anuario de estudios americanos,* 26 (1969):35-39. En él, el Sr. Siles alude a seis libros de cédulas reales, a '15 interesantes expedientes sobre la Guerra de la Independencia,' a documentación local referente a la Guerra del Pacífico, y a papeles de Donato Vázquez y Pantaleón Dalence--sin que se pueda saber del artículo en cuál de los repositorios orureños se encuentran estos fondos. Lo más probable es que están o en el Banco Central o en la Universidad de Oruro, ya que ésta, según el Sr. Siles, también posee manuscritos. Los datos facilitados en dicho artículo han sido complementados de otros recogidos por el autor y su esposa en 1973.

Aunque puedan alterarse las actitudes burocráticas, hasta el momento los fondos de Oruro han quedado asequibles a los investigadores. La Profesora Nash avisa que logró ver los manuscritos del Banco Nacional mediante gestiones que realizó en su favor el Dr. Josermo Murillo (Centro de Investigaciones Sociales, Universidad de Oruro). En la Corte de Justicia, hay que dirigirse al Presidente de la Corte. Para consultar los fondos manuscritos de la Biblioteca Municipal, parece prudente dirigirse no sólo a la dirección de la Biblioteca, sino también al Alcalde Municipal.

Varios abogados de la Corte de Justicia de Oruro informaron al autor en 1973 que existe en al pueblo de Poopó, Departamento de Oruro, un archivo judicial con expedientes del siglo XVI en adelante. No resultó posible averiguar esta noticia. Poopó se encuentra a unos 45 kms. al sur de Oruro en la carretera de Challapata y Potosí. No hay alojamiento en el pueblo, por lo cual habría que utilizar este archivo viajando desde Oruro. (PJB)

El Archivo Histórico de Potosí
Mario Chacón Torres

El Archivo Histórico de Potosí funciona en el edificio colonial de la Casa Real de la Moneda, ubicado en la esquina noroeste de la plaza "10 de Noviembre," que es la principal de la ciudad, donde también se halla instalado el Museo de Arte e Historia. La Casa, el Museo, y el Archivo están bajo la custodia legal de la Sociedad Geográfica y de Historia "Potosí."

La Casa de la Moneda conservaba en el local su archivo correspondiente, junto con los pertenecientes a los bancos, y sobre esos fondos a partir de 1941, fueron centralizándose allí otros archivos coloniales y republicanos, que existían en distintas instituciones citadinas, con lo que logró organizarse el Archivo Histórico, que resultó ser el central de Potosí, destinado a convertirse en departamental.

Es esencialmente de carácter administrativo y de extensión local, ya que la mayoría de los fondos provienen de reparticiones públicas que funcionaron en la ciudad; pero como administrativamente tuvieron jurisdicción regional más amplia, en varias secciones comprende al actual Departamento de Potosí, y en sus relaciones de correspondencia al resto del país, y aún más allá de las actuales fronteras de la república de Bolivia.

Cronológicamente, la documentación se remonta a la segunda mitad del siglo XVI (a partir de 1555), abarcando hasta la primera mitad del siglo XX (año 1950), es decir cuatro centurias, casi cómo la vida misma de la Villa Imperial de Potosí, que nació en el año 1545. La cantidad actual de los fondos del Archivo, hecha la medición, ha dado 317 metros lineales, de los cuales 172 pertenecen a la época colonial, y 145 a la republicana, que comenzó el año 1825.

Ocupa nueve salas intercomunicadas y debidamente adaptadas, con estantería y anaqueles de madera. Los legajos empastados en su época ocupan los estantes bajo vidrio, y los no empastados se hallan dentro de cajas especiales de cartón, llenando los anaqueles. Por lo general toda la documentación se encuentra en buen estado de conservación, debido a las condiciones climatológicas del medio, que es frío y seco, y al cuidado que se tuvo desde que ingresaron a la Casa de la Moneda.

La consulta es libre para todo investigador, durante los días hábiles (lunes a sábado, menos domingos y feriados) y en horario de oficina (9 a 12 y 14 a 17). El investigador dispone de una sala de estudio (separada de las del depósito), donde se encuentra el mueble fichero y el libro de registro de investigadores, quienes deben presentar sus documentos legales, para su identificación personal.

El Archivo se halla clasificado mediante el sistema de fichaje, habiéndose adoptado, como no podía ser de otra manera, el *principio de procedencia,* que establece que "los documentos deben guardarse en unidades separadas, correspondientes a sus orígenes en entidades orgánicas," formando secciones, y dentro de éstas las series respectivas.

En el mueble fichero, las tarjetas se hallan ordenadas por secciones, y dentro de cada sección el orden es cronológico. Cada ficha contiene una breve descripción de la unidad documental correspondiente, con las fechas extremas y número de folios, llevando junto a las siglas el número que indica su orden toponímico. Otros ejemplares de fichas, se encuentran en las cajas que forman el catálogo cronológico general.

Para adelantar una idea sobre el material del Archivo, bastarán unas notas acerca de las principales secciones que lo integran, con indicación de los fondos que existen.

EL ARCHIVO HISTORICO DE POTOSI

CAJAS REALES (C.R.)

Que como institución hacendaria se remontaría a los orígenes mismos de la población, presenta 900 ítems o libros empastados en cuero (36 m.), los mismos que cronológicamente van desde el año 1555 hasta 1825. Las series que lo forman son al rededor de cuarenta. Citaremos como ejemplos: acuerdos y diligencias, alcabalas, censos de indios, contaduría general, correspondencia, donativos y empréstitos a la corona, padrones de mitayos, quintos reales, y visitas de repartimientos.[1]

---

1. Merece la pena señalar que en la sección de 'Cajas Reales' se encuentran fondos referentes no sólo a la misma ciudad de Potosí, sino también, como es lógico, a toda la jurisdicción de la Caja Real de Potosí.

ESCRITURAS NOTARIALES (E.N.)

Comprende 270 volúmenes (28 m.), las dos centenas corresponden a la época colonial, y lo demás a la republicana del siglo pasado. La fecha más antigua es 1572 y la última 1886. Como es bien sabido, estos libros contienen contratos de trabajo, de enseñanza, compraventas, donaciones, testamentos, poderes, etc. Para un tiempo de más de tres siglos, con períodos de esplendor económico en la antes populosa ciudad, la cantidad de registros es muy reducida, evidenciando una gran pérdida, antes de su centralización en la Casa de la Moneda.[2]

CABILDO, CORREGIMIENTO, E INTENDENCIA (C.C.I.)

Constituyeron el gobierno local de la época colonial, lamentablemente apenas ha subsistido la serie de expedientes de pleitos entre particulares, con algo más del millar de unidades (8 m.), entre los años 1620 y 1825. En el Archivo Nacional de Bolivia, se conservan 33 volúmenes, correspondientes a los años de 1585 a 1817, de los libros de acuerdos del Cabildo de Potosí.[3]

Por ende, aquí hay libros de alcabalas de Cochabamba (1655-92, 1667-77, 1686-89), La Plata (1656-70, 1663-1702, 1756-63), y Tarija (1659-64). Existen también libros de censos de indios (1698-1745, 1714-75, 1752-73, 1765), padrones de yanaconas (1580-98, 1600, 1711), libros de tasas y de tributos de indios (1555-73, 1557-60, 1575, 1575-91, 1575-97) [de Colquemarca] y (1592-1604) [de Chucuito]. El tomo C.R. 63 es el libro particular de cuentas de un mercader limeño (1597-1625), sumamente interesante para la historia del comercio en la ruta México-Potosí. (JRB)

2. Incorporados en esta serie se encuentran varios libros inesperados--por ejemplo, los de alcabalas (1774-7, 1779-1811); visitas de cárcel (1816-24); asuntos del hospital de la Vera Cruz (varios años); fragmentos de escrituras notariales de Achacachi (La Paz) (1588), en E.N. 13. Escrituras potosinas de años posteriores a 1886 se pueden encontrar en el Tesoro Público de la ciudad; y otras en los despachos de notarios actuales y en posesión de personas particulares. (JRB)

3. Los fondos descritos en este párrafo se trasladaron a la Casa de la Moneda desde el Ayuntamiento de Potosí. Antes de efectuarse la traslación, publicó don Armando Alba una descripción de los manuscritos "Indice general del Archivo Municipal," *Boletín de estadística municipal de la ciudad de Potosí,* 1-19 (Potosí, 1928-9). Por desgracia, mientras todavía quedaba en al Ayuntamiento, esta colección sufrió pérdidas, por lo cual su contenido actual no corresponde del todo con el indicado en el inventario de Alba. La ordenación presente se debe al Dr. Guillermo Ovando Sanz; y por esta razón en el Archivo se refiere a esta sección, como 'las cajas de Ovando.' El material contenido en estas cajas se refiere, entre otras cosas, a tierras, temporalidades, tabacos, inquisición, misiones, guerra, y pleitos criminales. Los manuscritos, muchos de gran valor

IGLESIAS Y CONVENTOS (I.C.)

Bajo esta sección quedan agrupados los pocos manuscritos eclesiásticos que lleçaron al Archivo, 50 libros (2 m.), comprendiendo los años 1614 a 1830, aparte de los expendientes respectivos. Los fondos proceden concretamente de los ex-conventos de San Agustín, Santo Domingo, y la Merced; del Recogimiento de Niñas Huérfanas; y de la Iglesia Mayor. Los libros son de gastos ordinarios, inventarios, misas, y lo correspondiente a cofradías establecidas en tales iglesias.[4]

CASA DE LA MONEDA (C.M.)

El establecimiento local data de 1573, año de la construcción de su primer edificio (el actual corresponde al siglo XVIII). La documentación subsistente de los años 1626 a 1900, aparte de los legajos sueltos, suma 1,400 libros encuadernados (30 m. de los cuales cuatro quintas partes corresponden a la colonia). Entre las series de esta sección tenemos: compras de oro y plata, fundición de barras, labranza de monedas, contaduría, provisiones, nombramientos de oficiales, etc.[5]

BANCO DE SAN CARLOS (B.S.C.)

El Real Banco de San Carlos, institución de rescate, proveedora de azogue, y habilitadora en metálico a mineros industriales, se remonta a

---

histórico, tratan sobre todo de la región geográfica Potosí-Tarija. Hay papeles sobre actividades de guerrilleros en la lucha por la independencia; y otros sobre misiones fronterizas. (JRB)

4. De interés sobresaliente en esta sección para la historia agrícola son las cuentas de la hacienda de Tomola (1745-76) y para la historia de las obras de caridad, el Libro de administración del Recogimiento de Niñas Huérfanas (1702-21). Dieciocho libros en esta sección corresponden al período anterior a 1700. (JRB)

5. Para el contenido de los 'legajos sueltos' del archivo de la misma Casa de la Moneda, hasta 1700, véase el inventario elaborado por Armando Alba, "Archivo de documentos de la Casa Real de Moneda. Indice analítico. Parte primera: siglo XVII," *Boletín de la Sociedad Geográfica y de Historia 'Potosí'* 39 (Potosí 1951): 156-9. (Al parecer, la misma guía se volvió a publicar dos veces: en Buenos Aires, 1944, bajo el título *Sociedad Geográfica y de Historia 'Potosí.' Indice analítico. Archivo de documentos de la Casa Real de Moneda, Potosí*; e igualmente en *Sur. Boletín oficial de la Sociedad Geográfica y de Historia 'Potosí'* (Potosí, diciembre de 1943):165-203. De especial interés en estos 'legajos sueltos' son muchos pleitos relativos a actividades de la Casa de la Moneda y de su personal. (PJB)

1752, creado por la Compañia o Gremio de Azogueros, fue incorporado a la corona en 1779. Unos 500 libros indican su fondo (10 m.), comprendiendo el período de 1745 a 1825. Algunas de sus series son: auxilios a los azogueros, compra de metales, contaduría general, y expendio de azogue.

RAMO DE TEMPORALIDADES (R.T.)

Despues de la expulsión de los miembros de la Compañía de Jesús, ordenada por el rey en 1767, para la administración de los bienes temporales o materiales que le pertenecían, se formaron las Juntas de Temporalidades. Unos 300 ítems alcanza esta sección entre los años 1767 y 1825. La serie de Contaduría General o "cargo y data" se halla en legajos empastados, y el resto lo forman expendientes sueltos, conteniendo interesantes testimonios para la historia de la orden en Potosí, inventarios y posterior destino que se dio a dichos bienes.[6]

ADMINISTRACION DE TABACOS (A.T.)

Dependiente de la Administración General de Tabacos de Buenos Aires, el estanco de Potosí funcionó desde 1780 hasta 1825, habiéndose desligado de la institución matriz en 1810, al producirse la revolución argentina. Algo más de 100 ítems forman sus fondos. Todos los libros son de la serie Cuentas Corrientes.

PREFECTURA DEL DEPARTAMENTO (P.D.)

Creada en 1825 como el más alto organismo del gobierno departamental, con jurisdicción sobre todas las provincias y cantones que integran el departamento, representa al poder ejecutivo de la nación. Es la más extensa sección del Archivo (113 m.), abarcando los años 1825 a 1950. Comprende: correspondencia oficial (recibida y expedida), resoluciones prefecturales, disposiciones de orden interno, y expedientes administrativos.

TESORO PUBLICO (T.P.)

Si cajas reales fue en la colonia la recolectora y administradora del tesoro del rey, en la época republicana, correspondió sucederle al tesoro público, en la atención de la hacienda estatal. 300 libros debidamente

---

6. Hay referencias en esta sección a los productos de colegios jesuíticas en Charcas, Tucumán, y Paraguay. Las cuentas de cargo y data traen en general poco detalle. (JRB)

empastados (10 m.) constituyen su material entre los años 1825 a 1913.

BANCO DE RESCATES (B.R.)

Directo continuador del colonial de San Carlos, sirvió a la minería nacional. Cuenta con 200 libros (4 m.), conteniendo los años de 1826 a 1887. En esta sección, obviamente, las series son las propias de un establecimiento bancario de aquel tiempo.

BANCO DE HABILITACIONES (B.H.)

Denominado tambien "Refaccionario," fue creado en la presidencia del Mariscal Santa Cruz, para habilitar a la pequeña minería, y tuvo escasa duración. Presenta solamente 34 libros (0,90 m.) entre los años 1833 y 1847.

Debido a esta clasificación sistemática, las secciones de miscelánea colonial y miscelánea republicana han quedado muy reducidas, comprendiendo ítems procedentes de distintas reparticiones públicas, que por lo escaso ya no llegan a formar secciones especiales. Es aquí, donde también se encuentran las unidades documentales de procedencia privada o particular, ofreciendo piezas de interés histórico, ejemplo, documentos personales.

Periódicamente se irá recogiendo en este Archivo, los de otras reparticiones públicas en funcionamiento actual: Alcaldía Municipal, Corte Superior de Justicia, Jefatura Distrital de Educación, etc. En cuanto a los archivos eclesiásticos (parroquiales y conventuales),[7] se formará

---

7. El contenido de los archivos eclesiásticos de Potosí no se conoce todavía con entera precisión. El de la catedral posee una buena colección de libros parroquiales, en que todas las series llegan a la actualidad. Para la época colonial, las series faltan de continuidad. El primer libro de bautismos empieza el 5 de septiembre de 1611 (en él figuran también algunas confirmaciones). La serie de matrimonios comienza en 1640; y la de enterramientos, en 1680. Pese a que esta parroquia era de españoles, los libros parroquiales se refieren frecuentemente a indios y a mestizos.

El archivo conventual de San Francisco ha sido objeto de una investigación realizada por don Mario Chacón Torres, quien posee un fichero en que se registran todos sus fondos. El tomo más antiguo es el Libro de la Cofradía de la Madre de Dios de la Limpia Concepción . . ., 1587-1608. Para el período 1600-1850, subsisten 40 libros manuscritos, de los cuales la tercia parte son del siglo XVII. Son en general libros de misas, de inventarios, de capellanías, de actas, de profesiones, y de cofradías. Para el historiador de la economía serán de interés especial los libros de síndicos y de gastos, donde se anotan los precios de abastecimientos comprados por el convento. El primer libro de síndico empieza en 1676.

el Archivo Diocesano, lo que no impide a la larga su unión al central
de la Casa de la Moneda, de cuya conservación y servicio funcional,
garantizan los numerosos investigadores llegados desde lejanos países,
a estudiar el pasado potosino, que es indiscutiblemente, parte fundamental de la historia económica hispanoamericana.

El convento de Santa Teresa es de clausura. Por lo tanto resulta difícil consultar los manuscritos que pueden conservarse en el, aunque, en efecto, se cree que la mayoría se han destruido. Don Mario Chacón, habiendo logrado ver alguna parte de este archivo, encontró material, sin ordenamiento, relativo a bienes del convento.

Las series de libros parroquiales conservados en la parroquia de la Concepción se remontan al siglo XVII, y existe el proyecto de pasar el archivo a la Casa de la Moneda. Otras parroquias de Potosí poseen series de libros parroquiales, aunque con poco material anterior a 1700. (JRB)

Los Archivos de Santa Cruz
Hernando Sanabria Fernández

En hablando de papeles viejos, conviene empezar con la advertencia de que acá en el Oriente Boliviano la guarda y conservación de los tales ha tenido y tiene aún dificultades que no se presentan en otras regiones del país. El temple tropical con sus calideces receptoras e incubadoras de vidas minúsculas, aparte de su acción resecante y macerante sobre las cosas de débil consistencia; la copiosa vegetación que hospeda aquellas vidas y les proporciona los sustentos primarios; la cargada humedad de la atmósfera, en cuyo ambiente se expanden y reproducen las mismas, como en un caldo de cultivo, y la más cargada aún de las lluvias torrenciales que se filtra entre los febles materiales de construcción y se estanca en los muros, hasta impregnarlos y remojarlos, son otros tantos jurados enemigos de todo papel de antigua data.

En cuanto a vidas minúsculas, téngase entendido que se refiere a los insectos destructores y devoradores de papeles. Tenemos acá la poca envidiable fortuna de poseer una nutrida y variada fauna de papirófagos. A título de curiosidad y no sin temor a entrar en minucias con sus puntas y ribetes de necedad, citamos entre aquellos a cuatro especies de las mas conocidas y dañinas. El voraz *turiro*, del género de los termes, taladra hojas, pliegos, y legajos, hasta perforarlos de principio a fin y dejar en ellos una suerte de grotescas caladuras. El *pescadillo*, un pequeño áptero de dorso plateado, arremete contra los hilos de las costuras, y cuando los ha destrozado, pica en los lugares adyacentes, concluyendo por dejar bordes dentados como los de una sierra de carpintero. El *joichi*, variedad de la polilla común, ataca los lomos y los cantos, practicando menudos agujeros que van hacia lo hondo, para dejar allí las larvas que se nutren en la reblandecida celulosa. La vulgar y repulsiva *cucaracha* gusta de las gumosidades y los residuos grasos de las superficies, que obtiene royendo con sus incansables patas en cepillo. Tratándose de volúmenes empastados en telas o provistos de telas protectoras, opera de tal modo que sólo deja allí la urdimbre o las hebras sueltas.

Con respecto a la humedad constante, de más está decir que el moho de las paredes y los rincones irrumpe en los papeles hasta cubrirlos, en veces, de una pelusa verdegueante. Al querer echarla, el mísero papel invadido se desintegra en pedazos.

Clima e insectos no son los únicos agentes de destrucción y pérdida. Como en todas partes del mundo, el elemento humano tiene su parte, y muy señalada, no tanto en el deterioro como en la desaparición virtual de los viejos papeles. El maestro Gabriel René Moreno, en sabroso y curioso artículo sobre achaques del tema, atribuía al *ancuco* la extinción de valiosos documentos en la capital de la república, hacia mediados del siglo pasado. En Santa Cruz, emporio de dulcerías, nada ha hecho el tal, porque no es artículo de confección regional, ni tampoco lo han hecho sus congéneres, todos los cuales, que son muchos y muy variados, no han menester papeles para la vaciadura o la sustentación. Otro ha sido el expediente consumidor, si bien menos melifluo, igual en lo concluyente, y más todavía si se quiere.

Hasta bien entrado el presente siglo, la prefectura del departamento era poseedora y usuaria de un cañoncito de bronce, cuya antigüedad, según aseveración de entendidos, dizque se remontaba a los tiempos de la guerra emancipadora. Dos veces al año la benemérita arma era sacada de los trasfondos prefecturales al centro de la plaza mayor: la una el 6 de agosto, aniversario de la independencia, y la otra el 24 de septiembre, día de la efemérides regional. El fin era valerse de ella para solemnizar ambos históricos acontecimientos con ruidosas y elocuentes descargas, que en el programa oficial de festejos apuntábase con la denominación, también oficial, de "salvas de artillería."

Por cierto que para la descarga había de contarse previamente con la carga, y ésta tenía que hacerse con pólvora y taco. Nada más fácil y económico que emplear como taco papeles y más papeles. Los había, felizmente, a montones, en las dependencias prefecturales, en la notaría de tierras, en la oficialía de registros, formando rimeros y tongadas que así eran de inútiles como servían de estorbo.

El cañoncito fue, pues, aliviando de superfluidades los recintos de la casa de gobierno. ¡Qué de viejos papelotes, muchos de ellos de los tiempos del rey, hubo de consumir aquella boca que antes escupió metralla para patriotas y realistas!

No menos consumo han hecho, mas no para reventazones de intención patriótica, sino para llevarlos consigo, bien envueltos y cuidados, los visitantes extranjeros. Como resultado de estas diligencias, papeles nuestros de antigua escritura yacen en el Museo Británico, la Biblioteca Nacional de París, el Museo de Goteborg, y hasta en la Biblioteca Imperial de Viena, aparte, naturalmente, de lo que guardan celosamente, coleccionistas, anticuarios, y estudiosos de Europa y Estados Unidos. De entre los adquirentes forasteros, justo es decirlo y particularmente con referencia a los primeros en venir a estas tierras, la mayor parte los recibieron como obsequio, las más de las veces espontáneo, de parte de curas y corregidores, en los pequeños pueblos, y de funcionarios de jerarquía, de prefecto para abajo, en la capital departamental. Tal fue la forma en que hizo valioso recojo el sabio D'Orbigny en los pueblos de Chiquitos. El mismo lo cuenta como la cosa mas natural del mundo. Más tarde hicieron lo propio el conde Castelnau, el médico italiano Benatti, el francés Saac y, ya en el presente siglo, el alemán Hertzog, los suecos Erland Nordenskjold y Styg Ryden, y otros de nombres menos conocidos. Entre los últimos hubo ya el proceso de la oferta y la demanda y su consecuencia el tomo y recibo en numerario. Un prójimo entre chileno y paraguayo, Raúl del Pozo Cano, visitante de Santa Cruz por los años veinte, obtuvo franco acceso al por entonces descuidado archivo de la diócesis y tuvo allí la suerte de que se le pegaran a la faltriquera tal o cual documento relativo a las discutidas tierras del Chaco.

Mención aparte merece el recojo hecho en pueblos de las antiguas misiones de Chiquitos por el eminente hombre de ciencia y políglota ruso Baldomero Eberlein. Este no fue simple visitante, sino avecindado en San Javier y Concepción de la actual provincia Ñuflo de Chávez, de donde vino a fijar residencia definitiva en la propia Santa Cruz.

Poco restaba ya en aquellos pueblos de lo que fue su archivo y copioso respositorio de libros manuscritos. Eberlein adquirió los últimos, siendo lo más notable las copias de antifonarios y salterios, hechas por manos de hábiles calígrafos chiquitanos. En alguna otra ocasión hemos de referirnos a esta habilidad de los indígenas misioneros que, hasta donde conocemos, no tuvo pares o los tuvo muy pocos en el arte americano de los tiempos del rey.

Eberlein, al fallecer aquí mismo en Santa Cruz, hacia 1923, dejó todo lo suyo a un caballero alemán que le protegía. En poder de los descendientes de éste se conservan aquellos papeles, y en buenas manos como están, todo lleva a suponer que no correrán la suerte de ir a repositorios europeos. No ha muchos años tuvimos la complacencia de examinar aquellas piezas, verdaderas obras artísticas de caligrafía.

Con todo lo largamente apuntado se explica el porqué de lo reducido y pobre de nuestros archivos. De lo que queda, felizmente, y es materia principal de estas notas, nos ocupamos enseguida, breve y sucintamente. Será una mera reseña nominativa, ya que no disponemos de ningún conocimiento en la ciencia y el arte de la archivística. Por razón de lo último y necesidad que nos obliga, dividimos las referencias en secciones correspondientes a la procedencia y ubicación de los repositorios documentales que conocemos.

ARCHIVOS ECLESIASTICOS

Como quiera que la iglesia está en condiciones de guardar mejor los actuados que respectan a su actividad, los archivos eclesiásticos, a lo menos los de la capital, son los más nutridos y mejor conservados. El principal de ellos es, naturalmente, el de la curia diocesana. Se halla dividido en dos porciones, la una que corresponde a la actividad estrictamente episcopal y se guarda en las dependencias del obispado, y la otra, que pertenece al cabildo y está depositada en la sala capitular, contigua a la iglesia catedral. Ambas se hallan clasificadas de la misma manera y con iguales características, llevando numeración correlativa en los volúmenes o legajos de la respectiva materia. Los documentos más antiguos datan de principios del siglo XVIII.[1] Hay allí bastante de bueno y curioso, especialmente en lo relativo a la jurisdicción episcopal de Santa Cruz por más allá de los actuales lindes departamentales y nacionales, al movimiento parroquial en los días que precedieron a la guerra emancipadora y a la acción que cupo en ésta al clero diocesano.

---

1. Comunica Judith R. Bakewell que, visitando el archivo de la catedral en 1972, logró descubrir algunos pocos manuscritos del siglo XVI, y mayores fondos de material para el siglo XVII--aparte del material dieciochesco mencionado por el Dr. Sanabria Fernández--había varias visitas. Pese a los estragos causados por los insectos, los documentos eran utilizables. El Dr. Leandro Tormo Sanz (Instituto Toribio de Mogrovejo, Consejo Superior de Investigaciones Científicas, Madrid) ha realizado extensas investigaciones en este archivo, y, por tanto, posee conocimientos inigualados sobre sus fondos.

El vicariato apostólico de Cuevo, enclavado dentro de la jurisdicción político-administrativa del departamento, posee su propio archivo, formado en gran parte por los legajos referentes a las parroquias y misiones de su jurisdicción canónica que fueron recogidos del archivo diocesano de Santa Cruz. Hizo su catalogación, ordenada y metódica, el prelado Mons. César Ciggiani. Las piezas que contiene, agrupadas en no menos de doscientos legajos, tienen interés para el estudio del gentío guaranítico de la región, sus movimientos y agitaciones, sus desgracias y ocurrencias.

Entre las parroquias dependientes del obispado y de los vicariatos apostólicos de Cuevo, Velasco, y Ñuflo de Chávez, todos comprendidos en la jurisdicción política del departamento, poco es lo digno de interés y atención. Queda dicho atrás que de los pueblos que fueron misiones jesuíticas del núcleo de Chiquitos, todo lo mejor y más antiguo salió subrepticiamente, a extremos que hoy apenas si quedan libros parroquiales correspondientes a los primeros años de la república. En las restantes provincias, el único archivo que merece atención e interés es el del vicariato foraneo y parroquia de Vallegrande. En este hay documentos de alguna importancia, principalmente en lo que respecta a las distribuciones de tierras y entradas a parajes baldíos. Sus más antiguos libros de registro bautismal datan de la cuarta década del siglo XVII.

De entre las parroquias de la capital, el único archivo digno de alguna consideración es el de La Merced, antes titulada de "El Sagrario." Los libros, legajos, y papeles sueltos de mayor antigüedad se hallan en tal estado de deterioro, que bien pueden pasar por muestra acabada de la acción nociva de clima y fauna papirófaga, anteriormente anotada.[2]

ARCHIVOS JUDICIALES

Una ley de la república dictada pocos años atrás disponía la centralización en las capitales departamentales de todos los archivos pertenecientes a los diferentes tribunales del distrito judicial. La ley quedó escrita, como varias otras que se dictan, y los repositorios documentales de nuestros "juzgados" siguen como antes, o peor aún, hacinados en

---

2. El P. Lino Gómez Canedo se refiere en *Los archivos,* 1:507, a la posible existencia en el archivo conventual de San Francisco de Santa Cruz, de algunos manuscritos relativos a las misiones de Guarayos y Chiquitos.

estanterías endebles o inseguras, cuando no sobre improvisados anaqueles o destartalados mesuchos. Menos mal que compasivas o interesadas manos de actuarios y escribientes acomodaron y condicionaron los "expedientes," ordenándolos de acuerdo a los años en que fueron dictadas las sentencias resolutorias.

De entre éstos, en la capital es digno de mención el del Juzgado 1o. de Instrucción en lo Civil, cuyos legajos más antiguos datan de la última década del siglo XVIII. Hay en éste piezas de relativo valor, de las que puede extraerse bastante para la historia menuda de los años de la guerra por la independencia. Hemos visto y examinado litigios de esa temporada, en los que intervienen como autoridades juzgadoras las autoridades políticas y militares, a la alternativa entre patriotas y realistas, según lo determinaban los azares de la guerra. Allí aparecen proveídos de Seoane, Francisco del Rivero, Warnes, y el caudillo realista Aguilera. Corre entre una de las muchas diligencias para la recaudación de fondos con destino a las cajas de los ejércitos de la patria, una orden del general argentino Rondeau para requisar las iglesias de Chiquitos y Moxos.

Si se exceptúa al del Juzgado 1o. de Instrucción de Vallegrande, cuyos actuados más antiguos se remontan al segundo tercio del siglo XVII, los restantes de nuestro distrito judicial no tienen mucho que ofrecer al investigador de los días actuales.

ARCHIVOS NOTARIALES

Los repositorios de las escribanías, tan nutridos y valiosos en otros centros del país, se resienten en el nuestro por su poco volumen y corta antigüedad. Entendemos que los causantes de ello han sido, más que en otros casos, los agentes físicos, zoológicos, y humanos, que repetidamente tenemos que mencionar. Se habló ya, en los comienzos de esta anotación, de que los papeles de la notaría de tierras fueron a alimentar el material explosivo-patriótico del cañoncito de la prefectura, en los días de recordación histórica. Otro tanto puede decirse de la notaría de hacienda, bien que acá las instancias de la explosión demandaron menos cantidad de papeles viejos. Ambas notarías, fusionadas en una sola desde al año 1919, disponen de un repositorio tan corto como poco ordenado. Sus cursados más viejos apenas si llegan al 1830.

En cuanto a las notarías públicas, cabe anotar otro tanto. La que actualmente regenta D. Alberto Jordán pasa por ser la que tiene actuados de mayor antigüedad. Los primeros protocolos de ella datan de 1793. Y se conservan en regular estado. Una de las tres que funcionan en Vallegrande, a cargo en los días que corren, de don Imerio Mercado, registra como año inicial de sus matrices el de 1790. Desempeñaba entonces el oficio de aquella escribanía D. José Antonio de Arriaga, que antes había desempeñado igual oficio en Potosí.

Aunque no corresponde a esta sección, por no haber otra especial, mencionamos aquí el Archivo de la Municipalidad, y sólo de pasada. La razón es que el tal resulta tan menguado, que sólo dispone de documentos a partir de 1870. Igual o menos aún son los de las municipalidades provinciales, siempre con excepción de la de Vallegrande, cuyos primeros pliegos escritos datan de 1750, y la de Comarapa, en la que hay actuados correspondientes a 1830.

ARCHIVOS GENERALES

Incluimos dentro de esta denominación los repositorios documentales que no siendo propios de la institución que los posee, ésta los ha reunido y guarda, teniéndolos a disposición de quien quiera estudiar o investigar en ellos.

Tal es la Sección Manuscritos de la Biblioteca Central de la Universidad Gabriel René Moreno. Se ha formado dicha sección a base de los legajos de actuación político-administrativa, que fueron cedidos por la Prefectura del Departamento y de los entregados por la Jefatura del Distrito Escolar y respectivos exclusivamente a materia de educación.

Comprenden, los primeros, papeles diversos, de índole oficial: cartas, solicitudes, órdenes, procesos administrativos, revisiones de cuentas, etc. cursados entre los años 1824 y 1900. Están catalogados, provisionalmente, por años y materias, faltando hacerlo en pormenor por los asuntos de que versan. Su total se halla distribuido en 90 carpetas numeradas ordinalmente.

Lo que respecta a instrucción está simplemente ordenada y encuadernada por años, de 1890 a 1930. Consta de 28 volúmenes.

No ha mucho la Universidad adquirió la biblioteca del extinto sacerdote D. Adrián Melgar y Montaño, paciente investigador y puntual historiador, que dio a la estampa una docena de opúsculos y la obra en 2 volúmenes *Historia de la Provincia de Vallegrande*. Se encontró en dicha biblioteca una buena cantidad de documentos, en buena parte relativos el clero. Estos han sido detenidamente analizados y catalogados en orden a los asuntos de que versan y los años respectivos. Así en esta disposición y en una sub-sección especial, todo lo del P. Melgar yace en los contenidos de 16 carpetas. Creemos que es la mejor fuente de información, por no decir la única, sobre los acontecimientos locales durante la guerra de la independencia.[3]

Se dijo en el subtítulo "Archivos Generales" y no se ha enunciado sino uno solo, el de la Biblioteca Universitaria. A fin de justificar el plural, y sólo por ello, quien escribe estas notas se ve obligado a hablar de sí y mencionar cosa suya. Parte muy preciada de su biblioteca particular es el modesto acopio de documentos que cabe en sólo dos anaqueles de un estante. Reunidos pacientemente, ya por donaciones o obsequios, ya por otros medios que honran a cualquier poseedor, los hay de diversa procedencia y diverso tema, bien que todos atinentes al pasado nacional y especialmente al regional. Junto a los legajos de viejos manuscritos hay copias mecanografiadas de varios valiosos documentos, obtenidos de los archivos de Sucre, Lima, y Sevilla.

Se justifica aún más el plural con la indicación de que el modesto acopio está a disposición de propios y extraños. De entre los unos y los otros son ya bastantes los que lo han aprovechado, y sea en buena hora.

---

3. Comenta Judith Bakewell que, además de copias de manuscritos referentes a Santa Cruz, provenientes principalmente del Archivo General de Indias (Sevilla), contiene el archivo de la Universidad una transcripción del único libro de actas del Cabildo de Santa Cruz que sobrevive. El libro es del siglo XVII. Se guarda en la caja fuerte de un banco de la ciudad.

Los Archivos de Sucre
Judith R. and Peter J. Bakewell

Lamentablemente, no ha sido posible persuadir a ningún conocedor boliviano de estos archivos que haga una descripción de ellos. Por lo tanto, los datos que presentamos aquí no son nada más que una indicación somerísima del contenido de estos ricos repositorios chuquisaqueños. Utilizamos nuestros propios conocimientos del Archivo Nacional de Bolivia (que se concretan estrictamente a los siglos XVI y XVII), y extractamos el informe de L. Gómez Canedo, *Los archivos,* 1:490-98 y sobre todo, el artículo de Juan de Zengotita, "The National Archive and the National Library of Bolivia at Sucre" *Hispanic American Historical Review,* 29 (November, 1949):649-76. Es preciso señalar que en los 25 años que han pasado desde que publicó Zengotita su trabajo, la ordenación y la catalogación del Archivo Nacional han adelantado enormemente, gracias a los extraordinarios esfuerzos del director, el Dr. Gunnar Mendoza L.

ARCHIVO NACIONAL DE BOLIVIA: EPOCA COLONIAL

Situado, junto con la Biblioteca Nacional, en la calle España, Sucre. Horas laborables: ocho diarias--el horario cambia ligeramente según las estaciones del año.

El Archivo contiene fondos coloniales y nacionales. Las principales series coloniales, en gran parte restos del archivo de la Audiencia de Charcas y de los archivos de las cuatro notarías que existían en la ciudad de la Plata, son:

1. Cédulas reales, de 1543 hasta la independencia. Otros cinco tomos de cédulas recibidas en la Audiencia, 1561-1814, se encuentran entre los fondos de la Biblioteca Nacional, le que posee también ocho tomos de cédulas dirigidas a los oficiales de la hacienda real de la Plata, 1781-1822. En la Colección Rück (Biblioteca Nacional) existen además dos tomos de provisiones de virreyes del Perú (Velasco, 1596-1605 y Guadalcázar, 1621-28).

2. Acuerdos de la Audiencia de la Plata, 1561-1820. Estos se refieren principalmente a materias judiciales y a informaciones de méritos. Hay lagunas en la serie.

3. Acuerdos del Cabildo de Potosí, es decir, los "Libros de Cabildo" de Potosí, 1585-1817. En realidad esta serie forma parte de los fondos de la Biblioteca Nacional, pero se puede considerar como sección del Archivo. Consiste en 33 tomos, pero la serie completa hasta 1817 comprendía 61; entre los que faltan están los cuatro primeros tomos. El Dr. Mendoza posee una copia en microfilm de los "Extractos de los libros del Cabildo de Potosí, 1563-73," manuscrito descubierto por el Profesor Lewis Hanke en una librería bonaerense.

4. Archivo de Mizque, 1573-1863. Manuscritos referentes a la administración de la región de Mizque, al sur de Cochabamba. Podrían complementar esta sección los manuscritos notariales de Mizque conservados actualmente en el Archivo Histórico Municipal de Cochabamba (q.v.), y materiales sobre Mizque en el archivo de la Catedral de Santa Cruz. En la Colección Rück de la Biblioteca Nacional figuran algunos manuscritos sobre la retasa de la región Mizque, Santa Cruz (1734).

5. Informes sobre méritos y servicios de personas residentes en la región de Charcas, enviados por la Audiencia a la corona, 1583-1693. Pocos tomos.

6. Archivo de Mojos y Chiquitos. Manuscritos administrativos de la Audiencia de Charcas referentes a la dicha región oriental de la jurisdicción de la Audiencia. Son 41 tomos de manuscritos coleccionados por el gran bibliófilo e historiador boliviano, Gabriel René Moreno, en el siglo pasado. Abarcan el período 1767-1824. Se han juntado con estos documentos, otros de la Audiencia sobre el mismo tema.

7. Minería, 1565-1824. Documentos sobre minas, de toda índole. La litigación minera es especialmente reveladora del funcionamiento de la industria. Hay un fichero detalladísimo, obra del Dr. Mendoza, e inventarios de distintas clases de manuscritos, preparados por el mismo. El área geográfica abarcada por esta sección es amplia--desde el norte del Cuzco hasta el Paraguay y el norte argentino. En la Colección Rück (Biblioteca Nacional) hay material sobre la mita de Potosí, 1736-54.

8. Expedientes. Según L. Gómez Canedo, *Los archivos*, 1:492 "Son procesos de toda índole tramitados ante la Audiencia, con documentos anejos. Abarcan de 1550 a 1824 y suman unas 17,802 piezas." Hay

inventarios en los Nos. 2-7 del *Boletín y catálogo del Archivo General de la Nación* y en los Nos. 24-30 de la *Revista de la Biblioteca y Archivo Nacionales,* 1936-43. Además de litigación, esta sección contiene correspondencia entre la Audiencia y la corona, los virreyes del Perú, y otras autoridades menores. Hay material sobre asuntos indígenas. Merece la pena anotar, también, que la Colección Rück (Biblioteca Nacional) contiene una gran cantidad de manuscritos sobre incursiones indias en regiones pobladas durante el siglo XVIII.

9. Expedientes de abogados, graduados de la Universidad de San Francisco Xavier de la Plata, 1610-1824. Datos de valor biográfico.

10. Conmociones civiles en Potosí. En esta categoría entran los papeles referentes a la llamada "Guerra entre vascongados y otras naciones en Potosí," de 1622 a 1625.

11. Sublevación general indígena de 1780-83.

12. Papeles referentes a la Universidad de San Francisco Xavier de la Plata: de valor para la historia interna de la universidad.

13. Escrituras notariales. Una larga serie, de gran valor para la historia colonial de Charcas. Empieza en 1549 y termina en el siglo XIX. Los primeros libros contienen escrituras dadas en Potosí, y algunas provenientes de Panamá, Guatemala, La Paz, Chucuito, y de la región del Río de la Plata.

BIBLIOTECA NACIONAL: EPOCA COLONIAL

También posee fondos manuscritos. A algunos de ellos se ha hecho referencia en la lista precedente. Gómez Canedo menciona otros: *Los archivos,* 1:493. La colección de manuscritos reunida por Ernesto O. Rück, primer director del Archivo Nacional, se conserva en la Biblioteca, y en ella figuran piezas interesantes, como por ejemplo: una "Información" sobre la vida de Fr. Vicente Bernedo, O.P. (Potosí 1663), un "Extracto" de la *Crónica de la Provincia de San Antonio de los Charcas,* por Fr. Diego de Mendoza (1665), un libro de bautismos de Nuestra Señora de Copacabana y de sus tres parcialidades (1724-34), acuarelas pintadas por Melchor María Mercado durante sus viajes por Bolivia a mediados del siglo XIX.

En la Biblioteca Nacional se guardan también un millar de libros impresos antiguos, del período 1530-1804, la mayoría siendo de procedencia europea. Son principalmente libros sobre teología y otros temas eclesiásticos. Son restos de antiguas bibliotecas de convento. Hay, además, unos pocos incunables.

ARCHIVO Y BIBLIOTECA NACIONALES: EPOCA NACIONAL

1. Papeles de los Congresos y Ministerios, 1825-99.

2. Tribunal Nacional de Cuentas. Abundante documentación sobre asuntos financieros de la república, 1825-1928.

3. Archivo de Mizque. Véase el párrafo 4°, arriba.

4. Gran parte de las colecciones de Gabriel René Moreno, catalogadas en sus obras: *Biblioteca boliviana: Catálogo de la sección de libros y folletos* (Santiago de Chile, 1879); *Primer suplemento a la biblioteca boliviana: epítome de un catálogo de libros y folletos, 1879-1899* (Santiago de Chile, 1900); *Segundo suplemento a la biblioteca boliviana: Libros y folletos, 1900-1908* (Santiago de Chile, 1908).

5. Colección de periódicos bolivianos, 1825-1907, de René Moreno, encuadernada y bastante completa.

6. Colección de René Moreno de folletos bolivianos, siglo XIX y principios del siglo XX.

7. Colección manuscrita de René Moreno, "Poetas bolivianos" (1840-90).

8. Un tomo manuscrito "Correspondencia privada inédita entre el presidente de Bolivia Andrés Santa Cruz y su ministro Mariano Enrique Calvo" (1835-38). Es parte de la Colección de René Moreno.

9. Cuatro tomos de correspondencia entre el representante del Perú en Bolivia, Pedro Antonio de la Torre, y las autoridades bolivianas, 1831-1834. (Colección de René Moreno).[1]

SOCIEDAD GEOGRAFICA DE SUCRE

La mayoría de estos manuscritos son de los siglos XIX y XX, y se refieren a exploraciones geográficas de Bolivia. Hay mapoteca, con materiales de la misma época. Para el colonialista, poco de gran valor, aunque puedan interesar un libro de bautismos de una parroquia no identificada de Potosí, del siglo XVII y copias mecanografiadas de "los expedientes del Cabildo de la Plata, 1559-1838." Existen dos guías de los

---

1. Preciso es subrayar de nuevo que esta lista está extraída del citado artículo de Zengotita. En los 25 últimos años, la labor organizadora llevada a cabo por el Dr. Mendoza habrá revelado, sin duda, una mayor variedad de fondos nacionales en el Archivo y Biblioteca Nacionales. (PJB)

fondos manuscritos: el "Inventario viejo" (mecanografiado) y la "Guía del Archivo" (en manuscrito). L. Gómez Canedo, *Los archivos*, 1:496-97, ofrece títulos de otros manuscritos que le llamaron la atención.

BIBLIOTECA DE LA UNIVERSIDAD

Por lo que indica Gómez Canedo, *Los archivos*, 1:497-98, los manuscritos más antiguos se remontan a principios del siglo XIX. De aquella época hay materiales referentes a la Academia Carolina, en que estudiaron varios de los personajes que se distinguieron en las luchas emancipadoras del centro y del sur de Hispanoamérica.

ARCHIVO DEL CABILDO ECLESIASTICO

Se encuentra al lado de la sacristía de la catedral. Documentación a partir de 1572. Hay actas capitulares; expedientes, de contenido variado (1626-1879); reales cédulas (1619-1819); y otros muchos manuscritos de índole eclesiástica de los siglos XVII, XVIII, y XIX. Véase L. Gómez Canedo, *Los archivos*, 1:493-94.

ARCHIVO ARZOBISPAL

Situado en el Palacio Arzobispal. L. Gómez Canedo, *Los archivos*, 1:494, encontró únicamente "algunos libros de cuentas y parroquiales"; los que, sin embargo, podrían ofrecer algo de interés.

PARROQUIA DE SANTO DOMINGO

En este archivo, bien conservado, están los libros de la parroquia matriz de la ciudad de la Plata. Hay libros parroquiales, de los cuales el primero empieza en 1566. Las series de libros de bautismos, matrimonios, y defunciones no empiezan, sin embargo, hasta las primeras décadas del siglo XVII. Continúan, sin grandes lagunas, "hasta los tiempos modernos." L. Gómez Canedo, *Los archivos*, 1:495.

En el Oratorio de San Felipe Neri y en el Convento de la Recoleta, existen bibliotecas, las que han de contener, aparte de libros impresos, materiales manuscritos. Para una breve referencia a San Felipe Neri, véase L. Gómez Canedo, *Los archivos*, 1:495-96.

Los Archivos de Tarija
Peter J. and Judith R. Bakewell

El Sr. Juan Siles Guevara, quien había pensado preparar un informe sobre los archivos de Tarija, por desgracia no pudo viajar a aquella ciudad desde La Paz antes de la fecha en que se fuera a la imprenta esta capítulo sobre archivos bolivianos. Por consiguiente, no hemos tenido más remedio que recurrir, otra vez, a la obra del L. Gómez Canedo, *Los archivos*, 1:507-9. (JRB PJB)

CONVENTO FRANCISCANO

Manuscritos relativos a la historia del convento, desde el siglo XVII en adelante. Según las indicaciones de Gómez Canedo, parecería que la mayoría del material de los siglos XVII y XVIII es de carácter administrativo, aunque sí hay fondos para la historia de las misiones del convento en el siglo XVIII, así como otros para la historia de las misiones jesuíticas en la época colonial. Abundante material sobre las misiones del convento de la segunda mitad del siglo XIX. Este archivo fue fotocopiado en microfilm en 1948 para la Academy of American Franciscan History (Washington, D.C., EUA).

ARCHIVO DE LA PARROQUIA MATRIZ (CATEDRAL)

Libros parroquiales en regular estado de conservación. Libros de bautismos desde 1627, y de matrimonios desde 1629. Otros libros contienen una mezcla de bautismos, matrimonios, y defunciones. Hay algunos asientos anteriores a estos libros parroquiales.

ARCHIVO DE LA NOTARIA DE HACIENDA

Está en la prefectura de la ciudad. Escrituras notariales--al parecer generales, y no sólo de hacienda--de 1600 en adelante. Continuidad de la serie, desconocida.

ARCHIVO MUNICIPAL DE TARIJA

Escasos materiales. Sobrevive un solo Libro de Cabildo de Tarija aquí, desde el 5 de junio de 1671 hasta el 25 de mayo de 1683. Además, hay una pequeña colección de escrituras notariales, que se refieren principalmente a repartimientos de tierras. Un cuaderno remonta a 1576; otros son del siglo XVII. Podría haber pleitos coloniales.

CHILE

Introduction
William F. Sater

Patricio Estellé's essay is a first draft. He was planning to make some additions when he died of complications following an operation. His passing at the age of thirty-seven is a blow not only to his friends but also to Chile's intellectual life. His unfinished essay is being included as his memorial.

I should like to thank the numerous Chilean historians, librarians, and archivists who helped me in the preparation of this section. Without their patient aid, this work would never have been completed. It is to these kind men and women, and particularly to the memory of Guillermo Feliú Cruz and Patricio Estellé Méndez, that I wish to dedicate my section of this book.

Chilean historiography is extraordinarily rich and varied. Thanks to the efforts of José Toribio Medina, Guillermo Feliú Cruz, and Raúl Silva Castro, researchers can easily locate titles of books and pamphlets relating to their topics. The colonial epoch is covered by Medina's *Biblioteca hispano-chilena (1523-1817)*, 3 vols. (Santiago, 1897-99), as well as his *La imprenta en Lima,* 4 vols. (Santiago, 1904-1907), and *La imprenta en Santiago* (Santiago, 1961). Feliú Cruz published *Impresos chilenos 1776-1813,* 2 vols. (Santiago, 1943), as well as his one-volume *Historiografía colonial de Chile* (Santiago, 1968). The latter describes the research on the colonial period conducted by Chilean historians during the period 1796-1886. A second volume has not appeared and doubtless will not since Feliú Cruz unfortunately died in 1973.

Ramón Briseño analyzed the books, newspapers, and *folletos* published from 1812-1876. This study, *Estadística bibliografía de la literatura chilena,* 3 vols. (Santiago, 1965-1966) was republished in the mid-1960s. The latest version contains additions and revisions made by Raúl Silva Castro. The latter also analyzed the material published in Chile from

1877-1885 in his *Anuario de la prensa chilena,* a study which appeared in 1952.[1] The Biblioteca Nacional began to edit a yearly *Anuario de la prensa chilena* which listed material published in Chile. These volumes cover the output of the years 1886-1916.[2] The Dirección de Bibliotecas, Archivos, y Museos subsequently continued the series. Sixteen volumes have appeared from 1963-1966.[3] In 1966, the Biblioteca Nacional published a supplement covering the period 1877-1964.

Unfortunately, these guides are often not divided according to topic. Hence in order to compile a bibliography the researcher will have to read each entry, which is organized alphabetically and by year. While this is a time-consuming task, it is easier to accomplish it in the United States rather than thumb through the card catalogue in Santiago.

In addition to these guides, there is also the superb four-volume work of Guillermo Feliú Cruz, *Historia de las fuentes de la bibliografía chilena,* 4 vols. (Santiago, 1966-1969). The first book studies Spanish and Chilean historians during the colonial period as well as the influence of historical studies in Chilean bibliography. The second volume concentrates on the works of Ramón Briseño, Diego Barros Arana, Benjamín Vicuña Mackenna, and José Toribio Medina. The remaining volumes list various historians according to the decade of their birth while explaining their bibliographical speciality. This study is an invaluable source since it covers a variety of social science and scientific topics.

A substantial amount of information has been published about the National Archive. The Archive itself published *El Archivo Nacional: Antecedentes de su fundación y reseña de la labor realizada desde 1927 a 1945* (Santiago, 1946). Ricardo Donoso also wrote a somewhat dated but nonetheless excellent study of the Archivo Nacional which included a list of the catalogues describing the various components of the archive. The same historian also published an inventory of the Colección Fundo

---

1. Raúl Silva Castro, *Anuario de la prensa chilena, 1877-1885* (Santiago, 1952).

2. *Anuario de la prensa chilena publicado por la Biblioteca Nacional (1886-1916),* 31 vols. (Santiago, 1887-1927).

3. *Anuario de la prensa chilena,* 16 vols. (Santiago, 1963-1966), *Suplemento a los años 1877-1964* (Santiago, 1966).

Antiguo.[4]

Various archives have been inventoried and a catalogue has been published. Examples of these are: the *Colección de manuscritos de don José Ignacio Víctor Eyzaguirre*; the *Fondos Varios*; *Archivo Hidrográfico Vidal Gormaz*; *Archivo de la Real Audiencia de Santiago*; the *Archivo Claudio Gay*; the *Archivo de la Capitanía General de Chile*; the *Protocolos notariales de Valdivia, La Unión, Osorno y Calbuco, y alcabalas de Chiloé*; the *Archivo de Escribanos de Santiago*; the *Fondos Varios*; *Colección de manuscritos*; the *Archivo Tribunal de Minería*; *Archivo de Jesuítas* and the newest collection, the *Archivo de Jaime Eyzaguirre*. The latter is a twelve-volume collection of documents from the colonial and national period. All these catalogues can be purchased from the Archivo Nacional by writing to the Biblioteca Nacional.[5]

The Archivo has just received the personal papers of Pedro Aguirre Cerda, President of Chile (1938-1941) during the famous Popular Front. The collection consists of approximately sixty volumes covering the period 1912-1945. It is especially good for the years 1920-1928. The Archivo is preparing a catalogue.

The Archivo also contains the papers of various intendencies and ministries. The Archivo will publish soon a catalogue of the holdings of the Ministerio de Hacienda and the Ministerio del Interior. Almost all the holdings of ministerial and other government agencies have catalogues although they have not been published.

The published guides often can be supplemented by periodical literature. Some journal articles have described the Archivo del Museo de Medicina,[6] the Archivo de Escribanos de Valparaíso (1660-1700), and other repositories.[7] Tomás Thayer Ojeda studied the *sección de*

---

4. Archivo Nacional de Chile, *Revista de historia de América*, 11 (1941):47-78 and "Inventario de la Colección Fundo Antiguo en el Archivo Nacional," *Handbook of Latin American Studies* (Cambridge, 1937):547-572.

5. Write to Conservador del Archivo Nacional, Biblioteca Nacional Avenida Bernardo O'Higgins, Santiago, Chile.

6. Nina Ciacarelli and Vicente Aquirre, "Archivo del Museo de Medicina del Servicio Nacional de Salud," *Anales chilenas de la historia de la medicina,* 9-10 (1967-1968):277-287.

7. Antonio Dougnac Rodríguez, "Indice del Archivo de Escribanos de Valparíso, 1660-1700," *Historia,* 7 (1968):227-282; Teresa Esterio Stevens, "El Archivo de la Contaduría Mayor," *Revista chilena de historia del derecho,* 1 (1959):36-53. A brief description of the Archivo of the

manuscritos of the Biblioteca Nacional.[8] Information on foreign archival material relating to Chile can be found in Juan Luis Espejo's *Indice de documentos relativos a Chile, existentes en el Public Record Office de Londres, Archivo de las Ordenes Militares de Madrid, y Archivo General de Indias de Sevilla* (Santiago, 1915). Alejandro Soto Cárdenas' *Misiones chilenos en los archivos europeos* (México, D.F., 1953) provides a list of European documents that have been copied and which are available in Chile.[9]

Chile's principal research center is the Biblioteca Nacional which contains not only a superb collection of newspapers but also a large number of books and *folletos*. Although the library does not always contain a copy of every work published in Chile, it remains the premier institution. In addition to the Biblioteca Nacional, is the Biblioteca del Congreso, housed in the Congress at the corner of Morande and Companía, and the Anexo de la Biblioteca del Congreso, located at Huérfanos, 1117. These libraries contain copies of congressional debates, government documents, reports, and runs of Chilean newspapers and journals. The libraries also possess large collections of foreign books, magazines, and newspapers. The Central Library of the University of Chile also contains some additional material, including the superb library of the noted historian Eugenio Pereira Salas. Material on education can be found at the Museo Pedagógico. The Academia Chilena de Historia owns an archive which contains the still to be published papers of Bernardo O'Higgins as well as the Archivo Prieto. Church records can be found in the Archivo del Obispado de Santiago while records of the regular clergy are the

---

Ministry of Foreign Relations can be found in: Ronald Seckinger's, "A Guide to Selected Diplomatic Archives of South America," *Latin American Research Review*, 10 (1975):142-144. Researchers should be warned that documents dealing with outstanding problems such as relations with Peru, Bolivia, or Argentina, may not be available for use even though they have officially been declassified. This may be true even in cases where the information has already been published. In such cases, you will have to present your case for archival entry to the Foreign Ministry.

8. "La sección de manuscritos de la Biblioteca Nacional de Chile," *Hispanic American Historical Review*, 4 (1921):156-197.

9. For those interested in the trans-Pacific trade or Chile's relations with Australia, see Thomas Bader's, "Australian Manuscript Sources and Programs for the Study of the History of Latin America," *Latin American Research Review*, 9 (1974):105-115.

property of the various orders. Military topics can be researched in
Santiago at the Ministerio de Defensa and the Escuela Militar. Still,
the National Library should be the starting point in one's research. Its
facilities are comfortable, the hours ample, and the staff both helpful
and friendly. Another *sala* has been opened containing the vast personal
library of Guillermo Feliú Cruz. This is a superb collection of primary
and secondary sources which will be a great aid to the scholar.

Some provincial cites also contain important libraries. The University of Chile at Concepción, for example, is clearly the most important research center in the south. Its director, Juan de Luigi Lemus, himself an historian, is extremely kind and helpful. The library's holdings consist of some 300,000 volumes and 7,000 journals. There are some archives in the library including the papers of Cornelio Saavedra, a local figure important both in politics and the military. Apparently the library also contains the papers of the Rioseco family, important local landowners. The history library has purchased the private library of another important historian, Ricardo Donoso, and also embarked upon an interesting project, analyzing all of the colonial documents located in the Archivo Nacional--with the exception of those in the Contaduría Real--which pertain to the area south of the Maule River. These resumés are organized by topic and also include biographical information as well. Anyone working in the colonial history of this region would be well advised to visit Concepción. One could also contact Sr. de Luigi and explain his project to him.

Concepción itself contains the records of the *municipalidad* for the period after 1852. There are approximately 1,850 volumes although some were destroyed in the earthquake. There are also the records of the intendency (1912-present) as well as those of the Corte de Apelaciones. Those working in labor history might be interested in studying the archive of the Sociedad Lorenzo Arenas, a mutual aid society. In nearby Lota are all the records of the Compañía de Lota, a coal mining corporation. This would prove to be a superb topic for anyone working in economic history although Lota itself is somewhat dreary.

Valparaíso's principal library is the Severín. It does not contain any government archives, although it is trying to become a repository for the intendent's office. The library does, however, have some good newspaper runs. The Universidad Católica de Valparaíso has purchased the archive of the Valparíso daily, *La Unión*.

There are regional research centers in Punta Arenas as well as the Universidad Austral in Valdivia. By law the provinces are required to forward any document over fifty years old to the Archivo Nacional. Sometimes the legal requirements are not always rigorously observed, but more often than not, however, the Archivo in Santiago will have the most complete collection of material. Perhaps the only exception to this rule are parish records which often remain in the hands of local churches.[10]

---

10. For an analysis of articles on clerical history see the recent bibliographical study of Julio Retemal in *Historia*, 11 (1971-2):163-259. For an analysis of a provincial parish archive see: José María Casassa Canto's "Inventario de los archivos del Arzobispado de Antofagasta, de la Prelatura de Calama, y sus respectivas parroquias," *Anales de la Universidad del Norte,* 8 (1970):141-303.

The Political History of Colonial Chile
Jacques A. Barbier

Chileans have a long tradition of interest in their colonial past, an interest which has often found an outlet in the investigation of political and institutional themes. As a result, the modern researcher enjoys two major advantages in dealing with the field. The first is that he has a well developed historical literature available as a foundation for his own work. The second is that he can carry out his research with the aid of the impressive scholarly resources so carefully assembled by Chilean historians.

The researcher is particularly fortunate in having available several extensive bibliographies and collections of published documents. Of the former, those of José Toribio Medina are particularly useful since such works as the *Biblioteca hispano-chilena* and his studies of printing in Lima and Santiago, besides being invaluable as bibliographies, also contain priceless historical and biographical information.[1] As for the documentary collections, the two major ones (the *Colección de documentos inéditos para la historia de Chile* and the *Colección de historiadores de Chile*) are a logical starting point for any investigation of political topics.[2]

---

1. José Toribio Medina, *Biblioteca hispano-chilena*, 3 vols. (Santiago, 1897-1899); *La imprenta en Lima*, 4 vols. (Santiago, 1904-1907); *La imprenta en Santiago* (Santiago, 1961). The best bibliography of Medina's publications, many of which have been reprinted, is Carl Schaible, *Bibliografía de José Toribio Medina* (Santiago, 1958). As a supplement researchers can advantageously use Biblioteca Nacional (Santiago de Chile), *Impresos chilenos, 1776-1818*, 2 vols. (Santiago, 1963), and the very rare first volume of what was to have been Luis Montt's, *Bibliografía chilena*, 3 vols. (Santiago, 1904-1921), published in 1918.

2. *Colección de historiadores de Chile y de documentos relativos a la historia nacional*, 49 vols. (Santiago, 1861-1942); José Toribio Medina, *Colección de documentos inéditos para la historia de Chile desde el viaje de Magallanes hasta la batalla de Maipo,* 30 vols. (Santiago, 1888-1902); and the second series of the latter collection (6 vols.; Santiago, 1956-). Other collections exist.

Chilean-produced secondary works have also tended to be of high quality. Particularly important are the multi-volumed general histories which can guide the novice researcher through the intricacies of colonial chronology.[3] Secondary materials can be readily consulted in Santiago through the pleasant facilities of the Biblioteca del Congreso Nacional and the Biblioteca Nacional. The Chilean and periodical sections of the latter contain many items hard to find in North America, and both can be utilized through the convenient facilities of the Seminario Matta Vial. In general it can be said that reference and catalogue facilities in these establishments are inadequate. The staff, however, is helpful, and bibliographical control of secondary material has been much facilitated by the completion into recent times of a Chilean national bibliography.[4] Retrieval from periodical publications, however, remains a problem.

The crown jewels of the Biblioteca Nacional are, of course, the libraries of José Toribio Medina and Diego Barros Arana, housed separately in rooms bearing their names. Readers may use both through the luxurious facilities of the Sala Medina. These collections contain rare nineteenth-century works and some useful modern ones as well. Their glory, however, are their original manuscripts, archival copies, and precious colonial-period imprints. Of the documentary materials, those of Barros Arana have not always been readily accessible. The Medina manuscripts, however,

---

3. The best of these general histories remains Diego Barros Arana, *Historia jeneral de Chile*, 16 vols. (Santiago, 1884-1902). Others are Claudio Gay, *Historia física y política de Chile*, 28 vols. and 2 vol. atlas (Paris, 1844-1876); and Francisco A. Encina, *Historia de Chile desde la prehistoria hasta 1891*, 20 vols. (Santiago, 1940-1956).

4. The components of this national bibliography are: José Toribio Medina, *La imprenta en Santiago* (Santiago, 1961), [or. pub. 1891, covers to 1817]; Ramón Briseño, *Estadística bibliográfica de la prensa chilena* (Santiago, 1965), [or. pub. 1862-1879, covers 1812-1876]; and Biblioteca Nacional (Santiago de Chile), *Anuario de la prensa chilena* (Santiago, 1887-1927), [title varies, covers 1886-1917]. The gaps and oversights of these works have been corrected through a revival and completion of the *Anuario*. This has involved publishing annual volumes from 1963 onward, bridging the gaps in the existing bibliographies (1877-1885 and 1917-1962), and correcting the oversights of Briseño and the older *Anuario* through the publication of supplements. The moving force behind this project, Guillermo Feliú Cruz, has also provided researchers with valuable guidance through the older histories, bibliographies, and archival collections in his *Historiografía colonial de Chile* (Santiago, 1958), and *Historia de las fuentes de la bibliografía chilena*, 4 vols. (Santiago, 1966-1969).

are well catalogued and open to the researcher. All these papers are mainly copies of documents located in Spanish archives, and, along with similar collections in the Archivo Nacional, they make available materials otherwise to be found only in the Iberian peninsula. Save for the eighteenth-century pieces, most of them have been published. As for the imprints, although the printing press came very late to Chile, works of relevance to the country were often published in Spain and Peru. For such works, and for rare nineteenth-century books, the Sala Medina is without its peers.[5] Of particular interest to the political historian are the many *relaciones de méritos* which the Sala contains. These are useful sources of biographical information for Chilean officeholders and *pretendientes*.

Although the political historian of colonial Chile cannot avoid library work, it is in the archives that he will find his most valuable material. In Chile this means that he will spend much of his time in the Archivo Nacional; because of the centralization of archives, this depository contains practically all the surviving records of colonial civil institutions.

Working conditions in the Archivo Nacional are good: the reading room is ample in size, and the staff is both helpful and knowledgeable. General descriptions of the history and holdings of the archives are readily available so there is no need to describe all the collections here.[6] Since published descriptions of the holdings are sometimes

---

5. The published catalogue of the Sala Medina is Biblioteca Nacional (Santiago de Chile), *Catálogo breve de la biblioteca americana que obsequio a la nacional de Santiago J. T. Medina,* 9 vols. in 2 ser. (Santiago, 1926-1954). Printed books are catalogued in two original vols. (1926), and two vols. of supplements (1953-1954). Manuscripts are catalogued in a preliminary volume (1930), which serves as an index to Medina's *Colección de documentos inéditos para la historia de Chile,* and four numbered volumes (1928-1951).

6. Tomás Thayer Ojeda, "La sección de manuscritos de la Biblioteca Nacional de Chile," *Hispanic American Historical Review,* 4 (February, 1921):156-197; Ricardo Donoso, "El Archivo Nacional de Chile," in *Revista de historia de América,* no. 11 (April, 1941):47-78; Roscoe R. Hill, *The National Archives of Latin America* (Cambridge, Mass., 1945), pp. 36-45; Guillermo Feliú Cruz, *Historia de las fuentes de la bibliografía chilena,* 3 vols. (Santiago, 1968), 3:99-110; and R. H. Bartley and Stuart L. Wagner, *Latin America in Basic Historical Collections: A Working Guide* (Stanford, 1972), pp. 82-84.

confusing or contradictory, however, particularly in the case of collections without a printed catalogue, the researcher should be prepared to ask for guidance from the staff. Where whole runs of documents have been published (as in the case of most of the *actas* of the Cabildo of Santiago), the originals are not normally available to the public.

The Archivo Nacional contains two distinct types of holdings on the colonial period. Some are collections composed of donated or purchased papers. These are conglomerations of original documents, notes and copies which do not correspond to any particular administrative organism. More importantly, the holdings also include the surviving archives of the various branches of the administration. Both collections are generally composed of bound volumes.

The donated and purchased collections are obvious signs of the historical interests of the nineteenth-century Chilean intelligentsia. In this class are such well known archives as those of Benjamín Vicuña Mackenna, José Ignacio Víctor Eyzaguirre, and the combined collections of Claudio Gay and Carlos Morla Vicuña. Similar to these are the copies made in Seville and Simancas, the ex-cedulario de la Biblioteca Nacional, and the miscellaneous documents found in the Fondo Antiguo and Fondos Varios. These collections are particularly valuable for their private letters and papers and copies of Spanish documents. They also contain many pieces taken out of the official archives, however, and in some cases original volumes of such material (e.g. the Tribunal de Minería materials in the Vicuña Mackenna papers). Despite the fact that they have been extensively used in the past, researchers will still profit from using these collections. They contain material which can be found nowhere else, and consultation is often simplified by the existence of published catalogues.[7]

---

7. *Catálogo de la biblioteca y manuscritos de D. Benjamín Vicuña Mackenna* (Santiago, 1886); Archivo Nacional (Chile), *Catálogo de la colección de manuscritos de D. José Ignacio Eyzaguirre* (Santiago, 1944); Archivo Nacional (Chile), *Catálogo del archivo de Claudio Gay* (Santiago, 1963); for a brief catalogue of the Morla Vicuña papers see Feliú Cruz, *Historiografía colonial de Chile*, pp. 138-152; for an introduction to other collections of copies the researcher can use Alejandro Soto Cárdenas, *Misiones chilenas en los archivos europeos* (Mexico, 1953); Ricardo Donoso, "Inventario del Fondo Antiguo del Archivo Nacional de Chile," *Handbook of Latin American Studies*, 3 (1937):547-572; Archivo Nacional (Chile), *Catálogo Fondos Varios* (Santiago, 1952). Of some use for late eighteenth-century politics are the Jesuit papers whose Chilean manuscripts are described in Biblioteca Nacional (Santiago de Chile), *Catálogo de los*

They cannot, however, serve as the primary documentary base for political topics. Only the administrative archives can serve this function.

There are many administrative collections in the Archivo Nacional, of course, so only the most significant can be discussed here. The most important of these are the Archives of the Capitanía General and Real Audiencia.[8] The papers of the captains general are obvious sources for those activities of the colonial administration which came under the general heading of finance, *patronato,* war, and *gobierno político.* Less well known is the fact that they also contain judicial papers (for the governor was both a criminal and civil judge). The larger part of these documents consists of the multitudinous *expedientes* so characteristic of Spanish administration. Covering as they do every aspect of the governor's functions, they enable the researcher to follow in minute detail the formal decision-making process in the colony. This Archive also contains *reales cédulas* and *órdenes* sent from the mother country, *libros copiadores* of gubernatorial letters to Chilean, Peruvian, and Spanish authorities, and *bandos* meant for the general population. The last two types of documents, however, are effectively available only for the eighteenth century. Indeed, the closer one gets to the independence period the richer he will find these collections.

The Archivo de la Real Audiencia is a necessary complement to the Archivo de la Capitanía General. Since it is the depository of the papers of the highest colonial court, it naturally contains mainly judicial materials. It must be remembered, however, that decisions of Peruvian and Chilean authorities were often appealed to the audiencia or were questioned by the court itself, and that consequently a good number of these "judicial" matters on closer examination turn out to have been profoundly political. In addition to the political dimensions of its judicial role

---

manuscritos relativos a los antiguos Jesuitas de Chile que se custodian en la Biblioteca Nacional (Santiago, 1891).

8. José Toribio Medina, *Indice de los documentos existentes en el Archivo del Ministerio de lo Interior* (Santiago, 1884); as a supplement to the above see also "Indice de veinte volúmenes del Archivo de la Capitanía General de Chile," in *Revista chilena de historia e geografía,* No. 63 (Oct.-Dec., 1928):300-328; Archivo Nacional (Chile), *Catálogo de la Real Audiencia de Santiago,* 4 vols. (Santiago, 1898-1942). The Medina catalogue above is incomplete. Researchers should make use of the typescript inserts in the copies of the National Archive.

the audiencia also enjoyed a number of commissions of an administrative nature, served as an advisory body to the governors (and at times to the crown and viceroy as well), and served collegially as governor during a vacancy of the office. Documentation produced by all these roles are preserved in this collection. By far the larger, and as a mass most valuable, part of this documentation consists of the ubiquitous *autos* and *expedientes*. There are also some specialized papers, however, which the political historian cannot afford to neglect. Among these are the bound volumes of *reales cédulas* and the various *libros copiadores*. These last cover a greater time span than those of the *capitanía general* and include, among other things, the correspondence of the tribunal (including the order and resolutions it sent and received), and its *votos, sentencias*, and *reales provisiones*.

The most voluminous, and least used, of these great administrative collections are titled Contaduría Mayor. Notwithstanding their name, however, they contain documents from nearly all fiscal organs, documents which, despite the fact that the Contaduría Mayor was founded late, in 1768, cover nearly the entire colonial period. The existing organization and descriptions of these collections are utterly inadequate; consequently the researcher should benefit from discussing their state and history with a knowledgeable member of the archival staff. There are two series of obvious use to the colonial historian in this set. The first (Contaduría Mayor, Primera Serie), is made up of a variety of papers which were handed down to the modern period in loose form and were subsequently bound. The second (Contaduría Mayor, Segunda Serie), is basically made up of original account books which came down from the colonial period in bound form. This second series is by far the easiest to use, because a catalogue exists listing the titles and indicating the content of each volume. The first series, with its more varied documentation, is more important, however. This first series is broken up into sets of books (e.g. *aduana de Santiago, real hacienda, trámites administrativos, expedientes,* etc.) which refer to particular offices of government, broad areas of concern, or types of documents. For each of these branches there is a run of volumes arranged in ascending chronological order. Unfortunately the dates refer only to the oldest document in each volume (thus the first volume of a set might include papers from 1620-1821, the second volume 1621-1623, and the third volume 1624-1703!). This system makes consultation of these documents so cumbersome that historians have deliberately avoided using the collection. Thus, despite the fact that the documents of the Areche *visita* for Chile are located in this series, at least one Chilean historian travelled to Spain to consult them!

There are several other smaller collections of an administrative nature (notably those of the Tribunal de Minería, Consulado, Real Hacienda, and Intendencia de Concepción), but these are useful only for the late colonial period and certainly do not share the picturesque qualities of the Contaduría Mayor papers.

The last two major collections which must be mentioned are the Archives of the Cabildo and Escribanos of Santiago.[9] As regards the first it must be noted that although the *actas* have been published into the early years of the eighteenth century, other cabildo documents have not, and for most of the eighteenth century nothing at all has been published. The scarcity of other municipal corporations and the relative lack of competition from such bodies as consulados allowed the Cabildo of Santiago to wield more influence than it might otherwise have had. It cannot be ignored by political historians. As for the *escribano* papers, although scholars are presently inclined to think of them mainly in the context of social history, one should not forget that in the absence of a genuine system of party politics the political historian is often forced to have recourse to Namier-like explanations. If such a search for individual behavior needs to be launched, there is no depository of the individual to compare to the *escribano* papers.

In Chile the colonial political scene is a fertile field of research. The documentation is well preserved and the scholar can benefit from an existing infrastructure of secondary works, bibliographies, documentary collections, and research aids. Most importantly many vital questions remain unresolved. The most fruitful research topics may well prove to be those suggested by recent monographs on social and economic themes. The conclusions drawn in these works almost invariably presume the use of

---

9. For a guide to this latter section see Archivo Nacional (Chile), *Guía para facilitar la consulta del Archivo de Escribanos,* 3 vols. (Santiago, 1913-1927). The first volume covers to 1696, the second to 1760, the third to 1800. Only certain kinds of documents are described; thus, even though each volume of the guide is more inclusive than its predecessor, the researcher is often forced to operate without its help.

political power by some segment of Chilean society. For example, documented regional changes in labor institutions and landholding patterns during the eighteenth century imply that the Chilean elite had access to repressive force and could use the authority of the state to sanctify, if not realize, its economic pretensions. The political dimensions of such topics and such other areas as trade and the Araucanian wars are not sufficiently studied. Yet, with their relatively ready access to Spanish archives, this is an area where North American scholars seem to have a significant advantage over many of their Chilean colleagues. It can only be hoped that this combination of challenge and opportunity will bear fruit.

Archives and Their Usage: Economic History in Colonial Chile
Marcello Carmagnani

As the title indicates, we are not only primarily interested in suggesting different historical problems, which the various archives in Chile and other nations permit us to study,[1] but also in raising an important issue which until now has not received the scholarly attention which it merits and about which, consequently, our knowledge is speculative.[2]

One of these problems is relating the productive units of the economy, that is the *hacienda*, with mining and commercial activities.[3] A better and

---

1. The most important archives for the study of Chilean economic history during the colonial period are the Archivo Nacional in Santiago and the Archivo General de Indias in Seville. The latter contains the important section of the Contaduría, which includes the accounts of the royal Chilean treasuries in Concepción, Santiago, and Valdivia. The Audiencia de Chile section which houses the communications and proceedings sent to royal authorities; and Contratación section, which contains information dealing with the commercial relations between the colony and Spain. The collections of the Archivo Nacional--Gay Morla, Vicuña Mackenna, Fondos Varios, Fondos Antiguos, and the Fondo Medina, the latter being situated in the Sala Medina of the Biblioteca Nacional, contains copies of the documents of the Audiencia of Chile, of the originals to be found in the Archivo General de Indias. All these collections have been inventoried and have, as in the case of the Colección Vicuña Mackenna, Fondos Varios, and Fondo Medina, a printed catalogue.

2. The following works contain a good analysis of the sources utilized: Jean Borde and Mario Góngora, *Evolución de la propiedad rural en el valle del Puangue* (Santiago, 1956); Mario Góngora, *Origen de los inquilinos de Chile central* (Santiago, 1960), and *Encomenderos y estancieros. Estudios acerca de la constitución social aristocrática de Chile despues de la conquista, 1580-1660* (Santiago, 1970); Alvaro Jara, *Los asientos de trabajo y la provisión de mano de obra para los no-encomenderos en la ciudad de Santiago, 1586-1600* (Santiago, 1959) and *El salario de los indios y los sesmos del oro en la tasa de Santillán* (Santiago, 1961); Ruggiero Romano, *Una economía colonial: Chile en el siglo XVIII* (Buenos Aires, 1965): Carlos Sempat Assadourian, "Chile y Tucumán en el siglo XVI. Una correspondencia de mercaderes," *Historia*, 9 (1970): 65-109. See also Marcello Carmagnani, *El salariado minero en Chile colonial* (Santiago, 1963).

3. On the scarcity of works related to the agricultural productive units see Magnus Mörner, "The Spanish American Hacienda: A Survey of Recent Research and Debate," *Hispanic American Historical Review*, 53

more profound understanding of the dynamics of these productive units will allow us to understand better the prevailing means of production and the economic system in which these productive units developed. Proceeding in this fashion, we not only will analyze various archives but also relate them to the question under consideration.

It is equally important to bear in mind that an adequate analysis of productive units should go beyond the microeconomic and entrepreneurial aspects; it should also be analyzed as a sector of the economic system to which it belongs, thereby shedding light on the basic mechanisms of that economic system.

Keeping this goal in mind, we propose to analyze an agricultural, mining, or commercial enterprise. Our first task is finding the documents relating to a definite economic subsector. The Archive of the Jesuits in the Archivo Nacional in Santiago de Chile contains the material relating to the property of the Society of Jesus prior to its expropriation by the Spanish crown. This means that the documental base essential to our study is composed of the accounts of the *haciendas,* and among these still extant, it is preferable to select one whose documents cover a long period of time. We will use one or more complementary accounts to verify the extent to which the mechanism which we are trying to describe is or is not typical of a larger unit of the agricultural sector of the economy.[4]

To achieve this objective, we must verify the information by using the material contained in the archives of the Real Audiencia, the Capitanía General, Judicial, and Notarial, all of which are housed in the Archivo Nacional. The first two archives, like that of the Society of Jesus, have been inventoried, and a catalogue has been published. There is also a superficial but unpublished catalogue on the Judicial.[5] For

---

(1973):183-216. On the general scarcity of studies relating to productive units for the eighteenth century, see William Paul McGreevey, *A Bibliography of Latin American Economic History, 1760-1960* (Berkeley, 1968) and William Paul McGreevey and Robson B. Tyrer, "Recent Research on Economic History of Latin America," *Latin American Research Review,* 3 (1968):89-117.

4. On the use of this method of accounting for Peru see Pablo Macera, *Instrucciones para el manejo de las haciendas jesuitas del Perú (ss XVII-XVIII)* (Lima, 1966).

5. The section on the Archivo Judicial contains the judgments of least importance, and these can be found for almost all the old *corregimientos* of Chile. Unfortunately, there are rarely proceedings available prior to the eighteenth century and relatively few related to the eighteenth century.

the Notarial.[6] there is only a partially completed catalogue dealing with the section on wills and a complete but unpublished catalogue on the notarial deeds for Santiago in the sixteenth century and for Copiapó after 1800.[7]

Whoever wants to analyze these sources in order to study the agriculture sector should realize that the cataloguing of these sections of the Archive has been done according to the title of the litigation. For our study, what is particularly interesting are the *juicios de tierra*, the *alcance de cuentas*, and those of the Compañía. Moreover, many of these judgments contain agricultural accounts as well, although for short periods of time.

Those who wish to study the notarial deeds, on the other hand, will have to peruse all the *protocolos*. Although a time-consuming process, it is made easier by knowing the name of the land owner. The notarial deeds are extremely important because they provide us with both information on property holdings (generally to be found in testamentary documents) and the qualitative and quantitative information related to the marketability of foodstuffs and animal products. The deeds, and especially the inventory of holdings, will also permit us to verify the extent to which an agricultural unit formed part of a much larger economic complex.

All that which has been written about the sources dealing with agriculture is also valid for mining, the only difference being that this area of the economy does not have an all-inclusive source like that of the Archivo de los Jesuitas. Material on mining is to be found primarily

---

6. The notarial section of the Archivo Nacional clearly constitutes the least used source of documents. Nevertheless, it covers activity for some population centers for a good portion of the colonial period. It exists for the sixteenth century for Santiago and from the seventeenth century for La Serena. For other important urban centers like Valparaíso, Concepción, Chillán, and Copiapó, the *notariales protocolos* are preserved after the eighteenth century.

7. The catalogues for the *protocolos notariales* of Santiago and Copiapó can be consulted in the Centro de Historia Colonial of the University of Chile. The individual responsible for this catalogue and that of the Contaduría Mayor, Segunda Serie and the Archivo Gay Morla was Mario Góngora. The *sección* Gay Morla of the Archivo Nacional is particularly interesting for the qualitative documents relating to eighteenth-century Chilean agriculture.

in the archives of the Real Audiencia, Capitanía General, Judicial, and Notarial sections as well as in that of the Tribunal de Minería. The latter has yet to be inventoried. The particularly ambitious can use the Contaduría Mayor, Primera Serie, composed of 3,000 uninventoried volumes. This is unquestionably the least explored area of the Archive.

The material dealing with commerce is essentially the same as that for mining and agriculture. Other materials can be found in the relevant sections of the Fondos Varios, Fondo Antiguo, Tribunal del Consulado, and the Contaduría Mayor, Segunda Serie. All of these archival holdings, with the exception of that of the Tribunal, have an unpublished catalogue describing their contents. The Contaduría Mayor, Segunda Serie, also contains documents on the Casa de Moneda, clearly the largest commercial enterprise and private bank until the state took it over.

Until now, we have only mentioned the most suitable sources to analyze both qualitatively and quantitatively the problem of the productive units. Nevertheless, we know that this documentation (accounts and inventories) presents difficulties in their usage. Consequently, we believe it appropriate to discuss briefly the treatment of the information contained in these documents.

When dealing with accounts, it is imperative to determine if they are single- or double-entry. This can show the level of treatment of the information and also indicates the degree of technical development achieved by the managers of the estates, mining, and commercial firms. The fact that double-entry bookkeeping was rarely employed might indicate a lack of technical expertise.

Be they double- or single-entry, accounts should be converted into information which, unlike the archival material, will provide us not only with statistical data on the economic unit under consideration but also with the elements needed to understand its dynamics and to reconstruct its basic mechanisms.

Let us suppose that we wish to understand the functioning of some agricultural unit for which, in addition to its accounts, we also have one or more inventory of assets. These inventories will demonstrate the exact position of the economic unit within the production aggregate controlled by the same person or group of persons. The inventories, especially if they are particularly detailed, will also allow us to distinguish fixed capital (land and improvements) from working capital investments (livestock, stores of merchandise, etc.) and thus to reconstruct the basic elements of the economic mechanism.

Once the fixed and working capital have been ascertained, it will be necessary to determine the input of the final output--to distinguish the different productive elements which, when combined, produce the final output. In order to estimate the input, it will be necessary, basing our efforts on the accounts, to determine quantitatively, the most important output generated by the economic unit. In the event that the most important output might be wheat, we should immediately organize our data in order to ascertain the goods produced by the economic unit and imputable to wheat production. Within this group of goods, we should distinguish between those which are directly imputable (livestock, alfalfa, etc.) from those which are indirectly imputable (livestock, wine, beans, etc.). We should also try to determine the profits which are directly and indirectly imputable to the output of wheat and bought on the open market as well as those goods which are bought on the market and resold to farm laborers.

Proceeding in this fashion, we can break down the input into two areas: one which explains the input of labor and the other which is the input of goods. As a result of this separation, we can determine the degree of commercialization of the productive unit, defined as the percentage of the monetary expenses over the total expenses. This also, in turn, will permit us to determine the connection between the productive system and the form of circulation in order to see the modifications--determined through the percentages--which are produced in time in the productive system and to confirm the degree of self sufficiency of the productive unit at the level of input. By comparing them with the total revenues, real expenses also allow us to determine the gross profit of the productive unit to which should be added the other profits obtained from the *hacienda* store (*pulpería*) and from advance loans on goods to tenant farmers (*inquilinos*) and *peones*.

Having ascertained the total gross profits, we can try to calculate the net profits of the economic unit by using the information contained in the accounts related to the taxes paid (*diezmos*) and to the amortization of capital (yield from *censos*).

These calculations are not easy since they require beforehand a clear discussion of what is understood to be fixed and working capital. Is the real value of land really fixed capital? Is the real value of livestock really working capital? Is the real value of irrigation canals fixed capital or the result of the accumulation of the input of work of the productive cycle?

As soon as we have organized the documents which provide us with a monetary and non-monetary input-output matrix, we can then reconstruct the basic mechanism of the productive unit and the agricultural sector, and we can glimpse those mechanisms which tie the economic sector to the system as a whole. Only in this way can we learn the direct and induced effects generated by the economic unit.

Aggregation of the mechanisms will also permit us to comprehend how the owner of the productive unit took possession of the result of the productive cycle. It will thus be possible to observe the final uses of the income by the owner class. We can also verify if the part of their income not expended but invested instead in the purchase of new lands or in social status (hereditary titles, for example) effectively neutralized capital accumulation or whether this behavior was due to the fact that the productive system was not yet capitalistic.

We have thus examined the productive unit and the effect it produces. On the basis of new indicators such as that of total production--measured by *diezmo*--the internal circulation of the products--measured by the *alcabala*--and the external circulation of the products--obtained through the *almojarifazgo* and the *alcabala*--we can extend our model to a regional and then to a national scale, thereby verifying the role of the productive agricultural unit at the level of agriculture and total production.[8]

Whoever wishes to deal with the problem of the productive unit will have to raise these questions constantly because economic history can only bear fruit when the researcher begins his search for material on the foundation of a solid hypothesis and when he is aware of all the available methodological and technical instruments.

---

8. For information on the *diezmo, alcabala,* and *almojarifazgo* as sources of information on production, internal and external commerce, see Marcello Carmagnani, *Les méchanismes de la vie économique dans une société colonial: Le Chili (1680-1830)* (Paris, 1973), pp. 23-30, 130-146, 193-198.

Archival Resources for Chilean Economic History, 1800-1850
S. F. Edwards

It is necessary at the outset to stress an obvious point: the importance of doing your "homework" before going to Chile. By homework I do not mean simply the consultation of monographs and journal articles.[1] Pre-embarkation preparation, which will enhance productivity in the Archivo Nacional, should involve utilization of the various published collections of documents. For our purposes the oldest such collection is the *Colección de historiadores y de documentos relativos a la independencia de Chile* (Santiago, 1901 -   ) often cited as *CHIC*.[2] Although the volumes concentrate mainly on the years 1808-1830, they still contain some material from both earlier as well as later years. (So far forty volumes, as well as a partial index to the first thirty-seven of these, have been published.)[3]

Another important series is the *Colección de antiguos periódicos chilenos (CAPC)* (Santiago, 1952-   ), initiated by the late Guillermo Feliú Cruz in 1952. By the late 1960s, twenty volumes covering the years 1813-1825 had been published.[4] It is important to note concerning newspapers

---

1. Convenient listings of secondary works dealing with Chilean economic history can be found in Sergio Villalobos Rivera, "La historiografía económica de Chile: Sus comienzos," *Historia,* 10 (1971):7-56 and my "The Consolidation of Underdevelopment in Late Nineteenth-Century Chile: Some Bibliographical Bases and Suggested Research Strategies," *Annals of the Southeastern Conference on Latin American Studies,* 4 (1973):39-55.

2. The *Colección* was launched by Enrique Matta Vial in 1901. His successors included Tomás Thayer Ojeda, Moisés Vargas, Miguel Varas, and Guillermo Feliú Cruz.

3. Sergio Villalobos R., *Indice de la colección de historiadores y de documentos relativos a la independencia de Chile* (Santiago: Editorial Universitaria de Seminario de Historia de Chile, Instituto Pedagógico, Universidad de Chile, 1956).

4. The two major newspapers of the *patria vieja, Aurora de Chile* and *El Monitor Araucana*, have already been reprinted. Hence, Feliú Cruz began the series with the official newspaper issued during the *reconquista* together with two short-lived periodicals from 1813 and 1814. All of the *CHIC* volumes were published by the Biblioteca Nacional.

that microfilm copies of *El Mercurio* of Valparaíso (1826-   ) and *El Araucano* (1830-1877) are available in the United States. *El Mercurio* provides a great deal of economic information, particularly on commercial and financial matters. *El Araucano,* the official government newspaper, contains not only major laws and decrees, which generally appear in the compilation of Chilean laws, but also a host of minor notices and regulations which can be of value in researching a variety of economic questions.[5] Its articles dealing with economic questions are a good barometer of official thinking on such matters. Parenthetically newspapers, whether in *CAPC* or in the Biblioteca Nacional, do not become important sources of information on economic matters until the early 1840s. Periodicals prior to 1840, except the two already mentioned, were devoted almost exclusively to political questions; if they reported regularly on economic matters, they were usually too short-lived to provide any important runs of information. A most useful reference work for anyone using Chilean newspapers is Raúl Silva Castro's *Prensa y periodismo en Chile* (Santiago: Ediciones de la Universidad de Chile, 1958).

A third major source of published archival material is the *Archivo de don Bernardo O'Higgins (AO'H)* (Santiago: Archivo Nacional y Academia Chilena de la Historia, 1946-   ). While it contains thirty volumes and an appendix, to date only two categories have been completed. The most important republication of documents has been the official government newspaper for the years 1817-1823. The remaining volumes generally cover only the first year of don Bernardo's government (1817), but they show the wide variety of archival material to be covered for any particular topic.

An extremely important collection, especially for economic policy and legislation questions, is the *Sesiones de los cuerpos legislativos de la república de Chile, 1811 a 1845 (SLC)* (Santiago: Imprenta Cervantes, 1886-1909), all thirty-seven volumes--except the first--compiled and edited by Valentín Letelier.[6] Although each volume contains an index of persons

---

5. Newspaper reprints of official documents are occasionally the only source of information as to what the documents contained. On some occasions the documents might truly be lost, but quite often what occurred was removal of a particular document from the archives, perhaps to make a copy. Then it somehow never found its way back to the proper file. Hence, the newspaper might be one's only source of information unless one is lucky enough to uncover the document in the course of his work.

6. Volume One was prepared by Domingo Amunátegui Solar and appeared in 1887.

mentioned and topics discussed in the particular volume, the indices are not completely adequate. In pursuing a particular topic, it is absolutely essential to note for each session's *cuenta* Letelier's references to preceding and subsequent sessions dealing with the particular topic. This is the only way the legislative history of a measure, with the variety of opinions expressed in the legislature, can be traced. Volume indices, in other words, can be helpful, but they are not sufficiently comprehensive for a careful study of a particular measure. Volume One, edited by Domingo Amunátegui Solar, should be supplemented by the major newspapers of the *patria vieja* and archival material published by Fernando Márquez de la Plata.[7] Between 1846 and 1865 congressional debates, without any supporting or supplementary documents, were published monthly under the title *Sesiones del Congreso Nacional*.

Two other printed sources are particularly important. The annual messages of presidents and ministers provide one source of official thinking on some economic subjects. Such messages are reproduced in *SLC*. Those presented to the legislature from 1831 to 1861 together with many supporting documents omitted by Letelier for the years 1831-1845 can be found in *Documentos parlamentarios,* 9 vols. (Santiago: Imprenta del Ferrocarril, 1858-1861). Travel literature, the remaining printed source dealing with economic questions, must be used with caution. On some occasions, the writers were not in Chile for sufficient time to familiarize themselves with the entire economic scene. In these cases--and María Graham is a good example--they tended to rely on their commercially oriented countrymen and thus reflected all the merchant's prejudices and views. The pithy observations of John Miers and the in-depth work of Melville Gills, however, illustrate how important such material can be for your preparatory reading.[8]

Catalogues facilitate archival digging, and a few are available, some printed and some in typescript form only. The collections with printed catalogues include Vicuña Mackenna, Claudio Gay, and José Víctor

---

7. "Documentos de la primera junta de gobierno de 1810," *Boletín de la Academia Chilena de la Historia,* 11 (1938):106-407.

8. Concerning travel literature, see Guillermo Feliú Cruz, *Notas para una bibliografía sobre viajeros relativos a Chile* (Santiago, 1965).

Eyzaguirre, as well as the large and heterogeneous *Fondos Varios*.[9] The Ministry of the Interior, prior to the late nineteenth century when there was a proliferation of ministries, was responsible for many areas of economic life. One printed and one typescript index exist for this ministerial collection. The first, *Indice de los documentos existentes en el Archivo del Ministerio de lo Interior* (Santiago: Imprenta de la República, 1884) refers mainly to eighteenth-century material, although there are some entries for earlier and later periods. The copy in the Archivo Nacional contains typed insertions giving the specific contents of some of the volumes. The second index, a typescript in the Archivo Nacional, is titled "Catálogo de Ministerio del Interior, años 1818-1921." It is arranged by administrative divisions--*correos, telégrafos, intendencias,* etc.--but has few entries prior to 1830.

Two additional typescripts in the Archivo Nacional may also facilitate search for material. The first, "Catálogo de Ministerio de Hacienda, años 1823-1922," unfortunately contains very little material, aside from some references to foreign loan negotiations prior to 1850. The most useful typescript is "Archivo de la Contaduría Mayor, Primera Serie." It lists by categories--*aduanas, hacienda pública, obras públicas,* etc.--the specific volume numbers under each rubric in this huge collection.[10]

Turning now to specific research topics in Chilean economic history, it is necessary to stress the utility, at least during the initial phases of

---

9. *Catálogo de la biblioteca i manuscritos de don Benjamín Vicuña Mackenna* (Santiago: Imprenta Cervantes, 1886); *Catálogo del archivo de Claudio Gay* (Santiago: Dirección de Bibliotecas, Archivos y Museos: Archivo Nacional, 1963); *Catálogo de la colección de manuscritos de don José Ignacio Victor Eyzaguirre* (Santiago: Dirección General de Prisiones, Imprenta, 1944) and Archivo Nacional, *Catálogo Fondos Varios* (Santiago: Dirección General de Prisiones, Imprenta, 1952).

10. Upon closer examination my typescript suggests first, why it must be accepted as a tentative guide to the collection; it also suggests why the Archivo Nacional has delayed publishing it. A great many volume numbers are missing from the index. Volumes 1150-1157, for example, could be an important set of records, yet there is no way of knowing if they might be useful unless one checks each volume individually. The same can be applied to volumes 4783-4793, 4361-4747, 3722-3733, and other diverse sets of documents. There is also confusion arising from the fact that volumes 4759-4782 are listed as Estanco, 1739-1842 while volumes 4779-4780 are listed as Instituto Nacional, 1825-1836. Contaduría Mayor, Segunda Serie, contains a listing by dates of all decrees involving collection and expenditures of funds. It is useful, for example, in fixing the precise date a person went on the public payroll or when a particular law, such as a new tariff law, officially became operative.

Economic History (1800-1850)   77

investigation, of what might best be called a "legislative introduction" to a particular country and period. Too often, unless one has worked long years with the ideology and the idiom of a particular place and time, it is easy to miss some important bits of information. Laws are not necessarily of great importance to the economic historian, yet the ideas embodied in the preamble of a particular piece of draft legislation, whether dealing with coinage, mortgage laws, or protective measures for domestic industry, can prove useful. With the particular provisions of the proposed law, the preamble reveals not only the basic objectives of the current political leadership but suggests potential areas for fruitful archival investigation. Debates over such proposed measures in Congress, newspapers, and private correspondence greatly facilitate the researcher's speedy orientation to his period.

An investigator new to the country or to the first half of the nineteenth century is fortunate in Chile. Its national legislature has functioned almost continuously, whether appointed or elective, from 1818 onward. Yet, the *Sesiones del Congreso Nacional* should be considered only a prelude to archival digging. In the case of the Ministerio de Hacienda archives, a number of volumes contain material sent to the legislature as well as a number of volumes with congressional messages to this ministry.[11] The same applies to the Ministerio de lo Interior collection.[12] These volumes of correspondence after 1845 are absolutely essential since the *Sesiones del Congreso Nacional* contain only the debates. Valuable insights into official thinking on economic policy matters can be obtained, as stated earlier, from the annual presidential and ministerial reports; occasionally, an understanding of policy disputes at the highest level can

---

11. In the Ministerio de Hacienda collection, for example, volume 43, Correspondencia Cámara, 1818-1823, and volume 78, Correspondencia Cámara, 1824-1828, contain copies of messages sent to the legislature by the Minister of the Treasury. Messages from the legislature to the Minister are contained in, among others, volume 34, Senado, 1818-1820, volume 45, Senado, 1819-1837, and volume 101, Congreso, 1828-1849. Here might be a good place to mention that one cannot rely fully on the terminal dates for the papers in any volume. On occasion they contain supporting papers from an earlier date than that listed for the volume. (This might be yet another reason why some documents are missing from their proper place in the archival collection, as mentioned in note 5.)

12. The Ministry of Interior archives volumes dealing with the legislature are such numbers as 20, 67, 91, 107, and 135.

CHILE 78

be gleaned from the first four unnumbered volumes of the minutes of the Consejo de Estado for the years 1833-1852.

Identification of individuals participating in debates on national economic issues, at least on the official level, and the subsequent search for private correspondence in such archival collections as the Fondo Varios, is facilitated by two handy reference works. The first of these is Luis Valencia Avaria's *Anales de la república,* 2 vols. (Santiago: Imprenta Universitaria, 1951). It contains not only basic constitutional texts but also, more importantly, a complete listing of all chief executives, cabinet ministers, and members of the legislature with the exact dates of their exercise of official functions. Valencia, unfortunately, does not list the members of the Council of State, but Manuel S. Montt has since remedied this minor deficiency.[13] Both Valencia and Montt are essential tools for the identification of individuals active in the formulation of national economic policy during the first half of the nineteenth century.[14]

Coming now to more specific problems of archival research, I shall examine a few topics in some depth and, largely because of the work already done in some areas, discuss briefly some other possible subjects for investigation. Since an inadequate money supply was one of the persistent problems plaguing the Chilean economy during the first half of the nineteenth century, it might be useful to begin with topics concerning the supply of money and the closely related matter of interest rates which touched virtually all aspects of the economy

Chile did not officially adopt paper currency until 1861, so the matter of money supply focuses upon the production of the Casa de Moneda and the import and export of coins. Mint production is one of the easier and, at the same time, more difficult subjects to work with. For the uninitiated the major difficulty is the precise meaning of the technical terms used in archival records. Fortunately, Humberto Burzio clearly explains

---

13. "Personal del Consejo de Estado, 1833-1874," *Revista Chilena de historia y geografía,* 123 (1954-55):168-200.

14. The high-level considerations of various individuals must be considered in the light of personal petitions and requests. Thus, in the Ministerio de Hacienda collection volumes 72, 159, and 123, Solicitudes de Particulares indicate how existing laws and regulations are operating upon the more articulate common man.

most of them.[15] There are two major archival collections dealing with the mint. In Contaduría Mayor, Primera Serie, volumes 1332-1536 cover its operations from 1749, when it first began production, until 1839/40. In the Ministerio de Hacienda collection one should consult not only those volumes specifically entitled Casa de Moneda but the numerous volumes of Miscelánea and Contaduría Mayor.[16]

Reports and complaints about the adequacy of the currency can be found in a number of places. One of the more important sources is the correspondence between the Minister of Finance and the national legislature, provincial assemblies (when they existed), and other government offices both in Santiago and in the provinces.[17] Newspapers, especially from the 1840s onward, are another convenient source of information about the money supply. Reports of the Estanco's provincial agents, after it reverted to government management in 1826, occasionally contain information on financial conditions as does the collection Tribunal de Consulado.

Major aspects of monetary policy dealt with efforts to obtain an adequate supply of bullion for the mint, to introduce copper fractional currency, and, finally, efforts to establish a nationally chartered bank

---

15. *Diccionario de la moneda hispanoamericana,* 3 vols. (Santiago: Fondo Histórico y Bibliográfico José Toribio Medina, 1956-1958).

16. Ministerio de Hacienda, volume 25, Miscelánea, 1817-31, for example, contains material related to money supply because of a report of a technical team, which investigated La Moneda's operations in 1849, as well as papers, some dating from 1776, relating to proposals for the striking of copper fractional currency. Volume 58, Miscelánea, 1820-49, contains papers relating to the shipment of copper coins produced for the Chilean government in London in 1835 and 1836. Volume 100, Contaduría Mayor, 1827-49, in the same collection, contains papers relating to government efforts to buy bullion for minting in 1831. Such bullion purchases, for 1832, are found in Hacienda, Intendencia de Coquimbo, 1832. These are but two examples of the way in which an investigator must not be misled by the titles given to specific volumes, and the particularly useful nature of the Miscelánea and Contaduría Mayor volumes in the Ministerio de Hacienda archives.

17. In addition to the legislative-ministerial correspondence mentioned in note 15, one should also consult such volumes in the Ministerio de Hacienda collection, as an unnumbered one entitled Correspondencia Interior, 1817-1823, which contains copies of messages from the Ministry of Finance to other offices in Santiago. (Volume 93, for example, covers the period January 2, 1826 until November 6, 1829.) On the other hand, correspondence with offices outside Santiago are generally entitled Correspondencia Exterior (volumes 107 and 154 for example).

of issue. Chapter One of the 1901 edition of the *Resumen de la Hacienda Pública de Chile* (Santiago, 1901) contains a convenient compilation of the major pieces of monetary legislation.[18] Dimensions of the disputes over these issues can be traced in the correspondence between the Ministries of Hacienda and Interior and that of the national legislature and the provincial intendants; congressional debates, newspaper comments, and the private correspondence of key individuals also provide important, albeit at times frustratingly fragmentary, information on conflicting points of view.[19]

Official figures on coin imports and exports, as with all items in foreign trade, are difficult to estimate prior to 1844, since the government did not begin to publish trade statistics until that time. Even then, widespread smuggling tends to reduce the utility of such figures. The only way of estimating coin movements in and out of the country prior to 1844 is the laborious one of examining the volumes for the various customs offices, especially Valparaíso, in the Contaduría Mayor collection. Miscelánea volumes in the Ministry of Finance collection occasionally contain retrospective tables on official coin movements. Official figures should, of course, be supplemented by individual observations such as those of provincial intendants, foreign merchants, and newspaper commentators.

Interest rates are difficult to isolate. Quotations began to appear in newspapers from the 1820s, but a detailed study of prevailing rates must rely on lawsuits in the Colección Judicial and contracts in the Colección Notarial. Interest rates varied with the type of activity for which the money was borrowed. Lowest rates were generally for short-term commercial transactions, while higher ones prevailed for farmers and artisans. These charges for money thus played a role in such policy questions as agricultural expansion and industrial diversification.

The importance of the import and export trade in Chilean economic

---

18. This work was prepared by the Dirección General de Contabilidad for the Buffalo Exposition of 1901. In using other chapters of this work, such as those on government finances or foreign trade, one should be aware of the fact that the government changed its accounting procedures on a number of occasions during the nineteenth century and that the figures are not comparable over a long period of time.

19. An additional source of frustration and irritation arises from the fact that much public business was apparently conducted at evening *tertulias* or upon park benches along the Alameda.

Economic History (1800-1850) 81

history cannot be denied. Closely related to the export trade, of course, is the status of mining and agricultural production. In very general terms, mineral exports provided the bulk of the country's foreign exchange earnings, and hence influenced the volume of imports, while agricultural production affected the lives of the bulk of the population. Recent United States scholarship on mining and agriculture provide convenient summaries of conditions during the first half of the nineteenth century together with suggestions on the variety of archival sources which must be consulted in further investigations.[20]

The various factors influencing Chile's internal and external trade include transportation, money supply, commercial regulations--tariff levels, contract provisions, foreclosure procedures, etc.--as well as production in the two primary sectors of the economy. The legislative focus mentioned earlier would do a great deal to clarify the variety of factors helping to shape commercial life.[21]

---

20. Chapter Five of Leland Pederson's *The Mining Industry of the Norte Chico, Chile* (Evanston, Illinois: Northwestern University, Department of Geography, 1966) studies production during the nineteenth century. Arnold Bauer, "Expansión económica en una sociedad tradicional: Chile central en el siglo XIX," *Historia,* 9 (1970):137-235, contains useful leads to early nineteenth-century agricultural production.

21. Roads and bridges, for example, are one of the less spectacular aspects of economic life. The marshalling of technical and financial resources necessary to provide the country with an adequate system of land transportation is one that must be culled from the archives. The same applies for postal services. In these two cases, one must consult not only legislative records but also Ministry of Interior archives, such as volume 4 which contains, among other items, material pertaining to Correos. It is also necessary to explore the Ministerio de Hacienda archives for national expenditures on these two items and the pertinent volumes in Contaduría Mayor material. Concerning roads, one should also examine *cabildo* records when they exist, since municipalities were mainly responsible for the maintenance and improvement of local roads.

One moderately useful source of information for gauging levels of internal commercial activity is the sales tax *(alcabala).* Changes in this tax should be traced firstly in the legislative records, then in the Contaduría Mayor, Segunda Serie, to find when the new rate became operative. In the catalogue for Contaduría Mayor, Primera Serie, consulted there seems to be some confusion in numbering, but there are probably at least six volumes containing records of *alcabala* collections.

The government began publication of import and export information in 1844 under the title *Estadística comercial de la república de Chile.* Certain problems arise if one relies exclusively on the monetary values of imports and exports since the government relied on official valuations for various items rather than their true market value. Thus, to use this series effectively, it is necessary to rely exclusively on the volume

Mineral production and the variety of problems associated with it can be traced in a variety of archival areas. The Tribunal de Minería collection, an obvious starting point, must be used in conjunction with *cabildo* records of the major mining centers, such as La Serena, and the *aduanas* and *aduanas y tesorerías* volumes in the Contaduría Mayor series. In this latter collection it is important to concentrate not only on the mining ports of Copiapó, Coquimbo, and Huasco but also upon Valparaíso, since much of Chile's mineral production passed through this commercial center. Correspondence between provincial official and the Ministers of Finance and Interior, reports of Estanco agents, and the six Minería volumes in the Contaduría Mayor collection should also be consulted. More detailed information on mining industry operations can also be gleaned from the Judicial and Notarial collections, especially for the northern mining area called the Norte Chico.[22]

Landownership patterns, rural labor costs, and the profitability of agricultural enterprises during the first half of the nineteenth century constitute the three major themes in the country's agrarian history. The size of landholdings and the variations in the importance of pure size in relation to access to markets had social, political, and economic repercussions. Because of the paucity of studies dealing with this subject, one must begin from the raw archival sources. Wills, dowries, foreclosures are the types of papers that must be studied in both the Notarial and Judicial collections.[23]

The profitability of agrarian holdings cannot be gauged with any degree of precision at present. Toward mid-century the cadastral commission

---

figures given for each year's trade and then attempt to arrive at some approximate current market value for these items. If one desires a reasonably clear picture of imports and exports prior to 1844, he must examine the various *aduana* and *aduana y tesorería* records in the Contaduría Mayor, Primera Seria.

22. An illuminating discussion of the use of archival resources, albeit for the eighteenth century, can be found in Marcello Carmagnani, *El salariado minero en Chile colonial. Su desarrollo en una sociedad provincial: El Norte Chico, 1690-1800* (Santiago: Editorial Universitaria, Universidad de Chile, Centro de Historia Colonial, 1963), pp. 13-20.

23. Bauer's study cited in note 20 illustrates the manner in which these two archival sources can be used to good advantage.

attempted to fix the tax base for agrarian holdings, but just how much its final figures were influenced by size of holdings, access to markets, improvements on the property, or plain envy or animosity is difficult to assess.[24] Tithe collections provide a rough estimate of the relative prosperity of various areas of the country prior to the full implementation of the cadastral levies, yet these tithe figures present certain difficulties. They were usually farmed out by districts with only the most general indication in the official records of individual assessments.[25]

These observations on archival sources for Chilean economic history during the first half of the nineteenth century have dealt only peripherally with mining and agriculture and have concentrated on other subjects. The main reason is that mining and agriculture have already been studied more intensively than government finances, money supply, domestic and foreign trade, and commercial regulations. It is time, I believe, that economic historians stop treating the Chilean economy as if it were an esoteric plant that must be approached in the most gingerly of fashions. It may be time-consuming and awfully drudgery-ridden work, but in the long run, it can be a most illuminating and meaningful task.

---

24. The cadastral tax, first proposed by the government in 1831, was designed to raise $100,000 on a prorated basis. Hence, the estimated income of each piece of property did not reflect its actual value but rather a proportionate share of a region's total amount of tax. See the six unnumbered volumes on the *catastro* of 1833 in Contaduría Mayor.

25. Tithe collections are in the Contaduría Mayor, volumes 1141-1148. In the Ministerio de Hacienda archives attention should be paid to Miscelánea volumes. Volume 59, Miscelánea, 1820-49 contains the amount of the tithe for each province in 1834; volume 64, Miscelánea, 1821-33, contains many papers pertaining to the tithe, including the auctions for 1834 and 1835. In the Ministry of the Interior archives, volume 4 is but one example of material pertaining to the tithe, It contains some twenty folios pertaining to the work of the Junta de Almoneda y de Diezmos, 1827 á 1831.

Sources for the Study of Chilean Political History, 1810-1850
Patricio Estellé

The period from 1810 to 1850 has been of particular interest in Chilean historical bibliography. With the passage of time, certain fundamental works have appeared which are of special significance to the potential researcher. For a better understanding of the period, we should distinguish two important epochs: the first, the period of independence; and the second, often called the "Authoritarian Republic," which began in 1830 and corresponded to the presidential regimes of Joaquín Prieto and Manuel Bulnes.

Clearly such a classification emphasizes the essentially political aspects of the period under consideration, but the sources for both the independence and post-1830 periods might be broken down in the following manner:

COLLECTIONS OF DOCUMENTS

The most important collection of documents is perhaps the *Colección de historiadores y de documentos relativos a la independencia de Chile* (Santiago, 1900-   ). This series began to appear in 1900, and since then, a total of thirty-seven volumes have been published. There is also an *Index*, prepared by Sergio Villalobos, which was published in 1956. Another important source is the *Archivo de don Bernardo O'Higgins* (Santiago, 1916-   ). The first volume of this collection appeared in 1946, and so far a total of twenty-two have been published. The first twenty volumes have been indexed by Luis Valencia Avaria, *Indice temático de los 20 primeros tomos y un primer apéndice* (Santiago, 1965).

OFFICIAL DOCUMENTS

Memorias ministeriales are the yearly reports published by the different ministries which explain their activities. The various ministries are Guerra y Marina, created 21 April 1821; Interior, 14 August 1824; Hacienda y Justicia, Culto e Instrucción Pública, created 1 February 1837.

Mensajes presidenciales are presidential addresses delivered to the Congress upon the convocation of its ordinary sessions. Finally are the *Sesiones de los cuerpos legislativos de la república de Chile* (Santiago, 1887-1908), thirty-seven volumes covering legislative sessions from 1811 to 1845. Valentín Letelier edited this series.

LEGISLATIVE DOCUMENTS

The *Boletín de leyes y decretos del gobierno* (Santiago, 1823-1954) is a large body of legal documents which began to be published in 1823, has been supplemented, and continued publication until 1954. The *Leyes promulgadas en Chile desde 1810 hasta el 1 de junio de 1912,* 3 vols. (Santiago, 1912) was compiled by Ricardo Anguita. The scholar should also consult Cristobal Valdés, *Colección de las leyes y decretos del gobierno desde 1810 hasta 1923* (Santiago, 1946) and *Anales de la república* (Santiago, 1951), prepared by Luis Valencia Avaria.

GENERAL CATALOGUES

Perhaps the first of these works was that of Miguel Luis and Gregorio Amunátegui, "Catálogo de los libros y folletos impresos en Chile desde que se introdujo la imprenta," *Revista de ciencias y letras,* I (1857). In addition to the works of Briseño, Toribio Medina, Feliú Cruz, and Silva Castro, which were mentioned in the introduction, one should also consult: Luis Ignacio Silva, *Ensayo de una bibliografía histórica y geográfica de Chile* (Santiago, 1902); Luis Montt, *Bibliografía chilena precedida de un bosquejo histórico sobre los primeros años de la prensa del país* (Santiago, 1907); Emilio Vaisse, *Bibliografía general de Chile. Primera parte. Diccionario de autores y obras* (Santiago, 1915), and the *Revista de bibliografía chilena y extranjera*, published from 1913 until 1918.

THE PRESS

The indexes which exist dealing with the press are: Juan Bautista Alberdi, *Legislación de la prensa en Chile* (Valparaíso, 1846); Pedro Godoy, *Espiritú de la prensa chilena o colección de artículos escogidos de la misma desde el principio de la Revolución hasta la época presente* (Santiago, 1847); Ramón Briseño, "Cuadro sinóptico completo de los diarios y periódicos de Chile, 1812-1884," *Anales de la Universidad de Chile* (1886). Other works of interest are: Nicolás Anrique, *Bibliografía de las principales revistas y periódicos de Chile* (Santiago, 1904); *Semana retrospectiva de la prensa chilena. La prensa chilena desde 1812 hasta 1840* (Santiago, 1934); and *Colección de antiguos periódicos chilenos,* edited by Guillermo Feliú Cruz.

SPECIALIZED JOURNALS

Journals which should be consulted are *Historia,* published by the Catholic University of Santiago since 1960, as well as the *Revista chilena de historia y geografía* and the *Boletín de la Academia Chilena de la Historia.* The former has been published since 1911, and two indexes, one by René Feliú Cruz and the second by Francisco Santana, have been published covering the years 1911-1957. The *Boletín* first appeared in 1933. Raúl Silva Castro published an index in 1955 covering the first twenty years of the journal.

GENERAL HISTORIES AND BIOGRAPHIES

The signal works are: Claudio Gay, *Historia física y política de Chile* (Paris, 1844-1854); Diego Barros Arana, *Historia jeneral de Chile* (Santiago, 1844-1854); and Francisco Antonio Encina, *Historia de Chile desde la prehistoria hasta 1891* (Santiago, 1942-1952). Specific individuals have been discussed in José Toribio Medina, "Ensayo de una bibliografía de las obras de don José Miguel Carrera," *Revista del Museo de la Plata,* 4 (1892); Manuel de Salas, *Escritos de don Manuel de Salas y documentos relativos a él y a su familia* (Santiago, 1910-1914); José Zamudio, *Fuentes bibliográficas para el estudio de la vida y la época de Bernardo O'Higgins* (Santiago, 1946). Raúl Silva Castro published a *Bibliografía de don Juan Egaña* (Santiago, 1949) as well as edited *Escritos políticos de Camilio Henríquez* (Santiago, 1960). The Academia Chilena de la Historia is also editing a series of materials on Joaquín Prieto.

COLLECTIONS OF WRITINGS

Ernesto de la Cruz edited *Epistolario de don Bernardo O'Higgins* (Santiago, 1916-1919) as well as the *Epistolario de don Diego Portales* (Santiago, 1936-1937). Fernando Márquez de la Plata edited the *Correspondencia de don Bernardo de Vera y Pintado que se conserva en el Archivo General de la Nación Argentina y Biblioteca Nacional de Buenos Aires* (Buenos Aires, 1941). The writings of Mariano Egaña appeared in 1948, and the late Jaime Eyzaguirre edited the *Archivo epistolar de la familia Eyzaguirre, 1747-1845* (Buenos Aires, 1960).

FOREIGN TRAVELERS AND THEIR ACCOUNTS

Guillermo Feliú Cruz's *Notas para una bibliografía sobre viajeros relativos a Chile* (Santiago, 1962) is perhaps the most complete source for this subject.

Chilean Economic Development, 1850-1900: A Primary Source Guide
Robert Oppenheimer

The fundamental characteristic of the period from 1850 to 1900 was the expansion in all aspects of Chilean life, particularly in the area of economics. During the 1880s, Chile doubled in size because of the incorporation of vast quantities of territory in the northern desert and the southern forest regions. The population rose from 1.4 million persons to 2.8 million, and there was a major increase in the migration from rural to urban areas (the 1854 urban population was 20 percent, and in 1895 it was 45.5 percent). The number of population centers with more than 2,000 inhabitants increased from thirty-eight in 1865 to ninety-four in 1895, and three cities (Santiago, Valparaíso, and Concepción) became modern urban centers.[1] There was a substantial increase in the government bureaucracy, and a significant expansion of the transportation and communication networks, including railroads, roads, coast-trade, telegraph, regular mail service, and public works. This infrastructural development was a direct result of the tremendous expansion of the national economy, particularly in the exportation of mining and agricultural products.

In the second half of the nineteenth century, the national economy expanded tremendously, particularly the export sector. The concentration of production in this sector came at the expense of manufacturing and industrial growth.[2] This development process did not occur in a gradual upward progression, but in diverse cycles and spurts of rapid growth and acute depression. This cyclical economic development significantly influenced the various sectors and regions of Chilean society in diverse

---

1. Population statistics are from Carlos Hurtado Ruiz-Tagle, "Population Concentration and Economic Development: The Chilean Case" (Ph.D. dissertation, Harvard University, 1966), Tables 1, 2, 5, 7, and 9.

2. For statistics on exports see *La estadística comercial de Chile*, for the years in which it was published.

ways, affecting different economic groups, geographic regions, larger cities versus the smaller towns, and the urban versus the rural areas.

The worst aspect of this type of dependent export economy manifested itself in the inequitable distribution of wealth among the various sectors of the population. Only the few benefited significantly from the land, natural resources, capital, credit, education, political power, and social prestige. A new class of professionals, technicians, artisans, executives, managers, and bureaucrats emerged during the period and became a dynamic socio-political force in the twentieth century, but the majority of the population benefited little from the economic expansion, and this disproportionate distribution of wealth considerably increased social tensions. In the late nineteenth century, labor unrest, trade unionism, and class-conscious political movements (Marxist parties) appeared for the first time, although these did not become important factors until well into the twentieth century.

Economic development between 1850 and 1900 can be divided into two distinct stages of expansion. The first, from 1850-1879, was characterized by the initial participation of Chile in the modern industrial international economy, particularly with the increasing production of minerals. In the decades of the 1850s and 1860s, Chile became the world's leading producer of copper and a major producer of silver. The period was marked by two international disputes (the War with Spain, 1865-66, and the War of the Pacific, 1879-83), two internal revolts (1851 and 1859), and a series of economic crises which were closely tied to the world economic situation (the depressions of 1853, 1857-61, 1870-72, 1876-79). Chilean customs revenues, the major source of government revenue, fluctuated significantly in relation to internal political stability, war, and economic depression.[3]

The second stage from 1879 to 1900 was characterized by the development of the nitrate industry and the inflationary spiral. After the War of the Pacific, Chile became the world's leading producer of natural nitrates. Inflation became acute and is still one of the nation's most

---

3. Mining production and export figures can be found in: Alberto Hermann, *La producción en Chile de los metales i minerales más importantes de las sales naturales, del azufre i del guano desde la conquista hasta fines del año 1902* (Santiago: Imp. Barcelona, 1903). Custom revenues from *Resumen de la hacienda pública de Chile desde 1833 hasta 1914* (London: Spottiswoode and Co., 1914), p. 96.

serious economic problems. Inflation also became an important factor in the increasing social tensions which led to a number of major strikes and labor disputes in the late nineteenth century and early twentieth century. The inflationary economic policies of the government clearly benefited the upper classes. The inflated and depreciated currency reduced the importance of levying taxes, and favored landowning debtors and all who sold goods in foreign currencies for export. It also allowed employers to pay their workers in Chile's depreciated currency. The growth of the nitrate industry also exaggerated Chile's dependence upon foreign markets and investments. Finally, the period was marked by a *coup d'état* in 1891 which ousted President José Manuel Balmaceda. Balmaceda had sought to broaden the suffrage and democratize the government, but even more important, he had proposed economic reforms. He fostered measures to curb inflation, to implement land reform programs, and to curtail the growing influence of foreign investment. Eventually a coalition of landowners, exporters, and foreign investors who opposed his attempts at economic and political reform ousted him.[4]

An examination of bibliographical material available reveals a favorable situation for the study of Chilean economic history between 1850 and 1900. There have been a substantial number of general and interpretative economic histories of Chile, which include sections on the second half of the nineteenth century.[5] While few monographs and no general economic history of the period have been written, the works available provide a clear understanding of the period from the point of view of the various

---

4. Economic interpretation of Balmaceda's ouster is taken from Hernán Ramírez N., *Balmaceda y la counterrevolución de 1891* (Santiago: Ed. Universitaria, 1969). For an equally excellent political interpretation of the 1891 revolt, see Harold Blakemore, *British Nitrates and Chilean Politics, 1886-1896* (London: University of London, 1973).

5. This list includes what I consider representative of a particular point of view or the most important works on political economy: Francisco Encina, *Nuestra inferioridad económica* (Santiago: Ed. Universitaria, 1955); Julio César Jobet, *Ensayo crítico del desarrollo económico social de Chile* (Santiago: Ed. Universitaria, 1955); Daniel Martner, *Historia de Chile, historia económica* (Santiago: Univ. of Chile, 1929); Aníbal Pinto Santa Cruz, *Chile: Un caso de desarrollo frustrado* (Santiago: Ed. Universitaria, 1959); Hernán Ramírez N., *Historia del imperialismo en Chile* (Santiago: Empresa Austral, 1960); Gmo. Subercaseaux, *Historia de las doctrinas económicas en América Latina y en especial en Chile* (Santiago: Imp. Universo, 1924).

political and economic theories prevalent in Chile. Scholars have tended to emphasize the epoch after the War of the Pacific much more than pre-1879 Chile. In fact, little has been done to study the most salient economic characteristics of the first stage, including urbanization, economic growth patterns, depressions, and the impact of the initial period of economic expansion into the international markets. For the post-war stage of development, a number of studies covered such important topics as nitrate mining, monetary crisis, and the economic implications of the 1891 revolution, but most of these studies are very general and, again, deal mainly with the export economy and the political implications of the economic issues. Other topics covering the entire period--including free trade versus protectionism, state investment versus private interests, national entrepreneurs versus foreign investors, a gold based monetary system versus a paper-money system, and the role of government spending--have received little or no attention.

The first question a researcher in economic history must ask himself is this: "Do the empirical data exist to undertake studies in economic history"? The empirical data from the various archives, government agencies, newspapers, and company records are extensive but must be carefully scrutinized and checked for accuracy. In 1835 the first in a series of regular censuses was taken; for our period the censuses are for 1854, 1865, 1875, 1885, and 1895. These censuses not only included material on population growth but also information on professions, urbanization, and the number of foreigners in Chile. In 1844 the Oficina de Aduanas (Customs) began to keep annual *estadística comercial* (records of ship movements in Chilean ports by country of registry and port of entrance, listing importation of all goods and merchandise by port of entry and country of origin and exportation of all goods by port of debarkation and country of destination). In 1848 the Oficina Central de Estadística (Bureau of Statistics) began publishing a yearly statistical abstract (*Anuario estadístico*) and numerous miscellaneous statistical documents containing data on the population, agricultural production (*Estadística agrícola de la república de Chile*), mining production, and for the late nineteenth century, manufactured goods. The abstract also published irregularly information on public employees, roads, railroads, finance, crime, public instruction, and many other topics. In 1874 the *Registro civil* (Civil Registry) began to keep records on birth, death, and marriage, which had previously been kept by the church. Although many of the church records for Santiago were lost in the 1863 fire which destroyed the National Cathedral, parishes scattered throughout the country do have records covering the second half of the nineteenth century.

This statistical data can be corroborated by newspapers as well as regional and local government official reports found in the Biblioteca Nacional (National Library, hereafter referred to as BN). Newspapers such as *El Mercurio* and *El Ferrocarril* represented commercial interests and printed almost daily records on the commercial activities of Santiago and Valparaíso as well as information on other regions. Provincial newspapers printed extensive quantities of economic data on their regions, including ship movements, production statistics for mining and agriculture, licensing of businesses, and wholesale prices for commodities in Santiago, Valparaíso, and London. All newspapers advertised auctions, the selling of property, and printed annual reports of stock companies. These newspapers often carried on vigorous debates among themselves on various economic issues offering a clear indication of the different economic attitudes and philosophies prevalent in Chile and their application to the Chilean situation. Chile has a strong journalistic tradition, and its newspapers represented all prevailing political and economic philosophies in Chile. The *intendentes* and *gobernadores* (provincial and departmental officials whose equivalent in the United States would be state and county government heads) were required to submit annual reports to the Ministry of Interior on the state of affairs within their jurisdictional area. These reports often centered on economic matters, including infrastructural development, government construction projects, transfer of property, licensing of businesses, and production, and were published as part of the Ministry's annual report to Congress (all Ministries published these *Memorias*), or under separate cover, and are found in the BN.

The BN houses two major collections which are important to our survey of materials (the Sala Medina and the Sala General) as well as the newspaper collection. The Sala Medina contains the collected works of two of Chile's most distinguished historians, José Toribio Medina and Diego Barros Arana. Both collections are well catalogued and contain valuable miscellaneous documents and reports on Chilean economic history. The Sala General contains most of the general works and documents on Chilean history and has two catalogues: one by author and the other by subject. The subject catalogue has vague headings (administration, politics, economics, and religion), and neither catalogue is up-to-date (the BN is very understaffed). Books are shelved by size in a closed stack system. The only method to guarantee that every effort has been made to survey all works on a given topic is to peruse all the cards under a subject heading. The Sala General contains copies of all Congressional debates *(Sesiones del Congreso)*, the *Boletín de Leyes* (Bulletin of Laws), and the *Diario Oficial* (Official Government Publication of Laws, Decrees, and Pronouncements from 1877). The *memorias de las sociedades anónimas de Chile* (annual stock company reports) for the period are also housed in the Sala General. From 1854, the government required that all stock companies publish an annual report on their financial status and list all stockholders.

The *Cuentas de gastos y presupuestos generales* (government budgets) are available in the Sala General from 1845 to the present. These contain detailed balance sheets of each ministry and government agency and their proposed budgets. The *Rentas agrícolas* for 1852 and 1874 list all *fundos* (farms) over a specified value, their location, the owner, and the annual tax paid on the land. In 1873, the government required annual *Matrículas de patentes* (license tax rolls) of all businesses within a municipality to be published, and many of these are available in the BN or published in newspapers. Before 1874 some *matrículas* were printed partially or in full in newspapers. One can also find a variety of official reports, statistical surveys, travel accounts and miscellaneous documents on the Chilean economy in the BN. The *Boletines* of a number of national lobbies are available including the Sociedad Nacional de Agricultura, Sociedad Nacional de Minería, and the Sociedad de Fomento Fabril. These contain statistical abstracts, articles, and editorials on the economy and other valuable information.

The most important sources are the archives: the majority of which are housed in the Archivo Nacional (which is in the same building as the BN but administered separately and hereafter referred to as AN). The collections available for our period in the AN include the Ministry Archive, the Archivo Judicial, Archivo Notarial, Archivo de Fondos Varios, Archivo del Diccionario Eclesiástico, Archivo de Claudio Gay, and Archivo de Benjamín Vicuña Mackenna. Much of this material is well indexed, and the efficient and friendly staff knows what materials are available. The Archivo de Fondos Varios contains a myriad of different materials and must be scrutinized for material that might be of interest to the scholar. The Archivos de Claudio Gay and Benjamín Vicuña Mackenna contain the notes and observations of two of Chile's most astute observers of the nineteenth century. The Archivo del Diccionario Eclesiástico is a biographical dictionary of all priests in Chile in the nineteenth and part of the twentieth centuries.

The Archivo Judicial contains the transcripts and written records pertaining to all criminal and civil cases in Chile and is indexed by judicial department, volume, file number, and litigants. Disputes over land or water discuss in detail the properties involved. Probates of wills and divorce proceedings usually provide detailed listing of the property holdings of the deceased, the division of the property among the heirs, or property holdings of the parties to a divorce. Often when a will was held in probate for an extended period, the court kept accurate records of all transactions involving the subject properties, including accurate accountings of business operations or the administration of *fundos*. These could give us a clearer picture of the business practices of Chilean entrepreneurs.

The Ministry Archive contains the correspondence of the various ministries. The Ministry of Foreign Relations contains many reports on the role of Chilean consuls and ambassadors in promoting Chilean business overseas and the export economy. The most important for our purposes are those of Interior (AMI), Hacienda (AMH), and Industria y Obras Públicas (AMIOP). The Ministry of Interior was responsible for all roads, railroads, customs, telegraphs, public works, and internal security. Its Archive contains salaries and employee rosters of the ministry and all projects under the ministry's jurisdiction. Data on railroads, for example, include plans for construction, monthly progress reports, lists of employees, salaries, reports on working conditions, the accounts of the project, financing, and other pertinent data. After 1887, the Ministry of Industry and Public Works took charge of all transportation, communication, and public works projects and also collected data on industry and manufacturing. The AMH contains detailed data similar to that in the AMI for the agencies within its jurisdiction. The Ministry of the Treasury also kept detailed records on all aspects of national finances, including records on the external and internal debts, amortization of these debts, the national economy, production, government expenditures, *estancos* (government monopolies), banking, and the Caja de Crédito Hipotecario (National Mortgage Bank).

The Archivo Notarial contains all notarized documents which are catalogued by judicial department, *escribano* (notary), and year. Each volume has a table of contents indicating the persons involved and the nature of the notarized document. Wills, sale and purchase of property, contracts, statutes of stock companies, bankruptcies (also found in the judicial archives), and partnerships are among the various types of documents in the notary records. The Conservador de Minas also is included and contains all documents on the transfer of mine ownership, formation of companies and partnerships, the dissolution of the operation of a mine, and the declaration of claims. Also under separate volumes are the records of the Caja de Crédito Hipotecario.

There are also a number of archives located outside the AN. Much of the judicial archive of Santiago is housed in the basement of the Supreme Court Building (Palacios de los Tribunales). The Museo de Benjamín Vicuña Mackenna contains copies of all his works as well as personal notes and letters not in the AN. The various government agencies and departments maintain their own archives, which often contain some documents from the nineteenth century, though most of the material has either been donated to the AN or destroyed because of a lack of space. In my research I found this to be the case for the Archivo de los Ferrocarriles del Estado and the Archivo del Departamento de Tierras y Bienes Raíces Nacionales. The Archivo de las Juntas de Beneficencias (Municipal Public Welfare Agencies) can often be located in a particular municipality, if they still exist, but are not indexed or catalogued. Those for Santiago, for instance, are kept at the medical school of the University of Chile.

Though little has been done in terms of monographic studies of the Chilean economy in the second half of the nineteenth century, the empirical data are available to attempt studies on such diversified economic topics as national and regional production, regional growth patterns, urbanization, foreign investment, Chilean investment, entrepreneurial studies, sector studies (banking, mining, transportation, stock companies), managerial and administrative sector analysis, labor, tax structure, distribution of income and wealth, government spending, and others.

Notarial and Judicial Archives as Sources for Nineteenth-Century Chilean Economic History
Thomas F. O'Brien, Jr.

One of the major challenges facing students of nineteenth-century Chilean economic history is the gathering of information on specific economic enterprises. While statistical data on broad trends in the national economy are available, printed sources on private partnerships are nearly non-existent, and the published records of joint-stock companies are usually limited to an occasional semi-annual report or infrequent reference to these firms in the press. A similar lack of information exists in regard to members of the Chilean business community. Published biographical sources such as Virgilio Figueroa's *Diccionario histórico y biográfico de Chile,* 4 vols. (Santiago, 1920-28) tend to emphasize the political and literary accomplishments of prominent business figures. A partial solution to this lack of sources lies in the notarial and judicial archives of major economic centers such as Valparaíso, Santiago, Coquimbo, and Iquique.

The notarial and judicial archives are housed in the Archivo Nacional in Santiago. The notarial records are catalogued in chronological order and bound in separate volumes for each notary. The volumes for large urban centers such as Valparaíso contain carefully prepared alphabetical indexes which are nearly complete. Thus, while the Archivo Notarial de Valparaíso for a single year may amount to as many as 20,000 folios, it is still a usable, albeit time-consuming chronicle of economic history. These manuscripts are a rich source of data on economic enterprises and individual entrepreneurs.

Particularly useful are *estatutos* (company statutes) and purchase and supply agreements which provide information on the formation and operation of both private and joint-stock enterprises. Equally valuable are loan contracts which illuminate the financial structure of firms, their management of capital supply problems, and their ties to the domestic and international credit markets. In addition, the precise reasons for the failure of an economic undertaking are often delineated in notarized copies of bankruptcy proceedings.

Similar types of data contained in the archives can be employed in studies of Chilean entrepreneurs. Partnership contracts, records of loans and land purchases, wills, and *estatutos* permit one to trace the patterns of economic activity of individual businessmen, as well as to compile collective economic biographies.

There are, of course, limitations to the use of these manuscripts. Because of the sheer volume of the materials, using these archives without at least the name and place of origin of the enterprises or persons one wishes to examine would be an exercise in futility. Furthermore, the information they contain must be supplemented by other facts. Whether dealing with institutions or entrepreneurs, the archives provide only a partial picture of their economic development or careers, which often can only be made intelligible by other materials. Such complementary sources may include stock market reports and lists of shareholders published in the press.

On occasion the judicial archives can provide even more extensive data than the type found in notarial records. The entire history of a partnership agreement or financing arrangement may be traced out by one or both of the parties in a legal dispute. Still, a rather haphazard alphabetical and chronological index and the fact that the *pieza* for a single case may run to 200 or more folios makes these archives a cumbersome source to use. Furthermore, only a limited number of firms or individuals are likely to be involved in significant legal disputes. This source, then, should only be consulted in the later stages of a project when the possibilities of notarial research have been exhausted.

Notarial and judicial archives are a valuable and manageable source for economic history. They provide information on the origin, financing, and operation of economic enterprises often unavailable elsewhere. They are also a rich source of data on the careers of both prominent and less well-known members of the national business community about whom information has been sadly lacking. Historians who recognize their limitations will find these archives a most rewarding resource for the study of nineteenth-century Chilean economic history.

The Study of Chilean Political History, 1850-1925: An Introduction to Sources
Arturo Valenzuela

The years between 1850 and 1925 are critical in Chilean political history and require much more study. In the nineteenth century, Chile established a regime which proved to be remarkably stable and, initially, capable of adjusting to significant social and economic change. The administrations of Joaquín Prieto and Manuel Bulnes consolidated a system of presidential authority which permitted the cabinet, and to a lesser extent, the legislature, to play a significant role. Gradually, the legislature, the representative of opposition elements wedded both to tradition and to change, began to demand more power. This struggle between an increasingly powerful centralized secular state and the more conservative forces representing local and clerical interests finally led to the Revolution of 1891, which marked the first clear breakdown of the political system. This revolt, however, did not mark the collapse of a government of laws and institutions, only the shift of political power from the president to the congress. For the first time the triumph of provincial interest contributed to the consolidation of viable party networks extending from the central valley to the country's most remote localities. Political parties became the most prominent feature of Chilean politics, achieving a position of dominance before the rise of a modern national bureaucracy. Although the power of the president increased after 1925, parties continued to structure the political game until the military takeover of 1973.

The period between 1850 and 1925 was also significant because of the important transformations which occurred in Chilean society. Wheat and copper, which constituted Chile's principal exports, were replaced by nitrates, and, the nitrate industry, in turn, stimulated industrialization. Independent of this industrialization, Chile also began to urbanize at the turn of the century at a remarkable rate, thereby changing dramatically the character of social life. Increasingly, middle- and lower-class political professionals began to take over the traditional parties, which had been structured by local elites during the Parliamentary Republic, and an incipient working class began to organize both syndical and party movements.

Throughout this fascinating period, the single most important source for studying political history is the legislative documents. Foremost among these are the congressional debates of the Senate and the Chamber of Deputies.[1] Although initially the legislature did not enjoy much political power, it nonetheless provided a forum for debating the most important national issues. The debates are also excellent sources for studying the evolution of the various political factions which gradually crystalized into full fledged party organizations. During the Parliamentary Republic (1891-1924) they provide fascinating glimpses into political pacts, local brokers, and techniques for mobilization and control of the electorate. Furthermore, the debates are one of the most important sources for qualitative and quantitative information on elections.[2] Since each election had to be approved by the legislative body, it

---

1. For the period from 1811 to 1845 see *Sesiones de los cuerpos legislativos de Chile 1811-1845* (Santiago: Imprenta Cervantes, 1887-1908). After 1845 the debates were published in the *Sesiones del Congreso Nacional,* in separate volumes for each chamber. (The Duke University Library has a complete collection until 1930.) The best place to make use of these materials in Santiago is at the Library of Congress Annex.

2. The debates, supplemented by newspaper accounts, are the primary source for electoral and party information because comprehensive electoral results by party and commune were not published until 1912 when the Oficina Central de Estadística issued its *Censo electoral: Elecciones ordinarias de senadores, diputados y municipales, verificadas el 3 de marzo de 1912* (Santiago: Sociedad Imprenta y Litografía Universo, 1912). This same office published electoral results until the Dirección del Registro Electoral, established by the 1925 Constitution, assumed that function. Despite the paucity of electoral results, electoral registration figures were compiled as early as 1862 with the publication of the first *Censo electoral de Chile* by the Servicio Nacional de Estadística. This publication, which was continued throughout the period, provides basic information on the total registered population by province and department, and detailed information on the occupations of all those registered and the level of voting turnout in particular elections. The 1875-1876 *Censo electoral* included information on the general results of elections though, as noted above, data by commune and party were not published until 1912. No research has been done utilizing these electoral censuses. This resource, and the comprehensive population censuses to be noted later, provide the researcher with a wealth of aggregate data for a study of the political base of Chile's oligarchical democracy.

sometimes took months to scrutinize each election and to decide who was the winner.[3]

The existence of a viable legislature also meant that presidents as well as executive departments and agencies were required to report annually to the congress. These accounts are valuable sources for discerning the evolution of policies and major political controversies as well as the yearly evolution of the governmental bureaucracy. *Memorias* from agencies include financial data, progress reports on particular programs, statistics on personnel as well as agency arguments for new programs and larger resources for the coming year.[4] They occasionally provide good sources for the representation of particular interests tied to a particular agency. Thus the *Memorias* of the Ministry of War give a clear picture of the grievances of professional officers.[5]

For a biographical study of Congress and Chilean political elites, the scholar can use another set of materials. In the first place a few volumes exist which contain biographical data on particular congresses.[6]

---

3. Several key parliamentary and party leaders published their congressional speeches. For a sampling see Miguel Luis Amunátegui, *Discursos parlamentarios*, 2 vols. (Santiago: Imprenta y Litografía y Encuadernación Barcelona, 1906); Enrique Mac-Iver, *Discursos políticos y parlamentarios 1868-1898* (Santiago: Imprenta Moderna, 1899); Alberto Prado Martínez (editor), *Discursos y escritos políticos de don José Manuel Balmaceda 1864-1891* (Santiago: Imprenta Moderna, 1900). Speeches by Benjamín Vicuña Mackenna, José Manuel Irarrazaval, Manuel Rivas Vicuña, and other political leaders are also available in separate volumes.

4. The *Memorias* of the various ministries were issued in separate volumes, though for the early period a compilation is available. See Chile, Documentos parlamentarios, *Discursos de apertura en las sesiones del congreso i memorias ministeriales 1831-1861*, 9 vols. (Santiago: Imprenta del Ferrocarril). For presidential speeches see *Chile, pasado republicano de Chile. Colección de discursos pronunciados por los presidentes de la república ante el Congreso Nacional al inaugurar cada año el período legislativo*, 2 vols. (Concepción: Imprenta el País, 1899). Later speeches are published in the series Chile, Presidente, *Mensaje en la apertura de las sesiones ordinarias del Congreso Nacional*.

5. For an example of the use of the *Memorias* from the Ministry of War to deduce the interests of the armed forces see Arturo Valenzuela, "The Chilean Political System and the Armed Forces, 1830-1924," (M.A. essay, Columbia University, 1967).

6. A sampling includes Joaquín Rodríguez Bravo, *El Congreso de 1882, retratos políticos de sus miembros* (Santiago: Imprenta Victoria de H. Izquierdo, 1882); Alberto Prado Martínez, *Album del congreso chileno, 1900-1903-1906* (Santiago: Imprenta Turín, 1901); Alejandro Valderrama, *Album político* (Santiago, 1915). General political histories of the Conservative Party include Domingo Amunátegui Solar, *Pipiolos y peluçones*

Unfortunately, this task was undertaken systematically each year. However, good biographical dictionaries are available, particularly for the early period.[7] The Virgilio Figueroa volumes are particularly useful because they not only list individuals but entire families, thus making it possible for the researcher to trace the family background of elites. Finally, the Library of Congress has a filing system which includes biographical material of congressmen--but this file is not comprehensive until recent years.

A most impressive resource for the study of the Chilean politics, which has never been systematically used, is the "Fichero de Labor Parlamentaria," a comprehensive catalogue of all of the most important legislative measures initiated by each member of the Congress. These data are available from the early nineteenth century to the present. Included on cards for each member are lists of speeches, projects introduced, and

---

(Santiago: 1939); Marcial Sanfuentes Carrión, *El Partido Conservador* (Santiago: Editorial Universitaria, 1957); Ignacio Arteaga Undurraga (ed.) *Partido Conservador, XIV Convención Nacional, 1947* (Santiago: 1947). For the Liberals, the researcher should consult Oscar del Fierro Court, *El Partido Liberal: Su historia y doctrina* (Santiago: Editorial Universitaria, 1965); Benjamín Vicuña Mackenna, *El Partido Liberal Democrático: Su origen, sus propósitos, sus deberes* (Santiago: 1876). On the radicals see Florencio Durán Bernales, *El Partido Radical* (Santiago: Editorial Nascimiento, 1958), Luis Palma Zúñiga, *Historia del Partido Radical* (Santiago: Editorial Andrés Bello, 1967); Enrique Riquelme Vera, *Evolución del radicalismo chileno* (Santiago: 1943).

7. One of the single most useful sources for the study of Chilean political elites is Luis Valencia Avaria (ed.) *Anales de la República,* 2 vols. (Santiago: Imprenta Universitaria, 1951). This work includes a listing of all citizens who held ministerial and congressional posts from the founding of the republic until 1953 by presidency and legislative session. It also lists alternates for each congressional seat and the exact dates of service. Unfortunately the work does not identify the party affiliation of the office holders. A less reliable guide along the same lines is the *Monografía de la Cámara de Diputados* published by the Cámara de Diputados in 1945. The best biographical dictionary for the period in question is undoubtedly Virgilio Figueroa's impressive *Diccionario histórico, bibliográfico y biográfico de Chile,* 4 vols. (Santiago: Ballcels and Co., 1920-28). Since it lists individuals by family groupings, it is very helpful in identifying political backgrounds. The earlier Pedro Pablo Figueroa, *Diccionario biográfico de Chile,* 3 vols. (Santiago, 1897) is also a useful source. Other helpful reference works are Carlos Pinto Durán, *Diccionario personal de Chile* (Santiago: Imprenta Claret, 1921), *Chilean Who's Who* (Santiago, 1937), and the early editions of the *Diccionario biográfico de Chile* first published in 1937. Works such as Chile, *Abogados recibidos en Chile* (Santiago: Imprenta Nacional, 1899), listing all Chileans who had received a law degree until that date are also indispensable for a study of political elites.

periods served. For many members, data on party service and biographical information are included. Both this *fichero* and the biographical volumes mentioned above are located in an enormous card catalogue at the Annex of the Library of Congress.[8]

It goes without saying that another key resource for studies in political history is the corpus of formal rules and regulations which shape and reflect the principal characteristics of the political system, notably laws and decree laws. These can be found in special compilations as well as in the *Diario Oficial* available in the Library of Congress and the National Library.[9] Partial collections can also be found in the library of the Instituto Nacional de Estadística and the libraries of several governmental agencies. Not only are laws available, but the researcher can trace the legislative history of each piece of legislation by turning to specialized indices. The Library of Congress has a reference work called "Historia de la Ley" which gives the number of the law, the number of legislative steps which the law underwent, and the date of each of these steps. It is then possible to check the appropriate date in the legislative debates. After 1950, the index refers directly to page numbers in the *Boletines* of both houses of Congress.[10] Finally, important legislation generated a host of very valuable studies, analyzing

---

8. Access to these materials is not open to the general public. However, permission can be obtained from the Director of the Library. The excellent clipping service of the Library does not go back far enough to cover the period in question.

9. See Ricardo Anguita, *Leyes promulgadas en Chile desde 1910 hasta el 1° de junio de 1912*, 4 vols. (Santiago: Imprenta Litografía i Encuadernación Barcelona, 1912); Agustín Boza y Ricardo Anguita, *Legislación política, administrativa i judicial o sea colección completa de leyes i decretos dictados en Chile i vigentes en 30 de junio de 1898*, 2 vols. (Santiago: Establecimiento Poligráfico Roma, 1898). After 1893 laws are compiled in Chile, *Recopilación de leyes por orden numérico*. Until 1925 this compilation was done by the Consejo del Estado; between that date and 1932 by the Ministerio del Interior, and after 1932 by the Contraloría General de la República.

10. In locating laws and the legislative history of laws, the researcher should also turn to the excellent facilities of the Oficina de Informaciones del Senado. Materials from parliamentary commissions are available in this office and are open to researchers with permission. Unfortunately, most of the material kept in this office pertains to the most recent period.

the origin and history of the law in question and comparing it to previous legislation in the same area. Generally these studies were done as theses in partial fulfillment of the requirements for the acquisition of a law degree.[11]

In addition to the wealth of material generated by the legislative branch, the student of Chilean political history has at his disposition a voluminous amount of information in the archives of key governmental ministries. The Archivo Nacional in the basement of the Biblioteca Nacional includes documents of the Ministries of Finance, Interior, War and Navy, Foreign Relations, and others.[12] The documents are arranged by year and by subject matter though cataloguing after 1900 is not complete. For materials after that date the scholar should turn to the respective Libro de Partes. Comparative study is facilitated by the fact that similar subjects recur over the years. Unfortunately, some of the documents from 1850 are not completely legible, in part because of poor preservation techniques.

The Ministry of Finance has the largest archive. It includes not only accounts and financial data for public agencies but also documents on a whole host of institutions including the *aduana* or customs house, the treasury, railroads, and the nitrate monopoly. In addition, material is available for each of the various ministries and the country's intendencies. The archive of the Ministry of the Interior includes such items as correspondence from the various intendants and governors, government decrees, municipal records and budgets, and communications from other ministries. Unfortunately, the researcher will find that he may have to turn to other sources that are not as well catalogued. For example, there

---

11. As an illustration, the researcher interested in local politics, center-local linkages, and urban politics should consult the following works on the crucial municipal autonomy law of 1891: Agustín Correa Bravo, *Comentarios sobre la ley de municipalidades de 1891* (Santiago: Imprenta Cervantes, 1903); Agustín Correa Bravo, *Comentario y concordancia de la ley de organización y atribuciones de las municipalidades,* 3a ed. (Santiago: Librería Tornero, 1914); Joselín Maza, *Apuntes para un estudio sobre la organización local en Chile* (Santiago: Imprenta Claret, 1917); Luis Orrego Luco, *El gobierno local y la decentralización* (Santiago: n.p., 1890).

12. For references describing the Archivo Nacional see footnote 6 of the article on colonial Chile in this volume, p. 61.

is a Fondos Varios category which has materials that did not fit classification schemes of the various ministries. It contains materials relating to the Civil War of 1891, as well as some correspondence of Manuel Bulnes and José Manuel Balmaceda.

In addition to the archive of public documents, useful information can be found in special collections housed in the Archivo Nacional. The Benjamín Vicuña Mackenna collection includes valuable documents and clippings on key political events during the period in question, notably the civil wars of 1851 and 1859.[13]

While the lion's share of public documents pertaining to the period are found in the archives, some documents were never sent to the central authorities. Probably the most important groups of documents of this variety are the debates, correspondence, and accounts of the municipalities. These materials are an indispensable tool, not only for the study of local politics but also for understanding national events from a local perspective. Thus, the debates of the municipality of Collipulli in the province of Malleco provide a fascinating insight into the attitudes of local political elites toward the raging controversy over Balmaceda's rule in the late 1880s. Unfortunately, there is no national catalogue of those materials, and many municipalities have discarded old documents. Important collections can be found in the municipalities of Concepción and Valparaíso--and undoubtedly there are others.[14] The researcher, however, will be forced to travel to each one.

Key private organizations in Chile with important relevance for public policy have also kept important materials. The Arzobispado of Santiago has published historical documents and retains materials relevant to an

---

13. See the *Catálogo de la biblioteca y manuscritos de D. Benjamín Vicuña Mackenna* (Santiago: 1886). Other private collections are mentioned in footnote 7 of the article on colonial Chile. The most valuable single source for a study of the Parliamentary Republic is Manuel Rivas Vicuña, *Historia política y parlamentaria de Chile,* 3 vols. (Santiago: Ediciones de la Biblioteca Nacional, 1964). This work includes portions of a history that Rivas Vicuña never completed as well as an invaluable collection of documents, speeches, and letters from the period. One of its best features is an excellent index prepared by the Biblioteca Nacional staff.

14. The municipalities of Santiago and Valparaíso published their council debates during the Parliamentary Republic period.

understanding of the key controversies between church and state.[15] Similarly, the Sociedad Nacional de Agricultura, the Sociedad de Fomento Fabril and the Sociedad Nacional de Minería have libraries with materials that are relevant to political developments.[16]

An obvious very important source is the periodical literature. Most political groups published a newspaper or journal, even if for only a short period of time. For example, during the formation of the labor movement a whole series of papers appeared both in Santiago and in the nitrate fields. During the Parliamentary Period, specialized periodicals on politics are of great help in untangling the political complexities.[17] The Biblioteca Nacional has a superb collection of newspapers and magazines housed in a separate periodical compartment. Unfortunately, adequate indexes do not exist so the researcher must plunge in on his own. The Biblioteca del Congreso also has a good periodical collection which is often easier to use than the one at the Biblioteca Nacional. The beginning researcher should pay particular attention to *El Ferrocaril, El Mercurio,* and *El Mercurio de Valparaíso* (the latter two on microfilm).

This essay would be incomplete if it did not mention the excellent sources available to the social scientist for quantitative study of

---

15. See Arzobispado de Santiago, *Colección de documentos históricos* (Santiago, 1920).

16. The periodical publications of these associations are invaluable sources. See Sociedad Nacional de Agricultura, *Boletín de la Sociedad Nacional de Agricultura* (Santiago, 1869-1933); Sociedad de Fomento Fabril, *Boletín de la Sociedad de Fomento Fabril* (Santiago, 1884-1934). Some years of the first publication are missing in the Biblioteca Nacional (1916-1921); Sociedad Nacional de Minería, *Boletín de la Sociedad Nacional de Minería* (Santiago, 1883-1919). All three *boletines* contain a wealth of statistical information, and the *Boletín de la Sociedad de Fomento Fabril* has very good indexes. There is a great deal of information on the Chilean nitrate industry in the Biblioteca Nacional as well as in the headquarters of important nitrate firms. One publication which is particularly useful is Asociación Salitrera de Propaganda, *Circular semestral* (Santiago, 1897-1916). The Sociedad Nacional de Agricultura maintains a library which is open to scholars with permission.

17. For a study of the much neglected Parliamentary Republic the following magazines are very helpful: *La política ilustrada, Pacífico Magazine, Revista chilena.* A thorough study of the history of Chilean journalism is Raúl Silva Castro's, *Prensa y periodismo en Chile, 1812-1956* (Santiago, 1957). An excellent annotated listing of the labor press of the period between 1900 and 1930 is Osvaldo Arias Escobedo, *La prensa obrera en Chile* (Chillán: Universidad de Chile, Chillán, 1970).

political and social phenomena. Numerous reference works provide statistics on taxation and governmental expenditures indispensable for a study both of the expansion of the state and the impact of the state on society.[18] At the same time, comprehensive data are available on economic development and trade relations.[19] In addition, Chile has several censuses which make it possible to carry out aggregate analysis of political, economic, and social data.[20]

It must be noted that the beginning researcher has a wealth of secondary materials which provide general interpretations as well as empirical materials.[21] At the same time, a few bibliographical sources are

---

18. For monetary and fiscal policy see Víctor Celis, *Los ingresos ordinarios del estado, contribución al estudio de nuestras finanzas* (Santiago: Casa Editorial Minerva, 1922); Miguel Cruchaga, *Estudio sobre la organización económica i la hacienda pública de Chile* (Santiago: Imprenta de los Tiempos, 1878). For statistics see *Memorias de hacienda* which began publication in 1934; *Cuenta de la inversión de los caudales concedidos para el servicio público, 1845-65,* 4 vols.; Dirección General de Contabilidad, *Deuda pública de la república de Chile, 1899; Actas de la Comisión Mixta de Presupuesto, 1898-1922.* Many other primary and secondary works are available covering land values, debts, and exchange rates.

19. Commercial statistics for the republic of Chile are available in numerous sources. Among the most important are *Estadística comercial, 1840-1845; Estadística comercial de la república de Chile,* published by the Superintendencia de Aduanas from 1862 to 1910 and by the Oficina Central de Estadísticas after that date.

20. The first modern census conducted in Chile was that of 1854 with basic demographic information available by province, department, and commune. Occupational data are available only at the provincial level. The *Censo general de 1865* includes occupational information at the departmental level. The succeeding censuses of 1875, 1885, 1895, 1907, 1920, and 1930 added progressively more information.

21. For general works of this period the researcher should consult Diego Barros Arana, *Un decenio en la historia de Chile* (1841-1851), 2 vols. (Santiago: Imprenta Universitaria, 1906); Francisco Antonio Encina, *Historia de Chile,* vols. 9 through 20 (Santiago: Editorial Nascimiento, 1941-42); Ricardo Donoso, *Desarrollo político y social de Chile desde la Constitución de 1833* (Santiago: Imprenta Universitaria, 1942); Alberto Edwards, *La fronda aristocrática de Chile* (Santiago: Editorial Ercilla, 1936); Domingo Amunátegui Solar, *La democracia en Chile: Teatro político 1880-1910* (Santiago: Universidad de Chile, 1946); Gonzalo Bulnes, *Guerra del Pacífico,* 3 vols. (Santiago: Editorial Pacífico, 1911-19); Julio César Jobet, "Ensayo crítico del desarrollo económico y social de Chile," *Anales de la Universidad de Chile,* 109, no. 81-82 (1951)). Among the many memoirs the researcher should consult Abdón Cifuentes, *Memorias,* 2 vols. (Santiago: Editorial Nascimiento, 1936).

available to guide research, though the researcher, particularly of the most recent period, will find that these are not very plentiful.[22]

Finally, this author would like to encourage scholars studying Chilean political history to consider the use of oral history techniques. A surprisingly large number of political leaders who were active in the closing years of the period under discussion are still alive. In particular those figures who did not reach national prominence have a wealth of observations and information to provide interested scholars. They can provide insights on the formation of local party organizations, the structuring of party alliances, intra-party disputes, the origins of local syndicates, the operation of congress, and a whole host of other questions that are important not only in unraveling the past but also in interpreting the present.

---

22. Valuable bibliographical work on Chilean political history is being done by the research groups of the Biblioteca del Congreso. In particular see Bibliografía No. 49 on *Partidos políticos chilenos* (Santiago: Biblioteca del Congreso Nacional, 1973, mimeo). It includes 638 items arranged by party and covers history, political activities, programs, statutes, and biographies. A superb annotated bibliography for the study of Chilean economic history--with many useful references for the student of politics is Carmen Cariola and Osvaldo Sunkel's contribution to the SSRC Economic History project, which has been published by University of California Press.

Chilean Political History Since 1925
Paul W. Drake

Researching post-1925 Chilean political history is rendered both rewarding and perplexing by the *embarras des richesses*.* This essay will suggest ways of organizing and using the still unfolding panorama of scholarly resources in Chile. Earlier expeditions into the Chilean past have unearthed the major sources. The more standard research information can be extracted from the basic guides available in the United States or can be learned quickly in Santiago. Therefore, lesser known or seldom used materials will be emphasized here. In particular, this essay urges political historians to pay greater attention to a myriad of materials on the social and economic roots of political conflict and consensus.

Both the 1925 benchmark and the topical categories for this essay are partly arbitrary. The year 1925 did inaugurate a new constitutional era, but the origins of most subjects can be traced back to earlier years, and the research materials described below also contain information on pre-1925 politics. In addition, many sources classified under one topic also apply to others.

Unless otherwise indicated, sources are located in the Biblioteca Nacional (BN) or the Biblioteca del Congreso Nacional (BC). Even many of the materials slighted by past researchers lie not in secret gold mines but in these two main depositories. The difficulty is learning what exists and how to use it. Though buried treasure is rare, precious nuggets can be found by digging through smaller and private collections, some of which will be described below.

Researchers of twentieth-century history should beware that some of the information in this essay may have been invalidated by the military coup of September 11, 1973. For example, at the time of this writing,

---

*My thanks to Arturo Valenzuela and Peter Winn for their helpful suggestions.

the BC is temporarily closed to the public. Some resources on the left and labor are not as accessible as before. This transformation in the research climate has been taken into account as much as possible without restricting this essay's applicability to the current moment.

GENERAL SOURCES ON POLITICAL HISTORY

Academicians and politicians, often one and the same, can introduce the researcher to sources and to interview subjects. Chilean scholars can also reveal projects already underway and point out theses *(memorias de prueba)* which might go unnoticed otherwise. Historians can open relations with their Chilean counterparts at the Universidad de Chile, the Universidad Católica, the Centro de Investigaciones de Historia Americana, and the Sociedad Chilena de Historia y Geografía. Usually, students of twentieth-century politics will find that political scientists, sociologists, and economists in Chile are doing work close to their own concerns. These contacts can be acquired through such institutes as the Facultad Latinoamericana de Ciencias Sociales (FLASCO),[1] the Centro Latinoamericano de Demografía (CELADE), and the Centro para el Desarrollo Económico y Social de América Latina (DESAL).

After establishing contacts, the researcher will want to amplify bibliographic listings, though most of the key entries can be accumulated using research tools in the United States. Major additions can be culled from the card catalogues of the BN and BC, which are both partly organized by topics. The BC has been compiling subject bibliographies on its holdings. Most valuable is its complete guide to materials on *Partidos políticos chilenos* (Santiago, 1973).

An overwhelming number of standard and obscure secondary and primary sources, especially pamphlets, are stored in the BN and BC. Abundant literary insights have been only sparingly used. Hundreds of newspapers and periodicals are filed in the BN and the Annex of the BC. Many scholars have mined the major, long running publications, skillfully analyzed in Raúl Silva Castro, *Prensa y periodismo en Chile* (Santiago, 1958). Also worth consulting is Osvaldo Arias, *La prensa obrera en Chile* (Santiago, 1970). The more ephemeral and more partisan dailies, weeklies,

---

1. Though this is one example of a scholarly center whose activities have been sharply curtailed since the 1973 coup.

and monthlies have been relatively ignored, yet these smaller sheets are often more illuminating for political history than the more established press. Regional newspapers and journals have also been neglected. Some that appear to be generated by the outlying provinces are essentially carbon copies of capital city editions, but others reflect indigenous provincial sentiments. When using any Chilean newspapers and magazines, one must be acutely aware of the publication's regional and political affiliation, because both strongly color the content.

Some government ministries and university faculties or institutes maintain at least small libraries worth inspecting. Their holdings are frequently lean but potentially important, especially if a topic touches on the speciality of a ministry or institute, such as labor or urbanization.

Private and unpublished materials, encountered through personal networks or book dealers, are seldom as abundant or spicy as an historian might wish. Twentieth-century letter and diary collections, for example, seem to be rare. Although expectations should be modest when tracking private papers, the potential for tapping new sources is more than enough to justify the quest.

SOURCES ON PARTIES

Insightful histories of Chilean parties abound. Most party histories, however, have been written by partisan members of their organizations and hence are not very balanced or critical.

Outstanding primary sources, mainly party publications, fill the catalogue drawers at the BN and BC. First, are the copious party programs, propaganda, and broadsides. Second, national and provincial party convention reports include speeches, lists of leaders, and other pertinent information; pre-convention position papers highlight internal party debates. Third, party statutes contain rules, principles, and organizational blueprints. Fourth, some members of the Congress submitted reports to party and provincial leaders on their accomplishments for their constituents; these *cuentas* often comment on connections between national and local politics. Finally, there are national and provincial newspapers and periodicals, directly or indirectly party organs. For example, *Bandera Roja* (1931-33) was the official newspaper of the Communist Party, but *Frente Popular* (1936-40), under heavy Communist influence, expressed many opinions not attributable to the party.

The hunt for party archives can be frustrating. Generally, party records do not exist, at least in any coherent form, and tend to be scattered in private hands, packed with commonplace information, or are only partially open to nonmembers. The Socialists' party headquarters and the Communists' Museo Recabarren, for example, while accessible to outsiders prior to the coup and housing a few historical gems, possessed very little not in the BN or BC.

SOURCES ON POLITICAL LEADERSHIP

Both individual and collective biographies are waiting to be written, with ample sources on which to base them. Chilean politicians have a propensity to publish a great deal, easing the task of the biographer. For collective biographies, names of leaders can be combed from party publications and from lists of government officials, see Luis Valencia Avaria, *Anales de la república* (Santiago, 1951). Then the researcher can trace their socioeconomic backgrounds through the fine Chilean "who's who."   One pitfall with the published social directories is that they concentrate on the established elites and divulge less information about leaders of more lower-class, leftist movements. Also, the coverage of biographical data varies in mysterious ways, so it is advisable to corroborate social profiles from more than one source. Interest associations and clubs usually issue membership rosters, which supply a check on information gleaned from biographical dictionaries.

Oral history, an underutilized device in many historical projects, can fill some of the biographical gaps. In normal times, Chilean political participants have been extraordinarily receptive to interviewing. For an appreciation of the character and diversity of possible interview subjects, the researcher should scan the superb series of conversations with past political actors (1920s-60s) conducted by Wilfredo Mayorga in *Ercilla*, 1965-68.

SOURCES ON ELECTIONS

After surveying the secondary and primary literature on elections, such as party instructions for electoral behavior *(cartillas electorales)*, the researcher will come to grips with the extensive electoral data. First it is necessary to become familiar with changing electoral laws and districts. The index to the *Recopilación de leyes* at the BC will grant access to the legal rules of the game. Legal dissertations on Chilean suffrage are also useful. These laws, in conjunction with materials from the census bureau and the electoral registry, will make it possible to determine the rough geographic and socioeconomic makeup of electoral units. Electoral returns are reported at four diminishing levels: national, provincial, departmental, and communal. The composition of provinces and departments shifted on the map, especially in the 1920s-30s. Consequently, comparisons in electoral trends over time are safest at the community level.

Since 1938, votes have been recorded in the most regular, complete manner. Before then, the scholar may have to resort to second-best sources, because official returns do not always reach down to the communal level. There are, for example, a few lacunae in the 1920s and 1930s. In those instances, partially reliable local returns can be garnered from newspapers published during the days following the balloting. Several tabulations must be used for verification and matching community patterns with surviving official counts at higher levels. When necessary, these newspaper returns will provide imprecise but approximate trends in local voting.

Although an indispensable resource, many electoral records have somewhat limited utility. These limitations stem not only from the ways votes are recorded but also from some instances of fraud, particularly in earlier years and in the countryside. Another problem is that reliable census data does not always define electoral zones by sharp socioeconomic criteria. Some electoral documents give the names of the candidates by districts, others the numbers of votes received, and still others registration figures. Thankfully, all three sets of information are sometimes published in the same document. Despite drawbacks, Chile's electoral records are among the best in Latin America and deserving of intensive historical attention.

Most of the results, particularly for elections after the 1920s, are kept in the document center on the second floor of the Dirección del Registro Electoral. In the accounting office of the same agency, copies of past returns, notably from the 1950s on, can be purchased for nominal sums. Some of the same results are located at the BN, where microfilming is easier. Missing voting records can most often be acquired at the Dirección de Estadística y Censo library. There, the census volumes likely to encompass electoral inscriptions and returns are those entitled *Política y administración* or *Administración y justicia*, whether published by the Oficina Central de Estadística or its successor, the Dirección de Estadística.

SOURCES ON ADMINISTRATIONS

Secondary accounts of various administrations and administrative units are plentiful, especially *memorias de prueba* on programs, laws, and ministries or their sub-units. Legal studies and memoirs are important, though Chilean political reminiscences, while numerous, are not terribly candid about the inner workings of government. Most significant for studying the administrative hierarchy are government sources.

For the executive branch, presidential messages can be requested at the BN by year. Government ministries have both publications and collections laden with information. For example, national budgetary *cuentas* issued by the Ministerio de Hacienda can be requested by year at the BN, as can the *Ley de presupuestos*. Most government ministries, such as Interior, Foreign Relations, Agriculture, Social Welfare, and Industry and Public Works, have published *Memorias*, or annual reports. Some of their archives are housed at the BN. Lesser known sections of the bureaucracy, such as the Caja de la Habitación and the Caja del Seguro Obligatorio, produced critical studies of social conditions and programs. Perhaps the most imperative single source on government actions in the economy since 1939 is the Corporación de Fomento de la Producción (CORFO) with its high-quality publications and its library, containing mimeographed materials sometimes unavailable elsewhere.

For legislation, the researcher should see the *Recopilación de leyes* cited earlier and the *Diario oficial de la república de Chile*, where, at least since 1946, all approved laws and decrees have had to be printed before taking effect. The BC has the only complete collection of congressional debates during ordinary and extraordinary sessions of the Chamber of Deputies and the Senate. A useful BC guide to the debates, organized by the names of deputies and senators making initiatives, already exists. An even more impressive subject guide is still very incomplete, but there is a slender index by subject matter at the end of each bound series on a legislative session. The able staff at the BC can be extremely helpful.

Most sources on administration, as well as other topics, are centralized in Santiago. Materials in the outlying provinces and local repositories, however, rarely have been exploited and might yield bountiful returns to the intrepid scholar. For example, histories of local administration and politics could conceivably be written from the virtually untouched collections of debates, budgets, and petitions in municipal archives, such as in Concepción.

SOURCES ON PRESSURE GROUPS AND INTEREST ORGANIZATIONS

Though not part of the strictly "formal" political system, like the Senate or parties, organizations of like-minded social and economic groups command enormous power in Chilean politics. This essay can only hint at the plethora of groups and materials in need of systematic investigation. In recent years, some secondary literature has surfaced on functional elites and their organizations, but use of primary materials on such groups has only begun. Public, printed sources lodged in the BN and BC provide a respectable starting point for analyzing the political impact of private institutions. To date, few archival or manuscript materials have been discovered or used. Nevertheless, future historians should bend greater efforts to explore for caches of materials lying behind institutional walls because they may offer the brightest opportunity for fresh revelations on Chilean politics.

One definite target should be the economic sectoral organizations of Chile's privileged groups. The bulletins and other publications of the Sociedad Nacional de Agricultura and the Sociedad de Fomento Fabril can be perused, as can some of their private holdings. Quite often, these two organizations took politically significant stands in their public reports. Though less publicly political, the Sociedad Nacional de Minería and the Confederación de la Producción y el Comercio also exerted heavy influence and demand careful consideration.

At the other end of the social scale, organized labor merits more attention. Public documents and pamphlets can be read in the BN and BC. These are often filed under the major union leader's name and contain speeches, lists of officials, statements of principle, and reviews of actions. Researchers should also look at political party pronouncements on union activities. Through the Ministry of Labor, specifically the Dirección del Trabajo, fruitful archives can be investigated. This collection embraces petitions from urban and rural workers, studies and actions taken by governments, and documentation on strikes, unions, and working conditions. Harder to find are the internal records of the major unions, some preserved in private hands. To reconstruct the attitudes of the rank-and-file workers, oral history interviews can prove invaluable.

The military and the church, other obviously potent groups, present problems of accessibility to internal records, but church parish documents, for instance, can be used. Moreover, there are several public items, such as books and pamphlets by leading clergy and military figures. Indeed, Chile boasts some of the more forthright military memoirs in Latin America. There are also periodicals expounding church and military opinions, such as *La revista católica* or the *Memorial del ejército de Chile*.

Many other social groups warrant increased political study. Known documentation on student movements is thin, but tantalizing information can be obtained from pamphlets, magazines, and interviews. Especially in the 1930s-40s, the Student Federation of Chile (FECH),[2] as well as clusters of Communist, Trotskyist, and Falangist students, issued provocative manifestos and periodicals. Researchers can probe the political role of women through books by leading feminists, laws and court records, organizations like the Club de Profesoras, and personal papers and informants. Also waiting to be woven into the fabric of political history are Indian groups like the Mapuches, bureaucrats, and professional associations, such as those for doctors and lawyers, not to mention many other sectors of Chilean society on whom adequate but largely uncultivated sources exist.

As a final example, the records of ostensibly nonpartisan clubs and leisure or civic organizations are ripe for historical treatment. One case in point would be the aristocratic Club de la Unión and similar nerve centers of upper-class political activity. Such exclusive clubs often have membership lists, annual reports, and histories that cast light on the political proclivities and maneuverings of select social segments. Perhaps equally important were more middle class groups like the secretive Masons. The Masonic lodges' crucial participation in twentieth-century politics is difficult to study because of their conspiratorial nature and mystical reputation. Nevertheless, interviews, memoirs, exposés, and speeches, even by the Grand Master, do offer some insights.

---

2. Reportedly, the FECH archives were destroyed.

SOURCES ON THE SOCIOECONOMIC DIMENSIONS OF POLITICS

Related to the previous category, the sources sketched here apply broadly to the social and economic context of political life. This category does not plunge deeply into the social and economic history of the twentieth century, because that would require a separate essay. Instead, this heterogeneous final section only strives to acquaint the researcher with major secondary and primary resources available on larger economic and social trends.

The surviving social science institutes in Santiago offer many sources on social and economic currents, such as regionalism and income distribution, that shape political events. The institutes' studies, publications, and tiny but specialized libraries can be vital to historical projects. At least the major ones deserve mention.

For economic studies on Chile, the Economic Commission for Latin America (ECLA, CEPAL) has produced significant materials, and some of its unpublished works are shelved in its library at the United Nations building. The University of Chile's Instituto de Economía y Planificación has produced good theses, some of which are held in its own library. Unpublished economic treatises also exist at the Catholic University's Centro de Planificación (CEPLAN).

For more general social science research, FLACSO, CELADE, and DESAL, mentioned previously, are valuable institutes. For example, the FLACSO library maintained current journals and interesting literature on sociology and problems of development. The Centro de Investigaciones y Acción Social library serves the two Jesuit sponsored institutes, DESAL and the Centro Bellarmino. In addition, the Instituto de Organización y Administración de Empresas (INSORA) has some of its own data and publications. The Instituto de Ciencias Políticas y Administrativas can prove worth visiting for contacts, publications, and certain data collections, and the Instituto Latinoamericano de Investigaciones Sociales (ILDIS) holds its own in-house seminars and publications.

The thicket of individualized libraries within the separate faculties of the two major universities can make these resources more a barrier than an avenue to learning. For example, despite attempts at centralization, the University of Chile's library system sprawls over more than one-hundred distinct repositories. Still, a few specialized holdings, like those in sociology and political science, can be fairly useful.

Further sources for the study of socioeconomic influences on political history are produced or held by government agencies, many of the same ones instrumental for administrative studies. In addition to such agencies as the Dirección de Estadística and CORFO, the Ministry of Public Works puts out urbanization studies. Publications and documents from the Ministerio de Salubridad, Previsión, y Asistencia Social de Chile should be inspected, as should monthly economic reports from the Banco Central de Chile.

Nearly all the sources cited in other categories will enhance the historian's grasp of the social and economic substance of politics. The researcher will confront an awesome range of studies on every facet of Chilean development. Even though Chilean political history, however defined, is scarcely virgin territory, this multitude of materials has only begun to be tapped. Most often, the terrain has been explored by political scientists, economists, and sociologists rather than by professional historians. The contours of Chile's political experience have been charted, but the great historiographical issues are only beginning to emerge. Many post-1925 historical debates have not yet been generated, let alone joined. Hopefully, this small essay will help lead new researchers into this array of materials so that interpretations of Chile's recent past may become as rich as the resources upon which they can be built.

Sources for the Study of Chilean Labor History
Brian Loveman

Chilean labor history is a relatively underdeveloped area of study. Even in Chile the quantity and quality of literature on the labor movement are disappointing.[1] In English available works are extremely limited. Taken together, the most important of these provide a reasonable but sketchy descriptive overview of the origins and development of the labor movement as well as of the relationships between the labor movement and political parties.[2] But knowledgeable treatments of individual unions, union organization, working conditions, and working class social relations are nowhere to be found either in English or in Spanish. Scattered pieces of naturalist literature, for example, Baldomiro Lillo's stories about the coal mines (*SubTerra*) supplement our sketchy picture of what it meant to be a laborer in the early twentieth century in Chile.

In great part this lack of published information is due to an oversight by historians and social scientists interested in the Chilean labor movement. Available source material has not been tapped or exploited. Illustrative is the fact that even the most recent study of the Chilean

---

1. For a recent synoptic overview see Jorge Barría S., *El movimiento obrero en Chile* (Santiago: Ediciones de la Universidad Técnica del Estado, 1971).

2. Major works include Fredrick Pike, *Chile and the United States 1880-1962* (South Bend, Ind.: University of Notre Dame Press, 1963). Robert Alexander has written a number of works: *Labor Parties in Latin America* (New York: League for Industrial Democracy, 1942); *Communism in Latin America* (New Brunswick: Rutgers University Press, 1957); *Labor Relations in Argentina, Brazil and Chile* (New York: McGraw Hill Book Co., 1962); *Organized Labor in Latin America* (New York: Free Press of Glencoe, 1965). See also Alan Angell, *Politics and the Labor Movement in Chile* (London: Oxford University Press, 1972); Moisés Poblete Tronscoso and Ben G. Burnett, *The Rise of The Latin American Labor Movement* (New York: Bookman Associates, 1960); and James O. Morris, *Elites, Intellectuals and Consensus, A Study of the Social Question and the Industrial Relations System in Chile* (Ithaca, New York: New York State School of Industrial and Labor Relations, Cornell University, 1966).

labor movement (Alan Angell, 1972) makes no reference to the Chilean Labor Archive, fails to use systematically the numerous working class periodicals and newspapers as source material, and neglects as valuable sources of information many of the still-living pioneers of the Chilean labor movement in the twentieth century as well as Department of Labor functionaries.

The purpose of this article is to suggest the types of research opportunities which exist for the Chilean labor movement with special reference to the Chilean Labor Archive, the working class press, and the still-living labor movement pioneers.

THE CHILEAN LABOR ARCHIVE

No social scientist or historian has as yet made extensive use of the richest source of material on Chilean labor in the twentieth century--the Chilean Labor Archive. Since 1906 the Chilean Labor Department has maintained a documentary record of its operations, including its relations with worker organizations, employers, political parties, individual politicians, and other government agencies. These documents, housed in the Labor Department Archives in downtown Santiago, should eventually provide the raw materials for a number of studies on Chilean labor history, demography, economic and social development, politics, and the institutional development of the Labor Department itself. Because this archival material is generally unknown, it may be useful to describe the organization of the Archive generally and then, by reference to illustrative materials, indicate the breadth of documentary sources to be encountered in this archival collection.

ORGANIZATION OF THE ARCHIVE

From 1906-1930 the organization of materials in the Archive was rather haphazard. Bound volumes, often labelled simply *varios,* contain reports from labor inspectors, letters from government officials, workers, and employers, or police reports on so-called subversive activities. Only by reviewing these volumes page-by-page can an investigator determine if they contain any useful material. Although I have reviewed the material, it is difficult, if not impossible, to summarize it succinctly--except perhaps to say that it ranges from requests by functionaries for typewriter ribbons to detailed descriptions of working conditions and worker organization in the copper mines and nitrate fields. Early reports on strikes, evidence of labor mobility and the national labor market--including the governmental and "private" employment services--as well as the intervention by political parties in the coal fields, ports, and countryside can also be found, but only by laborious plodding through the thick bound volumes.

After 1930 materials are typically bound in volumes labelled *oficios, providencias,* or *telegramas* in addition to some more specialized volumes. The volumes labelled *oficios* usually contain documents that originated with the central headquarters of the Labor Department in Santiago. At times, accompanying these documents are copies of materials found also in the volumes called *providencias*. *Providencias* generally contain materials that originated outside of the Labor Department's Santiago offices. These include telegrams, reports by labor inspectors, letters from private citizens or organizations, communications from other government agencies, or from the national congress. The volumes labelled *telegramas* usually contain a numbered series of telegrams sent by Santiago personnel to officials in the provinces.

This general description of the organization of the Archive should not obscure the great variety of materials within each of these types of bound volumes nor suggest that anything like a perfect ordering of materials exists. Over and over again I was surprised by the type of materials I found in a particular volume and could discover no reason--except perhaps the year-end rush to get things bound--why materials appeared in one volume instead of another.

A relatively complex index system called a kardex provides a patient investigator with a log of incoming and outgoing communications for each year by province and by category. The Labor Department indexes some materials in the kardex according to whether it relates, for example, to other ministries, Congress, industrial unions, or various other subheadings. It also indexes materials according to regional and provincial location of the incidents involved--for example, a labor inspector's report on a strike in a farm in Aconcagua Province might be logged in the section of the kardex labelled Aconagaua under the title Labor Inspector Reports a Conflict. Sometimes these abbreviated titles can be of great assistance in searching out particular types of information. Often, however, they are so vague that only by reading the document can an investigator determine if the conflict in Aconcagua was in a factory of interest to him or on a farm that is of no current relevance.

TYPES OF MATERIALS

Despite the organizational problems an investigator encounters, this Archive will provide source materials for studies of particular farms or factories, the position of the working class in Chilean society, macroeconomic implications of labor policy, and administration of labor legislation. These materials may also allow detailed analysis of the evolution of individual unions from bakeries to farms to the copper industry, the role of particular labor leaders, and the linkages between unions, parties, and political movements. In addition, the institutional problems and development of the Labor Department is bared in the reports of labor inspectors, letters from citizens and interest groups, communications between the Labor Department, the Labor Ministry, and other governmental agencies and congressmen. Thus the archival materials will not only be a source for research on the labor movement but also provide political insight into the perpetual starvation budgets allocated to the Labor Department by governments committed symbolically to *leyes sociales* and operationally to less than benign neglect of the legal rights of workers and working class organizations.

SOCIO-ECONOMIC CONDITIONS

The reports, letters, surveys, copies of labor petitions, and related documents in the Labor Archive are a rich source of data on social and economic conditions in Chile after 1906. For example, one of the most important but little investigated aspects of economic development in Chile after 1880 was the great mobility of much of an important part of the labor force between nitrate fields, public works construction, and the countryside, yet no systematic study of this phenomenon exists. In the Labor Archive, materials can be found to allow reasonable assessment of the movement of workers between the southern and central valley provinces and the nitrate fields--and back again--as the nitrate industry responded to world demand. In addition to hundreds of telegrams indicating the number of men, women, and children carried by ships to northern ports, archival materials provide a look into conditions faced by the working class and the political problems associated with an expanding national labor market in an economy so dependent upon world markets. Thus, for example, during one of the periodic waves of workers returning from the north to central and southern Chile (1926), the Director of the

Labor Department urged that the state railway be used to prevent the "dangerous concentration of unemployment in this city." (Santiago, Oficio 3121, Communicaciones Enviadas, 1926, 2750-3168). Throughout the next decade control of unemployed workers and their movements were a key issue facing Chilean elites. By the end of 1931, the depression made this problem even more salient, as a report to the Minister of Interior from the Fifth Precinct in Santiago points out. This report continues in the same vein for Puente Alto, Lampa, Tiltil, Maipú, San Bernardo, Melipilla, San Antonio, and Buin. Reports of this sort (and others more detailed) allow not only a quantitative estimate of the massive unemployment experienced during the depression years, but also some sense of the earnings and living conditions of workers.

Also of interest is the effect on these unemployed workers when they were *forced* to work in the countryside. More often than has been imagined, unemployed workers carried labor militancy from mines and the urban sector to the rural areas, evident in a great number of reports in the *oficios* section of the Labor Archive.

In addition to reports on labor mobility and conflicts, archival materials provide relatively "hard" data on the cost of living, wages, housing conditions, medical services available to workers, and industrial accidents. This information is available, with gaps, from 1906 with industry-by-industry data available in many cases. One good source for such data is the annual or episodic labor petitions (*pliegos de peticiones*) submitted to management by workers' organizations or unions. These petitions often recount grievances as well as existing working conditions. (For the period after 1960 the offices of the various Juntas de Conciliación are also good sources for labor petitions, arbitral decrees and contract settlements, though *usually* copies will also be found in the Labor Department Archive.) Also of use may be the letters between authorities reflecting concern for labor conditions or current problems. These are often the result of complaints registered by workers or unions, which often resulted as a consequence, and referred to industrial accidents, non-compliance with labor legislation, working conditions, compensation, corruption of social security or labor inspectors, and so on. Systematic collection and use of such materials could add considerably to our knowledge of socio-economic conditions in twentieth-century Chile as well as to a more specialized knowledge concerning particular firms, industries, or economic sectors.

UNION DEVELOPMENT

Because the Labor Department was charged with overseeing the legally recognized unions (after 1924), supervising elections and union funds, investigating potential union officers, and resolving labor disputes, the archives are a rich source of information concerning union formation and membership. The *acta de constitución* of a union normally includes the date and place of legal foundation, the names of union officers, their ages, domicile, carnet number, military service record, and number of votes received by each. In addition, sometimes a complete list of founding members is available along with signatures or thumbprints--an indication of literacy levels in different unions or industries--and the amount of union dues fixed at the time of foundation. Because unions were required to elect their officers annually, archival materials could provide the raw data for long-term studies of leadership turnover, longevity, and generational conflict within unions. For scholars interested in micro-studies, it is not inconceivable, in some cases at least, that a majority of union founders, leaders, or even members could be interviewed concerning the evolution of particular unions over a three-or four-decade period. Occasional materials on internal corruption and forced dissolution are also available. While not a complete record of union activities, the Labor Archive is a very good starting point for micro-studies or even sectoral studies. Because of the extra-legal status of confederations, however, archival materials are much less complete, consisting in the main of documentary evidence of the various confederations' efforts to influence Labor Department policy towards individual unions, labor disputes in particular, or to protect groups of workers from arbitrary, illegal, or repressive actions on the part of employers. These materials, too, can be valuable but offer an incomplete source for reconstruction of the history and development of Chilean labor confederations.

POLITICS OF THE LABOR MOVEMENT

The internal divisions of the Chilean labor movement, particularly as these correspond to the influence of the major political parties in Chile, have been well treated by Chilean, American, and English authors. The most recent book, Alan Angell's *Politics and the Labour Movement in Chile*

(London and New York: Oxford University Press, 1972), repeats the now familiar theme of party-labor movement symbiosis that also, often, redounded to the disadvantage of workers bound by leadership with torn loyalties or constrained by the current party-line. Certain types of materials in the Labor Department Archive flesh out the macro-picture with information on politics within individual unions and between these and competing political parties or labor confederations. Internal politics was not always limited to politicking; sometimes refusal to cooperate with one group or another meant persecution or death for stubborn workers. The history of the coal fields of Lota is particularly difficult in this respect as a variety of workers' organizations competed for worker loyalty and membership. Labor inspectors' reports from the coal fields during the early 1920s are especially valuable for their insight into internal union politics as well as their description of social and economic conditions in the Lota-Coronel region. For example a report dated 25 junio 1925, No. 781, *Varios*, 1925, in addition to a general survey of industrial conditions in Concepción, application of labor law, and exploitation of women workers (earning one *peso* a day doing wash when bread sold for 90 *centavos* a *kilo*), contains a section concerning "different groups into which workers are divided in the region and their diverse ideological tendencies." Other reports provide information on the politics of workers' organizations in other industries and in the countryside from the 1920s until the present.

POLITICAL PARTIES, PARTY POLITICIANS AND THE LABOR MOVEMENT

A large amount of material on the relationship of political parties and individual politicians to working class organizations can also be found in the Labor Archive. From the local labor inspector to the Minister of Labor there is a constant awareness of the political nature of workers' movements and of the internal implications of labor disputes for specific unions. The commonplace experience of hearing workers' complaints and processing formal grievances transmitted via local party cells, congressmen, or senators make the reports of some labor inspectors acute political analyses. At higher levels, communications from party leaders, ministers, and Chilean presidents concerning labor matters are scattered throughout the Labor Archive awaiting the systematic analysis of students of politics and the labor movement.

OTHER MATERIALS

The above sub-titles have served to illustrate some of the different types of materials available in the Chilean Labor Archive. If one is interested in the number of horses purchased by the Labor Department from 1930-1950 or the scarcity of saddles and reins, this sort of information is also available. In short, any serious attempt to do labor history in Chile--beyond a regurgitation of the now existing overviews--should begin at the Labor Archive.

THE WORKER PRESS AND PARTY PUBLICATIONS

While not as overlooked as the Labor Archive, another source of relatively little utilized material on the Chilean labor movement is the worker press and political party journals. Osvaldo Arias' *La prensa obrera en Chile* (Santiago: Universidad de Chile, 1953) is a good starting point for a catalogue and description of workers' publications. But the type of materials in these publications is so varied, substantively and ideologically, that any overall characterization--except to note the short life-span of most--is difficult. It is possible, however, to illustrate the potential of these sources for enriching Chilean labor history by reference to various little-known but interesting periodicals.

Izquierda was a bi-monthly organ of the Izquierda Comunista (Trotskyite) party, which first appeared in early June, 1934. It is an excellent source of information concerning cleavages on the political left, internal disputes within the labor movement, and national politics in Chile (1934-1936). *Izquierda* is also a take-off point for study of Trotskyite activity and strength in Chile during this period. For example, the first issue of *Izquierda* reports on activities in Santiago, Talcahuano, Talca, and San Antonio. This first issue also carries a detailed discussion of the IV International. The last issue of *Izquierda* (August, 1936) features an attack on the USSR.

During its brief history *Izquierda* was stridently militant. Typical is the coverage of the massacre of *campesinos* at Ranquíl (1934). The Trotskyites urged a general strike to protest the government's action and come to the aid of the *campesinos*. Despite its significance as a source for Chilean labor history *Izquierda* goes unmentioned in every recent study of Chilean labor (to June 1974). A complete set *was* housed in the Biblioteca Nacional in Santiago prior to September 11, 1973.

The *Boletín de la Liga Nacional de Defensa de Campesino Pobres* is a short-lived, episodically issued organ of Chile's first national peasant leagues, founded by the Trotskyite-socialist Emilio Zapata in 1935. The *Boletín* carries news of organizational meetings; rural labor conflicts; activities of local *ligas* from north to south (an illustrative issue lists activities from *ligas* in Santa Fé, Chincolo, Alto Jahuel Limache, Colina, and Nos); the names of local leaders; and editorials concerning pending agrarian legislation or demands of the peasant leagues on the national government. Typical claims in the *Boletín* depict the *ligas* as a "liberating army" and "vanguard of the working classes." News items also appear detailing specific labor conditions and abuses committed by landowners against rural workers and peasants. The *Boletín* is thus an excellent source for national or rural labor in Chile, especially during the Popular Front period.

The daily newspaper, *La Opinión*, published by leading figures in the Partido Radical Socialista often included an entire page dedicated to "*actividades societarias*." On this page coverage of workers' organizations and groups like associations of retired persons ranged from reports on abuses against the working classes, current labor conflicts, anniversary celebrations by particular organizations, and union elections to efforts by labor organizations to influence national policy-making.

La Opinión provides a daily log of meetings of workers' organizations, cultural activities, and labor disputes as well as a moderate left view of national politics. This makes *La Opinión* a good starting place for any scholar looking at the Chilean labor movement and national politics from 1932 into the 1940s.

Numerous other periodicals and journals also exist such as *Combate*, *Arauco*, *FOCH*, *Acción*, *CTCH*, and *Consigna*. Each had a relatively short life, but taken together, they represent an important source for understanding the Chilean working class and leftist parties. They have been largely neglected by students of Chilean labor and Chilean politics.

LIVING SOURCES

The Chilean labor movement is, relatively speaking, quite young. Many labor pioneers (and early Social Security and Labor Department bureaucrats) are still alive and willing to contribute a deeper more detailed assessment of the Chilean labor movement, including the institutional responses by the Chilean state. Men like Héctor Escribar and Mariano Bustos, both contributors to the Labor Code of 1931, have much to tell us about the last forty years of Chilean labor history. Likewise, party activists such as José Campusano and Juan Ahumada Trigo--if they escape the most recent repression--have much experience that might clarify gaps in our own knowledge of the struggle of the Chilean working class. The potential contributions of "oral history" to ongoing research was brought home to me in my discussions with Emilio Zapata, Bernardo Yuras, and Carlos Acuña, all active participants in the formation of Chile's first National Peasant Leagues.

Not only do such personalities contribute from their own experiences, they often have personal documentation--letters, speeches, clippings, data on unions or party affairs, diaries--that are of great value. Often such important personalities in the development of the Chilean labor movement are retired--yet still lucid. At the risk of retreat into anecdotes, I recall an interview with Carlos Alberto Martínez in 1971 in which this leading figure of the Socialist Party in the early twentieth century recalled the addresses of the various printing houses in which he had worked over a number of years and provided lucid answers to my prepared questions. Yet, surprising as it may seem, this most obvious source of knowledge concerning the Chilean labor movement--the living sources--have been badly neglected. Indeed, because this source is passing from the scene, it would be of great value to organize an oral history project relating to the Chilean labor movement and to carry it out as soon as possible.

Civil-Military Relations in Chile
Frederick M. Nunn

Since Chile achieved its independence, civil-military relations have been an important aspect of that country's history. Despite the prominence of military leaders in politics and government in the independence and post-independence years, two successful nineteenth-century wars against Peru and Bolivia, a maritime conflict with Spain, the Civil War of 1891, and military involvement in politics and government (1924-32), few scholars have seen fit to study the military or its relations with the rest of society or with the political system. Accounts of past glories abound in the strictly defined field of military history, of course, but these do little to enlighten the reader and researcher with regard to the historical role of the military outside the area of war-making.

The *golpe de estado* of September 11, 1973, may alter this state of scholarly affairs, for to most observers the impossible had happened. The armed forces, led by the army, broke with tradition by becoming overtly involved in politics and government. South America's "leading democracy," Latin America's "most politically advanced country" (there is virtually no end to the sobriquets) had fallen victim to "militarism." This could result in some serious revision of traditional approaches to the study of Chilean history, notably the history of civil-military relations, with particular reference to the military's relations with the state. Crisis orientation has a way of directing scholars to new topics for study and re-examination, and Clio's disciples are no exception.

It is not my purpose here to discuss Chilean civil-military relations *per se*; there are places more appropriate for describing and interpreting the complexities of the topic in a scholarly fashion. Rather, the task, as I view it, is to point out some opportunities for research and to mention a hitherto slightly tapped source of data and research materials for the scholar.

RESEARCH OPPORTUNITIES

Most authorities agree that institutionalized civilian political leadership and orderly constitutional conduct of national affairs--in contrast to *caudillismo* and instability elsewhere in Spanish America--began in Chile in the 1830s. While it can be said that this is early by Spanish American standards, it can also be claimed that this stability may be due to the fact that for twenty years (1831-51) military men headed the national government. General Joaquín Prieto Vial, an independence leader, and his nephew, General Manuel Bulnes Prieto, hero of the 1837-39 conflict with Peru and Bolivia, established a kind of aristocratic, civil-military fusion which, as much as any other factor, was responsible for the army's relegation to "professional" activities, its external orientation (i.e., defense against threats by neighboring republics), and its apolitical stance until 1891.

These two decades surely need study if a sophisticated grasp of Chilean civil-military relations is to be achieved. The rise of the Basque-Castilian aristocracy; the structuring of the oligarchic, autocratic Portalian state; the triumphant war of 1837-39; the election of Bulnes and his successful conduct of government are topics which need to be approached from the standpoint of civil-military relations. So too does the decade of Manuel Montt (1851-61), Chile's first civilian president elected under the Constitution of 1833, for the role of the army was important in suppressing movements which sought to deny Montt the presidency, and then to topple his administration.

The Portalian system endured, though in modified form, until 1891. During the three decades between Montt and Chile's Civil War, civil-military relations provide additional opportunities for research, bearing in mind always that in nineteenth-century Chile the orientation of men in uniform was external, not internal.

First came the expansion of the Southern frontier--the military supported and protected extension of Euro-Chilean society and culture into Araucania--at the expense of the indigenous inhabitants. It need not be pointed out that the military frontier and territorial expansion were significant aspects of Chile's historical development. The development of regional history--a particularly stimulating research field--makes the last two statements all too obvious. Second, a myriad of opportunities exist for the War of the Pacific (1879-83), the second conflict in which

Chile bested her Andean neighbors. Though primarily viewed by military historians in terms of a confrontation between sea powers, the War of the Pacific provides the scholar an exemplary case study in relationships between the military in the field (as well as at sea) and civilian authorities at home. In dire economic straits, Chile was able to pursue this war to the end, and had there been any serious breach in civil-military relations, the war might not have been so important for Chile. A number of heroes emerged, new territories were added to the domain, and the economy more than revived.

Finally, in the pre-1891 period came the initiation of an expensive and extensive military modernization and reform program in 1885 with the contracting of the German Captain Emil Körner. Unlike Brazil, where civil-military relations underwent changes because army leaders believed they had been ignored after defending their country in the War of the Triple Alliance, the victorious Ejército de Chile was "rewarded by a grateful government." There is still much to be done on the development of the military profession in the late nineteenth century. Once the army became a professional organization and its ties to the ruling class weakened (as was the case after the War of the Pacific), relations between the military and the state underwent drastic change. Opportunities abound in the period between 1879 and 1891 for social, economic, and cultural historians as well as those interested in diplomatic and political themes. Needless to say, the Civil War of 1891 could well be approached from the standpoint of civil-military relations.

Beginning in 1891, Chile entered a new era, that of the "Parliamentary Republic" which endured until 1924 when the professionalized military assumed a political stance and subsequently helped establish a new political system under the Constitution of 1925. Even then it was not until 1927 that parliamentarianism was effectively curtailed by General Carlos Ibáñez del Campo, Chile's first army-bred chief executive in three quarters of a century. The forty years between Chile's Civil War and the fall of General Ibáñez in 1931 provide a number of worthwhile research topics; indeed, the bulk of research on Chilean civil-military relations has been concerned with this period.

During these years the army's orientation turned from the external to the internal. Thus we need to know more about the army as a professional organization and institution. While most scholars now agree that military professionalization did lead to political interests in Chile, we still need additional documentation of this phenomenon. Specifically, what was it about the professionalization process that might have caused antipathy toward the political system? How did the officer corps of the early twentieth century differ from that of the late nineteenth century, and what differences in the political system, society, and economy are significant? Do Chilean civil-military relations bear characteristics similar or dissimilar to those of other Latin American countries at that time? Are there ways and is it feasible to compare attitudes toward nation, state, and society during the critical 1920s to those of the critical 1970s? Does the lack of an imminent "external mission" or threat from across frontiers propel a military organization into internal affairs? What are the weaknesses of a political system which render it subject to military political action? These are but a few suggestions. Despite the fact, as stated above, that this period has been well investigated, ample opportunity for research still exists.

Reconstitution of the army following the Civil War needs study and analysis. Fertile ground for investigation could be army-navy relations and their consequent political, social, and economic ramifications with particular emphasis on the 1891-1918 period. The navy's continued prestige and the decline of the army's (with the German defeat in 1918) both influenced civil-military and inter-service relations.

The 1920s provide the first Latin American problem-oriented military *golpes*--those of 1924 and 1925 in Chile. Hopefully one day these will be studied by someone with a background in modern Spanish history who may see certain similarities between the Chilean experience and that of Spain under Miguel Primo de Rivera. Similarly, the Turkish experiment and Brazilian *tenentismo* provide examples for a study of military political attitudes toward state, nation, and society which can be compared and contrasted to those manifest in Chile during the 1920s.

Another aspect of Chilean civil-military relations definitely needing attention is the linkage between the officer class and civilian political parties and leaders; while considering itself unique, the Chilean army was by no means hermetically sealed off from civilian life. The relationship of military and society also underwent dramatic change after the turn of the century, and the social relationship that emerged contributed much to civil-military relations in the broader sense. The return to

Portalian-style authoritarianism in the 1920s was a civil-military movement during its rise and decline--led and championed by officers, but supported by influential civilians, then disavowed by both. That this was simply a military-middle sector alliance is an unsatisfactory explanation.

The fall of Ibáñez' government in 1931 ended one phase of Chilean civil-military relations and introduced another which lasted until 1973. The extremes of this most recent phase were marked by radical experiments in government and politics, and by military involvement. During 1931-32 the military continued to play a political role not unlike that between independence and the stabilization of internal affairs in the 1830s. Between 1970 and 1973 the military was again propelled into the arena of politics and government. It is significant that at critical stages of Chilean political development (1817-30, 1891, 1920s, 1931-32, 1970-73) civil-military solutions have been sought despite a strong "civilist" tradition. Concentrated study of Chilean civil-military relations with this in mind would reveal much about Chile's political and social development, generally examined without much reference to the military.

Here again is an abundance of topics for historical research--topics which suggest the use of interdisciplinary approaches and methodologies. What factors influenced military leaders (particularly those of the army) to support, if only briefly, socialist solutions to socio-economic problems in 1932? What in the nature of the polity convinced them to eschew political activism after 1932? Did the post-1932 composition of the officer corps differ markedly from the pre-1932 norm in ways that would influence civil-military political and/or social relations? Did professionalism preclude military interest in internal affairs after 1932--at least to the point of inhibiting action--whereas it had not earlier? Did political mobilization and awareness of those most likely to be conscripted into the rank-and-file militate against political activism by their officers? Is there a relationship between literacy level, political awareness, and the successful implementation of military discipline, and if so how does such a relationship affect the ability of officers to exert pressure on the state? How did the relationship between chief executive, defense minister, and service commander-in-chief contribute to the maintenance of civilian control of national affairs? Do military attitudes toward state, nation, and society indicate the presence or absence of an "ideological stance" or a "political profile" of the officer class, and how important is such presence or absence in a critical situation? How much does identification with, or alienation from the "ruling class" contribute to civil-military relations in a non-oligarchic sociopolitical matrix (i.e., post-1932 Chile as opposed to pre-1891 Chile)? Was the military's obedience and devotion to its assigned duties based more on "gradualism" in social and economic reform policy in the civilian sphere than on the principles of obedience and non-deliberation stated in the Constitution.

Since 1973 it is obvious that four decades of professional acquiescence did not insure Chile against military political action. It is equally obvious that no matter how democratic Chile appeared, serious shortcomings in the political-social and economic spheres influenced civil-military relations to take a new course. Furthermore, it is obvious that the armed forces represent no specific interest-group party or class (though they may represent some more than others) and that there is no evidence of elaborately preconceived "positions" on the role of the state or the proper remedies for national problems. These themes all need close examination with regard to civil-military relations. Assiduous attention to them may make it necessary to cast conclusions more in terms of Chilean *military-civilian* relations, particularly when considering recent events and their aftermath.

CONCLUSION

Chile has long stood out as a haven for scholars, its libraries and archives superior by Latin American standards. The Biblioteca Nacional with its collections of published and unpublished sources, the Biblioteca del Congreso, and the latter's Anexo, containing an extensive collection of documents, periodicals, and newspapers, are both full of materials necessary for the study of civil-military relations in the nineteenth and twentieth centuries, with particular reference to civilian relations with the military. The Biblioteca del Congreso's collection of congressional proceedings provide an ideal source of information on political issues and conflicts during crisis periods, and the Anexo's newspapers and periodicals are particularly useful for chronicling military political activity.

Nevertheless, the scholar of civil-military relations must go farther in Chile. The finest collection of primary and secondary source materials on this subject is in the Biblioteca del Estado Mayor General del Ejército de Chile (BEMGE). Formerly housed in the Ministry of National Defense (just across the Alameda Bernardo O'Higgins from La Moneda, the government house), the General Staff Library will soon be reassembled in space provided by the Escuela Militar. This Library, ably directed by Gonzalo Mendoza Aylwin, contains military journals (the most important being the *Memorial del Ejército de Chile*), officer rosters, memoirs, technical studies, recruitment studies, statistics, annual reports, conscription records, legislation, regulations, education and advanced training materials, and a small collection of secondary works all pertinent to the Chilean army in addition to an extensive collection of official and semi-official sources and general works relevant to other Latin American countries. Besides the *Memorial* there are other journals reflecting the interests and views of non-commissioned officers, enlisted men, and the different branches of the army which can be used to assess intra-service tensions or cohesion, always significant in the study of civil-military relations. The affable Sr. Mendoza is extremely knowledgeable, and his staff is most helpful to the scholar. In 1975 he became editor of *Armas y servicios* which combines the specialized publications just mentioned. *Armas y servicios* has been devised to include materials orienting the non-commissioned and junior officers to the problems encountered because of the assumption of a political role.

The moving of the collection began in 1972 and was somewhat retarded by the crisis of 1973, but it is hoped it will be functional in the near future. The collection compares favorably with those of other military archives and libraries in South America and is important for research in comparative civil-military relations as well as Chilean topics. No matter the specific topic in Chilean civil-military relations, research is not comprehensive unless use is made of appropriate materials in the BEMGE pertinent to military relations with state, nation, and society.

ECUADOR

Introduction
Jaime E. Rodríguez O.

Ecuador is a small country which has attracted little attention among foreign scholars. Since it had no great mineral wealth or major export crop until the twentieth century, Ecuador also attracted few foreign observers of any kind. The little that is known about the nation's past is the result of the efforts of Ecuadorians. Presently there are only a handful of professional historians in the entire country, and until recently, these men and women could not obtain employment in their chosen specialty because history was not a discipline studied in the universities. Nor could these historians support themselves with employment in archives and libraries where staff positions were few and poorly paid. With few exceptions, their work is not "scholarly" in the strict sense of the term, but they have forged a path which others may follow. Therefore, while history remains an underdeveloped field in Ecuador, the efforts of dedicated amateurs who have accomplished much under difficult circumstances should be applauded. Fortunately, Ecuador has begun to develop in recent years, and scholarship is advancing accordingly. New archives and repositories are now directed by active, progressive individuals, and history is now becoming a rigorous discipline in the universities and colleges. There is much to be done, but important first steps have been taken.

This section has been organized to provide scholars with information on Ecuador's historical sources. The first two essays discuss research opportunities in the colonial and national periods. They are not meant to be exhaustive, merely suggestive. The pieces which follow describe the principal libraries and archives of the country. Although it proved impossible to obtain descriptions of all important repositories, the editor was fortunate in obtaining contributions from scholars who have worked in a variety of national, provincial, municipal, clerical, and private repositories. Some were written by Ecuadorians, others by foreigners; together they have provided the most thorough description of Ecuadorian sources in any language. It is hoped this *Guide* will encourage more scholars to explore Ecuador's past.

Comments on the Historiography of Ecuador's Pre-Independence Period
Adám Szaszdi

The classical approach to historiography is--logically enough--to review past literature on the subject, analyze it and comment on it critically--perhaps eulogize it--and then, as an afterthought, to add a few comments on present trends and future perspectives. But I have decided to reverse the order of priorities for the following reason. To ignore the whole corpus of historical literature concerning Ecuador prior to 1808 must loom as an extreme proposition. I do wish to state, however, my appreciation for many--if not all--of the historians who, starting with Father Juan de Velasco have treated the colonial period. But I raise the question of usefulness, *aprovechabilidad*: usefulness not simply in the sense that a certain work might serve as an introduction to serious research on the subject but rather in terms of "definitive" contributions. By "definitive" I mean "not seeming to require immediate revision."

A few works qualify as "definitive." These appeared mostly during the past few years, though not exclusively so. I shall not list these since it would appear discriminatory, and in any case, would simply reflect my own preferences. On the other hand, I have raised the question of *aprovechabilidad* globally, in terms of *the historiography*, and not in terms of all and any individual contributions; and I opt for appraising those "definitive" works as the first steps in the right direction, the already-written parts of future historiography.

My previous statement that I appreciate the writings of many past historians is not limited to those I consider *aprovechables*. This might seem paradoxical, but I feel the same way about the great feats of the scholastics during the late Middle Ages, who integrated divine and human science into one single, complete explanation of the universe, this world and the other world. They achieved this integration through tremendous work and mental exertion: still, scholastic science is of little use, except as a source for the study of medieval thought.

But let me proceed with my task: guidelines for the writing of Ecuador's history before its independence from Spain. The first, a point I have just made, is that we must virtually begin anew. Second, we must define the purpose of present and future historical research and writing in a way that might justify the effort of doing it.

Beyond personal motivation, the question I am posing concerns the *razón de ser* of historiography. This varies, of course, from time to time and from author to author. Thus, Father Velasco was infused with American patriotism, while González Suárez pretended to show divine providence guiding the destinies of Ecuador step by step. Other authors are still trying to justify Ecuador's break with Spain, something which does not make much sense after 150 years of independence. Still others continue celebrating the victories won, 150 years ago. There are those who use history as an arm in the never ceasing struggle between the political right and the political left, to prove that their side was virtuous, while the other side had a monopoly of *bandoleros, cuatreros,* and *comanches*. Finally, the most progressive ideologues will present the novel proposition that the only reason for history at all is to prove that we can do without it, since don Carlos Marx provided the essential framework more than a hundred years ago. Yet, if we admit that the historian's task is to find and present the facts, interpret them, and try to reconstruct the missing ones through the use of logic, does he do all this simply as a virtuoso of his craft, or is there some other purpose beyond this professional consideration?

Even primitive peoples, by transmitting legends and myths from one generation to another, try to maintain a collective self-consciousness, a feeling of identity and belonging, which is actually a collective psychological necessity. This need is still present in modern society. Furthermore, somewhat optimistically I wish to think that the days have ended when the main purpose of government was to fill the pockets of government officials and those of their friends and relatives; to exercise petty--and not so petty--tyranny over the governed; and to assault, circumstances permitting, neighboring peoples. I wish to believe that the function of government is eminently that of administering and planning, serving a society whose daily life is steadily increasing in complexity.

For short-term planning, recent statistics are analyzed, the latest trends studied and projected forward. In the same way, the general trends, the vague goals toward which a society's future existence is oriented, are closely related to its awareness of its past. Essentially it is a question of whether this awareness of the past--this knowledge of history--is the knowledge of real or fictitious history. Those who knowingly adulterate history are schizoids who want to indoctrinate the people in a way that might serve their purpose of cutting all contacts with the real past. Those who adulterate history unknowingly are essential ignoramuses, but the results will be the same. It is similar to a planning board which makes decisions based on false statistics; for the final results it matters little whether the statistics were known to be false or not.

In the case of Ecuador, I ask only two questions: where is the usefulness of the proposition, with which all schoolchildren are indoctrinated in their history courses--and beyond them--that the fundamental national virtue is rebelliousness? And what is the specific goal of those who insist, explicitly or implicitly, that Ecuador is a Quechua nation?

To the contrary, I think that Ecuadorians should know that the formative stage of their nationality belongs to the period of 1531-1822, instead of being subjected to the nonsense of Atahualpa *fundador de la nacionalidad*. (Why not Huayna Capac or Túpac Yupanqui, for that matter?) It would be even a surprise to some reform-minded statesmen to know that something like ALALC or the Pacto Andino existed before 1820. To be sure, those of us who have worked in colonial economic history were aware of this even before the signing of the Acuerdo de Cartagena.

My third point is that Ecuador is in all respects, except the constitutional one, a federation of regions. Certainly, the adoption of a federal constitution at any time during the past 150 years would have been disastrous, since it would have favored the numerous centrifugal forces. But political convenience is one thing and geographical and social reality another.

I suggest, therefore, that the task of writing Ecuador's pre-1820 history be undertaken on a regional basis: that each researcher concentrate on one of these regions. These are not only determined by geography but also through their occupation by different tribes before the Spanish conquest and inclusion within different municipal jurisdictions during the Spanish period.

I. The coastal zone includes two main subdivisions: (1) Esmeraldas and (2) the Corregimiento of Guayaquil. The latter might be further subdivided: the province of Guayaquil proper (present-day Guayas, Los Ríos, and half of El Oro), and the province of Portoviejo (Manabi). But the history of both is so interwoven that their separation would not be a very practical solution. As far as the Galapagos are concerned, they fit into the maritime-naval aspects of the history of Guayaquil.

The second main geographical zone of the country is the sierra, the only one that had formed part of the Inca empire. This fact, together with the geographical factor, gives it its special character. It can be subdivided into various regions, corresponding to clearly delimited geographical units, which, at the same time, have been occupied by different tribes and, as mentioned above, belonged later to different municipal jurisdictions. Two main zones--grouping together various of these units-- are distinguishable here:

II. Northern Sierra. This includes the following regions: (1) Hoyas del Carchi y Chota (Mira)--Caranquis--Corregimiento of Ibarra (Provinces of Carchi and Imbabura). (2) Hoyas del Guayllabamba, Toachi, y Patate-- Quitos (alias Panzaleos)--Corregimiento of Quito (Provinces of Pichincha, Cotopaxi, and Tungurahua). (3) Hoyas del Chambo y Chimbo--Puruaes-- Corregimientos of Chimbo (Guaranda), and Riobamba, (Provinces of Chimborazo and Bolívar).

III. Southern Sierra, subdivided into (1) Hoyas del Chanchán, Cañar, Paute, y Jubones--Cañares--Corregimiento of Cuenca, (Provinces of Cañar and Azuay). (2) Hoyas del Puyango, Catamayo, Macará, y Zamora--Paltas-- Corregimiento of Loja, (Province of Loja and part of El Oro).

IV. Oriente (Amazonian basin). (1) Jaén de Bracamoros, Yaguarsongo, and Zamora. (These jurisdictions could also be included for purposes of study in one single group with Loja.) (2) Macas. (3) Quijos. (4) Maynas.

Independently of present-day borders, one can logically study such colonial provinces (Jaén, Maynas, and eastern Quijos) in the context of their historical relations; the same way as it would be sheer nonsense to redistribute the *legajos* in the Archivo General de Indias in a way to suit twentieth-century borders and administrative practices.

I see one general exception to this proposed scheme of a regional approach to Ecuadorian history: the study of institutions, such as the *audiencia* and the church on its episcopal level. It should be noted in this context, that the Province of Pasto, a well defined unit which now belongs to Colombia, was part of the Bishopric of Quito and not of Popayán, even though it belonged to the Gobernación of Popayán. On the other hand, most of the latter was included in the district of the Audiencia of Quito instead of the Audiencia of Santa Fé. This means that a systematic study of the Bishopric of Quito must also cover Pasto, and for the Audiencia of Quito one should certainly not leave out Popayán.

Turning to chronology my main interest was formerly the early nineteenth century; my wife was chiefly interested in the second half of the eighteenth century. Nevertheless, it did not seem to us reasonable to begin with the end of the colonial period, when there was nothing solid on which to depend for the previous two or three centuries. Thus we started our systematic research with the sixteenth century: ethnohistory, conquest, colonization, and from 1550 on, the beginnings of the new Indo-Hispanic society and its subsequent development. Of course, one can envision a situation in which a number of historians are doing research on the same region: in such a case, the chronological partition of the field among them is a logical solution.

To be sure, the traditions of our craft call for a division along disciplinary lines such as political, legal, economic, social, intellectual, and ecclesiastical history. These fields of history do exist. On the other hand my own practice is, and it is also my recommendation for future research in Ecuadorian history, to use an integrated, exhaustive approach. Two arguments support this position: first, the various fields of history are, in reality, interrelated to such a degree that to separate them is to adulterate history; secondly, when one labors through sundry, out-of-the-way *legajos* and other sources, it would be highly regrettable to pick out only those bits of information of immediate interest to the researcher, leaving behind all the rest for the next comer, perhaps one or two hundred years thence. Such a practice is comparable to the case of one who comes upon a cache of gems while searching for emeralds, leaving behind all the diamonds, rubies, and sapphires because he is not interested in them.

The next major point concerns standards of research. We should be exacting in our standards: go, whenever possible, to the primary sources;

strive to be exhaustive, instead of being satisfied with the first datum to come to our attention; establish heuristic priorities and practice the critical valuation of sources; see our subject within the widest possible context; have the capacity to infer conclusions even if they are not expressed explicitly by the documents; forget about writing *historias generales*; and avoid broad generalizations until all facts seem to be in. I know that my insistence on these standards must seem preposterous, since they are really nothing new. I mention them only because much of the past historiography on pre-1820 Ecuador is wanting in this respect.

My final point on the sources will be cursory. Among the printed sources are the *cronistas* and all other books written during the colonial period, including Father Velasco who will be useful for the eighteenth century. Then, we have the numerous *colecciones de documentos*, whether they bear this title or not, including the published *actas capitulares*. A similar category includes the printed catalogues of archives. A few works of modern historians are very useful, such as Jacinto Jijón's *Sebastián de Benalcázar*, which is merely a definitive study. A few others fall into this category; but others are useful only as an introduction to their subject. One should be very careful, however, with letting oneself be misled by certain standard interpretations. *Heroes* are not necessarily heroes, and *villains* perhaps were not villains. Certain foes of twentieth-century oligarchy seem to be unaware of the existence of an oligarchy before 1820. I also know of a conquistador who apprently has gained the sympathy of some modern *indigenistas* because he rebelled against the king: they do not know that the man in question was responsible for the "preventive action" of killing more than one hundred Indian notables of Quito in 1536.

Manuscript sources are abundant in Spain. First of all, the Archivo General de Indias in Seville, not only for the Audiencia of Quito section but for the other sections which also contain material referring to Ecuador. In addition, there are various depositories in Madrid in addition to the Archivo Histórico Nacional. The archive of Simancas is next in importance, but materials are also available in cities like Barcelona and Valencia and in the notarial and nobiliary archives all over Spain; such cities as Cádiz, Seville, Valladolid, and San Sebastián would be logical places to check, depending on the subject and the period. The same is true of parochial archives, where an immigrant's place of birth can perhaps be ascertained. Moreover key cities in Europe outside of Spain--Paris, London, Amsterdam, Rome--all house documents on Ecuador. (To be sure, a couple of silver chandeliers robbed by seventeenth-century pirates from the church of Guayaquil are said to be in the cathedral of Bristol.)

In Latin America, Lima and Bogotá are repositories for documents on colonial Ecuador. Archives of the former Gobernación de Popayán are of great value and interest; so are the materials on Ecuador in the archives of Mexico and Guatemala. This may also have been the case for Panamá, though probably not much of it survives.

In Ecuador, the survival rate of documents in the sierra has been rather high with the main problem formerly being their disorganization and lack of availability. Lately much progress has been made in cataloging and opening public repositories, though less has been done with private collections, which might even include *fondos* proceeding from public archives. The coast has been less favored, and humidity, fire, worms, and theft have all contributed to emasculate documentary collections. Still, there is much more than usually supposed: the municipal archives of Guayaquil and the newly created Archivo Histórico del Guayas-- largely because of the efforts of Julio Estrada-Ycaza--are a good example.

One more comment. Just as a few *guaqueros* are destroying the evidence of pre-Hispanic cultures by selling archaeological objects illegally, others are selling abroad manuscripts proceeding from public repositories. Some would argue that these expatriated documents are better kept in their new places, a poor argument, indeed, to justify theft or the encouragement of theft. If the trend continues, it should be no surprise if legitimate researchers be treated in the future as prime suspects. On the other hand, if somebody would search for material on Peguche, for example, the logical place to look would certainly not be Farmersville, Idaho, or--in the best of cases--Washington, D. C. Also another great enemy of research is the displacement of books or documents. We should all strive to create a consciousness of the need for international agreements against the pirating of documents.

And, a last word. Ten years ago I surveyed and analyzed Ecuadorian historiography. My appraisal of this past decade is--and why not speak of the last two decades as well--that these have been promising years.

I hope, I am convinced, that in 1990 somebody will survey this coming decade's work in terms of well deserved praise.

Research in the National Period
Jaime E. Rodríguez O.

The scholar contemplating research in Ecuadorian history has little to guide him. Few scholarly monographs have been written, and the existing general histories are full of errors and partisanship. Thus, irrespective of his research project and methodological approach, the scholar must be prepared to use primary sources. This generally means research in Ecuadorian repositories because few documentary collections have been published. The following remarks are intended to suggest possible directions for research in Ecuadorian history since independence.

Despite Ecuador's small size, regionalism has been an important factor for most of her history. Thus, Adam Szászdi's suggestion that research in Ecuadorian colonial history be carried out on a regional basis is also appropriate for the national period. The three major regions of Ecuador have been the coast with Guayaquil as its leader; the northern highlands controlled by Quito; and the southern *sierra* led by Cuenca. Throughout the national period, these three areas have maintained a shifting balance of power. The traditional rivalry between Guayaquil and Quito has often expressed itself in a competition for Cuenca's support. Economic factors have tended to favor an alliance between Cuenca and Guayaquil, but the more conservative social structure of the highlands has tended to create a community of interests between Quito and Cuenca.

While regionalism is often mentioned in works on Ecuador, no one has undertaken a systematic study of the phenomenon and its political, social, and economic effects either within the regions or the nation. The nineteenth- and twentieth-century history of Ecuador provides important opportunities for such investigations. The growth and decline of a region's dominance can be studied from a variety of perspectives. For example, population shifts, particularly in this century, provide evidence that the supremacy of the highlands is ending. The trend is easily discernible, but an explanation of the complex causal factors and the societal ramifications of the change can only be understood when detailed studies are undertaken by historians and other social scientists.

POLITICAL HISTORY

Although political history is the most studied aspect of Ecuador's past, the bulk of the publications in this area are partisan biographies. Little can be gained by continued debate on the personal merits of political leaders such as Juan José Flores, Gabriel García Moreno, and Eloy Alfaro. Rather, political studies should concentrate on broader questions. At the national level, much could be learned from the study of administrations. David Bushnell's masterful work, *The Santander Regime in Gran Colombia* (Newark, Del.: U. of Delaware Press, 1954) might serve as a model. Key periods could also be studied in this fashion. For example, one might investigate Ecuador during the Gran Colombian era (1822-1830) or the period of Liberal ascendancy (1895-1925).

Provincial government is another important area which has not been studied. How did it work? How did it affect provincial development or the lives of people within its jurisdiction? What were its relations to the national or to municipal governments? We cannot presently answer these fundamental questions. Yet several contributors to this section, Juan Freile-Granizo, Rosemary D. F. Bromley, Julio Estrada-Ycaza, and Michael Hamerly, indicate that the archives of provincial governments are voluminous. Similarly, we know virtually nothing about municipal government while there are extensive records of city government in the larger cities.

Institutional studies are also needed if we are to understand Ecuador's political history. This approach remains undeveloped. Our ignorance is such that we cannot say with certainty how institutions like the courts, the schools, and government monopolies functioned in the nineteenth century. Monographs on these subjects would also contribute greatly to our understanding of twentieth-century developments.

ECONOMIC HISTORY

The economic history of Ecuador is largely unstudied. Although we are aware of the main outlines of the history of Ecuador's exports, we know little about the development of the nation's internal economy. Important questions about regional markets, the development of a national market, and the relationship between Ecuador's internal economy and the world economy remain unanswered.

Indeed, nineteenth-century developments are shrouded in mystery. Did anything approaching a national market exist then? If one existed, was it large and how did it function? What regional markets existed? Were they the focus of the internal economy until the twentieth century? What role did the hacienda and the Indian communities play in the economy of the highlands? What were the size and role of various groups such as the artisans and entrepreneurs in the nineteenth century? Why did the early textile factories fail? What role did the church play in the economy? Did it serve as a bank as it did in Mexico? These are only a few of the many questions which can be asked about the internal economy of Ecuador during the 1800s.

The general outline of Ecuador's economy since the Liberals came to power in 1895 is better known, but the few existing scholarly studies generally concentrate on the period since World War II. Thus a variety of important questions await answers. The first years of the twentieth century witnessed improvements in transportation and communications; these, in turn, had a profound effect on the nation's internal economy. New industries and enterprises arose to take advantage of the expanding markets. Detailed studies are needed if we hope to understand their rate of growth and the extent to which the money economy penetrated the traditional subsistence sector. A number of other interesting problems, such as the relationship between the growth of national markets and the extension of effective state power, also need to be investigated.

Although the export sector has received more attention than any other part of Ecuador's economy, research has concentrated on post-World War II phenomena. We know the outlines of its history in the twentieth century but little about the nineteenth. Nor do we know much about the institutions, like banks, which developed to support exports, or the complex relationships between the internal and the export economy.

Unlike other Latin American countries, Ecuador was too poor to attract extensive foreign investment during most of her history. As a result, Ecuadorian enterprises were developed by Ecuadorians. Until late in the twentieth century, foreigners played only a minor role in the nation's economy. Thus, Ecuador offers an opportunity for students of comparative development to contrast Ecuadorian solutions to economic problems with those of nations where foreign influence was pronounced. Studies of the Ecuadorian economy may also provide important insights into the nature of economic dependence and the role of foreign influence in establishing investment patterns and controlling the direction and rate of growth.

SOCIAL HISTORY

Social history, like economic history, has been neglected in Ecuador, but as various contributors to this section have indicated, materials for social history are plentiful. A historian wishing to learn more about Ecuadorian society can approach the subject from a variety of perspectives. Historical demography and the study of internal migrations will provide clues to the nature of the political and economic relations of the country's regions. Acculturation studies and the analysis of relations among whites, mestizos, and Indians will provide important insights into Ecuador's history and into the general questions of nation building, social interaction, and social change.

Techniques like family reconstruction can help us understand the complex relationship between the cities and the countryside. Since Ecuador has always been a predominantly agrarian nation, it is important to trace the ties between the rural areas and the cities--the centers of power and change. Neither sector can be ignored if we are to comprehend the evolution of social structures. Both are important in understanding the functioning of the patron-client system, the slow growth of a modern class structure, and the coexistence of these two forms of social organization throughout the national period.

Abundant materials exist in municipal, notarial, parochial, and judicial records to study a variety of topics such as families, elites, artisans, workers, and servants. The techniques of social history are particularly important because they allow us to restore formerly neglected groups, like women, to the historical records. Although a few outstanding women have won fame through literature and art, as a group women have been ignored by Ecuadorian historians. This should not be allowed to obscure the fact that women have played a major role in Ecuador. Notarial records show that they were substantial property owners, petty traders, artisans, and shopkeepers and that they were active at all levels of society. The stereotype of the passive Latin American woman kept in the seclusion of the home remains only because social history is in its infancy. A study of the rise of the small middle class in Ecuador must give an important place to women.

This discussion of possible research topics is far from complete. An enterprising student will think of many more. The researcher is faced with great opportunities and challenges in Ecuador. The sources are abundant and are now beginning to be well organized. Research facilities, while not comparable to those in developed nations, are improving rapidly and are generally staffed with interested and helpful personnel.

Before concluding this essay, I would like to make one final observation. Although most foreign scholars working on Ecuador concentrate on monographic research, they should also consider editing and publishing documents. Few documentary collections exist, and if Ecuadorian history is to advance, all researchers must assume the responsibility for contributing fully to its development. This means that we must not only do the intellectually interesting and prestigious work of analysis and synthesis but also promote the wider dissemination of source materials.

The Libraries and Archives of Quito
Linda A. Rodríguez

Quito, the capital of Ecuador, has been an important economic, administrative, political, and intellectual center since colonial times. Accordingly, the repositories of the city are rich in historical materials. The good libraries and the most extensive archives in the country make Quito an excellent starting point for historical research in Ecuador. The following discussion will be limited to the more important repositories in the city; those institutions treated by other contributors to the Ecuadorian section have been omitted. Space limitations preclude an exhaustive discussion of any particular institution. In those instances where guides to archives already exist, the author refers the reader to the previously published work.

This essay seeks to alert the scholar to the types of sources which can be found in various repositories. In general, archives make colonial and nineteenth-century materials readily available to the investigator. Twentieth-century documents are usually housed in the institutions which generated them and may be consulted only with special permission. Since many depositories have much uncatalogued and unorganized material, the researcher should establish a good working relationship with personnel in these institutions. They can be very helpful in locating unclassified documents. The investigator will also find that most libraries and archives in Quito do not have facilities for reproducing documents, but in special cases, researchers can microfilm materials themselves or arrange to have the papers copied at one of several copying facilities in the city. Such arrangements can only be made if the scholar has good rapport with the director of the repository.

LIBRARIES

BIBLIOTECA NACIONAL

Ecuador's national library, the Biblioteca Nacional, is one of the oldest public libraries in Latin America. Formed from the books confiscated from the Jesuit libraries, it opened on May 25, 1772. The library's first director was the great Ecuadorian savant, Eugenio Espejo. Although the Biblioteca Nacional started with an excellent collection, lack of government support and, in a few cases, the negligence of its personnel led to its deterioration. For many years the National Library was housed in a former skating rink with a leaky roof and received only enough funds to pay its employees. Thus acquisitions were neglected. The library has recently moved to a better building in the center of the city, the former Central Bank Building at García Moreno and Sucre. Since 1948 the Biblioteca Nacional has been a dependency of the Casa de la Cultura Ecuatoriana, a national institute which fosters cultural and artistic endeavors. As such, the National Library is one of many competing institutions seeking support from the Casa de la Cultura, restricting efforts to expand the library and to organize existing material.

The Biblioteca Nacional has a large collection of rare books from the fifteenth through eighteenth centuries which were part of the Jesuit libraries; many were apparently used as texts in the colleges and the university. Thus, the volumes are an important source for colonial intellectual history. They are described in Biblioteca Nacional, *Sección de libros antiguos y raros* (Quito, 1959).

The library does not have a complete collection of Ecuadorian imprints. Nevertheless, despite extensive lacunae and many unorganized sections, the Biblioteca is a significant research center. It has many nineteenth-century imprints, particularly those published in Quito, and an extensive collection of northern highland newspapers and handbills. The library's holdings are estimated at 75,000 volumes. The Biblioteca Nacional once had an archive, but it was turned over to the Archivo Nacional de Historia when that institution was formed in 1948.

BIBLIOTECA MUNICIPAL

The Municipal Library of Quito is one of the best libraries open to the general public. It does not have as much material as the Biblioteca Nacional, but its holdings are better arranged and much more accessible.

Situated on Calle García Moreno 877 near the Plaza de la Independencia, the Biblioteca Municipal is open from 8 a.m. to 8 p.m. six days a week and during the afternoon on Sundays. The library's telephone number is 210-862. The Biblioteca Municipal has a representative collection of Ecuadorian imprints, and is particularly strong in highland newspapers and periodicals. Its holdings include a complete bound collection of the now defunct *El Día*, an important Quito daily, as well as published government reports and laws. Since the Municipal Library serves high school and university students, it is generally crowded and recent books are often in great demand. The scholar may prefer to seek contemporary works in other libraries. It is also advisable to request permission to work away from the noisy main reading room in a *sala de investigadores*. Such a request and access to rare materials is facilitated if the researcher has taken time to establish cordial relations with the director, Clemente Bognoli. Mr. Bognoli, an amateur historian, is generally eager to assist investigators.

BIBLIOTECA ECUATORIANA: AURELIO ESPINOSA POLIT

The late Father Aurelio Espinosa Pólit, S.J. organized the country's most comprehensive library of Ecuadorian materials. Located in the northern suburb of Cotocollao, the Biblioteca Ecuatoriana is currently under the direction of Father Julián Bravo, S.J. The mailing address is Apartado 160, Quito, Ecuador, and the telephone number is 530-420. The collection has recently been moved into new quarters at Prolongación 25 de Mayo in Cotocollao, which provides good facilities for investigators. It is normally open on Tuesdays, Wednesdays, and Fridays from 9 to 12 in the morning and from 3 to 6 in the afternoon and on Saturdays from 9 to 12, but researchers should telephone to make certain that the library will be open.

The Biblioteca Ecuatoriana has the nation's best collection of Ecuadorian imprints. It is particularly strong in nineteenth-century publications. The holdings are estimated to include 65,000 books, pamphlets, newspapers, periodicals, and handbills; most are catalogued and available to researchers. The library also has works on Ecuador published abroad. This section is incomplete, however, because the Biblioteca Ecuatoriana presently depends on gifts from foreign authors and institutions to augment its collection.

The library's documentary holdings are extensive; most pertain to the nineteenth century. The major strength of this section is the correspondence of Catholic writers such as Gabriel García Moreno and Juan León Mera, but there are also papers relating to Ecuadorian history in the colonial period and twentieth century. Saint Louis University, which microfilmed the nineteenth-century materials (1800-1894), reports that it photographed 140,000 pages of documents and that many more exist for the Liberal period (1895-1925). In addition to the library and archive, the Biblioteca Ecuatoriana houses collections of art and pre-Columbian artifacts.

BIBLIOTECA DE LA CASA DE LA CULTURA

The Library of the Casa de la Cultura, located in the first floor of the Casa de la Cultura building on Avenida 6 de Diciembre 332, is one of the best places to consult contemporary books and general reference works. Its relatively small collection of 12,000 volumes contains a good selection of Ecuadorian imprints. Working conditions are generally uncrowded and comfortable. The library keeps the same hours as the Casa de la Cultura. The telephone number of the library is 231-142.

BIBLIOTECA DEL PODER LEGISLATIVO

The Ecuadorian Congress has its own library, located at Calle 6 de Diciembre and Priedrahita in the new Palacio Legislativo. The telphone number is 235-971. The director, Licenciado Rafael A. Piedra Solís, is very helpful, and scholars will find that the library has good facilities for research. There is a photocopy machine in the building, and arrangements can usually be made to copy materials.

Since the Biblioteca del Poder Legislativo is designed for use by legislators, it has a complete set of laws and government reports as well as a collection of the various official newspapers published by the Republic of Ecuador. The library also houses the congressional archives. That repository has the records of all debates, reports, and resolutions of congress. This is an important source for historians because most of its holdings remain unpublished. At the turn of the century, the government began to publish the *actas* of congress, but only the volumes for the 1830s have appeared.

OTHER PUBLIC LIBRARIES

There are several other public libraries in Quito which have significant collections. The Universidad Central has the largest library in

Quito. The telephone number of the library is 233-627. Although most of
its holdings are not Ecuatoriana, it has a collection of national imprints.
Also the university library is the best place to consult journals. Some
of them, like the *Anales* of the Universidad Central, are important sources
since, at one time, it was the principal outlet for Ecuadorian intellectuals. The library of the Catholic University has a smaller but nonetheless useful collection. Since it received part of the Jijón y Caamaño
library, there are some rare items in its holdings. The library is on
the Catholic University campus at Avenida 12 de Octubre and Carrión; the
telephone number is 239-780. Another small library with a good corpus of
Ecuadorian imprints is at the Colegio Nacional Mejía, located on Vargas
989. The collection is particularly useful to late nineteenth- and early
twentieth-century materials. The Banco Central at Avenida 10 de Agosto
and Briceño has a valuable collection of documents and publications relating to economic topics; most of the holdings pertain to the period
after 1927. Anyone wishing to investigate Ecuador's twentieth-century
economic history should consult this collection. Although the library
of the Central Bank is not open to the public, qualified researchers
may obtain access to its holdings. Finally present-day newspapers like
El Comercio maintain their own archives and are generally open to researchers. In many cases it is easier to consult newspapers in these
collections than in crowded libraries.

PRIVATE LIBRARIES

The finest private library in Ecuador was amassed by the late Jacinto
Jijón y Caamaño. Situated in the Jijón mansion on Calle Versalles 1632,
the library is open to qualified scholars; investigators wishing to research there must obtain permission from Mrs. Jijón y Caamaño. Introductions from ambassadors and important Ecuadorian intellectuals will
facilitate entry. The telephone number of the library is 236-310. The
library is reputed to hold many extremely rare items. There is also a
valuable archive, which includes the papers of General Juan José Flores,
the first president of Ecuador. Its holdings include many priceless
colonial documents as well as papers for the nineteenth century. The
collection also houses the papers of Jacinto Jijón y Caamaño, a leading
Ecuadorian intellectual, and for many years, the leader of the Conservative Party.

The current director of Ecuador's Academia Nacional de Historia, Carlos

Manuel Larrea, also has an extensive library. The Larrea library and archives is in his home on 12 de Octubre 1699, a few blocks from the Catholic University. Don Carlos has been generous in allowing qualified scholars to consult his collection. The holdings include a number of colonial and early national documents and an important group of national imprints. Larrea's mailing address is Casilla de Correos #372 and his telephone number is 231-776.

ARCHIVES

ARCHIVO MUNICIPAL

The Municipal Archive is one of the most important repositories in Quito. Situated on Calle Espejo 1147 across from the National Palace, the Archivo Municipal is housed in one wing of the Museo de Arte e Historia (telephone number 210-863). It is open from 9 to 12 a.m. and from 2 to 6 p.m. Although there are no formal accommodations for investigators not employed by the city, visiting researchers are normally assigned a desk. There are no facilities for reproducing documents, but the archive does have a microfilm reader. Permission to work in the Archivo Municipal should be obtained from the director, Licenciado Luis Ortiz Bilbao whose mailing address is Apartado de Correos #3346, Quito, Ecuador.

The Archivo Municipal has materials from the founding of Quito in 1534 through the nineteenth century. (Twentieth-century documents are kept in the *secretaría* of the municipality located in the new municipal building on the Plaza de la Independencia. These materials are not generally available to researchers, but it may be possible to obtain permission to see specific documents from the city secretary who is in charge of municipal papers.) The materials in the Archivo Municipal are organized in bound volumes. The respository has a nearly complete set of "Libros de Actas del Cabildo de Quito," beginning with 1534 and continuing to 1900. These and the "Oficios dirigidos al Cabildo" provide a continuous source of documents on city government. The archive also has documents on slaves, lands, poor houses, schools, elections, population, etc. The holdings of the Archivo Municipal are described in "Lista de legajos manuscritos del Museo de Historia de la Ciudad de Quito," *Museo Histórico* I (May, 1949):31-35.

These papers are shelved alphabetically by volume title. However, researchers should realize that volumes with slightly different titles may contain related material. For example, although the volumes "Ingresos para la Manumisión de Esclavos," "Manumisión de Esclavos," and "Rentas de Manumisión" are in different sections of the archive, they all contain documents relating to the manumission of slaves. The municipality of Quito has published many of the documents in its collection in the series entitled *Libros de Cabildo* (35 vols.) and in the journal *Museo Histórico* (53 numbers).

ARCHIVO DE LA UNIVERSIDAD CENTRAL

Ecuador's Universidad Central has a well organized archive. Although the so called "Libro de Oro," which includes the earliest records of the university, dates from the sixteenth century, most of its documents are from the eighteenth, nineteenth, and twentieth centuries. The documents are either bound or in boxes. They are generally arranged chronologically by topic. Many of the papers consist of registries of entry into professional groups such as medicine, law, and engineering. There are also university financial reports, minutes of faculty meetings, lists of students and professors, course outlines, theses, and graduation records. These materials contain valuable information for the social history of Quito as well as for the intellectual history of Ecuador.

ARCHIVO ARZOBISPAL

The Episcopal Archive is located in the old bishop's palace on the Plaza de la Independencia. The researcher can arrange to use the Archivo Arzobispal by going to the *despacho* on the second floor. An employee in the office will then call the priest in charge of the archive. The investigator should be ready to explain his topic and the types of materials he hopes to consult. There is a typescript guide to the archive which the scholar may consult. The archivist will generally require a day or two to obtain the papers. The repository has a *sala de investigación* with two tables where the historian may work. But there are no facilities for the reproduction of documents.

The archive was originally organized by Father Juan de Dios Navas who divided the documents into three groups: colonial, independence, and republic. The papers were further subdivided into the following categories: (1) papal documents (2) interdiocesan papers (3) papers from foreign dioceses and religious institutions (4) civil documents (5) diocesan administration (6) pastoral letters and inspections (7) regular and secular clergy (8) benefices and seminaries (9) communications from the faithful (10) temporalities, and (11) relations between ecclesiastical and civil authorities. Many documents remain unclassified; a reorganization of the Archivo Arzobispal, which began in 1972, is continuing. Therefore, some of the old categories may have been abolished and new ones added.

There is a small church library in the same building which has a useful collection of publications on religious matters. It is particularly strong in nineteenth-century materials. The library has several tables and a small card catalogue. Since the volumes are arranged by topic in bookcases in the reading room, the researcher may locate materials not listed in the card catalogue by looking at various sections. Permission to use the library must be acquired from the priest in charge. He may be reached in the same manner as the curator of the Archivo Arzobispal.

ARCHIVO DEL CABILDO ECLESIASTICO

The Archive of the Ecclesiastical Cabildo is located in the *sala capitular* where the *quiteños* declared their independence. The colonial historian will find the archive particularly useful since it houses the documents of the Archdiocese of Quito which included all of present-day Ecuador and parts of Peru and Colombia. Materials on the national period pertain to a much smaller area because other dioceses were formed after independence. The archive has a complete set of *actas capitulares* from 1562 to the present. It also has a set of royal *cédulas* for the colonial period. The bulk of the documents pertain to the eighteenth, nineteenth, and twentieth centuries. Many, like the periodic parish reports, are important sources for social and political as well as for church history.

ARCHIVO DEL CONVENTO DE SAN FRANCISCO

The Convent of San Francisco, located at Cuenca 477, has an important archive. It has extensive records concerning the members, the activities, and the properties of the order. The holdings are strongest for the eighteenth and nineteenth centuries. The collection contains the following kinds of materials: documents concerning candidates to the order until 1800; *cofradías* from the sixteenth to the nineteenth centuries; papers relating to religious observances and indulgences; ten volumes on Franciscan *doctrinas* from the sixteenth through the eighteenth centuries; three volumes of *censos* from the sixteenth through the nineteenth centuries; accounts of the Convento Máximo for the eighteenth and nineteenth centuries; and books of Franciscan landholdings in the parish of Chimbacalle. These materials are important sources for social and economic history. Researchers wishing to use these papers should contact the priest in charge of the archive; the telephone number is 211-124.

ARCHIVO DE LOS JESUITAS

The Archive of the Jesuits in Ecuador was confiscated when the order was expelled from Spanish America in 1767. Some of the documents, pertaining mainly to Jesuit haciendas, were taken to Chile. [See Hermes Tobar, "Las haciendas jesuíticas de México: Índice de documentos existentes en el Archivo Nacional de Chile," *Historia mexicana* 20 (April-June, 1971):563-618; (July-Sept., 1971):135-189]. The materials which remained in Ecuador were returned to the Society of Jesus in 1862 by Gabriel García Moreno. These documents are divided into thirty-two *legajos* which contain detailed information on various aspects of the Jesuit order. Materials which may prove useful for economic and social history are: thirty-four volumes on land mortgages; three books of *censos*; thirty-five volumes of income and expenditures of the Convento Máximo and its dependencies; several volumes relating to *capellanías*; and a complete register of the members of the Cofradía de Rosía from its founding in 1588. An index to the documents of Jesuit archive was published in the *Boletín del Archivo Nacional de Historia* 12 (August, 1963).

ARCHIVO DE SANTO DOMINGO

The Archive of the Dominican convent, located at Flores 150 (telephone number 210-723), is presently under the able direction of Father José María Vargas, a distinguished historian. It has several hundred *legajos* pertaining to the colonial and national periods. Among these are papers on rents, royal *cédulas*, confraternities, properties, and correspondence between civil and clerical authorities as well as documents concerning the internal workings of the order such as official and ecclesiastical communications. The papers of the College of San Fernando, which are housed in the archive, include materials on education, texts, exams, etc.

The Convent of Santo Domingo also houses the documents which the late Father Enrique Vacas Galindo brought back from Spain. These consist of thousands of pages of typescripts and photocopies presently divided into 181 volumes. Many of the documents deal with the history of Ecuador's boundaries. Others relate to social, economic, and clerical questions in the colonial period. There is a catalogue of these materials in José María Vargas, *Misiones ecuatorianas en archivos europeos* (México, 1956), pp. 20-183. Luis Alfonso Ortiz Bilbao has compiled a detailed index of the documents bound in the thirty volumes of *cédulas* in that collection. The guide is being published in various issues of the *Boletín de la Academia Nacional de Historia* beginning with No. 160 (Dec., 1965).

ARCHIVO DEL MINISTERIO DE GOBIERNO

The Archive of the Ministry of Government is now being organized, but in the meantime, the documents are housed on the top floor of the Pasaje, a commercial center, situated in the 800 block of Calle García Moreno across from the Biblioteca Municipal. Researchers must obtain permission to use the archive from the director of the Archivo who has his office in the Ministerio de Gobierno located in the 1100 block of Calle Espejo, across from the Archivo Municipal.

The Ministerio de Gobierno has historically been concerned with the internal affairs of the country. It has materials on relations between the national government and the provinces, the police, health, taxes, Indian affairs, etc. Apparently, it retains the raw returns of various municipal, provincial, and regional censuses beginning in 1825. These materials are important sources for economic, social, and political history. The author visited the repository in the summer of 1975. At that time the materials were partially organized, but the archive lacked staff. Nevertheless, the investigator who is willing to spend some time searching for materials will obtain much useful information. The Ministry assured me that the archive would be "perfectly" organized in a year.

Professor Mark Van Aken, who returned from Quito in June, 1976, has kindly informed me that the Ministerio de Gobierno has been turned over to the Archivo Nacional de Historia. The National Archive is currently organizing these papers, which should be available to researchers in the near future.

ARCHIVO DEL MINISTERIO DE FINANZAS

The documents of the Ministry of Finance are available to researchers. Unfortunately, the papers of the old Ministerio de Hacienda and its successor the Ministerio de Finanzas have been divided. Approximately two-thirds of the documents are housed in the National Archive,and the remainder are located in the old Ministerio de Finanzas building on Guayaquil Street. Much of the material is in poor condition because it was previously stored in a former bull ring. The Centro de Historia y Geografía Militar aided in organizing the documents housed in the Guayaquil Street location. Special arrangements must be made to use this material. Working with these documents is difficult because of the bad physical condition of the building.

When the author began research in the National Archive in the summer of 1975, the Ministry of Finance materials were stacked in piles several feet high. A large part of the materials consisted of bound ledger books of various sizes; some were legal size and others were two by three feet and weighed as much as forty pounds. At first, the director of the archive was understandably loath to allow researchers to use the materials because they were covered with dust and because one had literally to climb on top of the documents to look through them. Moreover, there was the danger of being buried by an unstable pile of account books. The materials had no semblance of order, and one had to go through hundreds of volumes to find needed documents. Nevertheless, careful search can be extremely fruitful. Fortunately the documents in the National Archive have now been placed on shelves, which make them easier to use. But they still have no order. The director of the National Archive estimated that it would take about a year to organize the material.

The Ministry of Finance papers consist of three kinds of materials. First are the hard-bound ledger books containing tax, budgetary, and financial records of the national government. About eighty percent of this type of material is located in the National Archive and twenty percent in the Guayaquil street building. Some of these records are quite detailed, listing every expenditure by month. Others are general summaries of a year or a decade. Some contain the records of special enterprises such as the building of the Southern Railroad or the sanitation of the city of Guayaquil. These records actually begin in the colonial period--the eighteenth century--and continue in some instances until World War II. The eighteenth-century materials have generally been incorporated into the holdings of the Archivo Nacional. [See Juan Freile-Granizo, *Guía del Archivo Nacional de Historia* (Guayaquil, 1974).] The second type of material consists of correspondence about taxation, salaries of government officials, and government expenditures in general. Most of these papers are bound in chronological order. The majority of these documents are located in the Guayaquil Street repository. The third type of materials consists of carbon copies of official Ministry of Finance correspondence, receipts, etc. These apparently begin about 1940. The author did not go through these papers and is unable to give details. About half of these documents are located in the National Archive, the other half in the Guayaquil Street building. While the material in all three groups is extensive, it is not complete, with gaps in the collection.

ARCHIVO DE LA PRESIDENCIA

The materials which originally formed the Presidential Archive have been scattered. Some are now in the archive of the Centro de Historia y Geografía. (See the section on military archives.) Others may be in unorganized sections of the National Archive and the Archivo de Gobierno. Some papers have been lost. Remaining is a small archive situated in the first floor of the National Palace. Most of these papers date from World War II and are not open to researchers, but the records of the presidential advisory councils cover the period 1925 to 1944. Although it is not difficult to visit the Archivo de la Presidencia, it proved impossible for this researcher to obtain permission to use those materials. The director of the archive states that presidential permission can be obtained, but it takes time.

ARCHIVO DE LA UNIVERSIDAD CATOLICA

The Catholic University of Quito, the Pontificia Universidad Católica del Ecuador, has recently organized a small but important archive. At present it contains the papers of the Flores family. There are about 2,000 items covering the nineteenth century. Since two members of the family, Juan José Flores and Antonio Flores, were presidents of Ecuador, the collection is important for political history. Father Jorge Villalba,

S.J. is the director of the archive.

The repositories discussed above and the many others located in Quito have much material which has never been used by scholars. The volume and quality of these records present a challenge to the historian of Latin America. If Ecuadorian history is to develop, trained researchers must begin to utilize these sources.

The Archivo Nacional de Historia
Juan Freile-Granizo

This essay is a general introduction to the national archive of Ecuador, the Archivo Nacional de Historia, and is written in the hope that it will interest scholars in our--still to be done--history.* Although the Archivo Nacional has been in operation for some time, it is still not completely organized and various sections can only be described in a general fashion. The classification of documents is continuing. As it progresses, the researcher will find that this description is no longer applicable. Nevertheless, this essay may serve as a guide to the types of materials investigators can expect to find in the Archivo Nacional de Historia. [Also Juan Freile-Granizo has recently published a detailed guide to the colonial section, *Guía del Archivo Nacional de Historia* (Guayaquil: Archivo Histórico del Guayas, 1974).]

At the present time, the offices and the reading room (*sala de investigación*) of the Archivo Nacional are located in the second floor of the Casa de Cultura Ecuatoriana building situated on Avenida 6 de Diciembre 332. The telephone number is 236-843 and the mailing address is Casilla Postal 67, Quito, Ecuador. It is open every day, except Sundays and holidays, from 8 to 12 in the morning and from 2:30 to 6:30 in the afternoon. Permission to investigate in the archive should be obtained from the director, Alfredo Costales Samaniego.

The documents in the Archivo Nacional were gathered from various sources, and its holdings cover both the colonial and national eras. The following description is organized according to the origin of the documents and focuses on holdings in the colonial and early national period.

FONDO DEL ARCHIVO HISTORICO NACIONAL

Presidencia de Quito, 1600-1822

This series consists of six-hundred bound volumes, each containing

---

*Translated by Jaime E. Rodríguez.

approximately three-hundred folio pages on all aspects of colonial government. These include correspondence between the viceroys--from Lima or Santa Fé--and the presidents of the audiencia as well as correspondence among and between the officials of the audiencia--*gobernadores, regidores, tenientes,* etc.--and between private individuals and government officials. There is extensive material on social, political, economic, and religious matters. Papers on economic issues include *real hacienda* documents pertaining to tribute, stamped paper, tithes, tobacco monopoly, liquor and cards, temporalities, etc. These holdings may be used to reconstruct the fiscal history of the colonial period. Other documents refer to *real patronato*: material on bishops, ecclesiastical *cabildos*, and the various religious communities--the Augustinians, Carmelites, Franciscans, Dominicans, Jesuits, etc. There are also papers relating to the *salas* of the audiencia: *autos, sentencias, proveimientos, reales provisiones,* etc. Among the many other kinds of documents in this group are royal *cédulas,* royal and superior orders, and the records of private and official litigations.

Gran Colombia, 1822-1830

Documents relating to the Department of the South in Colombia are bound in volumes 601-664. There are also three volumes of the correspondence of José Manuel Restrepo (665-667) covering the years 1820-1830; a volume for Juan José Flores (668), and another for Tomás de Heres (669).

La República, 1830-1904

Some material in this section came from the Supreme Court. Volume 670 contains the proceedings against the assassins of Monseñor José Ignacio Checa y Barba; volumes 671-689 have correspondence to General Eloy Alfaro (1893-1903); and volumes 690-691 consist of the proceedings against the assassins of President Gabriel García Moreno. The high tribunal also gave the Archivo Nacional fourteen ledgers of documents pertaining to the death of Eloy Alfaro and his lieutenants, a volume of documents on the independence period, and materials relative to Ecuador's secession from Gran Colombia. These papers are kept in a locked cabinet.

Next to the volumes on Gran Colombia are 904 volumes titled República which contain documents that apparently came from the government of the Province of Pichincha. There is also a bookcase of official copybooks, at the end of the lower floor stacks, which also came from Pichincha.

Miscellaneous

This series is made up of a variety of documents: Real Hacienda--Quintos Reales, four volumes (1548-1587); Penas de Cámara, five volumes (1615-1791); and Jesuitas. The latter material comprises the so-called "Jesuit Library," which was confiscated when the order was expelled from Ecuador in 1767. It includes the manuscripts used as texts in the University of San Gregorio Magno and the College of San Luis. Some of these books were written in the Audiencia of Quito while others came from as far away as Granada. They deal with many disciplines and are an important source for the intellectual history of the period 1639-1761.

FONDO DE LA CORTE SUPREMA DE JUSTICIA

Materials in this series came to the Archivo Nacional from the Supreme Court. In many ways these documents complement papers in the Fondo del Archivo Histórico Nacional. One important group of documents is the *cedularios* which contain legislation from the crown. This includes not only the general *cédulas* and *órdenes* issued for the entire empire, but also the particular *cédulas* and *órdenes* issued for Quito. Some of these materials are bound in volumes while others are tied in bundles; they cover the years 1538-1820. Sixteen volumes of Autos Acordados, covering the period 1578-1812, provide sources for the internal legislative history of colonial Ecuador. They consist of local *acuerdos* on such varied matters as *obrajes*, Indians, local government, etc. Other materials on local government include a volume of Autos del Buen Gobierno (1767-1790); two volumes of Acuerdos de Hacienda (1791-1797); one volume of Acuerdos de Reos de Justicia (1779-1794); unbound documents on Sentencias--civil (1573-1607); a volume of Votos (1574-1630); and one of Visitas de Cárcel (1646-1649).

In addition, is material pertaining to the activities of the audiencia as an administrative body, including reports and correspondence between the audiencia and royal officials. Among these papers are twelve bound volumes of correspondence between the audiencia and the viceroys (1625-1778). Extensive documentation, some of it bound, also exists on a variety of matters including *asuntos religiosos*, civil suits, commerce, housing, *cascarillas*, slaves, *censos y capellanías*, mines, debts, slaughter houses, marriages, emancipation of minors, poverty, wills, criminal cases, and contraband which is listed under *ropas* in reference to *ropas de Castilla*.

The series also contains several groups of documents which I will discuss separately because of their importance. The Incorporación de Abogados (1732-1930) consists of documentation of lawyers, including family background and information on their education. There are seventeen volumes for the colonial period (1732-1822) and forty-six for the national period (1823-1930). The section on wills is also extensive and contains important materials for social history. One of the most voluminous sections of the Fondo de la Corte Suprema de Justicia is on Indians (*Indígenas*). Although this material has not been classified, the documents can be divided into the following groups: *tierras, cacicazgos, declaratorias de mestizos, sublevaciones, regimientos de pueblos de indios*, and *gobernadores de indios*. There is also a separate section on *cacicazgos* (1606-1817) which includes 111 bound volumes and eleven boxes. This material consists of matters brought before the president of the royal audiencia relating to Indian rights.

Other papers of the presidency of the audiencia include those pertaining to mails, prisons, *residencias, vínculos y mayorazgos, informaciones*--documentation on persons seeking favors from the crown, *padrones*--census reports, and *oficios*--materials referring to the administration of the audiencia, *encomiendas*, or *alcabalas*. Most of these documents are still in unclassified bundles.

Other materials in the Fondo de la Corte Suprema de Justicia have been tentatively organized. Among these are: Gobernación de Popayán (1570-1860), 229 boxes and seven bundles; Independencia, mainly proceedings against the leaders of the Revolution of 1809 and the Gobierno Superior de Quito (1810-1812), four bundles; Administración General de Tabacos, Naipes, y Pólvora (1772-1816), seventy-seven volumes; Dirección de Temporalidades, which administered Jesuit property after 1767, twenty-nine volumes; Administración de Alcabalas (1593-1822), ninety-five volumes; Real Hospicio y Lazareto de Quito, twenty volumes; Administración de Aguardiente (1767-1824), fifteen volumes; Real Contaduría (1755-1827), eighteen volumes; Real Hacienda (1671-1817), forty-two volumes; Real Caja (1644-1821), eighteen volumes; Varios de Hacienda (1671-1817), twenty-eight volumes. There are also thousands of individual papers listed simply under the headings of *diversos* and *hojas sueltas* and countless other groups of documents which cannot be mentioned because of space limitations.

FONDO DE LA CORTE SUPERIOR DE JUSTICIA DE QUITO

The documents in this series originated in appeals directed to inferior tribunals, normally to *alcaldes de barrio*. Unclassified material for the period 1808-1821 is included. In many instances, it is difficult to ascertain the source of the documents since the Superior Court, first formed by Simón Bolívar in 1822, functioned as a national supreme court after 1830, but most of these papers refer to local litigations.

FONDO DE ESCRIBANIAS DEL CANTON DE QUITO

The Archivo Nacional began receiving the Libros de Protocolos and the *juicios* of the six *escribanías* of the Cantón of Quito in 1956. These documents cover the colonial period, the nineteenth century, and the first three decades of the present century. The following discussion, however, is limited to holdings from the colonial epoch. The Libros de Protocolos contain notarial records on sales, dowries, wills, contracts, powers of attorney; in short, any transaction which required a notarized document. The section on *juicios* contains litigation on a wide variety of subjects. These court cases are an invaluable source of information for social, political, and economic history.

The colonial materials in the Libros de Protocolos are the following: Escribanía Primera (1582-1822), 412 volumes; Escribanía Segunda (1808-1822), six volumes; Escribanía Tercera (1642-1822), eighty-seven volumes; Escribanía Cuarta (1641-1822), twelve volumes; Escribanía Quinta (1587-1822), 114 volumes; and Escribanía Sexta (1581-1823), 105 volumes. The colonial section of *juicios* contains: Escribanía Primera (1604-1822), 100 legajos; Escribanía Segunda (1763-1827), ten legajos; Escribanía Tercera (1694-1824), forty-three legajos; Escribanía Cuarta (1649-1821), thirty-six legajos; Escribanía Quinta (1684-1825), nine legajos; Escribanía Sexta (1612-1822), forty-two legajos.

REGALOS

In 1966, the distinguished historian don Carlos Manuel Larrea gave the Archivo Nacional the following documents: the Registro de Escrituras of the *escribano* Gaspar de Aguilar (1597-1598), 703 folios; a contemporary copy dated 1760 of the *residencia* of Juan Pío Montúfar, President of the

Audiencia of Quito and Marqués de Selva Alegre, two volumes (855 and 766 folios respectively); and a Libro de Socorros of the Hacienda de Guachala from 1830.

CONFISCACIONES

This series consists of two volumes; a Libro de Cabildos of Riobamba (1594-1605) and a Libro de Protocolos of the *escribano* Pedro de Vallejo, also of Riobamba, for the year 1596.

ORIGEN DESCONOCIDO

Some documents relating to colonial financial questions are of unknown origin; they fall into two categories: Libros del Tesorero of the *cajas reales* (1568-1639), sixteen volumes, and Libros del Contador (1582-1649), nine volumes.

The Archivo Nacional de Historia will continue to receive documents from various government branches. At the present time, many documents are stored in warehouses and unavailable to researchers. Hopefully, the Archivo Nacional will soon receive the additional funds and personnel needed to organize, classify, and incorporate these important historical materials.

The Archivo Nacional de Relaciones Exteriores del Ecuador and the Biblioteca General del Ministerio de Relaciones Exteriores
Joedd Price

The Archivo Nacional de Relaciones Exteriores del Ecuador and the Biblioteca General del Ministerio de Relaciones are conveniently located in the same building just north of the Ejido Park on 10 de Agosto in Quito. Almost all the north-bound buses pass within a few blocks of the building. The Archivo and the Biblioteca are officially separate entities. The Archivo is a subdivision of the Department of Documentation in the Ministry of Foreign Relations and the Biblioteca is a section of the Cultural Department, but for all practical purposes they are the same for the researcher. Documents taken from the Archivo, for example, can only be used in the rooms of the Biblioteca.

The Biblioteca has no collection of documents per se. It contains only books, magazines, pamphlets, and other materials on Ecuador, especially its foreign relations. The Biblioteca contains nearly all of the *informes, reportajes,* and *mensajes* of the various ministers of foreign relations since the early nineteenth century. The library also has most of the books published on the well-known boundary dispute with Peru. One does not need special permission to use materials in the Biblioteca.

Documents in the Archivo, however, can only be used with the permission of the Minister of Foreign Relations. One simply writes a letter to him requesting authorization to examine documents of a certain nature and of a definite chronological period. If permission is granted, one secures the materials normally by asking the main librarian of the Biblioteca, Sra. Olga Moncayo de Pallares, to bring the documents from the Archivo. She will place the materials on your desk. If the library is not overly crowded, one can expect to have a desk and possibly a typewriter. If previous authorization is secured, one can have the Archivo photocopy certain documents, but this is relatively expensive. There are no microfilming facilities, but one may microfilm documents

Archivo de Relaciones Exteriores 171

himself if he secures permission and agrees to develop his own film.

There is no guide to the Archivo, though one is expected in the near future. There is an inventory of documents and a *registro* of existing documents, but these are for the private use of the Foreign Ministry.

The bound, but unpublished, volumes of correspondence sent to and received from the various Ecuadorian diplomatic missions are the most extensive collection of documents in the Archivo. For the nineteenth century, these volumes are listed by chronological periods. Unfortunately many of the important accompanying documents sent with the original correspondence are missing. There are numerous nineteenth-century documents which the Foreign Ministry still classifies as confidential and secret. Special permission to examine these has to be secured from the Foreign Ministry.

All documents in the Archivo are located in an "off limits" area of the building. The researcher may or may not be given permission to visit this area or sections of it. He cannot browse through the area to find exactly what is in the Archivo. He can never be certain that he has seen all the relevant documents for his research. To a large extent, he is dependent upon the attitude of the current Minister of Foreign Relations toward the research project.

Only one volume of documents at a time may be removed from the shelves of the Archivo, and it must be returned at the close of each day. Normally the doors of the Archivo and the Biblioteca are open from 8:30 a.m. to 12:30 p.m. and 2:30 p.m. to 6:30 p.m. Sra. Olga Moncayo de Pallares, the director of the Biblioteca, is capable and very cooperative.

There currently are plans to replace the old facilities with a new Archivo Histórico y Diplomático with all the modern facilities for research.

The Military Archives of Ecuador
Luis A. Rodríguez S.

The Ministry of Defense has overall authority on matters pertaining to the armed forces, including archives.* The Ministry is divided into three branches: the Subsecretaría (Under-Secretariat), which is in charge of general administration; the Junta de Defensa Nacional (Committee for National Defense), which is concerned with matters of national defense; and the Comandancia del Estado Mayor Conjunto (Office of the Chairman of the Joint Chiefs of Staff), which directs the army, navy, and air force. Each of these divisions of the Ministry of Defense has a current archive, which, after a number of years, (generally, a quarter of a century) is turned over the Archivo General del Ministerio de Defensa (AGMD).

The AGMD, located in Quito, is the principal military archive in Ecuador and is presently under the direction of Major Gonzalo Naveda. The archive is well organized and has good research facilities, including microfilm readers and cameras. It contains documents pertaining to the administration of the national armed forces from their establishment in 1830 to recent times. There are, for example, review lists for officers and men from 1830 to 1964, which contain biographical data on all military personnel and a complete service record. The records were kept for administrative purposes as well as to compute the pensions of military personnel. Since 1964, the armed forces have used the kardex system to maintain administrative control of personnel in the army, navy, and air force. Therefore, no review lists have been compiled since that time.

The AGMD also retains the orders of the various zone and district commanders. This material pertains to political and economic, as well as to strictly military matters. Finally, the Archivo General also keeps a complete collection of official newspapers and a collection of the laws, decrees, and resolutions passed in Ecuador. Since many of these documents

---

*Translated by Jaime E. Rodríguez.

have been microfilmed by Major Naveda, the researcher must use them in that form. Permission to use the archive must be secured from the Undersecretary of Defense.

The Archivo de la Auditoría Jurídica, also located in Quito, is another important military archive. It keeps records pertaining to retired officers and enlisted men and to widows and orphans who receive survivors benefits. Material in this repository dates from 1895. Investigators wishing to consult these documents must obtain permission from the auditor in charge of the archive.

There are three service archives which contain important historical material. The Archivo de la Comandancia General del Ejército has documents relating to the activities of the army, since its creation in 1830. The documentation in this repository is quite extensive. The Commanding General of the Army is authorized to permit scholars to use those materials. The Archivo de la Comandancia Naval holds papers relating to the history of the navy and the merchant marine. Those seeking to use documents in that archive should request permission from the Commandant General of the Navy. The Archivo de la Comandancia de la Fuerza Aerea is the youngest of the three service archives. Nevertheless, it has many documents pertaining to the formation and development of this branch of the Ecuadorian armed services. The Commanding General of the Air Force is in charge of this depository.

The military hospitals of Quito, Guayaquil, and Cuenca have archives with material concerning military health and sanitation. The directors of these hospitals should be consulted for permission to use those documents. Similarly, the headquarters of the military zones of Ecuador, located in Quito, Guayaquil, Cuenca, and Loja, have their own archives. The commanders of these zones have exercised considerable political power over the years. Therefore, their records are indispensable for an understanding of the politics and history of these regions. The headquarters of the naval zone in Guayaquil also has important materials. In all cases, the zone commanders must authorize investigation in these archives.

The army, navy, and air force also maintain archives in their schools, academies, and institutes. Perhaps the most significant, because of its long history, is the Colegio Militar Eloy Alfaro in Quito. The archive of this military academy contains extensive documentation, including cadets' applications, which provide information on their social and economic background and the performance records of students. There is also material on the history and development of the Colegio Militar. The director of the Colegio Militar controls access to these records.

An important military archive has recently been formed at the Centro de Historia y Geografía Militar in Quito. It consists of three general sections. The first, contains documents relating to civil and military affairs from 1820 to 1937, which formerly belonged to the old Ministerio de Hacienda, now called Ministerio de Finanzas. This material includes more than 10,000 items. Among the documents are many with financial information on taxation, subsidies, municipal rents, forced loans, and some records of the treasuries of Guayaquil and Cuenca. Dr. Luz A. Castro-Coronel is preparing a guide to these materials. It is hoped she will continue to catalogue new documents as they arrive. A second section contains papers of the office of the presidency. Documents in this group cover the years 1877 to 1960. There are more than 20,000 items, including records of export and treasury payments, proposals for tariff and bank reform, papers of the Changala hacienda and the Leonard Company, administrative records of the Southern Railroad, and a variety of other government documents. The third section consists of materials relating to the 1941 war with Peru. These documents are presently in the possession of the Third Department of the Chief of Staff of the Army. However, they will soon be transferred to the Centro de Historia y Geografía Militar. These materials have been microfilmed by Major Gonzalo Naveda and are also available in the Archivo General del Ministerio de Defensa. Permission to use the documents of the Centro de Historia y Geografía Militar may be obtained from the director of the Centro.

Scholars wishing to investigate various aspects of Ecuadorian military history will find ample material in the archives described above. Researchers with well conceived proposals have generally had little difficulty obtaining access to Ecuadorian military archives. Furthermore, Ecuadorian officers have generally made themselves available to national and foreign scholars, both for interviews and for assistance in research. However, all nations guard security matters carefully and research on sensitive contemporary topics may not be feasible. Thus the scholar should plan his project carefully and be prepared to modify his research design.

The Archives and Libraries of Cuenca
Michael T. Hamerly

Santa Ana de los Ríos de Cuenca, founded in 1557, is the third most important city in Ecuador and the second richest in historical records and research opportunities.* Cuenca, however, has had few professional historians of her own, albeit many *aficionados,* and apparently few foreigners have had recourse to her archives.

Hence it is not surprising that no guides to public and private depositories in Cuenca exist. Christian Vogel, a German scholar turned priest, includes a partial account: "Los archivos coloniales del Ecuador," published in the August 8, 15, 22, and 29, 1965 issues of *El Comercio,* a Quito daily. Brief statements may also be found in Lino Gómez Canedo, *Los archivos de la historia de América" período colonial español,* 2 vols. (Mexico: Instituto Panamericano de Geografía e Historia, 1961), 1:437; Michael T. Hamerly, *Historia social y económica de la antigua Provincia de Guayaquil, 1763-1842* (Guayaquil: Archivo Histórico del Guayas, 1973), pp. 10-11; José Reig Satorres, "Documentación ecuatoriana sobre derecho indiano," *Universidad* (Guayaquil), 10/11 (dic., 1970):59-88, 78 and "Complemento de documentación ecuatoriana sobre derecho indiano," III Congreso del Instituto Internacional de Historia del Derecho Indiano, Madrid, 12-23 de enero de 1972, *Actas y estudios* (Madrid: Instituto Nacional de Estudios Jurídicos, 1973):1079-1094, 1087-1089; and Jaime E. Rodríguez O., "New Research Opportunities in Ecuador," *Latin American Research Review,* VIII (Summer 1973):95-100. Of the above mentioned

---

*The author is grateful to the Doherty Charitable Foundation, Inc.; the Office of Education of the Department of Health, Education, and Welfare; and the Joint Committee on Latin American Studies of the Social Science Research Council and the American Council of Learned Societies for having financed his research in Ecuador, Peru, and Colombia between 1967-1969, 1971, and between 1974-1975.

authors, Gómez Canedo is the least useful. He erroneously states that there is a detailed inventory of the holdings of the Archivo Histórico de la Municipalidad de Cuenca (AH/MC) in José María Vargas, *Misiones ecuatorianas en archivos europeos* (México: Instituto Panamericano de Geografía e Historia, 1956), pp. 20-183, when in reality that inventory corresponds to the Vacas Galindo collection in the Dominican convent in Quito.

ARCHIVES

Two of the most important archives in Cuenca are the Archivo Histórico de la Municipalidad de Cuenca (AH/MC) and the Archivo Nacional de Historia: Sección del Azuay (ANH/SA). The AH/MC, the older of the two, is housed in the basement of the Museo Municipal "Remigio Crespo Toral" on the north bank of the Río Tomebamba at 7-97 Gonzalo S. Córdoba Street. The museum is open in the mornings between 8:30 and 12:00 and in the afternoons between 2:30 and 6:00, Tuesday through Friday, and between 10:00 and 12:00 a.m. Saturday and Sunday. The acting director of the museum and hence also of the archive is Sra. Rosa Moscoso Tamariz; the titular director is Ernesto Salazar González.

The Archivo Histórico de la Municipalidad de Cuenca has apparently never been catalogued. Stronger in holdings from the eighteenth and nineteenth centuries than the sixteenth and the seventeenth, the contents of the AH/MC may be divided into four groups: 1) the Libros de actas de cabildos de Cuenca; 2) Documentos; 3) several miscellaneous codices; and 4) a number of miscellaneous papers. There are at least twenty volumes of Libros de actas de cabildos: I, 1557-1563; II, 1563-1568; III, 1575-1578; IV, 1579-1587; V, 1587-1591; VI, 1591-1603; VII, 1606-1614; VIII, 1670-1680; IX, 1696-1697; X, 1701-1724; XI, 1724-1746; XII, 1751-1759; XIII, 1760-1773; XIV, 1776-1779; XV, 1779-1782; XVI, 1783-1784; XVII, 1791-1793; XVIII, 1796-1797; XIX, 1806-1851 (i.e., 1806-1829, 1827-1828, with the remainder of the volume being given over to Actas de la Junta Administrativa del año 1831, etc.); and XXII, 1826-1837. The first book is on display in the museum itself and has been published: *Libro primero de cabildos de la ciudad de Cuenca, 1557-1563*, transcribed and edited by Jorge A. Garcés G. (Quito, 1938; Publicaciones del Archivo Municipal de Quito, XII; 2d ed., edited by Víctor Manuel Albornoz, Cuenca: Dirección de Publicaciones Municipales, 1957). Garcés also transcribed Volume II of the "actas de cabildos," but it was not published. And presently Sr. Juan Chacón is supposed to be engaged in transcription for publication by the Municipalidad de Cuenca of vols. II through XIX. Volumes XX and XXI, corresponding to the years 1809-1825, were apparently taken home more than fifty years ago by Alfonso María Borrero, author of *Cuenca en Pichincha* (reprinted in 1972 by the Casa de la Cultura Ecuatoriana: Núcleo del Azuay), and never returned.

The Documentos comprise a dozen or more bound volumes of miscellaneous manuscripts, mostly municipal records and imprints. They have been folioed twice, originally in pen and the second time around in red pencil, but never indexed. The numbers do not correspond. I consulted the first eight volumes of Documentos for the years 1707-1749, 1761-1784, 1785-1791, 1792-1799, 1800-1810, 1822-1824, 1824-1827, 1828, 1833, and found most in a good state of preservation, but they are not bound in chronological order, and there are manuscripts from earlier as well as later years in each. The miscellaneous codices, which constitute the third group in the AH/MC, appear to consist mostly of account books. For example, there are three *libros de propios* from the late eighteenth century and a LIBRO DE HIJUELA EN QUE CONSTAN LOS CENSUTARIOS DE ESTE CONUENTO. HOSPITAL DE CUENCA. AÑO DE 1815.

The Archivo Nacional de Historia: Sección del Azuay (ANH/SA) was founded in 1964 by Dr. Miguel Díaz Cueva, its director through 1970, of whom more later. His successor and the present director is Sr. Marco Tello. The ANH/SA remains partially and provisionally organized. Located in a spacious room on the second floor (*primer piso*) of the Casa de la Cultura Ecuatoriana, Núcleo del Azuay at the intersection of Luis Cordero and Vásquez de Novoa, a block down from the main square (the Parque Abdón Calderón), the Casa de la Cultura is open Monday through Friday from 8:00-12:00 a.m. and 2:00-6:00 p.m. Parenthetically, just across the street on Luis Cordero is a used bookshop, El Rincón Literario, where national publications may be purchased cheaply.

The ANH/SA consists of four *fondos*: the books and papers through 1900 of the Archivo de la Gobernación, the Archivo de la Caja Real de Cuenca (Contaduría Mayor after 1822), the *protocolos* and *juicios* through 1900 of the Archivo de la Tercera Notaría, and the pre-1900 *protocolos* only of the Archivo de la Segunda Notaría. The contents of the Archivo de la Gobernación and of the Archivo de la Caja Real have not been kept separate and are not fully known. As in the case of the AH/MC, they appear to be stronger in eighteenth- and nineteenth-century holdings than sixteenth and seventeenth, and richer in demographic, economic, ethnohistorical, and social than political data. There are thousands of papers, bundled by year, as well as at least two hundred codices. The bundles or *legajos* range from the early seventeenth century through 1900, and thematically from *cartas cuentas* through *tornaguías*. In a national-period *legajo*, for example, one is likely to find communications from the Ministerios de lo Interior, Guerra y Marina, and Hacienda, as well as from the municipality, ecclesiastical authorities, and *jefes políticos*, carpetas containing population, military, and economic statistics, tax materials, and other commercial documents.

Dr. Díaz Cueva organized the codices by series and year. The *libros* comprise: *aguardientes* (one book), 1821; *alcabalas* (forty-one books), 1787-1796, 1799-1813, 1815-1820, 1822-1829; *copiadores de cartas* (nine books), 1776, 1780-1783, 1786-1792; *comunicaciones* (one book), 1788-1796; *contaduría* (one copy book), 1792; *guías* (eight books), 1786-1789, 1802-1819, 1828-1831; *hacienda* (one book), 1824-1829; *oficios* (six books), 1823-1830; *reales cajas* (ninety-three books), 1725, 1730-1731, 1741-1745, 1747, 1751-1754, 1757-1765, 1768-1769, 1772-1780, 1782-1784, 1786-1789, 1792-1797, 1800-1811, 1813-1820; *cajas nacionales* (fourteen books), 1821-1829; *reales cédulas* (five books), 1752-1794; *reales provisiones* (one book); *remates* (two books), 1773, 1800; *superiores despachos* (two books); *tabacos* (nine books), 1823-1828, 1831-1833; *títulos* (one book), 1790-1793; and *visita de pueblos del Gobernador Juan Antonio de la Carrera* (one book), 1781. From Jaén de Bracamoros, two books of *reales rentas*, 1811, 1818. And from Loja at least four books: *padrón de indios tributarios* (1765); *reales cajas* (1712-1715); *hipotecas* (1826-1827); and *registros* (1826-1827). In addition, the director keeps several codices in his office, including papers of Eugenio Espejo.

The *protocolos* and *juicios* of the Archivo de la Tercera Notaría through 1900 were transferred to the ANH/SA in 1969. The *protocolos* date from as early as 1567, and the *juicios* date from 1592. Hence the Archivo de la Tercera Notaría includes the oldest surviving notarial records for and in Ecuador. It is also important to note that the colonial *legajos* of the *fondo* of the Archivo de la Gobernación contain manuscripts from the sixteenth century, intermixed with papers from the seventeenth, making the ANH/SA one of the most valuable depositories in Ecuador. Recently, the *protocolos* of the Segunda Notaría, which date from 1700, but not the *juicios*, were also transferred to the ANH/SA.

The 1a., 4a., 5a., and 6a. Notarías, which are on the ground floor of the Palacio de Justicia have *protocolos* from 1869, 1776, 1777, and 1813 onward respectively, and the 1a., 2a., 4a., 5a., and 6a. Notarías, *juicios* from 1869, 1614, 1661, 1778, and 1813 onward. The Palacio de Justicia, which is located just across the street from the Parque Calderón at the intersection of Luis Cordero and Sucre, also houses another depository of interest, the Archivo y Biblioteca de la Corte Superior de Justicia del Azuay (ABCSJ/A) in a room on the second floor (*primer piso*). The contents of the library are unknown to me but may be presumed to be juridical. The archive itself is organized chronologically and consists of transcripts of *causas civiles* from 1831 through the present, and of *causas criminales* from 1835 through the present. Moreover, there is a manuscript catalogue for both groups.

Of the ecclesiastical archives I know little. El Sagrario, San Blas, San Sebastián, and San Roque have baptismal registers for 1700, 1670, 1701, and 1813 respectively, matrimonial records for 1693, 1749, 1728, and 1813, and burial registers from 1660, 1733, 1728, and 1813. Several earlier *libros de partidas de bautismos* from El Sagrario, San Blas, and San Sebastián are supposed to be in the Archivo de la Curia. Christian Vogel has a summary of the contents of the Archivo de la Curia in his article cited above. I was authorized to consult the Archivo del Cabildo Eclesiástico, but the priest assigned to supervise me was uncooperative. After my first visit, he made himself and the archive inaccessible. Housed in a cupboard in the Sagrario, I did find some papers from the seventeenth century. Reliable sources have the Archivo del Seminario as being stored in a slaughterhouse on the outskirts of the city. Permission to work in the ecclesiastical archives of Cuenca may now be obtained from the new archbishop, Monseigneur Ernesto Alvarez.

LIBRARIES

At least two public libraries in Cuenca are useful for research, the Biblioteca Municipal, which recently augmented its holdings through purchase of a large private collection, and the Biblioteca de la Casa de la Cultura Ecuatoriana: Núcleo del Azuay. The hours of the latter are 9-12 a.m. and 2:30-6:00 p.m., Monday through Friday. The Biblioteca of the local Casa de la Cultura houses the collection of two former illustrious intellectuals, Alberto Muñoz Vernaza and Miguel Angel Jaramillo. The Jaramillo collection is especially strong on national serials, for a catalogue of which see Miguel Angel Jaramillo, *Indice bibliográfico de las revistas de la Biblioteca JARAMILLO de escritos nacionales* (Cuenca: Casa de la Cultura Ecuatoriana, Núcleo del Azuay, 1953).

MUSEUMS

In addition to possessing fine examples of late colonial and nineteenth-century architecture, Cuenca is blessed with several excellent museums. The Museo Municipal Remigio Crespo Toral, mentioned earlier, is rich in colonial and national art and artifacts and has on permanent display a number of papers on the short-lived Republic of Cuenca of 1820. It is interesting to note that the latter were donated by the Municipality of Guayaquil to the Municipality of Cuenca in a fraternal gesture in 1920. The two other museums of historical interest are those of the nuns of the Immaculate Conception and of the Carmelites. Their monasteries date from 1599 and 1682 respectively and are located at 8-47 Vásquez and on Sucre across from the cathedral. The Museum of the Conceptas opens every afternoon promptly at 2:30 p.m. except on the first Sunday of every month. The Museum of the Carmelites, however, is closed to the public, but permission to visit it may sometimes be obtained from the archbishop.

PRIVATE COLLECTIONS

Many *cuencanos* have first-rate private libraries, which include manuscripts from the colonial and national periods. Apparently the two most important nowadays are those of Sr. Víctor Manuel Albornoz and Dr. Miguel Díaz Cueva. I have never seen Albornoz's library but understand from Dr. Díaz Cueva that don Víctor owns many nineteenth-century imprints and manuscripts. That of Dr. Díaz Cueva is one of the finest in Ecuador. His library possesses well over 6,000 books, pamphlets, and serials, beginning with the first Ecuadorian imprint issued at Ambato in 1755. He also owns several eighteenth- and nineteenth-century codices and papers, including a never published second edition of Eugenio Espejo, "La ciencia blancardina," 1793, with notes in Espejo's own hand. Also the holdings of Albornoz and Díaz Cueva are strong on local imprints, a press having been established in Cuenca in 1828.

Historical research in Cuenca is not easy, given the limited hours of the archives, libraries, and museums; dearth of copying facilities; lack of catalogues except for the ABCSJ/A; difficulty in securing permission to utilize some depositories; and the relative disorder in most. Still, the wealth of materials which await the researcher and the numerous lacunae in *cuencano* historiography as well as the possibility of filling in gaps in archives elsewhere more than compensate for those obstacles. It must be stressed that quantitative research into the demographic, economic, ethnohistorical, social, and urban history of Cuenca is feasible from the seventeenth through the nineteenth centuries. And it is precisely those themes and that approach which *cuencano* historians have slighted for the most part. It is also possible to research those themes for the second half of the sixteenth century, but it will be necessary to turn to other repositories elsewhere, especially the Archivo General de Indias in Seville for additional materials.

Finally, a few words of advice to prospective researchers. *Cuencanos* are conservative in politics and religion, traditional in dress and manners. Respect their views and conform to their standards, and you will find them cooperative and courteous. The friendship of local intellectuals is well worth cultivating. They tend to be highly literate, travelled, urbane, and sophisticated. Dr. Díaz Cueva is the key to successful research in Cuenca. In addition to being the former and founding director of the ANH/SA and a bibliophile, he is also an accomplished bibliographer and eager to aid researchers. Anyone contemplating research in Cuenca should contact him beforehand. His mailing address is Apartado 3, Cuenca, Ecuador. Víctor Manuel Albornoz, the former director of the municipal museum and archive, is also a useful person to know. He is an able biographer and competent historian. His *Fray Vicente Solano: estudio biográfico-crítico,* 2nd ed. rev., 2 vols. (Cuenca: Casa de la Cultura Ecuatoriana, Núcleo del Azuay, 1966), is an elegantly written, exquisitely detailed, and painstakenly researched biography of that nineteenth-century savant, and *Cuenca a través de cuatro siglos,* 2 vols. (Cuenca: Dirección de Publicaciones Municipales, 1959-1960) is a useful compendium of coeval descriptions of historic Cuenca and its hinterland, to cite but two examples of Albornoz's several important publications.

The Archives and Libraries of Guayaquil
Julio Estrada-Ycaza

LIBRARIES

BIBLIOTECA MUNICIPAL DE GUAYAQUIL (BMG)

The Municipal Library, the oldest library in Guayaquil, opened its doors on April 24, 1862, under the direction of Juan José Plutarco Vera.* The BMG began with one hundred volumes donated by don Pedro Carbo, and by the end of its first year had increased its holdings to 1,418 volumes. By 1892 it had 6,003 volumes and by 1899, 10,000, in addition to eight-hundred pamphlets, 3,000 prints, twenty-two maps, and 130 serial collections.

The present library building was inaugurated on October 8, 1958. The two floors are already inadequate to house the present collection of 34,904 volumes and numerous pamphlets, serial collections, and maps. The holdings of the BMG reflect its principal object, which is to provide study facilities and materials for high school and university students. It does not lend books. The current director is Dr. Abel Romeo Castillo, an historian.

The BMG has a few works from the eighteenth century, including several of historical interest. It possesses a copy of José Gabriel Pino Roca's transcription of the Actas del Cabildo de Guayaquil. The periodical holdings, which date from 1822, are especially useful. And the BMG has an historical archive, described below.

The BMG which is located on Diez de Agosto between Chile and Pedro Carbo, has microfilm equipment, a reader, and can facilitate photocopies. Its Post Office Box number is 6069 and telephone, 515-738. The BMG is open between 9-12 a.m. and 3-7 p.m., Tuesdays through Fridays; on

---

*I wish to thank Dr. Michael T. Hamerly who in addition to translating this chapter also provided me with much of the information on which it is based.

Saturdays between 9-12 a.m. and 3-6 p.m., and on Sundays, 9-12 a.m.

BIBLIOTECA DE AUTORES NACIONALES: CARLOS A. ROLANDO

This library was founded in 1913 by the late Dr. Carlos A. Rolando. It specializes in national works; indeed it may be said that its holdings consist almost exclusively of *ecuatoriana,* being surpassed in importance only by the Biblioteca de Autores Nacionales Aurelio Espinoza Pólit in Cotocollao, a suburb of Quito. Dr. Rolando attempted to collect all national publications, and in so doing has left a magnificent legacy. The Rolando Library pamphlet holdings are extensive, and its collection of local newspapers is the best in the country. As in the case of the BMG, its newspaper collections date from 1822. The Rolando Library also possesses some manuscripts from the eighteenth and nineteenth centuries described in the section on archives.

Presently the Rolando Library is housed in a wing of the BMG. Its director and hours are the same as the latter, and recourse may be had to the microfilming and photocopying facilities of the BMG. Its mailing address is Post Office Box 4179.

BIBLIOTECA DE LA CASA DE LA CULTURA ECUATORIANA: NUCLEO DEL GUAYAS

The Library of the local Casa de la Cultura was founded on July 4, 1945. The oldest book in its holdings is *El Iob de la ley de gracia retratado en la admirable vida del siervo de Dios, venerable Padre Fray Pedro Verraca . . .,* published in 1674. Its oldest newspaper collection is that of *El Guante* (1910-1925). Most of its holdings, however, consist of recent publications.

It is located in the Casa de la Cultura Ecuatoriana: Núcleo del Guayas, on Nueve de Octubre between Pedro Moncayo and Quito and is open between 9-12 a.m. and 2:30-8 p.m. The current director is Ms. Ruth Garaicoa.

ARCHIVES

ARCHIVO HISTORICO DEL GUAYAS (AHG)

According to Christian Vogel, "The great fire of 1917 destroyed all the notarial archives" in Guayaquil.[1] This is not true. One notarial

---

1. *El Comercio,* Quito, August 8, 15, 22 and 29, 1965.

archive was saved because the notary Federico B. Espinoza had his archive at home when the fire occurred. In 1961, Father Lino Gómez Canedo noted that this Archivo de Escribanos Públicos was to be found in the Centro de Investigaciones Históricas.[2] Shortly after the AHG was founded, it received the Archivo de Escribanos Públicos from the Centro de Investigaciones Históricas. Its contents are being catalogued and listed in the *Revista del Archivo Histórico del Guayas* (RAHG, 1972-   ). This *fondo* (EP) is of considerable value for research on the history of the city and province of Guayaquil. The oldest document in this collection dates from 1628.

In addition to the *fondo* EP, the AHG has acquired other documents, which are also listed in the *Revista*. Among these acquisitions, the oldest to date is from 1557 and concerns a remission of gold and silver to the crown. More interesting, in that it is one of the few early *expedientes* known regarding Indians of the littoral, is "Sobre los tributos de los indios de Yaguache, 1579," published in RAHG, 1 (June, 1972):69-97.

The AHG has obtained fourteen rolls of microfilm on Ecuador, especially on Guayaquil, from the Archivo Histórico Nacional in Bogotá. It also has some material from the Archivo General de Indias in Sevilla and intends to obtain microfilm copies from the latter of all sixteenth-century documents on Guayaquil and/or the coast.

As soon as a lot can be obtained from the Municipality of Guayaquil, the AHG will construct its own building. For the moment, it is housed in the Centro Cívico. The AHG has a working library of its own, which is continually being augmented.

The AHG is open to the public between 8:30 a.m. and 4:30 p.m., Monday through Friday. It has a microfilm reader and access to photocopying. It is publishing a semi-annual *Revista* and the *Actas del cabildo colonial de Guayaquil* (1972-   ). Four volumes of the *Actas* have appeared to date (I, 1634-1639; II, 1640-1649; III, 1650-1657; IV, 1660-1668). The original *actas* will be housed in the AHG when it is moved to its own building.

Its Post Office Box number is 1333 and telephone 358-369.

---

2. José Reig Satorres, "Documentación ecuatoriana sobre derecho indiano," *Universidad*, 10/11 (December, 1970):76-78.

ARCHIVO DE LA SECRETARIA MUNICIPAL (ASM/G)

The ASM/G, formerly the Archivo del Cabildo, is the oldest depository in Guayaquil. Unfortunately its invaluable contents were lost in the conflagration of December 7, 1636, but the Libro de Actas de Cabildo of 1634 which the notary had at home, no doubt to enter recent minutes, was saved. This volume is presently entrusted to the safekeeping of the Archivo Histórico de la Biblioteca Municipal (AH/BMG) as are those through 1800 (i.e., *tomos* I through XXIV). Tomo XXV, which begins in 1801, and subsequent volumes, however, are still in the ASM/G.

The ASM/G houses a number of series of considerable historical interest; a listing follows. Although these documents are extensive, they are not complete; in some instances there are gaps for various years. The eighteenth- and nineteenth-century series deal with a wide variety of topics. However the archive's tremendous volume of twentieth-century material which deals with strictly municipal matters is not included below due to space limitations.

Holdings of the ASM/G include the following:

   Documentos Varios, 32 vols., 1698-1886.[3]
   Autoridades Varias, 45 vols., 1814-1895.
   Oficios, 65 vols., 1830-1900.[4]
   Tenientes Políticos y Jueces, 38 vols., 1822-1895.
   Informes Varios, 16 vols., 1812-1895.
   Particulares, 36 vols., 1831-1895.
   Actas de la Junta Administrativa, 10 vols., 1826-1860.
   Estados de Caja, 4 vols., 1804-1825, 1827, 1829-1832, 1830-1853.
   Rentas de la Tesorería Municipal, 16 vols., 1832-1858.
   Representaciones, 35 vols., 1795-1894.
   Cámara Provincial, Actas, 3 vols., 1880-1882.
   Juicios de Imprenta, 2 vols., 1823-1861.
   Prefectura del Guayas, 3 vols., 1830-1833.
   Solares Municipales, 2 vols., 1886-1887, 1899-1893.
   Peticiones, 29 vols., 1876-1895.
   Jefatura Política, 17 vols., 1844-1894.[5]
   Jefatura de Policía, 40 vols., 1830-1895.
   Gobernación de la Provincia, 39 vols., 1845-1895.
   Gobierno de la Provincia, 4 vols., 1839-1844, 1860-1867.

---

3. The volume for 1820 was transferred to the AH/BMG in October, 1970.

4. This series is incomplete. The earliest currently available material dates from 1830 and continues with gaps through 1900. It is possible that the volumes missing from this series may be found later in the storage room (*bodega*) of the ASM/G, since according to an inventory of 1913, there should be a volume of *oficios* from 1812-1816.

5. According to the 1913 inventory, volumes from the years 1830-1836, 1854-1857, among others have been lost.

ECUADOR 186

A miscellaneous section of the ASM/G includes the following volumes:

> Denuncias, XXVII, 1870-1875
> Estatua Libertador Simón Bolívar, I, 1889.
> Gremio de Comerciantes, I, 1836.
> Inscripciones de Derecho de Llave, Casa Municipal, Mercado, 1827-1904.
> Junta Curadora de Niñas, I, 1834.
> Juzgado Civil, I, 1860-1861.
> Libro de Cuentas de la Casa de Orates, 1878.
> Núm. 1 Libro de Promesas, 1879-1884.
> Patentes de Aguardiente, I, 1836.
> Participaciones, XV, 1881.
> Patentes que Se Han Dado por el Consulado Español para Nacionalizarse de Ciudadanos Españoles, 1844-1851.
> Registro de los Electores del Cantón, 1872.
> Registro de los Títulos que Se Confieren a las Personas que Poseen Nichos en el Cementerio Católico de esta Ciudad, I, 1863-1889; II, 1863-1886.
> Libro Donde Se Anotan los Títulos de los Nichos en el Cementerio Católico; Solicitudes Varias, X, 1882.
> Actas de la Junta Electoral del Cantón de Guayaquil, 1866-1869.

The ASM/G, located in the Municipal Building, is open Monday through Friday, 9 a.m. to 1 p.m. and 2:30 to 6:30 p.m. and on Saturdays in the morning. Telephone is 511-580. No copying service is available.

ARCHIVO HISTORICO DE LA BIBLIOTECA MUNICIPAL (AH/BMG)

In the AH/BMG may be found documents of diverse public entities, from the parochial through the national level. The origin of this collection is unknown, but probably, over the years, the directors of the BMG, several of whom were historians, solicited historical materials from various officials. The holdings of the AH/BMG are valuable as the following list of series demonstrates, but there is little or no order within the series, and the documents were not properly classified before binding. Materials in the AH/BMG are classified as follows:

Gobierno

> Secretaría de Gobierno, 2 vols., 1831, 1845.
> Presidente y Gobernadores, 1 vol., 1841.
> Jefatura Suprema, Ministerios, 1 vol., 1859.
> Gobierno Robles, 2 vols., 1859.
> Gobierno del Guayas, 1 vol., 1860.
> Gobierno Provisorio, 2 vols., 1860.
> Secretaría General del Gobierno del Guayas, 1 vol., 1883.
> Secretario General del Jefe Supremo General Veintimilla, 1 vol., 1883.

Ministerio de Gobierno

> Secretaría de lo Interior, 1 vol., 1826.
> Ministerio de lo Interior y Secretaría, 1 vol., 1832.
> Ministerio de lo Interior, 24 vols., 1833-1891.

Ministerio de lo Interior y Relaciones Exteriores, 3 vols., 1836-1840.
Oficios del Ministerio de Gobierno, 1 vol., 1844.
Ministerio de Flores, 1 vol., 1845.
Ministerio General, 3 vols., 1845, 1850.
Ministerio Ascázubi, 1 vol., 1850.
Ministerio de lo Interior, Relaciones Exteriores, e Instrucción, 1 vol., 1854.
Ministerio de lo Interior y Justicia, 1 vol., 1860.
Oficios del Ministerio de lo Interior, 2 vols., 1872-1873.
Ministerio General de la Jefatura Suprema, 2 vols., 1876.
Ministerio de lo Interior a la Gobernación del Guayas, 3 vols., 1877-1879.
Ministerio de Estado, 1 vol., 1885.
Ministerio de Justicia, 1 vol., 1892.

Ministerio de Relaciones Exteriores

Secretaría de Relaciones Exteriores, 1 vol., 1825.
Ministerio de Relaciones Exteriores, 1 vol., 1838.

Ministerio de Educación

Instrucción Pública, 3 vols., 1873-1874, 1879.
Oficios de Instrucción Pública, 1 vol., 1875.

Ministerio de Obras Públicas

Ministerio de Obras Públicas, 2 vols., 1872-1873.
Oficios de Obras Públicas, 1 vol., 1873.
Oficios del Ministerio de Obras Públicas, 2 vols., 1873, 1875.
Obras Públicas, 1 vol., 1884.
Ministerio de Obras Públicas y Justicia, 1 vol., 1885.

Diversos Ministerios

Diversos Ministerios, 13 vols., 1822-1898.
Secretarías, 1 vol., 1824.
Ministerios, 2 vols., 1825, 1846.
Secretarías de Ministerios, 1 vol., 1827.
Ministerios y Secretarías, 4 vols., 1828, 1830.
Varios Ministerios, 3 vols., 1831, 1887, 1891.
Diversos Ministerios--Diversos Funcionarios, 1 vol., 1854.
Oficios Diversos Ministerios, 2 vols., 1895.
Ministerio de Relaciones Exteriores, Guerra y Marina, 1 vol., 1835.
Ministerio de lo Interior y Guerra, 1 vol., 1848.
Ministerio de lo Interior y Hacienda, 2 vols., 1851, 1870.

Ministerio de Hacienda

Ministerio de Hacienda, 123 vols., 1835-1898.
Oficios del Ministerio de Hacienda, 23 vols., 1841-1897.
Ministerio de Hacienda a la Gobernación del Guayas, 2 vols., 1877.
Oficios del Ministerio de Hacienda a la Gobernación del Guayas, 2 vols., 1886, 1898.

Dependencias de la Hacienda

Contaduría, 1 vol., 1825.
Contadurías y Correos, 1 vol., 1825.
Juntas de Hacienda del Guayas, 1 vol., 1825-1835.
Tesorería del Guayas, 13 vols., 1831-1890.
Administración de Rentas Interiores, 1 vol., 1837.
Oficios de Hacienda, 3 vols., 1841, 1883, 1887.
Oficinas de Hacienda, 15 vols., 1849-1889.
Tesorería de Hacienda del Guayas, 5 vols., 1864, 1873, 1888.
Comandancia [Contaduría?] de Diezmos, 1 vol., 1871.
Oficios de la Contaduría de Diezmos, 2 vols., 1872-1873.
Oficios de Hacienda a la Gobernación del Guayas, 1 vol., 1877.
Tesorería de Hacienda a la Gobernación del Guayas, 5 vols., 1877, 1879, 1891.
Tesorería de Hacienda, 6 vols., 1886, 1896, 1898.
Oficios de la Tesorería de Hacienda a la Gobernación del Guayas, 5 vols., 1893, 1897.

Aduana

Administraciones de Aduana, 3 vols., 1825, 1883, 1892.
Oficinas de Aduana, 3 vols., 1826-1828.
Aduana de Guayaquil, 1 vol., 1861.
Aduana, 2 vols., 1862, 1898.
Aduana y Contaduría, 1 vol., 1891.
Colecturía de Aduana, 1 vol., 1898.

Ejército y Marina

Causa Marítimas, 1 vol., 1822-1830.
Causas Militares, 15 vols., 1822-1876.
Oficios Militares, 2 vols., 1824, 1868.
Secretaría de Guerra y Marina, 5 vols., 1825-1835.
Comandancia de Marina, 5 vols., 1825-1835.
Comandancias Militares, 23 vols., 1825-1885.
Secretaría de Marina, 1 vol., 1827.
Ordenes Generales, 1 vol., 1829.
Estado Mayor General de Quito, 1 vol., 1831.
Comandancias Generales, 17 vols., 1831-1887.
Ministerio de Guerra, 48 vols., 1833-1876.
Guerra y Marina, 3 vols., 1834, 1842, 1889.
Marina, 3 vols., 1836.
Ministerio de Guerra y Marina, 7 vols., 1836-1839.
Asuntos Militares, 10 vols., 1836, 1872, 1892, 1898.
Ejército y Marina, 26 vols., 1841-1896.
Milicia y Marina, 1 vol., 1845.
Oficios del Ministerio de Guerra, 3 vols., 1851, 1873.
Comunicaciones Militares, 3 vols., 1852, 1878.
Ejército y Armada, 1 vol., 1855.
Jefes de Divisiones, Oficios, 1 vol., 1858.
Estado Mayor General, 3 vols., 1858, 1859.
Autoridades Militares, 1 vol., 1859.
Divisiones Ejército, 2 vols., 1859.
General Ejército, Comandancia General, 1 vol., 1859.
Varios Oficios Militares, 1 vol., 1859.
Jefes Políticos y Dependencias Militares, 1 vol., 1860.

Comandancia de Armas, 9 vols., 1860-1868, 1897.
Comandancia en Jefe del Ejército, 1 vol., 1861.
Jefes de Cuerpo y Otros a la Comandancia General de Guayaquil, 2 vols., 1861.
Ministerio de Guerra a la Comandancia General de Guayaquil, 2 vols., 1861-1862.
Comandancia de Armas de los Ríos, 4 vols., 1861, 1866, 1874.
Oficios de la Gobernación del Guayas a la Comandancia General, 2 vols., 1863, 1873.
Jefes de Cuerpos, 5 vols., 1865.
Varios Jefes de Cuerpo, 1 vol., 1865.
Comandancia General de Guayaquil, 7 vols., 1865-1871, 1888.
Comandancia General de Guayaquil al Ministerio de Guerra, 1 vol., 1866.
Comandancia General de Guayaquil a Varias Autoridades Militares, 1 vol., 1868.
Comandancia Militar de Jambelí, 1 vol., 1869.
Jefatura de Operaciones, 1 vol., 1869.
Oficios de la Comandancia Militar de Manabí, 1 vol., 1869.
Oficios de los Jefes de Cuerpos, 1 vol., 1871.
Oficios de las Comandancias Militares de Los Ríos, Manabí, Guaranda, a la Comandancia Militar de Guayaquil, 1 vol., 1872.
Oficios de la Comandancia General de Guayaquil a la Gobernación de la Provincia, 1 vol., 1872.
Oficios del Ejército y Marina, 5 vols., 1872-1876.
Comandancia Militar de Manabí, 1 vol., 1873.
Comandancia Militar de Los Ríos a la Comandancia General de Guayaquil, 1 vol., 1873.
Oficios de la Provincia de Guayaquil, 1 vol., 1873.
Oficios del Jefe de Artillería de Guayaquil a la Comandancia General, 1 vol., 1873.
Oficios de Varias Autoridades Militares a la Comandancia General de Guayaquil, 1 vol., 1873.
Artillería y Numeral, 1 vol., 1874.
Comandancia Militar de Babahoyo, 1 vol., 1875.
Dependencias Militares, 1 vol., 1876.
Varios Funcionarios de la Comandancia Municipal de Guayaquil, 1 vol., 1877.
Oficios Militares de Varios Tenientes Políticos, 1 vol., 1877.
Comandancia General de la División de Vanguardia, 1 vol., 1883.
Comandancia General del Guayas, 1 vol., 1884.

Gobernaciones Provinciales

Oficios al Intendente, 2 vols., 1822-1823.
Legaciones y Oficios al Intendente, 1 vol., 1823.
Intendencia del Guayas, 1 vol., 1824.
Intendencias, 5 vols., 1824-1828.
Prefecturas, 3 vols., 1829-1830.
Prefecturas del Guayas, 3 vols., 1830-1835.
Prefectura del Guayas y Azuay, 1 vol., 1833.
Gobernaciones, 1 vol., 1835.
Oficios de Prefecturas, 1 vol., 1835.
Gobernación del Guayas, 3 vols., 1835, 1855, 1861.
Gobernación de Manabí y Azuay. Dependencias Militares, 1 vol., 1849.
Varios Gobernadores, 5 vols., 1858, 1865, 1873, 1890, 1892.

Gobernación de Provincia, 1 vol., 1860.
Gobernadores de Provincias, 5 vols., 1860, 1863-64, 1869, 1872.
Gobernadores del Guayas, 1 vol., 1866.
Oficios de Gobernadores, 1 vol., 1868.
Gobernadores y Jefes Políticos, 1 vol., 1868.
Varias Gobernaciones, 1 vol., 1872.
Gobernación de Manabí, 1 vol., 1875.
Gobernadores y Consules, 1 vol., 1876.
Varios. Gobernación del Guayas, 1 vol., 1878.
Varios Oficios a la Gobernación del Guayas, 1 vol., 1879.
Gobernadores y Otros Funcionarios, 1 vol., 1882.
Gobernadores y Oficinas de Hacienda, 1 vol., 1885.
Gobernadores, 1 vol., 1889.
Oficios Diversos al Gobernador, 1 vol., 1898.

Municipalidades

Asuntos Municipales, 9 vols., 1823-1898.
Oficinas Municipales, 2 vols., 1826, 1828.
Jefatura Política, 3 vols., 1826, 1827, 1891.
Consejos Municipales y Prefecturas, 1 vol., 1831.
Corregimientos Cantonales, 12 vols., 1831-1845.
Corregimientos de Guayaquil, Babahoyo, Daule, y Santa Elena, 1 vol., 1837.
Corregidores, 1 vol., 1840.
Corregimientos de Guayaquil, 1 vol., 1841.
Varios Corregimientos, 2 vols., 1841, 1845.
Corregidores de Guayaquil, Morro, 1 vol., 1842.
Corregidores de Daule, 1 vol., 1842.
Corregimientos de Guayaquil, Daule, Morro, 1 vol., 1843.
Varios Jefes de los Cantones, 1 vol., 1846.
Oficios de Varios Jefes Políticos Cantonales, 5 vols., 1846-1857.
Jefes Políticos Cantonales, 32 vols., 1846-1890.
Oficios de Varios Jefes Cantonales, 1 vol., 1847.
Varios Jefes Políticos, 8 vols., 1847, 1876.
Oficios de los Jefes Políticos de Daule, Santa Elena, 1 vol., 1848.
Oficios de los Jefes Políticos, 8 vols., 1852, 1865, 1882, 1895.
Cantón Daule, 1 vol., 1854.
Jefes Políticos de Guayaquil y Daule, 2 vols., 1858, 1869.
Jefe Político de Machala y Santa Rosa, 1 vol., 1869.
Jefe Político de Daule, 3 vols., 1869, 1873, 1875.
Egresos de las Rentas Municipales, 1 vol., 1869-1910.
Jefe Político de Santa Elena, 1 vol., 1871.
Oficios del Jefe Político de Daule, 4 vols., 1871, 1872, 1876.
Oficios del Jefe Político de Guayaquil, 1 vol., 1872.
Oficios Varios, Jefes Políticos, 1 vol., 1872.
Jefe Político de Machala, 2 vols., 1873, 1876.
Oficios de Jefes Políticos de Machala, Santa Elena, 1 vol., 1875.
Jefes Políticos de Guayaquil, Daule, y Santa Elena a la Gobernación del Guayas, 1 vol., 1877.
Jefes Políticos de Guayaquil y Daule a la Gobernación del Guayas, 1 vol., 1879.
Oficios del Jefe Político de Yaguachi y de Varios Tenientes Políticos de Parroquias, 1 vol., 1895.
Jefaturas Políticas de Santa Elena, 1 vol., 1896.

Tenencias

    Tenencias Políticas, 1 vol., 1835.
    Oficios de Diversos Tenientes Parroquiales, 1 vol., 1872.
    Tenientes Políticos, 2 vols., 1873-1874.
    Tenientes Parroquiales, 1 vol., 1875.
    Tenencias Políticas y Juzgados, 2 vols., 1869.
    Oficios de los Tenientes Políticos del Gobernador, 1 vol., 1898.

Justicia

    Información sobre el Ciudadano Anastasio Ilarios, 1 vol., 1820.
    Causas Criminales, 18 vols., 1821-1884.
    Juzgados Políticos, 1 vol., 1825.
    Juzgados Municipales, 4 vols., 1826-1828, 1835.
    Corte Superior de Justicia, 3 vols., 1826, 1884.
    Jefaturas de Policía, 2 vols., 1830, 1857.
    Policía, 3 vols., 1831, 1889, 1892.
    Tribunales y Juzgados, 11 vols., 1841-1889.
    Juzgados. Policía. Varios, 1 vol., 1844.
    Comisaría General de Policía, 2 vols., 1855, 1872.
    Jefatura de Policía. Guayaquil, 1 vol., 1858.
    Tribunales y Juzgados. Varios Documentos, 1 vol., 1859.
    Policía, Tribunales y Juzgados, 1 vol., 1864.
    Juzgados y Policía, 2 vols., 1865, 1887.
    Tribunales y Juzgados de Policía, 2 vols., 1866, 1885.
    Municipio. Tribunales y Juzgados, 1 vol., 1869.
    Autoridad de Policía y Tenientes Políticos, 1 vol., 1869.
    Oficios del Ramo de Policía, 1 vol., 1876.
    Tribunales y Juzgados y Diversos Funcionarios, 1 vol., 1876.
    Oficios de Tribunales y Juzgados, 1 vol., 1877.
    Oficios de Policía, 1 vol., 1879.
    Policía y Juzgados, 1 vol., 1883.
    Autoridades de Policía, 1 vol., 1884.
    Policía y Varios, 1 vol., 1888.
    Criminal contra Pedro Pincay, 1 vol., 1888.
    Comisaría de Orden y Seguridad. Oficios del Intendente, 1 vol., 1893.
    Oficios de la Intendencia General de Policía, 3 vols., 1895.
    Intendencia de Policía, 1 vol., 1896.

Diplomáticos y Consulados

    Diplomáticos y Consulados, 1 vol., 1878.
    Diplomáticos y Consulares Dirigidos a la Gobernación del Guayas, 1 vol., 1879.
    Legaciones y Consules, 1 vol., 1889.
    Cuerpo Consular, 1 vol., 1897.
    Consulados y Bancos, 1 vol., 1898.
    Consulado de Venezuela, 1 vol., 1909-1915.

Censos

    Tenencias, Juzgados, Censos, 1 vol., 1831.
    Padrones, 2 vols., 1832.
    Censos y Padrones, 1 vol., 1837.
    Censo de Población, 1 vol., 1861.

Documentos Diversos

>Cuerpo de Bomberos, 5 vols., 1780-1904.
>Diversos Documentos, 1 vol., 1730 [1790]-1818.
>Documentos Auténticos, 2 vols., 1820-1909, 1831.
>Diversos Funcionarios, 104 vols., 1820-1902.
>Corregimientos y Comisarías, 1 vol., 1830.
>Varios Documentos, 3 vols., 1831, 1887.
>Jefatura de Policía y Marina, 1 vol., 1832.
>Hacienda. Guerra y Marina. Tribunales y Juzgados. Varios, 1 vol., 1833.
>Comandancias y Corregimientos, 1 vol., 1838.
>Oficios de Diversos Funcionarios, 4 vols., 1840, 1854, 1896.
>Varios Oficios y Documentos, 4 vols., 1845, 1847, 1878.
>Varias Oficinas, 1 vol., 1846.
>Diversos. Comunicaciones, 2 vols., 1851, 1856.
>Varios Oficios, 1 vol., 1852.
>Oficios Diversos, 4 vols., 1852, 1868, 1872.
>Varias Autoridades, 2 vols., 1861, 1872.
>Comunicaciones Oficiales, 1 vol., 1863-1867.
>Documentos Oficiales, 2 vols., 1864-1869, 1898.
>Consejo Académico, 1 vol., 1868.
>Sucesos Políticos, 1 vol., 1869.
>Varios Funcionarios, 2 vols., 1869, 1878.
>Diversos Oficios, 4 vols., 1870, 1888, 1896, 1898.
>Comité de la Estatua al Libertador Simón Bolívar, 3 vols., 1872-1889.
>Jefes de Departamento de Guayaquil y Santa Elena, 1 vol., 1873.
>Oficios y Documentos Varios, 1 vol., 1877.
>Decretos y Documentos Varios, 1 vol., 1879.
>Telegramas Oficiales, 10 vols., 1884-1902.
>Varios, 2 vols., 1886, 1890.
>Oficios de las Distintas Autoridades, 1 vol., 1889.
>Bancos, 1 vol., 1892.
>Decretos y Gobernaciones, 1 vol., 1896.
>Exposición de San Luis, Buffalo, 1 vol., 1901-1904.
>Historia del Ecuador, 1 vol., 1912.
>Manuscritos Inéditos, Quito, 1 vol., 1913.
>Historia de la Revolución del 9 de Octubre, 7 vols., (1920).

ARCHIVO HISTORICO DE LA BIBLIOTECA CARLOS A. ROLANDO (ACAR/G)

In addition to his valuable collection of national authors, described above, Dr. Rolando acquired many documents of considerable historical importance. Among these are a number of *legajos* of the Bethlemite Hospital in Quito dating from the seventeenth century, a copy book of official communications of Bartolomé de Cucalón y Villamayor, governor of Guayaquil (1803-1810), and various manuscripts and letters of Manuel de J. Calle.

ARCHIVO DEL REGISTRO DE LA PROPIEDAD (ARP/G)

According to an inventory of 1914, the Office of the Registro de la

Propiedad possesses the following series of documents:

  Registro de Propiedad, from 1826.
  Registro de Propiedad Literaria y Artística, from 1887.
  Registro de Sentencias, 1875-1883.
  Registros de Prohibiciones, from 1873.
  Registro de Exclusión de Bienes, from 1911.
  Registro de Hipotecas, from 1831.
  Registro de Embargos, from 1905.
  Duplicados de Bancos, 1872-1903.
  Repertorios, from 1870.
  Libros de Protestos, 1901-1907.
  Protestos, from 1907.
  Registro Mercantil, from 1907.

In addition, there are more or less complete indexes to these volumes, which include abstracts of their contents. This archive has barely been consulted by historians, but it is known that some of the nineteenth-century materials include histories of land holdings from at least the eighteenth century onwards. While no formal research facilities exist, it is possible to make special arrangements to use these documents. The Office of the Registro de la Propiedad is open to the public between 8-12 a.m. and 2-6 p.m., Monday through Friday. It is located in the Palacio de la Gobernación on Pichincha at the intersection of Clemente Ballén. Its telephone number is 532-385.

ARCHIVOS DE ESCRIBANIAS

Several of the public notaries of Guayaquil retain *legajos* of former notaries possibly including some from the colonial period and without question a number from the last century. Their specific contents, however, are unknown, and it would be difficult to research in these archives since such "old paper" is not properly preserved but stored in improvised warehouses. The AHG has solicited the transfer of all materials over sixty years of age and by the time this *informe* appears expects to have begun the classification of such material.

ARCHIVO DE LA CORTE SUPERIOR (ACS/G)

Apparently this archive preserves most of its papers from the inauguration of the Superior Court of Justice (1830?) through the present. It also retains the papers of the old Archivo de la 2ª Escribanía. Trial transcripts and notarial records exist from as early as the 1840s. including a 1916 "Ynventario General del Archivo de la 2ª Escribanía del Cantón Guayaquil entregado por el Sr. Alejandro Jaime Martínez a su sucesor Sr. Amable García R. Agosto 22, 1916." According to the latter, there should be *juicios* from 1832 onward. Unfortunately, the papers of the ACS/G are presently stored without order in a room in the Palacio de la Gobernación. As in the case of the notarial archives, the AHG has solicited the transfer of these historical materials.

ARCHIVO DE LA CURIA (ACD/G)

Most holdings of the Archivo de la Curia Diocesana de Guayaquil date from the erection of the bishopric in 1838. However, the ACD/G also has many documents from the colonial period apparently including one *expediente* from the sixteenth century. This is surprising because until recently this archive was housed in wooden buildings, exposed to the constant threat of fire.

It is important to note that several inventories of the ACD/G have been located; inventories were carried out in 1852, 1862, 1874, 1878, 1921, and most recently in 1956. Christian Vogel published a resumé of this archive,[6] but it is incomplete and should be used with caution.

The existing bound series in the ACD/G are:

Comunicaciones, 69 vols., from 1838.
Libros Copiadores de Oficios, 46 vols., from 1854.
Libros [of the Ecclesiastical Chapter], 7 vols., from 1688.
Sínodos Diocesanos [of Riobamba], 1 vol., from 1869.
Asuntos Judiciales, 48 vols., from 1686.
Confirmaciones, 36 vols., from 1838.
Dispensas Matrimoniales, 183 vols., from 1709.

Also there are a large number of unbound *legajos*, including five of *testamentos, escrituras, y contratos* (1697-1899), the *protocolos* of the notary José Ignacio Moreno from January 31, 1759 through January, 1760, and of the notary Gregorio Ponce de León from 1765-1767.

Other bound vols. are:

Libro de Cuentas de la Fábrica de la Casa de Huérfanos (1872-1879) which includes the Libro de Cuentas de la Fábrica del Palacio Episcopal (1874-1879).
Libro de Actas de la Junta Constructora de la Iglesia del Sagrado Corazón de Jesús (1891-1908).
Libro de Actas del Comité Reconstructor del Templo de Santo Domingo (1898-1910).
Memorandum de la Construcción de la Nueva Catedral de Guayaquil (1922-1934).

---

6. *El Comercio*, Quito, August 8, 15, 22 and 29, 1965.

Libro de Actas de la Junta de Construcción de la Catedral de Guayaquil (1948-1954).

This archive is located in the Archbishop's Palace on the corner of Chimborazo and Clemente Ballén. It is in a separate room with air conditioning and has metal stacks. Although it has no fixed hours, permission to consult its holdings may freely be obtained from the archbishop.

PARISH ARCHIVES

The three historical parishes in Guayaquil are El Sagrario, La Concepción (i.e., La Merced), and San Alejo. The oldest and most important is El Sagrario, the only parish until 1792(?) when La Concepción was founded. San Alejo dates from 1861 but existed as a vice parish from the late eighteenth century.

El Sagrario has baptismal, matrimonial, and burial registers from 1695, 1701, and 1704 respectively. It is located at the intersection of 10 Agosto and Chimborazo, next to the cathedral. The church of La Concepción and its archive were lost in the great fire of 1896. Its successor parish, La Merced, has baptismal, matrimonial, and burial records from 1898. Its address is Víctor Manuel Rendón and Pedro Carbo. San Alejo has baptismal, matrimonial, and burial records from 1827, 1867, and 1887 respectively. Its address is Eloy Alfaro 302 and Luzárraga.

Because the registers of La Concepción were lost and not all of those of El Sagrario and San Alejo have survived, it is necessary to turn to other sources to fill in the gaps. These include the burial records of the Junta de la Beneficencia, mentioned below, and bills of mortality sporadically published in the irregular *Rejistro Municipal* (1833-1861) and *Gaceta Municipal* (1862-1925) among other newspapers of the last century.

ARCHIVO DEL CEMENTERIO Y/O FUNERARIA DE LA JUNTA DE BENEFICENCIA

The General Cemetery and the Funerary of the Junta de Beneficencia have burial registers from 1862 onward. Neither office has an historical archive in the strict sense, but the personnel are cooperative. The address of the Funerary is Vélez 119, and its telephone number is 512-765.

ARCHIVO DE DON PEDRO ROBLES CHAMBERS

Don Pedro Robles Chambers is the most prestigious genealogist in Ecuador. He has formed a valuable archive over the years, complemented by an extensive card file. Since it is a private collection, access to it is limited and dependent upon permission from the owner who, however, is willing to honor specific requests for data.

The Provincial Archives and Libraries of Ecuador
Rosemary D. F. Bromley

The scholar intending to conduct historical research in Ecuadorian provincial archives, outside the major cities of Quito, Guayaquil, and Cuenca, must be prepared to work on uncatalogued and unclassified documents in institutions unaccustomed to the researcher. Provincial archives lack regulations or controls, just as they lack facilities for the student. Nevertheless, once permission to investigate the repository has been granted, the researcher is usually willingly accommodated. While the archives do not possess copying facilities, arrangements can generally be made to take documents outside the institution for copying, and, if necessary, even to a neighboring town. With the time and determination to work on unsorted material in rather makeshift conditions, the researcher is generally rewarded by a wealth of regional information.

Ecuadorian provincial archives are of four major types: municipal, gubernatorial, parochial, and notarial. The important urban centers of highland Ecuador generally have a long history of municipal government, beginning with their functions as *ciudades* or *villas* during the colonial period. Theoretically, the papers of the colonial *cabildos* were inherited by the *municipios* of the national period, but inevitably the number of manuscripts has diminished. The *municipios* do, however, normally house the largest collections of historical manuscripts to be found outside Quito, Guayaquil, and Cuenca. Permission to work in a municipal archive has to be obtained from the secretary. Once permission is granted, the researcher is allowed access to the archive during the working hours in the institution, usually from 8 a.m. to mid-day and from 2 p.m. to 5 p.m. for five days a week. Working days are normally from Monday to Friday, but where the weekly market is held on a Saturday, the urban administrative offices are generally open on that day and closed on Monday.

Municipal archives are most rewarding for students of the nineteenth and twentieth centuries. The archives contain accounts of municipal business, copies of out-going letters, collections of incoming correspondence, and miscellaneous statistical data. Accounts of municipal business are found in leather-bound volumes, usually titled Libros de Actas. The dated entries summarize all matters discussed by the municipal council and itemize the measures passed. Copies of letters sent by the president of the municipal council are preserved in special volumes and range over a wide variety of affairs. Incoming letters are often grouped according to the institutions of origin. Letters from the provincial *gobernación* and the cantonal *jefatura política* form the largest body of inter-institutional correspondence. These letters relate to all matters of public concern, including the erection of buildings, road construction, provision of educational and hospital facilities, administrative changes, and expenditure of tax revenues. Another corpus of material originate from the *comisaría*, a department within the *municipio*. These letters refer to town affairs, such as street improvements, water supply, market-place and shop regulations, the imposition of fines, and the upkeep of the prison. Correspondence from the municipal treasury is usually less voluminous and concerns tax collection and municipal income and expenditure. Lastly, apart from various letters from parish and cantonal officials, correspondence from local citizens forms a large and disparate body of material, covering such matters as property and water disputes, tax complaints, and petitions to erect new buildings. Documentation of a statistical nature varies considerably in quality and quantity between different municipal archives but becomes uniformly available from the 1930s. It includes population censuses, electoral registers, and schedules for the collection of taxes on property, commerce, and other goods and activities.

   The *municipio* of Latacunga maintains its archive in a spacious room on the second floor of the municipal building, which fronts on the main square. The manuscripts are ordered chronologically and tied in packages, each consisting of four-hundred to eight-hundred papers. The fifty-eight packages containing nineteenth-century documentation are stored in labelled wooden boxes, while the more copious twentieth-century material is stacked on the shelves. The oldest papers date from 1658 and are legal records of property sales. No more than four-hundred or so sheets remain from the seventeenth and eighteenth centuries, however. The document collection at Latacunga, as in other central highland towns, must have been reduced by the earthquakes of 1698 and 1797 and depleted by pilfering. Apart from a few manuscripts of the 1820s and 1830s, the bulk of the papers concerns events from the mid 1840s onwards. By 1860, documents are sufficiently numerous to warrant a separate package for each year. Within the packages, the majority of sheets have been tied into numbered *legajos,* with a brief indication of their contents. Libros de Actas run in a continuous series from 1846 and are scattered amongst the relevant packages. The archive has a good collection of correspondence and many books of copied municipal letters. There are registers of electors which begin in 1825, but these are not common until the mid-nineteenth century. While only a very few tax listings survive from before 1920, the archive does hold the detailed schedules of two population censuses taken in 1846 and 1857. For the twentieth century, most correspondence, and records of municipal meetings and electoral listings, are preserved in the archive, but nearly all the tax records are kept in the archive of the municipal treasury on the ground floor of the same building. Here lie an excellent series of urban and rural property registers, lists of telephones, and records of electricity and water consumption, all covering most years since the mid 1920s. The records are stacked on shelves in approximate chronological order.

The municipal archive of Ambato was laid out in a large room in the municipal building during 1971. All manuscripts, excepting the most recent, are bound in thick leather-covered volumes, each containing six-hundred to seven-hundred numbered pages. The volumes are ordered chronologically, and while none has an index, the papers are organized so that all letters from a particular institution form a continuous sequence. The oldest manuscript is one of 1807, but the collection is patchy until the late 1850s. For the nineteenth century as a whole there are only twenty-three volumes, and it is not until the 1910s that annual volumes become necessary. Clearly many nineteenth-century documents have been lost or destroyed. The collection of correspondence is good, but the series of Libros de Actas beginning in 1851 is incomplete, and there are no nineteenth-century electoral registers or population censuses and few tax listings. The quantity of documentation increases considerably for the twentieth century, and there are sixty-seven volumes for the 1940s alone. No tax schedules are housed in the municipal archive, however, and those dating from before 1950, mostly those of the 1930s and 1940s, are deposited in the municipal store. In a hut adjacent to the old town prison, this store is completely disordered, and dust-covered volumes are piled haphazardly alongside building equipment. Tax listings from the 1950s onwards are maintained in the archive of the municipal treasury.

The municipal archive of Riobamba has an extensive manuscript collection tied in numbered bundles and arranged on shelves. The archive occupies an interior room of the municipal building by the Plaza Maldonado. While this room does not afford space for a researcher, a desk can be made available in the adjoining office. The oldest documents are from 1797 and concern the earthquake damage to Riobamba in that year and the plans for the refoundation of the town on its present site. These, and a hundred or so other papers of 1798 and 1799, including Actas de Cabildo, are locked away separately by the secretary. On the open shelves are twelve bundles, each of five-hundred to seven-hundred sheets, containing documents from 1822 to 1860. After 1860 documentation is prolific--between one and three bundes for every year. The series of Libros de Actas is continuous from 1822. Apart from the bound Libros de Actas and volumes of copied letters and tax schedules, each bundle simply contains several hundred loose and unsorted letters of a particular year. The outstanding feature of Riobamba's municipal archive is the excellent collection of nineteenth-century tax data. Scattered among the bundles and inscribed in the Libros de Actas are detailed lists, beginning in 1824, of the apportionment of irrigation water, schedules for the taxation of property owners and merchants commencing in 1835, records of urban shops, and registers of urban and rural properties from the 1850s onwards, and many other miscellaneous tax listings. There are numerous registers of electors from the mid-nineteenth century, and some parish population censuses for 1856, 1860, and 1882. The most valuable demographic sources in the archive are the copious nominal listings for the Contribución del Trabajo Subsidiario, levied between 1852 and 1896. The twentieth-century holdings of the *municipio* are dispersed, and the bundles in the archive contain only the correspondence, records of municipal business, and copies of the local gazette. The electoral registers, the telephone, water, and property records, and other tax schedules are simply heaped in the store, which is located within the main municipal building. Only the most recent records, dating from the 1950s onwards, are kept in good order in the appropriate municipal departments.

The municipal archives of cantonal capitals are smaller and less well maintained than those of the provincial centers. The archives of the *municipios* in Píllaro and Pelileo in the province of Tungurahua are two examples. Their small, disorganized collections have both been seriously depleted, at Píllaro by fire and at Pelileo in the destruction caused by the 1949 earthquake. Other institutions in the same cantonal centers also hold minor document collections. The archive of the *jefatura política* in Pelileo houses a set of bound correspondence, arranged in chronological order on shelves, dating back to the mid-nineteenth century. The equivalent repository in Píllaro is in complete disarray. The documents lie piled haphazardly on top of a large cupboard, and the oldest extant manuscripts are from the 1890s. The *jefatura política* of Quero, also in Tungurahua, holds a small body of bound correspondence, dating back only to the 1920s. From these few examples, it appears that the archives of cantonal capitals possess only limited documentation from the late nineteenth century.

A governor's archive exists in every provincial capital and is housed in the buildings of the *gobernación*, usually on the main square. The researcher can obtain access to the archive with permission from the governor. The *gobernación* is open for the same five working days each week as the *municipio* but has working hours which generally extend to 6 p.m. rather than 5 p.m. Each manuscript collection should at least date back to the appointment of the first governor in the town, in the year when the province was established. In the central highlands, the provinces of Cotopaxi (formerly León) and Tungurahua were not created until the mid-nineteenth century, and the corresponding governors' archives date only from that time. In the governors' archives investigated by the author, documents were not only fewer in number but lacked the organization of those in the *municipios*.

To some extent the information to be gleaned from the two types of repositories is similar. The standard contents of a gubernatorial archive are letters received from various central government ministries, from provincial, cantonal, and parochial authorities, and from local citizens. There are also volumes containing copies of letters sent by the governor and a few records of council meetings, particularly from the late nineteenth century. None of the governors' archives, however, possesses the large collections of tax data available in the *municipios*.

The governor's archive in Latacunga contains a disordered quantity of documentation in which the earliest manuscripts are from the 1850s. The papers are stacked on shelves and on the floor of a small room, and it is up to the researcher to ferret through the piles to glean what he can. In the repository at Ambato, the volume of material is far smaller, and the bulk comprises books of copied letters, the earliest dating from 1860. These books are stored in a large cupboard, and they are easily sorted as the year and destination of the letters is marked on the cover of each volume.

Riobamba undoubtedly possesses the richest gubernatorial archive in the central highlands, not only because the collection commences in 1822 but also because a particularly large number of manuscripts have been preserved. The documents are tied in dated bundles and occupy a small interior room on the second floor of the *gobernación*. While there is no strict ordering of the bundles, the oldest papers are stored in a large cupboard. The more recent documents and pamphlets are stacked on shelves and on the floor. A distinguishing feature of Riobamba's gubernatorial archive is the existence of various detailed population censuses, dated 1825 and 1836, and aggregated population statistics for the 1840s. There are also numerous sheets of parish economic information submitted to the governor by the local officials. For the student interested in tracing nineteenth-century developments in the province of Chimborazo, this archive clearly has almost as much to offer as that of the *municipio* in Riobamba.

Ecclesiastical parish archives usually contain registers of baptisms, marriages, burials, and occasionally confirmations, records of marriage testimonies, and some correspondence. All the registers and papers are kept in the parish buildings, usually in the priest's house, adjacent to the church. Before venturing into a parish archive it is wisest for the researcher to seek permission from the appropriate bishop, although many parish priests are happy to allow the student access to their archives without such formalities. While a large number of ecclesiastical parishes have been founded in the last 150 years and are unlikely to contain colonial records, at least a hundred parish archives in Ecuador should hold registers from the eighteenth century. In the major towns, the parish archives are generally located in the episcopal building. Here the registers of all the urban parishes are usually united and put in the charge of a priest or nun, who opens the archive at regular working hours in order to answer inquiries. A desk or table can normally be made available for the researcher. Outside the towns, access to parish documents is by special arrangement with the priest. Working conditions are makeshift, and there may be little or no electric lighting for the consultation of documents in the late afternoon.

The author investigated ten urban and rural parish archives during 1971-1972. In Latacunga, Ambato, and San Felipe (Cotopaxi) the parish archives hold records from the seventeenth century, while in Riobamba and San Sebastián (Cotopaxi) there are registers from the early 1700s. In Cajabamba (Chimborazo) and San Bartolomé (Tungurahua) the series of registers commence in the 1740s, but in Patate (Tungurahua) and Sicalpa (Chimborazo) there are no records prior to the late eighteenth century. The last parish archive investigated, that of Tisaleo (Tungurahua), possesses registers dating from its foundation as a parish in the early nineteenth century. As a group these ten archives are probably fairly representative of ecclesiastical parish archives all over Ecuador. In all the archives, registers prior to the late eighteenth century are invariably disordered, with many pages missing and with sheets rendered illegible through decay. For the close of the colonial period, the gaps are fewer, but not until the national era can the researcher be relatively assured of finding a complete record. The organization of the baptism, marriage, and burial entries between different registers, and the amount of detail the entries contain, varies considerably from parish to parish and from one year to another.[1] In the most populous parishes, baptisms of white and Indian children were inscribed in separate registers, at least until the 1830s. Burials and marriages were usually recorded in one book for all ethnic groups.

Notarial archives are found in all the principal towns. These often contain the oldest documents available in provincial centers, but their holdings are usually disordered. Unfortunately, access to these private archives is not always easy, and the foreign researcher is often unwelcome if a local historian is in the process of investigating the archive

---

1. See Rosemary D. F. Bromley, "Parish Registers as a Source in Latin American Demographic and Historical Research," *Bulletin of the Society for Latin American Studies* 19 (1974):14-21.

contents.

Libraries, outside the major cities, rarely contain any books which are not more easily consulted elsewhere. The municipal libraries of Latacunga and Riobamba both hold small, general collections, which are only worth consulting for the local monographs and pamphlets not readily available in Quito or Guayaquil. Ambato has two good libraries. The oldest, belonging to the Colegio Bolívar, has a large number of nineteenth-century volumes and many locally printed books. The other library in the Casa de Montalvo holds a fine set of local newspapers, in addition to a good collection of nineteenth-century publications. It provides pleasant and comfortable surroundings for the reader.

A wealth of historical information lies virtually untapped in many of Ecuador's municipal, gubernatorial, parochial, and notarial archives. These provincial document collections, while often disorganized and lacking the facilities of the major repositories, can yield invaluable regional material, particularly relating to the nineteenth and twentieth centuries.

PERU

Introduction
Leon G. Campbell

The appearance of the *Research Guide to Andean History* comes at a time when scholarly interest in the Andean area is growing, evidenced by an increasing number of historians and social scientists identifying themselves as Andeanists.[1] With the creation in 1970 of the Andean Studies Committee of the Conference on Latin American History, our organization has progressed even further by providing a forum whereby important research is discussed and common interests publicized. This *Guide* is the most recent effort of the Committee to provide a practical basis for the organization. Strength, however, emanates from the membership and accordingly, all younger scholars are encouraged to join the Committee.[2]

A random sample of the historiographical literature on Peru indicates the great quantity of work being done in this field, exceeding that of the other Andean countries.[3] Despite the quantity, the quality of

---

1. In Howard F. Cline, compiler, *Historians of Latin America in the United States, 1965* (Durham, North Carolina, 1966), fifty-seven historians identified themselves as Andeanists, thirty-one of these being Peruvianists. In the second edition of the guide, expanded to include social scientists, 248 persons identified themselves as Peruvianists. *National Directory of Latin Americanists, 1970* (Washington, D.C., 1971).

2. Professor Brooke Larson, Department of History, New School for Social Research, New York, New York, 10011, is currently Executive Secretary of the Committee, which meets annually in conjunction with the American Historical Association meeting.

3. See for example, Watt Stewart, "Jorge Basadre and Peruvian Historiography," *Hispanic American Historical Review,* 29 (May, 1949):222-227; J. León Helguera, "Research Opportunities: The Bolivarian Nations," *The Americas,* 18 (April, 1962):365-374; Fredrick B. Pike's "Bibliographical Essay," in his *Modern History of Peru* (London, 1971), pp. 321-332; and the sections on Peru in Charles C. Griffin, ed., *Latin America. A Guide to the Historical Literature* (Austin and London, 1971). Independence is briefly described in J. A. Puente Candamo, "Historiografía de la independencia del Perú," *Revista de historia de América,* 59 (1965):280-293. Also illustrative are the sections by John TePaske on the Spanish colonial period and Frederick M. Nunn on Chile and the Andean Republics in Roberto Esqueñazi-Mayo and Michael C. Meyer, eds., *Latin American Scholarship since*

Peruvian historiography has not been uniformly impressive, especially that dealing with the postcolonial period, as a variety of scholars have noticed.[4] In recent years, however, this situation has begun to change. Works appearing on the Peruvian colonial era have been remarkable for their insights and skillful use of new methodological tools. Similarly, those studies now being done of the early national and modern eras in Peruvian history demonstrate less of an emphasis on heroes, martyrs, and political-military developments in favor of fresher approaches to the past which utilize social and economic data and emphasize regional distinctions.

The publication of the *Research Guide to Andean History* constitutes a recognition of the gains made in the field and an invitation to younger scholars to extend and amplify the knowledge of the Peruvian past. Even the most venerable topics, including the last Inca revolts (1780-1783) and the War of the Pacific (1879-1883), demand re-interpretation, while enormous areas such as urban, agrarian, ecological, and contemporary social history remain virtually unexplored.[5] By bringing to these and other topics the insights allowed by the methodologies and techniques now available to scholars in every field, we are permitted to approach more closely the realities of the Peruvian past than ever before.

The Peruvian section of the *Guide* has been organized along lines which I found reasonable and useful for the reader preparing to undertake field research. It is divided into three parts: 1) research in specific chronological periods; 2) research in special methodologies and topics; and 3) major documentary collections. Without any pretension at completeness, I have sought to provide a description of the ongoing work in each chronological period, the important trends which have appeared, lacunae remaining, and to describe some of the problems and priorities remaining for researchers. While the contributors to the section vary somewhat in approach, their choices of particular sources and topics for discussion and their description of these subfields are the result of years of study of these particular areas. Secondly, I have also chosen to include

---

World War II. Trends in History, Political Science, Literature, Geography, and Economics (Lincoln, Nebraska, 1971), pp. 5-22 and 73-102.

4. Cited by Nunn in Esqueñazi-Mayo and Meyer, eds., *Latin American Scholarship*, pp. 85-86.

5. As an example of this need in the former area, see my research article, "Recent Research on Andean Peasant Revolts, 1750-1820," *Latin American Research Review*, 14 (Spring, 1979):3-49.

certain selected topics, such as the Peruvian Indian, which are of importance to almost every scholar at work in the field and which illustrate as well the depth of research being done in specific areas which cross disciplinary boundaries. Because of space limitations I have provided a brief description only of major archival and library holdings, intended to suggest to the reader some idea of the rich body of documentation available in Peru. This of course omits smaller departmental and personal archives which may be of considerable historiographical importance.

John R. Fisher of the University of Liverpool, whose research has been concentrated on the administrative and economic developments in Peru during the later colony, describes the archival resources in both Spain and Peru for the study of the colonial period. Students interested in this period are also encouraged to consult the research articles by James Lockhart, Karen Spalding and Frederick Bowser which survey current work on specific social groups in fuller detail.[6] The periods of Peruvian independence and the early republic to 1930 are covered respectively by Paul B. Ganster of Utah State University and Jesús Chavarría of the University of California, Santa Barbara. Ganster's particular familiarity with the ecclesiastical archives in Peru and elsewhere gives an especially clear picture of research opportunities concerning the church and church-related topics, while Chavarría's comments about the origins of Peruvian nationalism also open up a number of fresh areas for research. Peter F. Klarén of George Washington University draws upon his detailed knowledge of the social and economic history of contemporary Peru in describing the sources available for the study of this period. His attention to family papers and memoirs, business records and hacienda archives, and professional and personal archives is especially welcome in that it alerts researchers to the existence of these often-neglected resources, many dealing with several centuries of Peruvian history. Finally, Daniel M. Masterson indicates the archives and individuals in Peru and the United States which can aid the scholar researching the Peruvian military.

Part II considers certain topics and methodologies of unusual importance to the Peruvian historian. Anthropologists John V. Murra and Patricia Netherly of Cornell University survey existing source materials

---

6. See the articles by James Lockhart, Karen Spalding, and Frederick Bowser on colonial social history, the colonial Indian, and the colonial African in Peru, all in *Latin American Research Review*, 7 (Spring, 1972).

available for the study of Andean ethnohistory and describe ongoing developments in this field, one of the most rapidly advancing areas in Andean-oriented research. Of especial interest is Murra's attention to sources located in Bolivia and Argentina and Netherly's detailed description of those materials located in the northern coastal region, neither of which have been before described in print. Thomas M. Davies, Jr., of California State University, San Diego, describes the many sources, both governmental and private, available for the study of the Peruvian Indian, a subject which is today receiving even greater attention by scholars. Susan Ramírez-Horton takes us through the many forests of fashioning hacienda history. Her detailed review of the multiplicity of sources available for the study of the Peruvian hacienda, the ingenious approaches possible toward these documents, and the obstacles and pitfalls in their use provide a whole new dimension for our understanding of the socioeconomic history of Peru. Although these are but some of the newer methodologies and topics to receive attention from historians, they, along with oral history projects and other non-traditional approaches, suggest the development of important alternative views of the past which can broaden our perspectives and test hypotheses that may be more venerable than valid. Elinor C. Burkett of Frostburg State College warns, however, that certain pitfalls await the unwary scholar preparing to do research utilizing certain of these newer methodologies and sources. Taking Peruvian notarial archives as an example, Burkett illustrates both the problems and possibilities of work in this field, providing insights into some of the obvious and less evident yields of archival data, as well as practical information on diverse subjects such as microfilming, letters of introduction, paleography, and family feuds, which are not always explicitly dealt with by mentors or research directories, but which can spell the difference between a successful field research venture and a disastrous one.

Part III contains a series of short pieces describing the major libraries and archival collections in Peru.[7] Guillermo Durand Flórez, the

---

7. Among the several general archival guides for Peru and Rubén Vargas Ugarte, *Biblioteca peruana. Manuscritos peruanos en las bibliotecas y archivos de Europa y América*, 5 vols. (Buenos Aires, 1947); Lino Gómez Canedo, *Los archivos de la historia de América*, 2 vols. (Mexico, 1961), and Raúl Porras Barrenechea, *Fuentes históricas peruanas* (Lima, 1963). Useful for working in the Lima area, although somewhat dated, is Howard

Director of Lima's Archivo General de la Nación, illustrates his familiarity with this important repository, which has for so long been so useful to scholars of the Andean area, and in the process complements J. R. Fisher's description of Lima's other important archives and Vincent Peloso's survey of the Archivo Agrario. The *Guide,* however, recognizes that archives and libraries abound outside of Lima as well, that require explanation as scholars begin to recognize and write about Peru's distinctive regional development. Donald L. Gibbs of the University of Texas at Austin, a specialist in the history of Cuzco, provides considerable information on the resources for historical study located in that important city, which for four centuries has been one of Peru's most important administrative, economic, and religious centers. Hernán Horna, a young Peruvian scholar, describes the archival holdings of Trujillo, an important city of northern coastal Peru. This piece, when considered with that of Klarén and Ganster's description of the Archbishop's Archive of Trujillo, gives researchers a fairly complete idea of the available resources in this important area. Fernando A. Ponce, another Peruvian completing his doctorate at the University of Texas at Austin, rounds out the section with a description of the archival resources of Arequipa, southern Peru's important urban center, placing special emphasis upon the parish records located there. As a further aid to scholars, Ganster provides additional information concerning the microfilm holdings of the Mormon Genealogical Society headquartered in Salt Lake City which has been extremely active in the Andean area, especially in the filming and assembling of parish records. Researchers will also benefit greatly from the list of addresses and personnel of the major Peruvian archives kindly compiled by Sra. Tita Monzón de Davies. Finally, a list of dissertations in the field of Peruvian history written at universities in the United States is available through Xerox University Microfilms International with guides published periodically.[8]

Karno, "Some Notes on Social Science Research in Peru," *Noticiero* (September, 1970):13-22, which includes a list of booksellers and other practical information. A recent guide to specialized libraries is the *Directorio de bibliotecas especializadas del Perú* (Lima, 1972) which describes libraries in both the public and private sectors of Peru.

8. See, for example, Carl W. Deal, ed., *Latin America and the Caribbean: A Dissertation Bibliography* (Ann Arbor, Michigan: University Microfilms International, 1978). The guide is available from the publisher, University Microfilms International, 300 N. Zeeb Road, Ann Arbor,

Even such a brief overview of recent Peruvian historiography as that described in the pages which follow indicates that the quality of scholarship has greatly improved in recent years. Many of the contributors to this section have been in the forefront of the group of revisionist scholars who have contributed fresh insights into the Peruvian past, and I am profoundly grateful to all of them for their dedicated efforts in making their work and knowledge of Peru available to others. It is anticipated that their efforts will be especially useful to graduate students and prospective researchers who already appreciate the cultural differences existing between our country and Peru and seek further knowledge of the Peruvian past. This process promises an extension and improvement of relationships between Peruvian and North American scholars which have generally been cordial and always beneficial. Those persons preparing to investigate the Peruvian past will certainly benefit from knowing Peruvians in general and Peruvian scholars and archivists in particular. Better than I they will explain that the study of Peru and its past is sometimes frustrating, oftentimes fruitful, but always fascinating.[9]

Michigan, 48106.

9. Since these lines were written, a large number of important works on Peru by both Peruvian and foreign scholars have reached print, giving further credence to the assertion made above. While it would be both impossible and presumptuous to list all of them, the titles that follow constitute a representative sample of the work of historians that has been done in the last five years. They also reflect the emerging trend towards regional studies and to the subjects of class and ethnicity, which are discussed fully by the contributors to the *Research Guide*. Timothy E. Anna, *The Fall of the Royal Government in Peru* (Lincoln and London: University of Nebraska Press, 1979); Leon G. Campbell, *The Military and Society in Colonial Peru, 1750-1810* (Philadelphia: The American Philosophical Society, 1978); Jesús Chavarría, *José Carlos Mariátegui and the Rise of Modern Peru, 1890-1930* (Albuquerque: University of New Mexico Press, 1979); Thomas M. Davies, Jr. and Víctor Villanueva, eds., *300 documentos para la historia del APRA* (Lima: Editorial Horizonte,1978); Alberto Flores Galindo, comp., *Túpac Amaru, 1780. Sociedad colonial y sublevaciones populares* (Lima: Retablo de Papel, 1976); Howard Handelman, *Struggle in the Andes: Peasant Political Mobilization in Peru* (Austin and London: University of Texas Press, 1975); Robert Keith, *Conquest and Agrarian Change: The Emergence of the Hacienda System on the Peruvian Coast* (Cambridge, Mass.: Harvard University Press, 1976); Franklin Pease G.Y., *Del Tawantinsuyu a la historia del Perú* (Lima: Instituto de Estudios Peruanos, 1978); Magnus Mörner, *Perfil de la sociedad rural del Cuzco a fines de la colonia* (Lima: Universidad del Pacífico, 1978); Karen Spalding,*De indio e campesino. Cambios en la estructura social del Perú colonial* (Lima: Instituto de Estudios Peruanos, 1974); Pierre van den Berghe and George P. Primov, *Inequality in the Peruvian Andes: Class and Ethnicity in Cuzco* (Columbia and London: Univ. of Missouri Press, 1977).

Resources for the Study of Colonial Peru
John R. Fisher

Notwithstanding its imposing title, the modest aim of this article is simply to introduce the inexperienced researcher to the major archives in Peru and Spain for the study of colonial Peru. It should be borne in mind, of course, that many libraries in the United States contain valuable collections of manuscripts relating to Peru. These should be examined, or at least sampled, at an early stage, if only to provide an idea of the paleographical problems likely to be encountered in the major Hispanic repositories. Those requiring information about published material, both primary and secondary, on colonial Peru should consult, in addition to the usual general bibliographies on Spanish American history, the following specialized works: Raúl Porras Barrenechea, *Fuentes históricas peruanas* (Lima, 1963), and Rubén Vargas Ugarte, *Historia del Perú. Fuentes* (Lima, 1945). Carlos Moreyra y Paz Soldán's *Bibliografía regional peruana* (Lima, 1967) is also a useful introductory work.[1]

ARCHIVES IN SPAIN

ARCHIVO GENERAL DE INDIAS (SEVILLE)

For all but the most specialized topics, drawing upon materials available only in Peru, it is advisable for the researcher to begin archival work in Spain. The archives there tend to be not only better-housed and better-administered than those in Peru but also more coherent in the extent and organization of their documentation. For most dissertations material from sources in Peru will be of crucial importance, but in many cases its fragmentary nature makes it intelligible only when studied in the light of what has been learned from the vast holdings of the Archivo

---

1. One might also consult, Fernando Silva Santisteban, "Algunos archivos históricos y repositorios de Lima," *Fénix*, 12 (1958):145-182.

General de Indias. A good description of the history and general organization of this magnificent archive is provided by José Mariá de la Peña y Cámara, *Archivo General de Indias de Sevilla. Guía del visitante* (Madrid, 1958). Those with a special interest in the sixteenth and seventeenth centuries might find it useful to begin work in Sections I (Patronato), II (Contaduría), and IV (Justicia). The most widely used, however, is Section V (Gobierno), which contains some 18,000 of the archive's total holdings of 42,000 *legajos*. They consist mainly of the records of the Council of the Indies and other metropolitan organs of government and cover virtually all aspects of the government of the Indies over three centuries: the most prominent general categories of material are instructions and resolutions sent to America by the Council, reports, petitions, complaints, etc. submitted to Spain by a wide range of authorities and officials in the empire--viceroys, audiencias, governors, bishops, treasury ministers, *visitadores,* etc.--and papers relating to the discussion and resolution within the Council of matters referred to it. The legajos in this section are classified into fifteen groups, fourteen of them corresponding to individual audiencia districts, and a fifteenth--Indiferente--mainly for material that cannot easily be classified geographically. The Audiencia de Lima division contains 1,638 legajos with a chronological coverage from 1529 to 1849. There are an additional 82 bundles in the Audiencia de Cuzco group, which runs from 1787. A useful guide to the latter is Carlos Daniel Valcárcel, *Documentos de la Audiencia de Cuzco en el Archivo General de Indias* (Lima, 1957). Rubén Vargas Ugarte, S.J., *Manuscritos peruanos en el Archivo de Indias* (Lima, 1938) gives some indication of the contents of the Lima section, but the only general catalogue available is the manuscript inventory in the Archive itself. This provides a brief indication of the contents of each legajo, with dates, but in most cases gives no clue to the precise contents. Hundreds of legajos are simply described as Cartas y Expedientes, for example, or Duplicados del Virrey.

Approximately two-thirds of the Audiencia de Lima legajos are grouped under the general heading, Consejo y Ministerios, and are then further classified into the following self-explanatory groups: *gobernación y gracia; hacienda; guerra; marina; consulado; comercio; eclesiástica.* The bulk, but by no means all, of the documents here relate to the period of interest, but it is advisable for all students whatever their topic, to devote a few days at the outset to reading right through the inventory. Those for the Audiencias of Panamá, Santa Fé, Charcas, Buenos Aires, and Chile should also be examined, particularly by students concerned with Peru in its widest sense rather than the rump viceroyalty of the late eighteenth century. The inventory of the Indiferente Section should not be missed. Part of it is devoted to Indiferente del Perú (legajos 258-414), but there is also much of relevance to the viceroyalty in the larger Indiferente General, in many ways the most interesting division in the whole Archive. For a guide to its contents see José Torre Revello, *El Archivo General de Indias de Sevilla* (Buenos Aires, 1929). The citations employed in this and other old works are now out-of-date, but they can easily be checked in the inventories.

The remaining sections of the Archive are more specialized, and researchers will determine whether or not they wish to consult the inventories according to their particular interests. Section III (Contratación) is large and, like Sections XII (Consulados) and XV (Tribunal de Cuentas), valuable for commercial and economic history. Section IX (Estado) has important papers for the study of the independence period: see Pedro Torres Lanzas, *Independencia de América. Fuentes para su estudio. Catálogo de documentos conservados en el Archivo General de Indias de Sevilla*, 6 vols. (Madrid, 1912). Section XVI (Mapas, Planos, Dibujos, y Estampas) contains important pictorial material relating to Peru. The official guide is Pedro Torres Lanzas, *Relación de los mapas, planos, etc. del virreinato del Perú existentes en el Archivo General de Indias* (Barcelona, 1906). The Archive has a supplementary list of items added to this group since 1906. For a good guide to town-plans in the Archive as a whole, see Pedro González y González, *Planos de ciudades iberoamericanos y filipinas existentes en el Archivo de Indias*, 2 vols. (Madrid, 1951). Sections IV (Justicia) and VI (Escribanía de Cámara de Justicia) are also worth exploring. The holdings of the latter extend only as far as 1761 but are continued in Section VIII of the Archivo Histórico Nacional, Madrid (see below).

When visiting the Archivo General de Indias for the first time, it is advisable--and this is a general rule for Spanish archives--to bring along a letter of introduction addressed to the director (at present Srta. Rosario Parra Cala). If possible avoid Seville during the summer (July-August) when the Archive opens only in the mornings. There is an excellent microfilm, photographic, and photocopying service. It is useful while in Seville to make contact with the Escuela de Estudios Hispanoamericanos (Alfonso XII, 16), which readily allows access to its excellent library. This contains mainly published material, but it also has some important sets of documents, including the papers of Viceroy José Fernando de Abascal. The Archivo General de Indias, too, has a reasonable collection of published works, which can be used off the premises.

ARCHIVO GENERAL DE SIMANCAS (VALLADOLID)

Most of the papers referring specifically to the Indies which had been stored at Simancas were supposedly transferred to the Archivo General de Indias in 1785, but a combination of inefficiency and, more important, inevitable overlapping between peninsular and American affairs means that Simancas remains an important archive for the student of the Spanish empire in America. My experience of it is limited to eighteenth-century material, particularly in Sections IX (Secretaría de Guerra), X (Secretaría de Marina), and XVII (Hacienda. Dirección General de Rentas); the last of these has valuable material on trade in the 1778-1795 period (legajos 568-580). For themes such as defense, which were of general imperial significance, it also contains important material for earlier centuries, and references to Peru naturally abound. There is no published catalogue, but for a sound general description of the archive see Dirección General de Archivos y Bibliotecas, *Guía del Archivo General de Simancas* (Madrid, 1958). Students working there normally commute by bus from Valladolid.

ARCHIVO HISTORICO NACIONAL (MADRID)

After the Archivo General de Indias this is the most important single repository for Americanists. On its general organization see Luis Sánchez Belda, *Guía del Archivo Histórico Nacional* (Madrid, 1958). It is organized thematically rather than geographically, so there is no single section on Peru. Those interested in social history, however, will find many invaluable *relaciones de méritos y servicios* of Peruvians in Section VIII (Consejos). For a brief general guide to this section, which contains some 1,550 legajos dealing with the work of the Council of the Indies after 1761, see Angel González Palencia, *Extracto del catálogo de los documentos del Consejo de Indias conservados en la Sección de Consejos del Archivo Histórico Nacional, Madrid* (Madrid, 1920). See, too

Archivo Histórico Nacional, *Indice de relaciones de méritos y servicios conservados en la Sección de Consejos* (Madrid, 1943). Further items of particular interest in this section are the legajos containing the residencias of a number of Peruvian viceroys. The Section on Ordenes Militares is also a fruitful area for those seeking biographical data. See Guillermo Lohmann Villena, *Los americanos en las órdenes militares,* 2 vols. (Madrid, 1947), Aúrea Javierre Mur and Consuelo Gutiérrez del Arroyo, *Guía de la Sección de Ordenes Militares,* 2 vols. (Madrid, n.d.); Manuel C. Bonilla, "Documentos relacionados con el Perú existentes en el Archivo Histórico, Madrid," *Revista del Centro de Estudios Históricos-Militares,* 5 (1950-1951):114-127. Those interested in the defense of the viceroyalty should look through the card-index to Section III (Estado), which contains almost 9,000 legajos on foreign affairs from the reign of Philip V until that of Ferdinand VII.

BIBLIOTECA DE LA REAL ACADEMIA DE LA HISTORIA (MADRID)

The most important item here for Peruvianists is the 125-volume "Colección Mata Linares," assembled in the last quarter of the eighteenth century by the famous *oidor* Benito de la Mata Linares. The first volume of the catalogue to the collection has now been published: Remedio Contreras and Carmen Cortés, ed., Real Academia de la Historia, *Catálogo de la Colección Mata Linares* (Madrid, 1970). The other outstanding collection of documents, the "Colección Muñoz," assembled by the eighteenth-century scholar Juan Bautista Muñoz, is not confined to Peru, but it contains many items of great value for the history of the viceroyalty, particularly on the sixteenth century. For an excellent catalogue, see Real Academia de la Historia, *Catálogo de la Colección de don Juan Bautista Muñoz,* 3 vols. (Madrid, 1954-1956). Those interested in the independence period should look at the smaller "Colección Torata," which refers mainly to the career of General Jerónimo Valdés.

OTHER MADRID ARCHIVES

The manuscript section of the Biblioteca Nacional contains diverse documents relating to Peru--see Julián Paz, *Catálogo de manuscritos de América existentes en la Biblioteca Nacional* (Madrid, 1933)--as does the Biblioteca del Palacio. One of the most interesting collections in the latter consists of the nine volumes of papers of Báltasar Jaime Martínez Compañon, the famous bishop of Trujillo in the late eighteenth century.

For this and other items, see J. Domínguez Bordona, *Manuscritos de América* (Madrid, 1935).

The Archivo de las Cortes Españolas contains reports from Peru for the critical 1810-1814 period. Those using it might also wish to consult the papers of the Junta Central and the Consejo de Regencia, which are kept in the Archivo Histórico Nacional: José Garreta and Ignacio Olavide, *Indice de los papeles de la Junta Central Gubernativa del Reino y del Consejo de Regencia, publicado por el Archivo Histórico Nacional* (Madrid, 1904).

Suggestions for Further Reading:

E. J. Burrus, "An Introduction to Bibliographical Tools in Spanish Archives and Manuscript Collections Relating to Hispanic America," *Hispanic American Historical Review,* 35 (1955):443-483.

Lino Gómez Cañedo, *Los archivos de la historia de América. Período colonial español,* 2 vols. (Mexico, 1961).

Dirección General de Archivos y Bibliotecas, *Guía de fuentes para la historia de Ibero-América conservadas en España,* 2 vols. (Madrid, 1966-1969).

Dirección General de Archivos y Bibliotecas, *Guía de las bibliotecas de Madrid* (Madrid, 1953).

Dirección General de Archivos y Bibliotecas, *Guía de los archivos de Madrid* (Madrid, 1952).

ARCHIVES IN PERU

ARCHIVO NACIONAL DEL PERU (LIMA)

Although now officially called the Archivo General de la Nación, this archive, the most important in the country, is still generally referred to by its older name. For a summary of its somewhat checkered history, see María Castelo de Zavala, "El Archivo Nacional del Perú," *Revista de historia de América,* 20 (1945):371-386. Its extensive holdings are based upon what have survived of the documents of the viceregal Secretaría de Cámara and the civil papers of the Audiencia de Lima, together with those of more specialized institutions, in particular the Cajas Reales, Tribunal de Cuentas, Contaduría General de Tributos, Rentas Estancadas and Temporalidades, and Inquisición. A card catalogue exists for some of the smaller sections such as Superior Gobierno and Derecho Indígena, but the bulk of the material, although arranged reasonably systematically, is uncatalogued. This fundamental problem is minimized to some extent by the readiness of the staff to allow direct access to the stacks. The main groups of documents in the Sección Histórica are as follows: Real

Audiencia--some 800 legajos on civil jurisdiction and approximately 40 on criminal jurisdiction (a far larger collection of legajos on criminal affairs is housed in the adjacent Archivo de la Corte Superior, which, like the Archivo Nacional is located in the Palacio de Justicia), 1544-1835; Real Hacienda--a vast amount of material, mostly seventeenth- and eighteenth-century, organized by *cajas* and also according to particular sources of revenue in some cases (*tributos, tabacos, etc.*); Propiedad y Derecho Indígena--23 legajos on *mitas, encomiendas, cacicazgos, reducciones, etc.*; Temporalidades--an extensive collection of papers on the administration of former Jesuit properties after 1767, particularly useful for data on haciendas and colleges; Compañía de Jesús--legajos on various activities of the Jesuits from the mid-sixteenth century; Superior Gobierno--close to 40 legajos on administrative topics, mostly eighteenth-century, but some earlier; Cabildos; Residencias--26 legajos on the period from 1570 to 1812; Inquisición--over 100 legajos dealing primarily with property (*autos de fé* are in the Archivo Arzobispal--see below); Minería--the archive of the former Tribunal de Minería, primarily eighteenth and early nineteenth centuries; Caja de Censos de Indios--70 legajos covering the period from 1565 until 1826; Judicial Militar--mostly eighteenth-century; Consulado--material subdivided into various categories (*administrativo, aduanero, etc.*).

A separate Sección Notaría Judicial contains the invaluable protocols issued by the notaries of the viceregal capital during the three centuries of Spanish rule in Peru, classified both chronologically and alphabetically. There are a total of 162 for the sixteenth century, 2,067 for the seventeenth, and 1,200 for the eighteenth. See Archivo Nacional del Perú, *Indice de notarios de Lima y Callao cuyos protocolos se hallan en el Archivo Nacional del Perú (siglos XVI, XVII, XVIII, XIX y XX* (Lima, 1928). The most famous single item here is the Protocolo Ambulante, compiled by the notaries who accompanied the first conquistadores.

The archive still has a large quantity of unclassified papers, which are gradually being sorted and allocated to the respective sections. There is a photocopying and microfilm service, but those wishing microfilm must provide their own film for two copies. Hours for the non-vacation months are more than generous: 8 a.m. to 7:30 p.m. The director, Dr. Guillermo Durand Flórez, can be relied upon not only to be most hospitable but also to provide information on and introductions to various provincial archives which are gradually being organized under his supervision. The *Revista del Archivo Nacional,* which has appeared fairly regularly since 1920, contains a considerable amount of information on various sections.

ARCHIVO HISTORICO DEL MINISTERIO DE HACIENDA Y COMERCIO

Theoretically this archive lost its separate identity in 1970, when it was incorporated into the Archivo Nacional del Perú, but, in practice, its holdings are still housed apart, in the basement of the Palacio de Justicia. Its Sección Colonial contains approximately 1,760 manuscript volumes and more than 1,500 separate expedientes and documents. They consist essentially of the remnants of the archives of the Tribunal de Consulado, the Casa de Moneda, and the Real Hacienda; they cover the period from 1602 until independence. For an excellent guide, see Federico Schwab, *Catálogo de la Sección Colonial del Archivo Histórico* (Lima, 1944). The Consulado papers--210 volumes in excellent condition--are of particular importance not only for economic and commercial topics but also for the social history of Lima, containing as they do, abundant information on the guild's membership and internal organization. The Casa de Moneda papers provide precise details from year to year on the mintage of gold and silver. A further group of volumes of particular interest are those containing *cédulas* and viceregal orders relating to financial affairs: see Federico Schwab, *Reales cédulas, reales órdenes, decretos, autos y bandos que se guardan en el Archivo Histórico del Ministerio de Hacienda y Comercio de la República del Perú* (Lima, 1947). The unbound papers are classified into two main groups: the Colección Miscelánea and the Colección Santamaría, for which card catalogues are available. The physical amenities in this archive are poor, but its holdings are of tremendous value, and it deserves greater attention from historians. For additional information on its history and organization, see Federico Schwab, "El Archivo Histórico del Ministerio de Hacienda y Comercio del Perú," *Revista de historia de América,* 21 (1946):29-44.

BIBLIOTECA NACIONAL

A large part of the manuscript collection of the Biblioteca Nacional was destroyed by fire in 1943, but, following this disaster, the surviving items were thoroughly catalogued. The Sala de Investigaciones now contains two excellent card catalogues, one arranged chronologically, the other by subject matter, for the estimated total holdings of 120,000 documents. Many of these refer to the republican period, but the holdings on colonial Peru are extensive and, above all, easily located. As in national libraries the world over, the documents derive from many separate sources, so that there is no particular thematic unity. The diversity means, however, that every researcher can expect to find something of interest here. Those working on the sixteenth century should not miss the notarial registers of the early *escribanos* of Lima, Arequipa, and Cuzco; seventeenth-century holdings include a copy of the Ordenanzas of Toledo, made in 1604, and the *memorias* of a number of viceroys; the eighteenth-century and late colonial papers are particularly useful for economic history--tributes, mining, etc.--and there are also frequent references to rebellions and civil disturbances. The Biblioteca usually closes in April. There is an efficient photographic service.

ARCHIVO GENERAL DEL MINISTERIO DE RELACIONES EXTERIORES

One has to be both persistent and insistent in order to obtain access to this repository, which is housed in the Torre Tagle palace. Although the bulk of its material naturally relates to the post-1821 epoch, it has three or four filing cabinets literally crammed full of colonial material. Nobody in the archive knows much about this, but it seems to consist primarily of material ransacked from other archives at the time when Peru was preparing her arguments in her respective boundary disputes with Ecuador and Bolivia. For some indication of what might be available, see Guillermo Lohmann Villena, "La sección manuscritos de la Biblioteca del Ministerio de Relaciones Exteriores del Perú," *Handbook of Latin American Studies, 1940* (Cambridge, Mass., 1941):518-520. When I worked there in 1968, some of the items mentioned here could not be found--notably the forty volumes of *consulado* papers--but other interesting items turned up, particularly on Cuzco in the eighteenth century. My advice is to get in and root around.

ARCHIVO ARZOBISPAL (LIMA)

An extraordinarily rich archive, not only for the ecclesiastical history of Peru since 1543, when it was opened, but also for social history: there is abundant material on topics such as *visitas, obras pías, diezmos,* property, divorce, etc. The 2,600 legajos are organized into twenty sections; for a general description see Rubén Vargas Ugarte, S.J., "El

Archivo Arzobispal de Lima," *Handbook of Latin American Studies, 1936* (Cambridge, Mass., 1937):443-448. The documents are stored chronologically, but there is no detailed catalogue. For those not concerned primarily with religious history as such, the most fruitful sections are likely to be I (Sección Histórica), III (Comunicaciones Oficiales), VII (Legados y Obras Pías), XIII (Cofradías), XIV (Visitas Pastorales),and XX (Varios). To obtain admission, present a letter stating credentials and research interests. In my experience access is usually permitted, although I know of a recent case in which it was refused to a female researcher.

OTHER ECCLESIASTICAL ARCHIVES

The Archivo Arzobispal in Trujillo, located in the Palacio Arzobispal, is now partially catalogued--indirectly as a result of the damage caused by the 1967 and 1970 earthquakes--and open to *bona fide* researchers. It contains excellent documentation on the diocese beginning ca. 1611. Microfilming is normally permitted on application. The archives of other dioceses, notably Arequipa and Cuzco, are also inevitably of great importance, but it is impossible to generalize about access to them.

Ecclesiastical archives as a whole are the most underused in Peru. The convents of the leading orders in Lima and other cities are known to contain extensive records dating back to the very foundation of the viceroyalty, but permission to use them is very difficult to obtain, even for Peruvian scholars. One suspects that, in some cases, this is more because the convents are ashamed of their poor organization than because of deliberate secrecy. There is less difficulty with parochial records, which consist primarily of registers of births, baptisms, marriages,and deaths, of great importance for demographers. The Parroquia del Sagrario de la Iglesia Metropolitana in Lima, for example, has twenty-two baptismal registers, twelve matrimonial registers, and eleven registers recording deaths for the period from 1567. The Parroquia de San Sebastián of Lima has similar records from 1561. Such documents are perhaps of even greater value for rural areas, where communities were less mobile. Access in every case is at the discretion of the parish priest.

MUNICIPAL ARCHIVES

The *libros de cabildos,* or minute books, of the municipal corporations of the viceroyalty are sources of prime importance for the urban history of colonial Peru, providing abundant information about public administration, the foundation of towns, commercial life, markets, public hygiene, the administration of justice, social relationships, etc. Some, particularly for the sixteenth century, have found their way into the United States Library of Congress, but the records still in Peru are reasonably intact for most of the major towns and cities. Except for Huamanga, whose *libros* are in the Biblioteca Nacional, they are to be found in their respective municipal libraries. The *Libros de Cabildo* for Lima are available in published form for the period from the foundation of the city until 1639; for the rest of the colonial period they may be consulted in the excellent Biblioteca Municipal, which holds altogether forty-five volumes. The first three volumes of the *Libros de Cabildo* of Trujillo have recently been published, too (Lima, 1969); the remainder are available in manuscript form in Trujillo. There, as elsewhere, the volumes for the late seventeenth and early eighteenth centuries, when *cabildo* activity was at a low ebb, tend to be less informative than those for earlier and later periods. The first volume for Arequipa has been lost, but the Archivo Municipal there has twenty-six well-preserved *libros de actas* from 1546 to 1812. Access is usually granted willingly to these and other municipal archives. A small number of Peruvian scholars, of whom Waldemar Espinoza Soriano is the best known, have recently been making increasing use of the records of indigenous communities, which are particularly important for demographic data arising out of *visitas*.

In addition to its minute books, the Biblioteca Municipal of Lima contains thirty-one *libros de cédulas y provisiones,* which contain either originals or copies of the vast amount of municipal legislation issued by the crown, successive viceroys, the Audiencia of Lima, and the Cabildo itself. Volume I, for example, contains the *cédulas* granting Pizarro and Almagro the government of Peru. Nearly all the volumes have indices of their contents. See Juan Bromley, "Los libros de cédulas y provisiones del Archivo Histórico de la Municipalidad de Lima. Indice de sus documentos," *Revista histórica* (Lima), 19 (1952):61-202.

OTHER PROVINCIAL ARCHIVES

Most of the non-ecclesiastic archives outside Lima are rich in notarial records but disappointing as far as general administration is concerned. In Arequipa, for example, the excellent Archivo Histórico Departamental, contains a large number of *libros de protocolos notariales,* the earliest of which dates from ca. 1556, but nothing on such themes as financial administration. The notarial records alone, however, are of immense importance and are particularly numerous for the eighteenth century for those interested in social history. The Archivo Histórico del Cuzco, opened in 1949 under the supervision of the Universidad Nacional del Cuzco, is the exception to the general rule in that it contains not only the registers of the Cuzco notaries but also papers from the Real Audiencia del Cuzco and other official institutions. The *Revista del Archivo Histórico del Cuzco,* edited by Manuel Jesús Aparicio Vega, frequently publishes individual documents and partial guides to the contents of the archive.

In the majority of towns and cities in Peru notarial records remain in private hands, although it is usually not difficult to obtain access to them. In Trujillo, for example, a large number of registers are held by one of the city's principal notaries, Sr. Amayo: his cellar contains approximately 250 volumes for the colonial period alone. The Archivo Nacional is reportedly about to begin transferring these and other collections to Lima, but it seems that there will be some delay before this occurs. In Huancavelica, to give another example, colonial papers are kept in complete confusion in a windowless room in the municipal building. To read them one has to carry them into the Plaza de Armas--although again local officials do their best to be helpful.

Research on Peruvian History: Independence and the Early Republic (1780-1870)
Paul B. Ganster

Traditional historiography of the Peruvian independence and early republican periods generally has viewed the epoch in heroic terms. It has been maintained that the precursors, dating from the rebellion of Túpac Amaru in the 1780s, produced a national consciousness which provoked a confrontation between the Peruvian people and the abusive leadership of Spain. Eventually this confrontation led to the rupture of political ties with Spain and resulted in independence. Historical writing about this period has emphasized the actions of great men, from the precursors to the independence heroes to later caudillos and political leaders. The importance of rebellions against the royal officials, the great military campaigns, and the subsequent national and international political developments were continually stressed, to the exclusion of other aspects of the historical past. This traditional view of the epoch has been sustained and strengthened by the activities commemorating the 150th anniversary of Peruvian independence in 1971, and has resulted in numerous publications that are very traditional in outlook. [See, for example, José Ignacio López-Soría, *Descomposición de la dominación hispánica en el Perú* (Lima, 1973).]

In recent years this approach to Peruvian history has been challenged by a new group of scholars who have provided a fresh interpretation of the era--both for Spanish America in general and for Peru in particular. This new historiography maintains that independence came about as a result of conflicts in Europe and that in Peru independence was conceded by outside armies, not won by Peruvians. [See Timothy E. Anna, "Economic Causes of San Martín's Failure in Lima," *Hispanic American Historical Review,* 54 (November, 1974):657-81, and Heraclio Bonilla, et al., *La independencia en el Perú* (Lima, 1972).] Furthermore, independence is interpreted as a military and political occurrence that left the basic nature of the colonial period unaltered. A lucid, provocative statement of this revisionist position is to be found in the essay by Heraclio Bonilla and Karen

Spalding in "La independencia en el Perú: Las palabras y los hechos," in Bonilla, et al., *Independencia,* pp. 15-63.

This revision of the traditional view of independence and the emergence of the republic underscores the need for a new approach to the period. Historians must now go beyond the usual Lima-centric, political, and formalistic studies. It is imperative that historical writing reach a better understanding of the most basic social and economic conditions in the country from the late colonial times to 1870, when the complex phenomenon known as modernization begin to make significant headway. Bonilla and Spalding, in their article, and Jorge Basadre, in his various works. [See, for example, *Historia de la república del Perú,* 11 vols., 5th ed. (Lima, 1961-64) and *Introducción a las bases documentales para la historia de la república con algunas reflexiones,* 2 vols. (Lima, 1971).] These works have pointed out many crucial areas in need of research. The remainder of this article will continue along the same vein, identifying additional areas that merit serious investigation. Also, it will be suggested where the data necessary for these studies might be found.

First, however, an introductory note about sources is necessary. Much of the history of the period under consideration has been written from the available printed materials. These sources are, at times, surprisingly rich and varied, and consequently must not be neglected. Clearly the best way to approach the printed materials for the independence and early republican period is through Jorge Basadre's *Introducción a las bases documentales.* Written by Peru's leading historian of the republic, this volume represents the culmination of a life's work. Introductions to each sub-period covered in the work provide keen insights into the historical problems of that epoch, although from a fairly traditional perspective. As a result, *Introducción a las bases documentales* is of great value not only for Basadre's detailed knowledge of printed sources of the period, including such items as obscure pamphlets and broadsides, but also for his views and theses on Peruvian history. Annotations for many of the items listed in this great opus are useful. Unfortunately, no equivalent to Basadre's work is available for the late colonial period, but, Rubén Vargas Ugarte's *Biblioteca peruana,* 12 vols. (Lima, 1935-57) does provide a comprehensive listing of Peruvian imprints up to the 1820s. Vargas lists the location of each item and frequently includes useful annotations.

Excellent collections of imprints from the independence and early republican period are available both in Peru and in the United States. The private collection of Félix Denegri Luna in Lima and that of the Biblioteca Nacional del Perú (BNP) are the single most complete holdings of such materials. Also of some interest is the Colección Vargas Ugarte, now housed at Huachipa, near Lima. In the United States, both the Library of Congress and Yale University have significant collections of nineteenth-century Peruvian imprints.

Guides to Peruvian archives and manuscript collections are not as thorough as might be desired. Printed catalogues of the holdings of individual archives include only those for the Archivo Histórico of the Ministerio de Hacienda, now located in the Archivo General de la Nación (AGN). Most of the Lima archives have general lists of the contents of the different sections of their manuscript collections, and card files of some individual sections are available at both the AGN and BNP. The AGN also has several indexes, including those to testaments and to rural and urban property titles. The completeness and accuracy of catalogues and indexes varies widely, and investigators should take the time to check the accuracy of these. No adequate general guide exists for all Peruvian archives—in fact, there is not a good guide even to one archive, although the articles included in this volume will go a long way to meeting the need. (I am presently preparing a guide to the Archivo Arzobispal of Trujillo, which I reorganized in 1971-72. It will indicate the types of documents contained within each section of the archive and will be broadly applicable to all ecclesiastical archives in Peru.)

There are several collections of Peruvian manuscripts in the United States which should be brought to the attention of the potential investigator. The Lilly Library at Indiana University has extensive holdings on the late colonial and independence periods, covering such topics as revolts, church matters, the wars of independence, and general government affairs. Also, the collection includes a fair number of congressional documents for the period 1826 to 1870 and a considerable amount of correspondence and other material relating to church matters, laws, and the military for the same time period. Juan Friede has published an excellent description of the Peruvian manuscript holdings of the library, "Peruvian Manuscripts in the Lilly Library," *The Indiana University Bookman*, 9 (April, 1968):3-38.

The Rosenbach Foundation in Philadelphia also has a significant collection of Peruvian manuscripts dealing with the independence movement and early national history. Totaling about 500 documents, the collection covers events from the revolt of Túpac Amaru through the wars for independence and into the early years of the national period. A calendar of these manuscripts is now being prepared for publication.

The standard collections of printed documents and primary sources, including laws and legal codes for this period, are thoroughly covered by Basadre in his *Introducción a las bases documentales,* and will not be discussed here, but a publication by the Comisión Nacional del Sesquicentenario de la Independencia del Perú, the *Colección documental de la independencia del Perú,* 30 vols. (Lima, 1971-72) deserves mention. Published as part of the official celebration of the 150th anniversary of Peruvian independence, the collection consists of documents on a wide variety of topics for the period 1780 to 1822 that relate to independence. Although uneven in quality and representative of the "official" interpretation of the period, the volumes do bring together many useful items in a readily accessible form. [See Frank Safford's review of this collection in the *Hispanic American Historical Review,* 54 (August, 1974):522-24).]

A better understanding of the late colonial period is necessary in order to deal adequately with the independence and early republican eras. Only through reaching a clearer and fuller knowledge of the nature of the society, economy, and the major institutions and corporate entities of Peru on the eve of the political separation from Spain will it be possible to determine effectively changes or continuities for the period from colonial times to 1870. First and foremost, a more comprehensive picture of the social structure of Peru during the late colonial period is necessary. In recent years, a number of studies have come out that make substantial headway towards providing a clearer picture of society and in relation to the rest of Peruvian life. For example, Leon Campbell, Mark Burkholder, and Paul Ganster have focused on elite groups, while Karen Spalding has examined rural Indian society in the central sierra: Leon Campbell, "A Colonial Establishment: Creole Domination of the Audiencia of Lima During the Late Eighteenth Century," *Hispanic American Historical Review,* 52 (February, 1972):1-25; Mark Burkholder, "From Creole to Peninsular: The Transformation of the Audiencia of Lima," *Hispanic American Historical Review,* 52 (August, 1972):395-415; Paul B. Ganster, *A Social*

History of the Secular Clergy of Lima During the Middle Decades of the Eighteenth Century (Ann Arbor, 1974); Karen Spalding, *Indian Rural Society in Colonial Peru: The Example of Huarochirí* (Ann Arbor, 1967). Also of related interest is John Fisher's *Government and Society in Colonial Peru: The Intendant System, 1784-1814* (London, 1970). Studies of this sort should be carried forward through the independence and the early republic to 1870. In this fashion, changes in the structure and composition of society would stand out in bold relief. Social history is also needed for the same period to add depth and meaning to the traditional institutional and political histories that have been produced thus far. For examples of the types of applications of social history, see the article by James Lockhart, "The Social History of Colonial Spanish America: Evolution and Potential," *Latin American Research Review,* 7 (Spring, 1972):6-45. Much of what has been done by social historians for the colonial period could also be undertaken for the nineteenth century with only minor modifications of techniques.

Traditional historiography has tended to deal with the urban and rural masses only at times when these groups have risen in rebellion or otherwise have become involved in political events (see Basadre, *Introducción a las bases documentales,* I, pp. 198-200). Very little research has been done concerning the composition of these groups, their relationships with the broader society, or their change and evolution through time. This neglect is due, in part, to the elitist genealogical and great-man traditions of Peruvian historical writing, but it is also due to the types of sources available. Members of the lower levels of society tend to appear less frequently in the ordinary documentation of the period than do their more affluent fellowmen.

Nonetheless, archival sources are adequate for the study of urban, lower-class groups, and to a lesser extent, for their counterparts in rural areas. Even though it might be impossible to study an individual or even a particular family from this section of society, it is definitely possible to study the class as a whole. Except for the very lowest elements, such as the *léperos* or vagabonds, the popular classes participated in the activities of organized society on a regular basis and in many different ways. That participation frequently generated some sort of written record. These people were married, produced children, and had them baptised; they died, owned small amounts of property, rented rooms or apartments, bought and sold goods, became involved in civil and criminal law cases, made wills, joined *cofradías,* and so forth. Birth, marriage, and death were all recorded in the parish records, and these are extant for both rural and urban areas and are to be found in both local parish archives and the central archives of the bishoprics and archbishoprics. Cofradía records, which contain significant socioeconomic data about persons of all levels of society, are scattered through the ecclesiastical archives in Lima and the provinces. They also may be found in the Beneficencia Pública in Lima, the AGN, and to a lesser extent, in the manuscript collection of the BNP. At times, parish archives, particularly those in rural areas, have important holdings of cofradía records. Marriage and divorce cases in the ecclesiastical archives and in the AGN provide very interesting information on the daily lives of the persons of the lower strata of society.

The AGN also has other types of records of a more secular nature that contain pertinent data on the lower levels of society. Particularly useful are the civil and criminal law cases which have incidental information on many social types. Notarial records are similarly useful and provide a wide range of detail about everyday affairs for the entire spectrum of society. The series of notarials for Lima is virtually complete for the period under consideration. The same types of sources exist in provincial cities, but both the legal and notarial archives tend to be poorly organized and access is difficult, if not impossible. Preservation of documentation in provincial cities and rural areas is poorer than in the metropolitan center, and research on social history of the provinces is correspondingly more difficult.

All of the above sources contain information on the middle elements of society as well as on the elite groups. Additional data on these individuals are to be found in the records of the corporations, tribunals, and ministries with which they were associated in one capacity or another. Genealogical studies traditionally have concentrated on elite families, and these provide useful information for the period from the end of the colonial period through the early republic. Of particular interest is the *Revista del Instituto Peruano de Investigaciones Genealógicas,* 14 vols. (Lima, 1946-65). Individual articles and monographs of a genealogical nature are too numerous to mention, but an important example of this genre is Swayne y Mariátegui's *Mis antepasados* (Lima, 1951). Private family archives often extend back into the period under consideration and should be consulted whenever possible. Other family archives have passed into the collections of public archives and libraries and thus are more accessible. The BNP has parts of some of these and the Sección Histórica of the AGN contains the papers of the family of Mariano Felipe Paz-Soldán.

It is not, of course, possible nor desirable to isolate entirely the study of society and social classes from economic and political currents. Rather, society and social history are intermingled with fundamental aspects of economic history, such as that of the agrarian sector, where basic questions remain unanswered. Land ownership and land tenure during the first part of the nineteenth century are not well understood nor is the problem of the social value of landholdings versus the economic value of that resource. The role of capital and the debt structure of the agrarian sector also have not been adequately researched. Of major interest is the evolution of the *censos,* or mortgages, during the early republic and the related topic of the significance of the 1839 law of abolition of *mayorazgos*. In light of the beginnings of modernization of coastal agriculture by the late 1840s, the fate of the Indian villages and small landholders has not been thoroughly investigated. Finally, it should be pointed out that most of what we know about nineteenth-century agriculture in Peru pertains to the coast; the situation in the sierra remains largely unknown.

A number of these problems will be dealt with by Juan Engelsen, a UCLA graduate student, in a forthcoming dissertation, "The Rejuvenation of Agriculture and the Formation of a Plutocracy on Coastal Peru, 1825-1880." Engelsen links changes in the landowning aristocracy to agricultural developments, and both of these are related to internal and external economic changes, such as the growth of guano exports and the changing demand on world markets for agricultural products.

Printed sources for agrarian history are adequately covered by Basadre in his *Introducción a las bases documentales*. Manuscript sources remain largely unexploited. Fortunately, an excellent guide to documentary sources is available in the work by Susan and Douglas Horton, "Sources for the Investigation of Peruvian Agrarian History," LTC (Land Tenure Center, Madison, Wisconsin), 84 (February, 1973). This guide lists the types of documents useful for agrarian history, what they typically contain, and where they may be found. Also included is a description of the

Independence and the Early Republic 231

holdings of the recently established Centro de Documentación Agraria in Lima which has the archives of many of the haciendas affected by the recent agrarian reform laws.

Many other aspects of the economic history of this period merit attention. Studies by Basadre; W. M. Mathew, "The First Anglo-Peruvian Debt and Its Settlement, 1822-1849," *Journal of Latin American Studies,* 2 (May, 1970):81-98 and "The Imperialism of Free Trade: Peru, 1820-1870," *Economic History Review,* 21 (December, 1968):562-79; H. Bonilla, *La expansión comercial británica en el Perú* (Lima: Instituto de Estudios Peruanos, 1974) and "La coyuntura comercial del siglo XIX en el Perú," *Revista del Museo Nacional,* 35 (1967-68):159-87; Jonathan Levin, *The Export Economies* (Cambridge, Mass., 1960), among others, have made great strides toward describing the broad economic relationships between Peru and Europe and dealing with the presence of British and other foreign merchants in Peru from the late colonial years through the early republic. Most of these efforts have been grounded in trade statistics available in Europe. What is needed now is to relate these international relationships to the domestic economy and to the economically active groups through studies based on the rich manuscript collections in Peru. Ernesto Yepes del Castillo has initiated this broader use of sources with his *Perú, 1820-1920: Un siglo de desarrollo capitalista* (Lima, 1972), but a great deal more remains to be investigated. Interesting and fruitful research topics include, for example, the changes occurring within the community of Peruvian merchants during the independence period, the precise nature of effects of the new flood of imports on the merchants and domestic industry, the Peruvian involvement in the whaling trade, the significance of contraband trade during independence and the early republic, and the manner in which the traditional coastal-sierra relationship was affected by the modernization of coastal agriculture and technological advances in transportation. The question of who received the guano money and how that windfall was utilized is of paramount importance. Mining for this period also must be restudied just as it has been for the late colonial period in John Fisher's, *Silver Mines and Silver Miners in Colonial Peru, 1776-1824* (Liverpool, 1977). The decline of mining is constantly referred to in the literature on independence and the early republic, yet there is some indication that the total production of the mining sector did not decline as drastically and as permanently as once supposed. [See for example, H. Bonilla, "La coyuntura comercial."]

The principal source of documentation of economic activity in Peru during this period is the Archivo Histórico del Ministerio de Hacienda in the AGN. Fortunately for the researcher, a number of catalogues for this archive have been published, and the staff is in the process of producing supplements: Perú. Ministerio de Hacienda y Comercio: *Catálogo de la Sección Colonial del Archivo Histórico* (Lima, 1944); *Catálogo de la Sección Republicana, 1821-1822* (Lima, 1945); *Catálogo de la Sección Republicana, 1823-1825* (Lima, 1946); *El Índice del Archivo del Tribunal del Consulado de Lima* (Lima, 1948); Lima. Archivo General de la Nación: *Catálogo de la Sección Republicana del Archivo Histórico de Hacienda, 1826-1830* (Lima, 1972); *Catálogo de la Sección Republicana del Archivo Histórico de Hacienda, 1831-1835*, No. 2 (Lima, 1974). A wide variety of documents is in this archive, and the researcher is referred to the catalogues cited above for content descriptions.

Some consulado records are in the AGN, as are the records of the Archivo Judicial; the latter contain the civil and criminal law cases of the republican period and form an extremely important source for the study of merchants and the economy during this period. Similar collections are to be found in the provincial cities, which is also the case of the Archive of the Corte Superior in Trujillo, containing a large amount of litigation from the republican era. Mining records may be found in the Minería Section in the AGN.

The notarial records of the capital and the provincial towns of Peru are potentially an excellent source of material for economic history. They are valuable for the study of individual merchants, entrepreneurs, artisans, and people of other economic levels. Among the categories of documents found in these registers are sales of real and other types of property, obligations of a financial or commercial nature, mortgages (*censos*), testaments which frequently list inventories of personal estates, and so forth. It should be noted that information on the economic activities of the clergy, including the clergy in rural areas, frequently is to be found in the ecclesiastical archives in the sections dealing with law cases.

Considerable attention has been focused on the upper levels of the political bureaucracy since independence; likewise the changes in legal forms have been dealt with by Francisco García Calderón, *Diccionario de* la legislación peruana, 2 vols. (Lima, 1860-62) and Jorge Basadre, Los fundamentos de la historia del derecho, 2nd ed. (Lima, 1967) and Historia de la república. Still, very little research has been done on the effect of these changes on the day-to-day functioning of the bureaucracies involved. Of course, this type of data is crucial for understanding the ultimate effects of political and legal changes on the general populace. For example, did the political unrest and turmoil at the top cause a serious decay in the functions performed by government bureaucracies? Was the membership of these bureaucracies radically altered over time? Did a basic continuity in administration exist for the early republic? The only way to answer these questions is to go directly to the records of the various branches of government involved and to determine whether and how the daily functioning of government changed or remained the same. The effects of the new legal codes must be studied through cases showing direct application and enforcement of the law vis-à-vis individuals.

Finally, a better assessment of the Peruvian church is needed. The central question is the change in the role of the church in Peruvian life over the period from the beginning of independence to 1870. The church exercised enormous influence on the populace during the colonial period, but existing studies give little information on how this relationship fared during and after independence. [See, for example, Rubén Vargas Ugarte, Historia de la iglesia en el Perú, vol. 5 (Burgos, 1962).] Changes in the temporal authority of the church are most evident and are the result of a progression of secular and liberal attacks that culminated with the constitutions of 1856 and 1860. Specifically, state collection of tithes was eliminated, the fuero eclesiástico was abolished, secular education was pushed, among other things. While these legal measures are well known, little has been done to measure their effects on the daily functioning of the church. Less obvious but equally important questions, such as the changing composition of the clergy, also have been neglected. The best sources for the study of these topics are in the ecclesiastical archives, specifically the archivos arzobispales. Convent archives, such as that of La Merced in Cuzco, also contain material relating to these questions. Civil archives, particularly the AGN, have sections dealing with church matters, and should be consulted.

The period of independence and the early republic, as can clearly be seen from the above discussion, is in need of basic studies based on the rich manuscript collections in Peru. Previously, the attention of historians was focused primarily on national and international political events, resulting in an incomplete understanding of the period. Most urgently required now are studies of the composition of society, the economy, and the major institutions of the epoch. In terms of sources, these studies must go beyond the printed materials and take advantage of the largely untouched archives available to the investigator.

Research on Peruvian History: 1870-1930
Jesús Chavarría

Of the various guides on the historical literature of republican Peru available to the researcher, Jorge Basadre's *Introducción a las bases documentales para la historia de la república del Perú con algunas reflexiones,* 2 vols. (Lima: P. L. Villanueva, 1971) is the indispensable general source. It is not only the product of a lifetime's work but also the work of a master craftsman in the field of historical writing. There is no better place to start for "non-Peruvian graduate students intending to undertake research" on the period, 1870-1930. Chapters XVII to XXII provide a many-faceted account of primary and published materials more than sufficient to initiate consideration of the period, 1870-1930, its principal problem, and problems.

The principal, or primary problem of the era is, of course, how to account for its general significance; that is to say, what does the period *mean* in relation to the 150-year existence of republican Peru? Its principal or leading problems, on the other hand, reflect the many parts and aspects of the social process characteristic of the general epoch. Such aspects fall under different categories such as economy, social structure, politics, and culture, though they are inter-dependent within a fundamental and dynamic organic unity, the human society of Peru. Indeed, one of the particular strengths of Basadre's *magnum opus* is the attention given to cultural production, ranging from such institutional activities as education and science to concern with *costumbres, cuentos, leyendas, y tradiciones*.

As will be seen, the most recent monographs on our period suggest that its primary problem (the problem of its general significance) be viewed as a time when the "onset of modernization" takes place in Peru. Even research on the half-century following independence tends to confirm this view, as do also some general works on the entire region of Latin America. In a seminal book, *Historia contemporánea de América Latina*

(Madrid: Alianza Editorial, 1969), Tulio Halperín Donghi proposed that beginning in the 1880s--"*años mas, años menos*"--ensued a period that he characterizes as a "maturation of the neo-colonial order," the result of modernization (p. 280). A somewhat dissimilar study, D. C. M. Platt's *Latin America and British Trade, 1806-1914* (London: Adam and Charles Black, 1972) would appear to corroborate Halperín Donghi's periodization in saying that the years between the early 1800s and the 1850s were a time of "modest expansion, not of radical change" in the social order of the region, and that the "take-off point in the economic relationship between Latin America and the outside world" did not come until the latter part of the century (the years of "maturation" in Halperín Donghi's term) (p. 3). However, not all of the recent research on Peru employs the concepts of neocolonialism and dependency used in the *Historia contemporánea,* so agreement is not universal on the question of just what kind of society "modernization" produced.

The two leading students of Peru's nineteenth-century economy, William M. Mathew [see "Anglo-Peruvian Commercial and Financial Relations, 1820-1865, With Special Reference to Antony Gibbs and Sons and the Guano Trade" (Ph.D. dissertation, London School of Economics and Political Science, The University of London, 1964); "The Imperialism of Free Trade: Peru, 1820-1870," *The Economic History Review,* 21 (December, 1968):563; and four other articles, including "Antony Gibbs & Sons, the Guano Trade, and the Peruvian Government, 1842-61," in: D. C. M. Platt (ed.), *Business Imperialism: An Inquiry Based on British Experience in Latin America Before 1930* (Oxford: Clarendon Press, 1977), and the to be expected magisterial *The House of Gibbs and the Peruvian Guano Monopoly* (to be published by the Instituto de Estudios Peruanos)]; and Heraclio Bonilla [see his "Aspects de l'histoire économique et sociale du Pérou au XIXe siècle, 1821-1879" (Thèse de doctorat, Ecole Pratique des Hautes Etudes, Université de Paris, 2 vols., 1970), and "Auguste Dreyfus y el monopolio del guano" (Lima: Instituto de Estudios Peruanos pamphlet, 1973)] generally confirm the periodization of Platt and Halperín Donghi, and, while not employing the concept of neocolonialism, they do use that of dependence. Mathew has been the most restrained in characterizing the relationship between Great Britain and Peru in the early part of the century, in contrast to Bonilla who sees the fifty-year period following independence as a "conquest" and "domination" of Peruvian commerce and finance by Great Britain. Nevertheless their works highly complement each other. To a degree, their views support some of the generalizations made in an earlier study by Jonathan V. Levin, *The Export Economies* (Cambridge, Mass.: Harvard University Press, 1960), though Mathew has on several occasions called attention to "ambiguities" in Levin's work [see his "The First Anglo-Peruvian Debt and its Settlement, 1822-49," *Journal of Latin American Studies*, 2 (May, 1970):81-82]. Mathew's focus on the early period's leading foreign merchant house, The House of Gibbs, and Bonilla's on the era's principal and fascinating foreign entrepreneur and financier, M. Auguste Dreyfus, provide a magnificent economic and social portrait of the age from the perspective of national institutions with a high degree of historical specificity. Mathew's work in particular is a model of traditional British historical craftsmanship, though increasingly venturesome in interpretation.

Not so reticent about generalizing are two other monographs, Ernesto Yepes del Castillo's *Perú, 1820-1920, un siglo de desarrollo capitalista* (Lima: Instituto de Estudios Peruanos, 1972) and William A. Bollinger's "The Rise of United States Influence in the Peruvian Economy, 1869-1921" (Master's Thesis, University of California at Los Angeles, 1971). As one reviewer remarked about Yepes's work, "Crucial assertions appear as received truths rather than hypotheses requiring substantiation." [See R. Thorpe's review in *Latin American Review of Books*, 1 (Spring 1973):191-193.] Yepes's work, though a high gloss of Peruvian economic developments, is nevertheless a useful study because of its Peruvian documentation (unlike Mathew and Bonilla, whose works rest mainly on British and French government and private papers), and general line of interpretation and periodization. Bollinger's study, on the other hand, though more historically grounded and exceptional for a master's thesis, uses historical evidence principally, it seems, to support a highly abstract "theoretical model" (the André Gunder Frank "metropolis-satellite" dependency model) which leads the author to deal, almost exclusively, with market relations and to generalize on that basis.

All of these studies, excepting Mathew's, have one thing in common: they all agree that at the turn of the century Peruvian economic relations with the capitalist West underwent a highly significant modification. In the words of Bonilla, the economy at the turn of the century changed owing to the direct "placement of British capital in the agricultural and mining sector" ("Aspects de l'histoire économique," 2:380); and, in those of Bollinger, "during the 1869-1921 period the Peruvian economy began to be integrated into the internal market of the United States" (p. 14). So these studies, whether they use Halperín Donghi's concepts or not, tend to support the thesis of a "maturing neocolonial order" for the period, 1870-1930.

By no means do these works conclude the many tasks still required for reconstructing the main outline of the Peruvian economy in the nineteenth century, but they do provide a basis for intelligent discussion about its general characteristics, and even more important, with an invaluable canon of historical explanation: the economic canon. So far, economic studies have almost exclusively focused on the export-import sectors of the economy, and there is now a great need for continuing research along the lines of Francois Chevalier's pioneering effort, "L'expansion de la grande propiété dans le Haut-Pérou au XXe siècle," *Annales,* 21 (July-August, 1966):821-25. Also to be consulted is his "Official *Indigenismo* in Peru in 1920: Origins, Significance, and Socioeconomic Scope," in Magnus Mörner (ed.), *Race and Class in Latin America* (New York and London: Columbia University Press, 1970). There is a need for research on agrarian developments on a regional basis, and also for studies on the impact of the extractive and related industries on the highland's ecology. There is also a great need for relating events in the economic sphere to events in other social domains, such as the pioneering study of rural insurrection by Jean Piel, "A propos d'un soulèvement rural péruvien au début du vingtième siècle: Tocroyoc (1921)," *Revue d'histoire moderne et contemporaine,* 14 (October-December, 1967):375-405. Among graduate students working on Latin America at the Ecole Pratique des Hautes Etudes, VIe Section, the Sorbonne, I found widespread interest, and ongoing research, on Andean history: problems dealing precisely with the impact of modernization on the Andean social world at the turn of the century and on the peasant insurrections that it unleashed.

In my own work [see "The Intellectuals and the Crisis of Modern Peruvian Nationalism: 1870-1919," *Hispanic American Historical Review,* 50 (May, 1970):257-278; "Desaparición del Perú colonial, 1870-1919," *Aportes,* 23 (January, 1972):120-153; and "José Carlos Mariátegui, Revolutionary Nationalist; The Origins and Crisis of Modern Peruvian Nationalism, 1870-1930" (Ph.D. dissertation, The University of California at Los Angeles,

1967)], I have sought to characterize the spirit of the age as a time of high nationalist awareness, and in a forthcoming study of José Carlos Mariátegui, I view the period in terms of a Peruvian modernization that intensified dependency and produced a neocolonial society distinguished by a variety of nationalist ideological formulations and movements. These were times of giant nationalist intellectuals, of men and women like Manuel González Prada, Javier Prado y Ugarteche, Clorinda Matto de Turner, Manuel Vicente Villarán, Juana Manuela Gorriti, José de la Riva Agüero, Francisco García Calderón, Víctor Andrés Belaúnde, José Carlos Mariátegui, Víctor Raúl Haya de la Torre, Luis Alberto Sánchez, Jorge Basadre, Raúl Porras Barrenechea, and many more individuals of intellectual quality.

It is also a period of giants in the political sphere. Howard L. Karno's "Augusto B. Leguía: The Oligarchy and the Modernization of Peru, 1870-1930" (Ph.D. dissertation, University of California at Los Angeles, 1970) deals with the era's most successful and fascinating political leader. Leguía presided over one-quarter of the era as President (1908-1912 and 1919-1930), and over four more years as Chief of Cabinet for the imperial president, José Pardo (1904-1908). Karno posits a socioeconomic oligarchy politically organized around El Partido Civil, and its undoing by a proscribed *civilista*, the enigmatic Augusto B. Leguía. His study assimilates considerable and notable economic data in characterizing the *civilista* bourgeoisie and its hegemony and weighs excellently the high stakes of political dramas of the age. While the study is not entirely convincing in its attempt to present Leguía as an innovator and modernizer, it ably portrays him as the *caudillo* of an ascending middle-class (incidentally from which derived his "progressive" image).

Karno may not succeed in presenting Leguía as a modernizer, but Carl F. Herbold's, Jr., "Developments in the Peruvian Administrative System, 1919-1930: Modern and Traditional Qualities of Government under Authoritarian Regimes" (Ph.D. dissertation, Yale University, 1974) does succeed in showing that he contributed fundamentally to the modernization of Peruvian government bureaucracy and administration. To such a degree did Leguía contribute to the modernization of government administration that it later became "notable for its augmented strength and penetration of national society and its 'rationalization' to serve the authoritarian leadership" (p. ii). Herbold's study is a sophisticated handling of the problem of modernizing bureaucracies, especially in its use of biographical profiles of middle-management and ministerial elites. It suffers perhaps one weakness: its conceptualization of the social process tends to be somewhat static.

From all of these recent studies emerges an ever clearer explanation of the process of modernization in Peru; how the fact that the impetus and resources for change and modernization essentially come from the outside and largely determine the kind of modernizing process that unfolds. A case in point is Peter F. Klarén's "Origins of the Peruvian Aprista Party: A Study of Social and Economic Change in the Department of La Libertad, 1870-1932" (Ph.D. dissertation, University of California at Los Angeles, 1968), published in 1973 by the University of Texas Press. Klarén's study ably shows how the modernization of the north coast sugar industry, beginning in the late nineteenth century, eventually produced a social and political situation that led to the emergence of the Peruvian Aprista party, an essentially authoritarian and traditional political organization that cultivated an innovative and, indeed, even revolutionary style through the adept manipulation of ideology and political program. Relying on, among other sources, the archives of the Cámara de Comercio, Agricultura y Industria del Departamento de la Libertad, Klarén reconstructs an exceptional socio-economic background for the analysis of political events.

The new social history must do more than explain events at the level of material base, social structure, and political hegemony; it must also explain events at the level of superstructure. Basadre's *Bases documentales* is an excellent guide for locating some of the standard sources for investigating how socioeconomic modernization affected society at the level of culture and even consciousness. Basadre's own *Historia de la república del Perú*, 11 vols. (Lima: Ediciones "Historia," 1961-68), includes considerable learned discussions of intellectual and literary events. But the indispensable general guide for cultural history is Luis Alberto Sánchez's *La literatura peruana*, 5 vols. (Lima: Ediciones de Ediventas, 1965), its sins of omission and commission notwithstanding. Also important are Sánchez, *Valdelomar o la belle époque* (México: Fondo de Cultura Económica, 1969); Luis Monguió, *La poesía postmodernista peruana* (Berkeley and Los Angeles, Mexico: University of California Press and Fondo de Cultura Económica, 1954); and Mario Castro Arenas, *La novela peruana y la evolución social* (Lima: Ediciones Cultura y Libertad, n.d.).

And we have not even mentioned the need for research on race and class relations, and a good deal more, though this is a good place to mention Magali S. Larson's and Arlene Eisen Bergman's *Social Stratification in Peru* (Berkeley: Institute of International Studies, 1969), for an excellent discussion of the problem and problems of dealing with Peruvian social structure. An interesting characterization of Peruvian women and of Lima's social mores for our period can be found in William W. Sanger, *The History of Prostitution* (New York, 1910), pp. 367-369. For urban studies on Lima itself, see Richard M. Morse (ed.), *Lima en 1900* (Lima: Instituto de Estudios Peruanos, 1973), and also his "The Lima of Joaquín Capelo: A Latin American Archetype," *Journal of Contemporary History*, 3 (July, 1969):95-110.

The cumulative contribution of these studies has been to throw the configurations of nineteenth-century society and culture into sharp, dynamic relief. Events not only achieve concreteness at the level of economic relations but also at the level of social, political, and cultural relations, so that we get a truly dynamic impression of a world in the throes of change and modernization. As such, the real historical situation of Peru begins to emerge, especially in relation to how Peruvian events are affected by outside, foreign interests and influences. One can conceive of this new historiography as an emerging, new social history in the sense that it is research that focuses on the social process itself, on those conjunctures when economic, class, political, and cultural forces intersect, converge, and thereby produce real events (rather than generalizing as has been done in the past, from limited and often highly ethnocentric perceptions of "political" data and events). In these studies the student will find a rich bibliography of sources, to include government and private papers, newspapers, private archives and collections, periodicals--in short, a rich literature that has contributed vastly to our knowledge of this crucial era: the emergence of modern Peru, 1870-1930.

Among the many libraries the student will want to keep in mind are La Biblioteca Nacional, especially its collections in the Sala de Investigaciones; La Biblioteca Pública de la Cámara de Diputados with its collection of congressional debates; El Archivo de la Beneficencia de Lima; El Archivo Histórico de Arequipa; La Biblioteca Central de la Universidad Nacional Mayor de San Marcos (and the various *facultad* libraries); La

Universidad Nacional de Ingeniería; La Pontífica Universidad Católica del Perú (especially the library of the Instituto Riva-Agüero); Universidad Nacional Agraria; the Ministerio de Hacienda; El Archivo de la Dirección Nacional de Estadística y Censo; and, last but not least, the private library of Dr. Félix Denegri Luna, whose kindness to researchers on the history of Peru is well-known. Of the many bibliographical guides available, some of the principal ones are: *Anuario bibliográfico peruano*, the *Boletín de la Biblioteca Nacional, Boletín bibliográfico, Documenta,* and *Revista histórica*. Also useful is Carl Herbold, Jr. and Steve Stein, *Guía bibliográfico para la historia social y política del Perú en el siglo XX, 1895-1960* (Lima: Instituto de Estudios Peruanos, n.d.).

Sources for the Study of Twentieth-Century Peruvian Social and Political History
Peter F. Klarén

The "great man" historiographic tradition in Peru is today increasingly being called into question by a new generation of young Peruvian historians. Not long ago, a furious debate was touched off in the Lima media by the publication of a revisionist interpretation of the Peruvian independence movement.[1] Accused of unpatriotically debunking the nation's traditional heroes, the revisionists on the contrary sought only to add a new social and economic dimension to the interpretation of this movement. More recently this debate focused on the use of certain textbooks in high school classes and revolved around the issue of whether history should be taught as a complex and intricate web of economic and social forces, cultural traditions, and ideas and not merely as the heroic deeds of a few great men. The purpose of this article is to contribute to furthering this tendency by focusing on some potentially valuable new source materials for the study of twentieth-century Peruvian political and social history.

FAMILY PAPERS AND MEMOIRS

Like other historiographic traditions in Peru, the art of the memoir, whether it be political or simply autobiographical, is poorly developed. The general dearth of this historical genre may be due to the hazardous and generally precarious nature of Peruvian politics, which constantly threatens those who venture forth into its often dangerous waters. Indeed, in the highly charged and often polarized world of Peruvian politics, where power has been wielded by a very closed and reduced circle of families, the political memoir has been consciously eschewed because of the potential threat it represented to the practitioner's immediate heirs

---

1. Heraclio Bonilla, et al., *La independencia en el Perú* (Lima, 1972).

and family. Then too, in view of the society's general stage of development, it would be wrong to expect, perhaps, a tradition of autobiographical writing akin to say England or France, even though most members of the country's political elite may at one time have studied at Oxford or the Sorbonne.

This is not to say that such writing is nonexistent in Peruvian historiography. Such important twentieth-century political figures as Víctor Andrés Belaúnde, Luis Antonio Eguiguren, José Luis Bustamante y Rivero, and more recently Luis Alberto Sánchez among others have all contributed intelligent and sometimes revealing memoirs. Far less common, however, have been the formal writings of business and agricultural leaders, who, precisely because of the interrelationship between business and politics in Peru, have long been in a position to cast light on the dynamics of politics. The only published memoir of a planter, whether he be in sugar or cotton, with which this writer is familiar is that of the Trujillano Rafael Larco Herrera, *Memorias* (Lima, 1947). And while it is sometimes valuable in detailing the economic growth of the sugar industry along the north coast, the Larco memoir largely eschews controversy and does little to lay bare the inner workings of local or national politics.

Perhaps this reason alone makes the discovery of the Aspillaga Anderson papers such a landmark in the field of modern Peruvian social, economic, and political history; for while the papers of this leading sugar planting family do not constitute a printed or published memoir in the formal sense, they happily go far beyond that genre in their revelations of the inner dynamics of coastal society. Thanks to the 1969 agrarian reform, we have the raw material to reconstruct the social and economic life of a major plantation along Peru's north coast. More importantly for our purposes the Aspillaga papers provide one of the richest sources yet found for the study of Peruvian politics.

The Aspillaga papers are housed in the Centro de Documentación Agraria (CDA) located in the Rimac District (Paita 429) only a short walk from the Plaza de Armas. They include the business records (account books, *planillas,* official correspondence, and the like) of the plantation Cayaltí, one of the largest sugar plantations in the country, and cover a virtually unbroken 100 years of the plantation's existence since its purchase by the Aspillaga family in 1869. The partially catalogued business correspondence carried on between the administrators of Cayaltí (some fifty miles southeast of Chiclayo) and the *gerente* or central administrative offices in Lima comprises the most noteworthy section of the papers.[2] From the 1920s this correspondence flowed at regular weekly or biweekly intervals between and among the Aspillaga brothers, who alternated administering in the field at Cayaltí and managing the Lima headquarters.

On one level, these letters reveal the everyday workings of the plantation, ranging in subject matter from the latest price quotations on the Liverpool market to the problems of labor recruitment and supervision, from crop rotations and irrigation techniques to the purchase of fertilizers, from government export policies and taxes to the daily food ration provided for field workers--in short the daily details of operating a million dollar agricultural enterprise. On another level, the letters provide some extraordinary material on the mechanics of local and national politics, for the brothers discuss, sometimes in the most intimate manner, those aspects of local and national politics which interconnect and mesh with the world of big business and high finance. What emerges in some respects is a confirmation of the Peruvian left's longstanding critique of the nation's political evolution--namely the interconnection between economic success and political favors among an oligarchical elite. True enough there are many nuances in the socio-political picture which perhaps assuage the wholly black interpretation of a ruthless elite bent on dominating and subjecting the downtrodden *mestizo* and Indian worker. The Aspillagas do not come out, so to speak, *all* bad, but there is enough here of blacklisting, buying of local officials, the formation of company unions, and the general anti-labor conspiracies indulged in regularly by the coastal planter oligarchy to outrage even the most moderate observer of the Peruvian political scene. Moreover, the back-and-forth flow of power from Cayaltí and the prefect's office in Chiclayo and the powerful Sociedad Nacional Agraria (SNA), significantly only a short walk from the Aspillaga offices in downtown Lima, stands out in sharp relief. It is this interplay between local and national interests which is starkly revealed in the Aspillaga papers and which will doubtless make this the richest single source for the study of twentieth-century Peruvian politics for some time to come.

---

2. Mark Sonnenblick, "Catálogo general de la hacienda Cayaltí," mimeo (Lima: CDA, 1971).

BUSINESS RECORDS AND HACIENDA ARCHIVES

Other hacienda and business records recently acquired by the CDA also cast valuable light on the structure of the Peruvian body politic. Take, for example, the archives of the sugar plantation Casa Grande, the largest of its kind on the west coast of South America, if not all the continent. Founded in the 1880s by that intrepid German immigrant, Juan Gildemeister, who made a fortune in the Peruvian nitrate business before plunging into the sugar business shortly after the War of the Pacific, Casa Grande became the prototype of the expansionist hacienda along the Peruvian coast during the late nineteenth and early twentieth centuries.[3] The Casa Grande archives, unfortunately, are still housed at the plantation which is located some thirty miles north of Trujillo. Judging from the sheer quantity of materials, the reconstruction of Casa Grande's business and labor practices will not be an easy task. A preliminary inventory of the archive by Colin Harding and Juan Granda O.[4] runs to some twenty-seven single spaced pages and indicates the existence of over 1,000 documents (account books, letter books, *planillas*, and the like) going back to the 1880s. That a portion of the company's official correspondence is written in code is perhaps enough to indicate the political significance of these archives. Along with other hacienda records held by the CDA, which are listed in a preliminary fashion in the first *Boletín* of the Centro de Documentación Agraria in 1973, they promise further to illuminate the process of oligarchical politics. At the same time these records will certainly deepen our knowledge of other socio-political phenomena such as the formation of a rural proletariat and the emergence of organized labor in the countryside. For the first time, we have precise and detailed information on a number of important subjects, ranging from the *enganche* system, labor recruitment, and migration to tenancy and syndicalism.

---

3. Peter F. Klarén, *La formación de las haciendas azucareras y los orígenes del Apra* (Lima, 1970) and *Modernization, Dislocation and Aprismo: Origins of the Peruvian Aprista Party, 1870-1932* (Austin, Texas, 1973).

4. Colin Harding and Juan Granda O., "Inventario del archivo de la ex-empresa Agrícola Chicama S. A. Hacienda Casa Grande," mimeo (Lima, 1973).

PROFESSIONAL ASSOCIATION ARCHIVES

Equally important for the study of Peruvian politics are the archives of various professional associations which have strongly influenced the shape and direction of public policy throughout the century. One of the more notable of these organizations, particularly as commerce and industry have become increasingly significant in the economic evolution of the nation, has been the Chamber of Commerce, with its local branches or counterparts in the provinces. Both Jorge Basadre and Rómulo Ferrero on the national level[5] and Peter F. Klarén[6] on the local level have made valuable use of the records of such organizations, which often, like the proverbial forgotten trunk of letters in the attic, must be diligently tracked down by the historian turned detective. The reports, letters, and memoranda of the various departmental and municipal chambers provide a wealth of information on important socioeconomic and political matters.

Perhaps even more important are the newly available records of the powerful Sociedad Nacional Agraria (SNA). Another historical windfall from the 1969 Agrarian Reform Law, the SNA archives promise to yield significant new material for the study of agrarian history and politics, so very important in a largely rural society such as Peru. Most of the official SNA records have been transferred to the Centro de Documentación Agraria, now the Archivo del Fuero Agrario, and like the Aspillaga papers they are now in the process of being organized and catalogued by the CDA staff. The SNA was founded in 1896 largely as a pressure group for the nation's sugar planters, but the halcyon days of its power and influence appear to have occurred after World War I when the organization began to broaden its already elitist coastal membership, first to include the nation's cotton growers and later its rice growers and cattlemen (1930s and 1940s). Moreover, reflecting the emergence of more "middling" agricultural and merchant groups during the 1920s and 1930s, the SNA moved during the latter decade to broaden its membership and thereby extend its influence among medium and small sized farmers. All of these changes, as well as the increasing influence of the state in the operation of the

---

5. Jorge Basadre and Rómulo Ferrero, *Historia de la Cámara de Comercio de Lima* (Lima, 1963).

6. Klarén, *Formación* and *Modernization*.

Society in the late 1920s, make the records of the SNA for our purposes a particularly significant resource.

The range of materials located so far in the SNA archives is, to say the least, staggering and will occupy a legion of historians for quite some time. Like the Aspillaga papers, most of the SNA archive now occupies one entire room of the CDA. Among other things it includes all official correspondence of the organization, the minutes or *actas* of the Junta Directiva and other official committees, a myriad of official reports and memorandums, both printed and unprinted, literally bundles of statistics gathered in all realms of Peruvian agriculture and trade, financial records and account books, drafts of proposed laws, petitions to congress and the president, position papers, membership records, and finally visitation reports. Perhaps the richest single subject in all of this material is that dealing with the various proposals for agrarian reform, which during the 1950s and 1960s elicited a fury of activity from the SNA. In addition to the official records of the SNA, a valuable newspaper clipping file, bound in over eighty volumes and covering the period from the late 1920s through the 1960s, occupies still another room of the CDA. These files cover a wide variety of subjects relating to agrarian matters clipped from all the Lima dailies as well as several provincial newspapers. Outside of the very spotty and incomplete file kept by *La Prensa* for the 1950s and 1960s, the SNA series comprises the only collection of its kind in the country. Finally, the original SNA library, which houses some 5,000 volumes and includes all SNA official publications as well as a wide variety of national and international works devoted to agricultural matters, completes this very substantial archive.

While the inherent wealth of much of this material is unquestionable, a note of caution is in order. The content of both the correspondence as well as the *actas* are not always as revealing on intimate or delicate political matters as one might expect. Much of the daily political business of the SNA was transacted on a face-to-face, personal level so that a minimum of "sensitive" topics was committed to writing. Since the location of the SNA headquarters in Lima was only a short walk to the Presidential Palace, Club Nacional, Congress, or the main offices of the large exporters, more business was conducted in the secrecy of informal meetings and conversations than in formal meetings where notes or minutes might be taken. The fact that these sources do not reveal the "sensational," however, by no means negates their importance.

PUBLIC AND PRIVATE LIBRARIES

Until relatively recent times Peru has been dominated economically and politically by a relatively small, coastal based elite, the proverbial forty families. This fact as well as the predominantly capitalist character of its economic system explains why so many of the country's artistic and literary collections have remained in private hands to this day. As a result, a discussion of private libraries becomes as important perhaps as those, like the National Library, of a public nature.

Without a doubt the most important private library in the country is the collection of Dr. Félix Denegri Luna which is housed in his private home in Miraflores. Although Dr. Denegri long ago lost count, his library is calculated to hold some 20,000 items. The richest aspect of this collection is the materials from the independence and post-independence period which has long been Dr. Denegri's research interest and in which he has published widely. For our twentieth-century concerns, however, the Denegri Library has considerable strength, particularly in the area of provincial materials of a social and economic character and political pamphletry in general.[7]

Other private libraries deserve mention here. Despite recent political changes, the Club Nacional, located in the Plaza San Martín, continues to function and, surprisingly, contains a very large collection of Peruviana. Modeled along the lines of the venerable and staid nineteenth-century British clubs, the Club Nacional houses a large reading library for its members replete with comfortable smokers, librarians in white uniforms, and a well-organized Dewey-decimaled card catalogue. While the proper connections will be necessary to gain admittance, for some its unique pamphlet and twentieth-century *revista* sections will be worth the effort.

Likewise those interested in the history of Lima, particularly its recent dizzying growth to a city of almost four million during the last one-half century, will want to consult the holdings of the Lima urbanist and architect, Juan Gunther. Purported to be the finest library of its kind in Peru, it has served as the basis for a number of recent

---

7. Carlos Moreyra y Paz Soldán, *Bibliografía regional peruana* (Lima, 1967).

dissertations on urban topics.

In foreboding contrast to the previous libraries stands the former collection of the great Peruvian educator and politician, Javier Prado, still located in the decaying family home in Barranco. This is one of the unfortunate tales of political rancor (which abound in Peru) mixed with general disinterest and neglect on the part of the Prado family which we need not go into here. Suffice it to say that while largely abandoned and little used, the library is still accessible to the persistent. The real strength of the Prado collection lies in its immensely rich collection of late nineteenth- and early twentieth-century pamphlets on economic and political issues. On the famous Dreyfus loan alone, the library contains possibly twenty to thirty rare pamphlets. For some it may well be worth the trials of admission.

The largest and most complete library in the country, of course, is the National Library. Its Sala del Perú (located in the Sala de Investigaciones Bibliográficas) complemented by the Raúl Porras Barrnechea collection and its newly expanded and reorganized newspaper and periodical section[8] provide the starting point and main base for the study of social and political movements in the twentieth century. While the main cataloguing system of the library is still incomplete and lacking somewhat in cohesion, each section and collection of the library has its own subject-author catalogue which should also be consulted. The Sala de Investigaciones also contains the important Zegarra collection, consisting of several hundred pamphlets from the late nineteenth and early twentieth centuries. Like those of the Prado library, these pamphlets, mostly polemical in tone and content, cover a wide range of social, economic, and political matters for the period--from hacienda disputes over water rights to schemes for expanding the coast's railroad network. In addition the library holds an extensive collection of prefect reports or *memorias*.[9] Published regularly between the 1890s and 1930, these reports, depending

---

8. Raúl Porras Barrenechea, *El periodismo en el Perú* (Lima, 1970) and *Fuentes históricas peruanas* (Lima, 1963).

9. Antonieta Ballón and María Caridad Esparza, "Catálogo de las memorias de prefectos, alcaldes y presidentes de juntas departamentales del Perú," *Boletín de la Biblioteca Nacional,* 10 (December, 1953):341-68.

on the caliber of the prefect, offer a wide ranging collection of valuable information on local administration. Often on the basis of local visitations, a prefect would describe the general economic and social conditions prevailing in his department as well as the state of public order. Gaps in the Library's holdings can be filled by turning to the pages of *El Peruano* where these reports were also published.

There are several other public or semi-public libraries in Lima and the provinces which should also be mentioned. Both San Marcos (Biblioteca Central) and La Católica (the Riva-Agüero library) universities have major libraries which are not only substantial in themselves but also contain copies of many theses written on twentieth-century Peruvian economics and politics.[10] The same can be said for several provincial universities, such as the one in Trujillo which houses a number of theses relating to the socioeconomic development of northern Peru. In Lima the library of the Banco Central de la Reserva del Perú holds an extensive collection of official economic and social statistics as well as numerous publications relating to the national economy, as does the newly formed library of the Centro de Documentación del Sector Agraria (sixteenth block of Javier Prado) on agro-political matters.[11]

Finally, considering the preponderant role it has played in shaping the course of Peruvian politics, we would be remiss in not mentioning some of the major archives relating to Peruvian matters in the United States, particularly in the nation's capital. The National Archives in Washington, for example, not only holds the important diplomatic files on Peru, but also a wealth of material relating to commerce and finance compiled by consular officials. Moreover, in addition to the well-known Library of Congress Hispanic Collection, the Department of Agriculture

---

10. Universidad Nacional Mayor de San Marcos, *Nómina de graduados y catálogo de tesis de la Facultad de Derecho* (Lima, 1942).

11. Other valuable works which the researcher might consult are Jorge Basadre, *Historia de la república del Perú,* 12 vols. (Lima, 1968) and *Introducción a las bases documentales para la historia de la república del Perú con algunas reflexiones* (Lima, 1971); C. Herbold and S. Stein, *Guía bibliográfica para la historia social y política del Perú en el siglo XX (1895-1960)* (Lima, 1971); Héctor Martínez, *Bibliografía indígena andina peruana, 1900-1968,* 2 vols. (Lima, 1968); José Matos Mar and Rogger Ravines, *Bibliografía peruana de ciencias sociales (1957-1969)* (Lima, 1971); and Guillermo Ruillón, *Bio-bibliografía de José Carlos Mariátegui* (Lima, 1963).

Library contains a substantial collection of materials relating to agrarian matters. Yale University's holdings on Peruviana are also quite rich, particularly foreign travel accounts and the like.

Clearly the checklist of resources for the study of Peru in this century could be vastly extended beyond these few pages. Various archives on both the local (notary publics, newspapers, municipal records) and the national level (government ministries) could be enumerated. Time and space restraints cut short such an effort, but it is hoped that the present brief survey will provide a solid point of departure for researchers. *Ahora, a trabajar!*

Research on the Modern Peruvian Military: A Selective Guide
Daniel M. Masterson

The scholar who proposes to study the modern Peruvian military must be prepared to exploit a wide range of field sources and to develop a basic proficiency in the techniques of oral history. Archival materials in the United States will also provide a very important supplement for the researcher, and this data can frequently supply a check on the validity of published primary sources in Peru.

The main repositories for primary documentation in Peru are the Sala de Investigaciones of the Biblioteca Nacional del Perú, and the Centro de Estudios Histórico-Militares del Perú. The primary archival collection to be consulted in the Sala is the Colección de Volantes. This collection contains handbills, manifestos of various legal and clandestine civilian and military organizations, and other forms of political propaganda. It is contained in folders arranged in one- to five-year groups for the period after 1914. Also housed in the Sala are the records of Peruvian congressional proceedings, *memorias* of armed forces ministers of government, presidential addresses, and annual reports to the congress. The main newspaper and periodical archive for Peru is located in the basement of the Biblioteca Nacional.

Nearly all the primary sources dealing with military affairs that are available to scholars are located in the Centro de Estudios Histórico-Militares. The staff list for the army officer corps are contained in the Escalafón General del Ejército. These lists are available for most of the years after 1939 and provide information concerning length of service, dates of promotion, active-duty status, and limited biographical data. The general orders for the army in addition to decrees of military governments, information on armed forces foreign study missions, and punitive action taken against armed forces dissidents are found in Ordenes Generales del Ejército. Similar data for the other armed services and police are provided in the Ordenes Generales de Marina, Ordenes Generales de Aeronaútica, and Ordenes Generales de Guardia Civil y Policía. The source for military legislation is *Legislación Militar del Perú*.

Peru's leading service journals, including the *Revista militar del Perú*, *Revista Escuela Superior de Guerra*, *Revista de marina,* and *Actualidad militar* are also located in the Centro. These journals are important sources for military theory and the professional attitudes of the armed forces. The leading service journal is the *Revista militar*. It replaced the *Boletín del Ministerio de Guerra y Marina* in 1919. The *Revista militar* was published monthly until 1950, then four to six times yearly thereafter. The *Revista Escuela Superior de Guerra* first appeared in 1953 and soon became a leading outlet for the more progressive military theories of Peruvian army officers. First published in 1962, *Actualidad militar* serves as a form of newsletter for the armed forces. This journal is the most useful source for detailed personal information regarding military personnel. The researcher can work in the Centro with a letter of introduction. It is located on the Avenida Nueve de Diciembre in central Lima and is open from 9:00 a.m. to 2:00 p.m. Monday through Friday. The staff of the Centro is efficient and very helpful. The scholar who wishes, for example, to use a camera for copying purposes should have no difficulty in doing so.

Personal interviews can be very useful for the student of Peruvian civil-military affairs. Those interviews that proved particularly helpful for my research were with former army Major Víctor Villanueva Valencia; Ricardo Pérez Godoy, Peru's Prime Minister in 1963; Fernando Schwalb López Aldaña; and APRA leaders Víctor Raúl Haya de la Torre, Ramiro Prialé,and Armando Villanueva del Campo. Víctor Villanueva, a former army activist and presently the leading authority on the Peruvian armed forces, should be consulted by all foreign scholars concerned with the modern Peruvian military. He is accessible and quite helpful. General Pérez Godoy also consented to complete a questionnaire dealing mainly with his role in the military government that assumed power in July, 1962. Many of his replies were frank, and he was willing to comment upon the most sensitive issues of his brief presidential tenure. Haya de la Torre granted two lengthy interviews in which a wide range of issues regarding APRA's role in national politics in the period 1930-1968 were discussed. He and other party leaders were contacted at the APRA headquarters (Casa del Pueblo) on the Avenida Alfonso Ugarte on most weekday evenings after 8:00 p.m.

The chief sources of primary documentation in the United States regarding modern military affairs in Peru are the National Archives in Washington, D. C. and the Federal Records Center in Suitland, Maryland. The Records of the Department of State Relating to the Internal Affairs of Peru, Record Group 59, Serial file 823.00 (Political Affairs) and 823.20 (Military Affairs) are now available through 1949. Particularly helpful for the review of internal military affairs in Peru are the Military Intelligence Document File, Record Groups 165 and 319. Access to Group 319 is restricted after 1945, but with a clearance from the Department of the Army (Office of the Adjutant General), one is able to review documents classified as "secret" through 1951. All notes taken on classified documents must be reviewed by officials at the Records Center or by the Department of the Army. But this process is generally handled swiftly and efficiently by the personnel involved. It is advisable for the scholar interested in examining these materials to contact officials at the General Services Administration, National Archives and Records Services, Washington, D.C. 20409. This should be done at least two months in advance of the proposed research visit. This will enable the staff at the Records Center to detail available materials and initiate any necessary declassification procedures that may be required.

Considering the diversity and breadth of the field sources available to the student of the modern Peruvian military, research on this topic will prove to be a highly interesting and rewarding experience.

Ethnohistory
John V. Murra

While many notions, not necessarily conflicting, prevail as to what ethnohistory deals with, let us agree for the purposes of this *Guide* that there is an *Andean* version or vision of institutions and events. The task before us is how to recover that version.

The most notable contributions have in the past come from European archives: the 1,200-page "letter to the king" of Guaman Poma,[1] from Copenhagen; the oral traditions of Huarochirí,[2] from Madrid. Nothing comparable in detail and importance has been located in the Andean region itself. It is not impossible, however, that the ecclesiastic repositories of the several orders and dioceses will still reveal manuscripts written by Andean authors, for example, Cristobal de Molina, who is known to have written books.[3] In the case of Guaman Poma additional materials about his life are known to exist in private hands but are inaccessible to scholars.

No one has yet located the Andean equivalents of the Nahuatl notebooks of the informants of Sahagún in Meso-America. We still lack the preliminary notes of the great compilers of Andean dictionaries, put together in the waning years of the sixteenth century.[4]

---

1. Felipe Guaman Poma de Ayala, *Nueva crónica y buen gobierno* (Paris: Institut d'Ethnologie, 1936).

2. José María Arguedas, trans. *Dioses y hombres de Huarochirí* (Lima: Museo de Historia e Instituto de Estudios Peruanos, 1966).

3. Raúl Porras Barrenechea, *Crónicas pérdidas, presuntas y olvidadas sobre la conquista del Perú* (Lima: Sociedad Peruana de Historia, Serie Monografías II, 1951).

4. Ludovico Bertonio, *Vocabvlario de la lengva aymara* (Juli, Perú: 1612. Photostatic reproduction, La Paz, 1956). Diego González Holguín, *Vocabvlario de la lengua general de todo el Perv llamada lengua Qquichua* (Lima: 1608. Contemporary edition, Universidad de San Marcos, 1952). I have discussed elsewhere the interest in the linguistic and other papers of the earliest Andean lexicographer, Domingo de Santo Tomás; see John V.

Some of the richest materials for Andean ethnohistory are in the Archivo Histórico of Cuzco, now part of the Instituto Nacional de Cultura there. The former director of the Archivo and editor of its *Revista,* Dr. Horacio Villaneuva, is now in charge of the Instituto. In a 1970 issue of the publication (no. 13), he has reproduced some extraordinary data about the valley of Yucay, once the home of several royal lineages; their lands later fell into the hands of some of their Kañari retainers.[5] Another recent and most efficient use of this still inadequately catalogued collection has been made by our French colleague Nathan Wachtel,[6] who studied the "destructuration" of the Andean world in its former capital.

By law, notarial and *escribanía* records from all over the department of Cuzco should have been turned over to this Archivo. Only the formerly Jesuit collection now remains at the University. Many papers remain in private hands: see for example the sources consulted by María Rostworowski de Diez Canseco in preparing her recent papers on royal and other land tenures.[7] Most of them, however, remain unavailable for study: for example, before his death some years ago, Dr. J. Uriel García published in Mexico[8] some tantalizing information about royal family holdings in and about Cuzco, quoting a *"cadastro"* of such lands from 1550, a very early date as Andean records go. He also referred to a document in which someone was selling Machu Picchu in the eighteenth century. It is assumed that such records remain in the hands of the family, relocated in Lima.

Murra, "Current Research and Prospects in Andean Ethnohistory," *Latin American Research Review,* 5 (1970):3-36.

    5. Compare this information with that provided by two articles, one annotated by Josyane Chinese and the other by María Rostworowski, both dealing with the population of that valley at about the same time, published in the fourth number of *Historia y cultura* (Lima, 1970).

    6. Nathan Wachtel, *La vision des vaincus: les Indiens du Pérou devant la conquête espagnole* (Paris: Gallimard, 1971).

    7. María Rostworowski de Diez Canseco, "Nuevos datos sobre tenencia de tierras reales en el incario," *Revista del Museo Nacional,* 31 (1962): 130-64. Also, "Nuevos aportes para el estudio de la medición de tierras en el virreinato e incario," *Revista del Archivo Nacional,* 28 (1964): 3-31.

    8. José Uriel García, "Sumas para la historia del Cusco," *Cuadernos americanos* (1959):133-51. México.

A similar concentration of notarial, *cabildo*, and other papers has taken place in Arequipa, where the Archivo Departamental, Quesada 102, Yanahuara, is under the direction of Dr. Guillermo Galdós Rodríguez. While much of the material deals with the Andean population of nearby valleys, the jurisdiction of Arequipa included the inhabitants of the Lluta, Azapa, Vítor, and Camarones valleys, now in northern Chile, and the corresponding parts of the *altiplano,* in what was the Audiencia de los Charcas. Dr. Alejandro Málaga has published the indices of Arequipa materials in the National Archives and of those in the National Library. He has also prepared for publication a resumé of the 1572 *visita* by Viceroy Toledo of the southern half of the kingdom (up to Cuzco--the text itself and the northern half are still lost). The Arequipa group (Málaga, Quiroz Paz-Soldán, Juan Alvarez) has recently brought out a first and maybe last issue of *Inédita*. They are preparing a new *revista* of the Universidad de San Agustín where colonial history and archeology, ethnohistory and contemporary ethnology will all be welcome.

Considerable concentration of ethnohistorical sources has taken place in the Archivo Nacional, Lima. While much of the material deals with circum-Lima valleys, there is also a lot from the rest of the viceroyalty, frequently beyond the borders of 1974 Peru. A quick consultation of the sources quoted from that Archive by Wachtel will indicate how much can still be located in that frequently used repository, beyond the well-known *visita* of Iñigo Ortiz, with which the old *Revista del Archivo Nacional* opened its first issue in 1920. People familiar with this Archivo over the years have reported the disappearance of sources, some of them already catalogued, and ethnohistorical materials are alleged to be among them. The untimely death of Felipe Márquez Abanto has removed the one person truly familiar with its contents and with a particular flair for Andean materials.

Among those using the Archivo intensively in recent years has been the Seminario de Historia Rural Andina, led by Pablo Macera, who with his students has been concentrating on eighteenth-century social and economic organization.[9] The most dramatic recent results have come from María Rostworowski's efforts since 1970 to document the coastal ethnic groups inhabiting the Chillón, Rímac, and Lurin valleys. Since these populations

---

9. Among its publications see Nicolás Sánchez Albornoz, *El indio en el Alto Perú a fines del siglo XVII* (Lima, 1973).

were destroyed so early, the feeling here as elsewhere along the coast has been that the ethnography of the litoral was beyond reach. Even from the preliminary data published,[10] we can see that an ethno-ecologic atlas of the Andes in 1532, coast as well as highlands, can still be achieved.

I have asked Patricia Netherley, who has worked intensively in north coast archives, to provide us with an up-to-date report on opportunities for research about the irrigated coastal kingdoms.* The age-old discrepancy, between the north coast, where archeological information is so good but where the historical ethnography was neglected by the foreign excavators, and the highlands, where we had ample chronicles and administrative records but little archeology, is finally being resolved.

Also in Lima is the Archivo Arzobispal. More than twenty years ago, when George Kubler was a visiting professor at San Marcos, an attempt was made to use this treasure trove for ethnographic purposes. Eventually Pierre Duviols was able to continue this study; the quality and relevance of this material, particularly for Andean religion, can be seen by perusing his recent book,[11] and his account of the sources used. As indicated above, and confirmed by Ms. Netherley, one can expect to find information about the Andean population at virtually every diocesan level, even where no formally constituted, public archives are reported.

The Biblioteca Nacional also has in its manuscripts collection some of ethnohistoric significance. Their quality can be assessed by consulting the material footnoted in Rolando Mellafe's article.[12] The late José María Argüedas published one of these sources in extenso in the first issue of *Historia y cultura,* which he sponsored. Some of the papers missing from the rather complete notarial records at Huánuco can also be

---

10. Maria Rostworowski, "Las etnías del valle del Chillón," *Revista del Museo Nacional,* 38 (1972-73):250-314; also, "Plantaciones prehispánicas de coca en la vertiente del Pacífico," *Revista del Museo Nacional,* 39 (1973-74):193-224.

11. Pierre Duviols, *La lutte contre les réligions autochtones dans le Pérou colonial: l'éxtirpation de l'idolâtrie entre 1532 et 1660* (Lima: Institut Français d'Etudes Andines, 1971).

12. Rolando Mellafe, "Consideraciones sobre la visita . . ." en Iñigo Ortiz de Zúñiga, *Visita de la provincia de León de Huánuco en 1562* (Huánuco, 1967), pp. 325-44.

*See Ms. Netherly's report at the close of this article.

located at the National Library. In recent years, under the leadership of Graciela Sánchez Cerro, the Biblioteca Nacional has added to its holdings reproductions of primary sources which had drifted into foreign collections.

One should not leave Lima without mentioning again the private collections of primary sources not open to the public. Some are of the kind mentioned above, brought to Lima because the heirs of the provincial elite have increasingly chosen to live in the capital. Others are in the hands of living collectors, some recognized scholars in the field, who may or may not will their treasures to public institutions; their importance derives from the fact that they were selected with a professional eye.

Excellent materials on the populations of the *altiplano* on both sides of the Bolivia-Peru border can be located in the Sucre and Potosí archives. They are well catalogued by Dr. Gunnar Mendoza and Mario Chacón, respectively. While most scholars have used them for "colonial" history,[13] involving the Andean population only marginally as "Indians," working off their *mita* in the mines, one could readily use the same materials to understand that same population's social, political, or religious organization. When in 1973, Luis G. Lubreras and the writer organized a seminar dealing with the resources of the *reinos lacustres* of the *altiplano,* we discovered that we did not even know where the borders of the several kingdoms had been. Using materials from the two repositories, we discovered that it would not be difficult to locate these *mojones* to begin drawing up an ethnographic atlas of who inhabited the Collao, as a first step in understanding the Andean component of Charcas life. The litigation records preserved at Sucre and the censuses of *mitayos,* listing them by lineage and moiety at Potosí, were particularly useful.

In recent years, ethnologists like Tristan Platt studying the contemporary Macha, Nathan Wachtel for the Chipaya, and Philip Blair for the Aymara, have all been able to locate records which gave them centuries of historical perspective about the ancestors of the very populations they were meeting, thus avoiding artificial constructs of what "Indian" life may have been in the past.

---

13. Joseph M. Barnadas, *Charcas: orígenes históricos de una sociedad colonial, 1535-1565* (La Paz: Centro de Investigación y Promoción del Campesinado, 1973).

Beginning with the late eighteenth century, some of the materials dealing with these same populations were transferred to Buenos Aires and are available at the Archivo de la Nación there. The fact that Boleslao Lewin was able to produce his work on the rebellions of Thupa Amaru II and Tomás Catari from this archive will give an idea of the usefulness of the collection. Nicolás Sánchez Albornoz and his students have recently catalogued and surveyed this repository. In a very brief foray in 1974, I was able to locate here information about some inhabitants of San Pedro de Atacama (now in Chile) who were moving across the cordillera to Salta, more about the kingdoms on the shores of Lake Titicaca and the distribution of the Uru, and the prices of foodstuffs in the same area.

One does not always think of Córdoba or Tucumán as centers of Andean studies, but since those areas were settled from the highlands and maintained long-standing contacts with the Andean region, one can frequently locate good information there. Córdoba has had the advantage of Professor Aurelio Tanodi's long tenure as paleographer and archivist.[14] Good information on the inhabitants of northwest Argentina can also be located at the archives in San Salvador de Jujuy, recently under the direction of Dr. Guillermo Madrazo.

A final observation. As useful as any one of these repositories, if not more so, are the papers held by hundreds of Andean communities. They justify current control or support their claims to holdings lost in centuries past. Some *comunidades* will have only transcripts made for them by notaries in town; others may have large leather boxes storing thousands of pages of original titles, later reconfirmations, litigation records or minutes of council meetings; individuals also have frequently come into possession of important papers from the past. Holding such community records is frequently denied by the custodians and justifiedly so.

Copies of some of these documents and, alas, sometimes even originals, have been included in the proceedings which led in recent decades to the "recognition" of the *comunidad* by the Ministerio de Trabajo y Asuntos Indígenas of Perú. Since 1968, these records have been transferred to the Ministry of Agriculture. Land reform authorities in the several Andean

---

14. Aurelio Z. Tanodi et al., *Libro de mercedes de tierras de Córdoba de 1573 a 1600* (Córdoba: Universidad Nacional, Instituto de Estudios Americanistas, serie documental, V, 1958).

republics have also sometimes gained access to such previously village-held documentation. Where originals and not copies are involved, the danger of loss is very real.

*Sources for the ethnohistoric study of the peoples of the north coast are located in Trujillo, Chiclayo, and Piura, in archives now under the care of the Archivo de la Nación and the respective dioceses.

The first three volumes of the *Libros de Cabildos* of Trujillo have been published. I was unable to spend time in the Archivo de Piura, which has the services of an archivist, but I am assured that it is a good source.

The most fruitful single repository for the ethnohistory of this area is the notarial protocols and *expedientes*, now under the control of the new Archivo Regional de Trujillo. This includes the papers of the *notarías* of Baldomero Jara and of Higinio Gutiérrez as well as the records of the Beneficencia Pública. Notarial protocols touch on every aspect of colonial life: wills, bills of sale of Indian-held lands, leases of acreage between Indians and Spaniards or other Indians; contracts of indenture as craftsmen or laborers are frequent and include much valuable information. The material from the Archivo Jara is abundant and extends from the sixteenth century. The Trujillo material is noteworthy because of the continuity of the holdings; although there was almost always more than one notary, the records of both survive.

Similar records from the Lambayeque valley, which were held in Zaña, were destroyed by a flood in the first third of the eighteenth century. A notarial archive from about 1740 is still in the hands of a notary in the town of Lambayeque. I presume that if Piura notarial records are extant, they are also still in the hands of working notaries.

The Archivo Arzobispal of Trujillo includes records referring also to Piura and Lambayeque throughout the colonial period. It has recently been reorganized by categories and the documents put into chronological order within each category. This greatly facilitates its use, although a general catalogue is not available. Some of the materials dealing with the Peruvian period in the life of Bishop Martínez Compañón, such as his inspection of his dioceses, are in this archive.

Parish records form another primary source of ethnohistoric information. There are some in the archepiscopal archive in Trujillo. Others are still to be found in the parishes themselves; for example those from metropolitan Trujillo, Mansiche, and Huanchaco are in the church of the Sagrario in Trujillo.

The Archbishopric of Chiclayo is interested in gathering up colonial parish registers, but to my knowledge they remain in the parishes. In both Chiclayo and Trujillo permission to use the archive must be obtained from the archbishop or the auxiliary bishop.

In both dioceses are parishes with records of baptism extending back to the last quarter of the seventeenth century; they are continuous to the present. Two parishes in Lambayeque have records extending back from 1650. In addition to fairly complete baptismal records, probably less complete marriage and death registers identify individuals by their named social grouping, the *parcialidad*. (PN)

Indian Historiography in Republican Peru
Thomas M. Davies, Jr.

Since Indians (defined culturally) have comprised a majority or near majority of the population of Peru since colonial days, any study of Peru in the republican period must deal in some way with the economic, social, political, and legal problems involved in Indian integration. Still, although almost every work dealing with Peruvian affairs devotes some attention to Indian integration and Indian problems in general, most of this material is scattered throughout hundreds of books, pamphlets, and articles, and since most Peruvian books lack indexes, the task of the researcher is extremely difficult. Moreover, it is hard to find documentary sources for the study of Indians and Indian integration which thrust the researcher into the exciting but frustrating role of private detective.

Fortunately, several bibliographical sources exist which are of inestimable aid to those interested in pursuing various facets of Peruvian Indian affairs. Jorge Basadre has published a masterful study, *Introducción a las bases documentales para la historia de la república del Perú con algunas reflexiones*, 3 vols. (Lima, 1971), which will serve for years as the basic point of departure for all Peruvianists. Likewise, the bibliography in Basadre's *Historia de la república del Perú*, 16 vols., 6th ed. (Lima, 1968-1969) is extremely valuable. There are many other Peruvian bibliographies of a general nature, but the most complete is the *Anuario bibliográfico peruano*, 13 vols. (Lima, 1945-1969), published by the Biblioteca Nacional in Lima. Other important bibliographies include Carlos Moreyra y Paz Soldán's *Bibliografía regional peruana* (Lima, 1967); Mariano Felipe Paz Soldán's *Biblioteca peruana* (Lima, 1879); Raúl Porras Barrenechea's *Fuentes históricas peruanas* (Lima, 1954); Gabriel René-Moreno's *Biblioteca peruana*, 2 vols. (Santiago de Chile, 1896); and Alberto Tauro's *Bibliografía peruana de historia, 1940-1953* (Lima, 1953).

An important source for Indian affairs, particularly for anthropological studies, is Héctor Martínez et al., *Bibliografía indígena andina peruana (1900-1968)* (Lima, 1969). There are also two bibliographies which came out of the highly significant Cornell-Peru Project at Vicos in the Callejón de Huaylas: Henry F. Dobyns and Mario C. Vázquez, *The Cornell Peru Project: Bibliography and Personnel* (Ithaca, 1964); and the bibliography in Henry F. Dobyns, Paul L. Doughty, and Harold D. Lasswell, eds., *Peasants, Power, and Applied Social Change: Vicos as a Model* (Beverly Hills, 1971). The bibliography in my own doctoral dissertation, "Indian Integration in Peru: A Half Century of Experience, 1900-1948," (Ph.D. dissertation, University of New Mexico, 1970) contains well over one thousand entries.

Major documentary sources are scarce. In its many moves from ministry to ministry, the Bureau of Indian Affairs (created in 1921 by Augusto B. Leguía) misplaced its files for the period 1921-1948.[1] There are extensive files available, however, for the period after 1951 in the archive of the Instituto Indigenista Peruano (created in 1946 by José Luis Bustamante y Rivero). The Indian *comunidad* registry in the Ministerio de Trabajo contains documents relative to the recognition process (begun in 1926 by Leguía) and some papers dealing with *comunidad* boundary disputes, but there is no indication of the impact of specific pieces of Indian legislation.

The administration of Manuel Odría (1948-1956) constitutes a major turning point in government-Indian relations. There were numerous, large-scale projects undertaken in the various regions and departments such as the Cornell-Peru Project at Vicos, the Puno-Tambopata project, and programs in Cuzco, Ayacucho, and Junín. Although these projects did involve government agencies as well as Peruvian scholars and technicians, much of the impetus, funding, and direction came from international organizations, foreign universities, and private foundations such as the United Nations, Cornell University, and the Ford Foundation. The files of these projects are invaluable for the study of Indian affairs in the 1950s and 1960s.

---

1. Dr. Dan C. Hazen found the elusive files of the Bureau in 1973 and utilized them in his superb doctoral dissertation, "The Awakening of Puno: Government Policy and the Indian Problem in Southern Peru, 1900-1955" (Yale University, 1974). Unfortunately, as a part of its attempts to corporativize the agrarian reform program, SINAMOS split the archive into as many parts as there were regional offices of SINAMOS, so there is every reason to expect that the archive is again lost, particularly in view of the rather severe downgrading of the agency in the post-1975 period.

The extensive archives of the Cornell-Peru Project, including field notes and reports, are located at Cornell University and are of value to all students of Indian affairs, particularly those interested in applied social change.

Unfortunately, most private document collections as well as most of the twentieth-century Catholic church records are closed to the researcher. An exception is the archive of Manuel Bustamante de la Fuente, now open and housed in the Archivo Nacional, which is extremely valuable for the period 1930-1948. The late Pedro Ugarteche performed a great service by editing and publishing portions of his own archival material on former president Luis M. Sanchéz Cerro, *Sánchez Cerro, papeles y recuerdos de un presidente del Perú,* 4 vols. (Lima, 1969-1970). The complete archive, donated to the Biblioteca Nacional in 1971, contains many additional documents. It is to be hoped that other Peruvian families will make their private manuscript collections available to scholars.

Finally, there now exists in the Centro de Documentación Agraria a documentary source which is unique in all of Latin America. When the military junta expropriated the northern coastal sugar and cotton plantations in 1969-1970, it confiscated these hacienda records, one set of which dates back to the 1870s. These files have not been "laundered" but provide rather a daily and monthly record of financial and political events. Their value to social historians in general is incalculable, but they should also furnish a detailed record of the *enganche* labor system by which Indians from the sierra were lured down to the plantations and then forced into debt peonage.

The Indian publication record of the Peruvian government has been uneven. There were almost no official studies published before 1920 and very few in the next two decades, but several *boletines* are important, such as those published by the Ministerio de Fomento in the 1920s, by the Ministerio de Salud Pública, Trabajo y Previsión Social in the 1940s, and by the Ministerio de Trabajo in the 1950s and 1960s. The work *La política indigenista en el Perú* (Lima, 1940) is also important. The best and most complete collection of early Indian legislation is *Legislación indigenista del Perú* (Lima, 1948) published by the Ministerio de Trabajo y Asuntos Indígenas. The formation of the Instituto Indigenista Peruano in 1946 led to an increasing flow of Indian studies which increased with the advent of international Indian programs in the 1950s and 1960s and with the formation in 1959 of the Plan Nacional de Integración de la Población Aborigen. Many of these studies are in typescript or mimeograph form and are deposited in the library of the Ministerio de Trabajo. The Instituto Indigenista also published the important journal *Perú indígena* between 1948 and 1967. Although largely anthropological in its emphasis, the journal contains articles vital for every aspect of Indian affairs.

The most important governmental source for Indian affairs are the *Diarios de los debates* of the Senate and House of Deputies of the Peruvian Congress. These volumes contain not only debates on proposed Indian legislation, but also lists of all the *oficios, proposiciones,* and *pedidos* presented on behalf of individual Indians, Indian *comunidades,* and *hacendados*. With the exception of the Constituent Congress of 1931 (lasting from 1931 to 1936), the congressional debates are reasonably well indexed. The annual *Mensajes al Congreso* of the various presidents contain the official analysis of the success or failure of administrative Indian programs.

Several Peruvian scholars have compiled collections of Indian laws. The most important are Magdaleno Chira C.'s *Observaciones e indicaciones básicas de legislación indígena elevadas a la comisión parlamentaria respectiva de la honorable asamblea constituyente de 1931* (Lima, 1932); J. V. Fajardo's *Legislación indígena del Perú* (Lima, 1961); Atilio Sivirichi's *Derecho indígena peruano: proyecto de código indígena* (Lima, 1946); José Varallano's *Legislación indiana republicana: compilación de leyes, decretos, jurisprudencia judicial, administrativa y demas vigentes sobre el indígena y sus comunidades* (Lima, 1947); and Manuel Velasco Núñez's *Compilación de la legislación indigenista concordada* (Lima, 1959). My own work *Indian Integration in Peru: A Half Century of Experience, 1900-1948* (Lincoln, 1974) contains an appendix listing all the major Indian legislation from 1900 to 1948.

Since the late nineteenth century, all political parties and leaders have taken cognizance of the "Indian problem," and all have mentioned it in some way in their campaign literature and platforms. Some presidents such as Augusto B. Leguía and Fernando Belaúnde Terry even emphasized Indian integration, but the greatest body of *indigenista* literature produced by a political party is that of the Alianza Popular Revolucionaria Americana (APRA) and its founder Víctor Raúl Haya de la Torre. There are hundreds of Aprista books and pamphlets, but the most important are those by Haya de la Torre himself, including *El antimperialismo y el Apra* (Santiago de Chile, 1936); *Construyendo el Aprismo: artículos y cartas desde el exilio (1924-1931)* (Buenos Aires, 1933); *Espacio-tiempo-histórico: cinco ensayos y tres diálogos* (Lima, 1948); *Política aprista* (Lima, 1933); *Por la emancipación de América Latina: artículos, mensajes, discursos (1923-1927)* (Buenos Aires, 1927); and *Treinta años de aprismo* (México, 1956).

Other important works on Aprismo include Harry Kantor, *The Ideology and Program of the Peruvian Aprista Movement*, 2nd ed. (Washington, D.C., 1966); Alberto Baeza Flores, *Haya de la Torre y la revolución constructiva de las Américas* (Buenos Aires, 1962); Eugenio Chang-Rodríguez, *La literatura política de González Prada, Mariátegui y Haya de la Torre* (México, 1957); and Luis Alberto Sánchez, *Raúl Haya de la Torre o el político. Crónica de una vida sin tregua* (Santiago de Chile, 1934).

For a critical analysis of Aprista *indigenismo* see my article, "The *Indigenismo* of the Peruvian Aprista Party: A Reinterpretation," *Hispanic American Historical Review*, 51 (November, 1971):626-45. Others critical of APRA include Fredrick B. Pike, *The Modern History of Peru* (New York, 1967) and "The Old and the New Apra in Peru: Myth and Reality," *Inter-American Economic Affairs*, 18 (Autumn, 1964):3-46; Magda Portal,¿*Quiénes traicionaron al pueblo?* (Lima, 1950); Víctor Villaneuva, *La tragedia de un pueblo y un partido: páginas para la historia del Apra* (Santiago de Chile, 1954); and Luis Eduardo Enríquez, *La estafa política más grande de América* (Lima, 1951).

As noted above, there are hundreds of books and pamphlets which include some treatment of Indians, but lack of space precludes mentioning them all. One great trove of anthropological data is found in the works of dozens of scholars who were associated with the Cornell-Peru Project at Vicos. Alan R. Holmberg, founder and long-time director of the project, produced over thirty articles and books, and all students of Peruvian Indians owe him a debt of gratitude. One of his more important articles is "Changing Community Attitudes and Values in Peru: A Case Study in Guided Change," in Richard Adams, et al., *Social Change in Latin America Today* (New York, 1960):63-107. Mario C. Vázquez V. also made major contributions, particularly with *Hacienda, peonaje y servidumbre en los Andes peruanos* (Lima, 1961), and *Educación rural en el Callejón de Huaylas:*

Vicos (Lima, 1965). Other Vicos scholars whose works stand out include
William W. Stein, *Hualcán* (Ithaca, 1961), *Countrymen and Townsmen in the
Callejón de Huaylas, Peru: Two Views of Andean Social Structure* (Buffalo,
1974) and "The Struggle for Free Labor in Rural Peru: Vicos, 1872-1971"
(mimeograph, 1974); Henry F. Dobyns, *The Social Matrix of Peruvian Indigenous Communities* (Ithaca, 1964) and with Allan Holmberg, Morris Opler,
and Lauriston Sharp, *Methods for Analyzing Cultural Change* (Ithaca, 1968);
Paul L. Doughty, *Huaylas, An Andean District in Search of Progress* (Ithaca,
1968); and the works of Carlos Monge Medrano, Héctor Martínez, Harold D.
Lasswell, William P. Mangin, J. Oscar Alers, William C. Blanchard, and
Clifford R. Barnett.

The Instituto de Estudios Peruanos (IEP), under the very able direction
of Dr. José Matos Mar, has compiled an admirable publication record, including a number of excellent works dealing with Indians and Indian problems. The IEP began by publishing numerous mimeographed papers and
research projects which emanated from round tables and conferences held
at the Instituto. Examples of these papers are: Fernando Fuenzalida,
et al., "Modernidad y tradición local en una comunidad de indígenas del
valle de Chancay" (Lima, 1967); Wesley W. Craig, Jr., "El movimiento
campesino en la Convención, Perú: la dinámica de una organización campesina" (Lima, 1968); and José Matos Mar, et al., "Proyecto de estudio de
'Los movimientos campesinos en el Perú desde fines del siglo XVIII hasta
nuestros días'" (Lima, 1967).

More recently the IEP has published a number of highly significant
volumes on Indians including the following: Carlos I. Degregori and Jurgen
Golte, *Dependencia y desintegración estructural en la comunidad de Pacaraos* (Lima, 1973); Alberto Escobar, ed., *El reto del multilingüismo en
el Perú* (Lima, 1972); Fernando Fuenzalida, et al., *Estructuras tradicionales y economía de mercado: la comunidad de indígenas de Huayopampa*
(Lima, 1968); Fernando Fuenzalida, et al., *El indio y el poder en el Perú*
(Lima, 1970); and Robert G. Keith, et al., *La hacienda, la comunidad y
el campesino en el Perú* (Lima, 1970).

Several scholars stand out both for the depth of their analyses and
the quality of their interpretations. In addition to those already mentioned, the following authors and works deserve special mention: José
María Argüedas, *Evolución de las comunidades indígenas* (Lima, 1957);
Felipe de la Barra, *El indio peruano en las etapas de la conquista y*

frente a la república: ensayo histórico-militar-sociológico y con proposiciones para la solución del problema indio peruano (Lima, 1948); Luis M. Castillo Delgado, *El procedimiento en la administración de justicia indígena* (Cuzco, 1966); Hildebrando Castro Pozo, *Del ayllu al cooperativismo socialista* (Lima, 1936) and the classic *Nuestra comunidad indígena* (Lima, 1924); Jorge Cornejo Bouroncle, *Las "comunidades" indígenas: la explotación del trabajo de los indios* (Cuzco, 1948) and *Tierras ajenas: estampas de la vida andina* (Cuzco, 1959); José Antonio Encinas, *Contribución a una legislación tutelar indígena* (Lima, 1918); José Uriel García, *El nuevo indio* (Cuzco, 1930); Manuel González Prada, *Horas de lucha* (Lima, 1908); George Kubler, *The Indian Caste of Peru, 1795-1940: A Population Study Based Upon Tax Records and Census Reports* (Washington, D.C., 1952); Máxime H. Kuczynski and Carlos Enrique Paz Soldán, *Disección del indigenismo peruano: un examen sociológico y médico social* (Lima, 1948); Roberto Mac-Lean Estenós, *Sociología del Perú* (México, 1959); José Carlos Mariátegui, *Siete ensayos de interpretación de la realidad peruana* (Lima, 1928); Dora Mayer de Zulen, *El indígena peruano a los cien años de república libre e independiente* (Lima, 1921); Moisés Poblete Troncoso, *Condiciones de vida y de trabajo de la población indígena del Perú* (Geneva, 1938); Pedro Erasmo Roca Sánchez, *Por la clase indígena: exposición y proyectos para una solución del aspecto legal del problema indígena* (Lima, 1935); Moisés Sáenz, *Sobre el indio peruano y su incorporación al medio nacional* (México, 1933); Julian H. Steward, ed., *The Andean Civilizations*, Vol. 2 of *Handbook of South American Indians* (Washington, D.C., 1946); Luis E. Valcárcel, *Ruta cultural del Perú* (México, 1945), and *Tempestad en los Andes* (Lima, 1928); Carlos Valdez de la Torre, *Evolución de las comunidades indígenas* (Lima, 1921); and Juan José Vega, *La emancipación frente al indio peruano: la legislación indiana del Perú en la iniciación de la república, 1821-1830* (Lima, 1958).

Finally, there is a large body of material which has been heretofore ignored by most scholars: the thousands of doctoral dissertations on file at various Peruvian universities. While it is true that some of these dissertations are inadequate, many are excellent studies which contain valuable data found nowhere else. The theses at the Universidad Nacional Mayor de San Marcos and at the Universidad Católica del Perú are generally the best, but there are some fine individual efforts at the various provincial universities.

Much research remains to be done on Indians and Indian integration in Peru, and it is hoped that scholars in all disciplines will undertake detailed studies in the future. Except for the revolt of Túpac Amaru II in 1780, Indian uprisings in Peru have been insufficiently studied. In large part this is due to the scarcity of data on the various revolts and to actual suppression of such data by local *hacendados*, government officials, and oligarch-owned newspapers. Some very preliminary work has been done by Peruvian historian Jorge Basadre and by French sociologist Jean Piel, but much more is needed if we are to understand the dynamics and history of Indian movements and revolts in the nineteenth and twentieth centuries. Local and regional newspapers constitute one untapped source, as do personal interviews with participants in such revolts.

We also need more detailed studies of Indian legislation on a departmental or regional scale in order to view the successes and failures of national laws and legislative programs. Such studies should also delineate the true power alignments between the rural landed oligarchy and the coastal commercial elite at various points in history. There is also a need for analysis of the relationship between a president's Indian program and his efforts in other areas of social welfare. Indeed, there are a myriad of economic, political, and social topics which need to be studied. Many Peruvians will tell you that Peru is Lima and Lima is Peru, but the truth is that Peru is the Indians, and we need to know much more about them.*

---

* A number of years have passed since I originally wrote this article, and of course, a great deal has been published in the interim. Space limitations preclude an extensive analysis of those materials, but the following works can serve as basic points of departure. The review *Allpanchis Phuturinqa* (first published in 1969 by the Instituto de Pastoral Andina in Cuzco) has achieved a level of sophistication rarely found in interdisciplinary publications of this nature. Some of the more important monographs are: Giorgio Alberti and Enrique Mayer, eds., *Reciprocidad e intercambio en los Andes peruanos* (Lima: Instituto de Estudios Peruanos, 1974); Giorgio Alberti and Rodrigo Sánchez, *Poder y conflicto social en el valle de Mantaro (1900-1974)* (Lima: Instituto de Estudios Peruanos, 1974); Stephen B. Brush, *Mountain, Field and Family: The Economy and Human Ecology of an Andean Valley* (Philadelphia: University of Pennsylvania

Press, 1977); Manuel Burga, *De la encomienda a la hacienda capitalista: El valle del Jequetepeque del siglo XVI al XX* (Lima: Instituto de Estudios Peruanos, 1976); Alberto Escobar, José Matos Mar, and Giorgio Alberti, *Perú ¿país bilingüe?* (Lima: Instituto de Estudios Peruanos, 1975); Alberto Escobar, ed., *El reto de multilingüismo en el Perú* (Lima: Instituto de Estudios Peruanos, 1972); Gabriel Escobar, *Sicaya: Cambios culturales en una comunidad mestiza andina* (Lima: Instituto de Estudios Peruanos, 1973); Wilfredo Kapsoli E., *Los movimientos campesinos en Cerro de Pasco, 1800-1963* (Huancayo: Instituto de Estudios Andinos, 1975) and *Los movimientos campesinos en el Perú, 1879-1965* (Lima: Delva Editores, 1977); José Matos Mar and Jorge A. Carbajal H., *Erasmo: Yanacón del valle de Chancay* (Lima: Instituto de Estudios Peruanos, 1974); Pierre de Zutter, *Campesinado y revolución* (Lima: Instituto Nacional de Cultura, 1975). The agrarian reform law of 1969 and the subsequent actions of the Peruvian military government produced a plethora of studies on *campesinos* (officially, Indians are to be called only *campesinos*), and while this literature is far too vast to include here, the researcher should be aware of its existence and importance.

Sources for the Study of Peruvian Hacienda History
Susan Ramírez Horton

The great estate or *hacienda*[1] is commonly recognized as one of the most fundamental social and economic institutions in Spanish America. Its formation speeded European settlement and acculturation of the native population. Within a few decades of the conquest, the estate developed into the basic socioeconomic unit of production in an agrarian society. Under the aegis of owner and overseer, a subordinate labor force produced first cattle, wheat, and other foodstuffs to meet a local demand and later sugar, indigo, and similar products to supply a growing regional market and the western world. Interpersonal relations within the confines of the rural domain reflected the hierarchical, multi-racial society of the towns and cities. In short, the estate served, and still serves in many areas of Latin America today, as a unit of social organization, which also produced the material basis of wealth for a significant sector of the elite.

Despite the hacienda's importance, there have been few notable studies of that institution. Magnus Mörner's systematic review of the literature summarizes the research that has been done and pinpoints the controversial aspects of the hacienda and the neglected areas which deserve further study.[2] Such institutional aspects of the hacienda as its formation, growth, and development, levels of profitability, labor regime, sources of financing, and access to markets await future treatment. Likewise, many aspects of the social dimension of the estate including interpersonal

---

1. The word "hacienda" is a terminological convention. It is used here as a generic term for several different forms of the great estate in Spanish America, e.g., cattle ranches (*estancias*), mixed farms, and plantations.

2. Magnus Mörner, "The Spanish American Hacienda: A Survey of Recent Research and Debate," *Hispanic American Historical Review*, 53 (May, 1973): 183-216.

and cross-cultural relations; the paternalistic and/or feudal versus the rational, entrepreneurial character of the landowner; and the prestige versus economic value of land are topics which remain to be developed.

Information exists on these social and economic dimensions of the great estate as well as on more general topics of rural life[3] of interest to historians, economists, sociologists, and those in other disciplines. A partial explanation for the dearth of historical research on estates and rural economies and societies is that few scholars appreciated the potential richness of the sources or knew where to locate them. It is my purpose here briefly to indicate and discuss hacienda records, the kind of information each type contains, and their principal repositories. Although my examples are drawn from personal research experience in Peru, they are indicative of where to look and what might be found in other Andean countries.

Since the hacienda's formation, its owner generated many documents in its role as production unit, employer, rural population center, and tax payer. For analytical purposes, hacienda records[4] are loosely categorized into internal and external documents. External documents are *public* records involving the hacienda or its owner(s) and other outside individuals or institutions. Internal documents are *private* papers which were initially intended for circulation among hacienda personnel and usually written to facilitate administration. The types of external or public hacienda documents which will be discussed are land titles, wills, contracts, and court cases; internal or private hacienda documents include account books, personal correspondence, and administrative reports. Neither the categories nor the types are mutually exclusive. Private documents are sometimes found or quoted at length in public documents and vice versa.

---

3. For a discussion of sources for the study of Peruvian rural life, see Susan and Douglas Horton, "Sources for the Investigation of Peruvian Agrarian History," Land Tenure Center Paper, No. 84, Madison, Wisconsin, February, 1973.

4. I define "hacienda records" as papers in which the hacienda or its owner is one of the principal parties directly involved. This article, therefore, does not deal with primary sources, such as the minutes of town council meetings (*libros de cabildo*), parish registers, tax and title records, population censuses, diaries of inspection tours (*visitas*), traveler's accounts, newspapers, and maps. These sometimes contain valuable information and insights regarding the hacienda and related topics and should not be overlooked.

Similarly, evidence in a court case dealing with land may include land titles and wills as well as account books and letters. The concepts, however, will facilitate our discussion.

Although the content of hacienda documents varies greatly, the information they contain and their use can be generally described as follows. *Land titles* record the transfer of property rights. Spaniards originally received land as an outright grant or *merced* from the governor of the district, the viceroy, or the town council (*cabildo*). These early titles include the name of the grantee, the general location of the land, and the conditions of the grant: that the grantee reside nearby and work the land for a certain number of years, that the grant not be prejudicial to third parties, and that the land not be sold or donated to the church. Subsequently, the crown issued titles for a fee to individuals who held land illegally (without title). This legalization process and the titles themselves are called *composiciones*. Composiciones name the landholder, give the approximate area and general location of the property, and record the amount paid to the crown for the title. The crown authorized composiciones several times before the wars of independence;[5] and for each subsequent *composición,* titles became more elaborate and specific. By the eighteenth century, they usually cited the specific boundaries, the exact area, and the value of the land. After its original alienation from the crown, land was transferred by sale or donation.

Bills of sale and *donations* indicate the parties and property involved, the area and boundaries of the estate, its price or value, the conditions of the transfer, any outstanding debts or mortgages, and sometimes a list of the buildings, capital equipment, livestock, and personnel (resident Indians and/or slaves) included in the transactions.[6] Land titles provide data with which to reconstruct chronologies of landownership, to trace expansion, to determine methods of land acquisition, and to describe labor regimes. Problems associated with land titles are 1) they do not offer comparable data on the same property: early land titles rarely cite specific boundaries with which to compare later surveys, and land area may be given in different units or omitted; and 2) the names

---

5. For the north coast of Peru in 1591, 1642, 1712, and 1787.

6. Slavery was abolished in Peru in the 1850s.

of the properties may change or disappear as when one estate is absorbed into another.[7]

Wills and last testaments provide information on the estate and its owner. They begin by presenting biographical information on the deceased (his *calidad personal*) and normally name his parents and heirs. Such knowledge is extremely useful in reconstructing genealogies and tracing landownership. Testaments also list other rural and urban properties and business interests, which suggest the importance of the hacienda to the overall economic position of the owner.

Contracts are of various kinds. Mortgage contracts (*censos*) appear early in the colonial period and remain important to this day. Landowners borrowed funds from private individuals and institutions, mortgaging their property as security. One sub-type common in colonial times is the *capellanía* or *obra pía*.[8] Wealthy people left large sums of *pesos* in their wills to establish these chantries and legacies. The trustee invested the principal in real estate and used the annual interest (usually 5%) to carry out the wishes of the deceased: to contract a priest to say masses for the founder's soul, to sponsor a religious celebration, to offer dowries to poor damsels or fellowships to support seminary students, and to fund specific charitable acts or good works. Landowners contracted with the trustees for the funds. Mortgage contracts typically mention the mortgage arrangement--principal, rate of interest and repayment schedule, the value of the estate, an indication of its capital equipment, a list of other mortgages and debts, and the conditions of the lien, including a clause prohibiting the partition of the property while the principal is outstanding. Series of mortgage contracts reveal changes in technological complexity, fluctuations in the rate of interest, and terms of credit. The availability of credit and debt burden are two factors which help explain relative expansion and prosperity or stagnation and decline of haciendas over time.[9]

---

7. On land titles see: Enrique Torres Saldamando, "Reparto y composición de tierras en el Perú," *Revista peruana*, 3 (1879):28-34.

8. The importance of the sub-type is suggested by the large sections of ecclesiastical archives filled with such documents. The church often served as the beneficiary and/or the trustee of such foundations.

9. See Susan Ramírez-Horton, "The Sugar Estates of the Lambayeque Valley, 1670-1800: A Contribution to Peruvian Agrarian History," Land Tenure Center Paper No. 97, Madison, Wisconsin, November 1973.

Owners also signed contracts when they sold their products, made major acquisitions, or hired labor. *Sales contracts*[10] yield information on prices, markets, and credit terms. *Labor contracts* indicate the conditions under which laborers and administrative personnel were hired. Such contracts reveal wages, salaries, housing arrangements, and other perquisites of the employed, as well as their major obligations, duties, and responsibilities. Sales and labor contracts provide a basis for statements on the local price structure, division of labor and specialization, origin and racial composition of the work force, and forms of payment. They also reveal the hacienda's position in regional and international labor, commodity, and financial markets. The value of sales contracts and labor contracts as sources is diminished by the fact that the former reflect transactions involving credit and future delivery and the latter register stable labor agreements. Cash sales, especially before the systematic collection of the sales tax, were not always recorded in writing. Seasonal and temporary laborers did not always sign contracts. Finally, *rental contracts* include the parties involved, the boundaries of the property, the life of the agreement, and the rental terms. Rental contracts indicate tenure arrangements, and when used in conjunction with land titles and mortgages, they can help complete histories of landownership, technological innovation, and territorial expansion.

Court cases dealing with land, water, and natural resources; the administration of wills and estates; bankruptcy proceedings against a landowner (*concursos de bienes*); and legacies are particularly rich sources. Records of court cases are as interesting from the point of view of the case itself (e.g., a dispute over land between neighboring estates or between a Spanish landowner and an Indian community) as for the documents presented as evidence. Inserted in the papers dealing with one case are many of the individual documents listed above.[11] Judicial proceedings also generate their own documents on the estates, including detailed inventories and appraisals. These contain information on personal assets such as slaves, livestock, buildings, hand tools, processing facilities, household effects, fields under cultivation, and cropping patterns.

---

10. One type of contract discussed above is the bill of sale as a land title.

11. Other sources are notarial registers.

Because of the volume and variety of the material presented as evidence and bound in one judicial record, court cases are revealing sources of information on an estate. Litigation records, however, must be used with caution. Lawyers exaggerate, distort, and conceal information. Testimony should be read with a critical eye and an alert mind for contradictory statements.

These external hacienda records characteristically provide information on the physiognomy of the estate: the names of owners, the size of estates and the work force, the product mix, etc.; and on its relationship to the geographic and institutional setting in which it exists. These papers do not usually include minutiae on daily operations and administration, factor costs and profitability, or information on social relations. Students of these aspects of the estate must rely on internal hacienda documents.

Account books are good sources of details on the economic, financial, and social aspects of the estate. Administrators or accountants recorded earnings and expenditures with a notation of the source or purpose of each transaction. Because they note small transactions and temporary labor arrangements, use of account books is one way to overcome the deficiencies and inherent biases of sales and labor contracts to arrive at an overall picture of the estate's economic activities during a specific time period. A careful reading of accounts will often also reveal input and produce markets, investment patterns, wages, credit sources, and prices.

During colonial times and on some of the small haciendas to this day, the scale and complexity of the operations allowed the accounts to be recorded in one volume. As the organization of production became more elaborate, several sets of accounts were kept. The number of separate accounts and the aspect of production each covers differ from one hacienda to the next. In general, the larger and more complex the hacienda, the greater the number of separate accounts. On one large sugar plantation, for example, a separate accounting for labor and cash flow existed for each aspect of production such as field work, administration, sugar refining, and distilling. These sub-accounts were aggregated periodically in detailed reports for a central office.

Volume of production and profitability, two statistics which are vital for the economic analysis of the estates and which one would expect to be able to calculate from accounts, have in the past proven difficult to find or compute. The reasons for this are several: 1) accounts rarely balance. Errors in adding and subtracting appear frequently. 2) Most of the surviving ledgers found among litigation-related papers reflect atypical periods--when estates were embargoed and administered by the church or the state. Under such conditions the sale of products was restricted; administrators could sell products only with the permission of the court, which often implied long periods of delay. 3) In other cases, account books are incomplete; they either omit the accounts of the factor's end of marketing and supply and/or do not record the transactions for an entire year.

The problems of working with more than one set of accounts for one estate are 1) the annual summaries give aggregate statistics without an adequate explanation of their meaning or how the numbers were calculated; 2) the accounts for all aspects of production for one period may prove difficult to locate; and 3) many haciendas have internal accounting conventions, abbreviations, methods, and procedures which make understanding the accounts difficult.

Personal correspondence from owners and administrators to relatives, neighbors, private firms, government officials, and others deal with the problems and details of administering an estate: labor recruitment, long- and short-term marketing strategies, and investment, and the rationale for changes in technology, cropping plans, and other matters. Also, divulged in personal correspondence is the social tone of the times or the nature of interpersonal relations--between owner and administrator, between an owner and his subservient labor force, and between owners themselves.

Personal correspondence became more voluminous with the passage of time and improvement of communications. Twentieth-century correspondence from the administrators and owners of one Peruvian estate, for example, included separate bound volumes for each of the following: *cartas internas*--correspondence between the main office and other hacienda offices; *cartas externas*--letters to and from foreign and Peruvian firms, landowners, labor contractors, public institutions, officials, and others; *cartas oficiales*--letters to and from governmental offices regarding legal rights to land and water, taxes, and legislation; *cartas judiciales*--letters between hacienda administrators and attorneys, concerning land, water, labor, taxation, agrarian reform, and other legal issues; and *cables*--copies of cables and telegrams. One danger in using letters as a source is that they present the views and perceptions of the writer and rarely discuss adequately the opposing side of a controversial issue.

Administrative reports are a last type of private hacienda document. They include periodic reviews of field operations and crop yields; technical reports, concerning processing and packaging; and statements on marketing conditions, shipping, and labor needs. Ordinarily, owners and administrators wrote these papers for internal consumption. The contents, therefore, are largely factual. Investigators should be alert, however, for the interjected comment which represents the management's point of view.

External documents are the most abundant sources for the study of the hacienda. They have survived the depredations of insects, water, humidity, mold, neglect, and patent human destruction better than their internal counterparts, because their value as legal documents and records was recognized, and they were housed and preserved accordingly in public offices and archives. The following outline indicates the major repositories in Peru and the sections or collections which contain public documents.[12]

    I. Biblioteca Nacional del Perú: Sala de Investigaciones (Lima)
        A. Colección Porras Barrenechea: Manuscritos
        B. Colección Astete Concha
        C. Sección Manuscritos
    II. Archivo General de la Nación (formerly the Archivo Nacional del Perú) (Lima)
        A. Sección Histórica
            1. Titúlos de propiedad
            2. Temporalidades (the Jesuit archives)
            3. Derecho indígena
            4. Aguas
        B. Sección Notarial y Judicial
            1. Real Audiencia
            2. Diarios notariales
        C. Sección Hacienda (formerly Archivo Histórico del Ministerio de Hacienda)
    III. Archivos Arzobispales (Lima, Trujillo, etc.)
        A. Sección Testamentos
        B. Sección Capellanías

---

12. For a more detailed discussion of these archives see Susan and Douglas Horton, "Sources," pp. 30-36. Entries are annotated here only when significantly different from or omitted from the above listing.

C. Apelaciones: court cases from other bishoprics, regarding church owned properties or claims of ecclesiastical authorities against landowners for debts.
IV. Archivos Notariales
V. Archivos Regionales (de Trujillo, Cuzco, etc.): recently established regional archives designed to house notarial records and judicial records for an entire district.
VI. Registros de Propiedad e Inmuebles (see below)
VII. Private collections

The Registros de Propiedad e Inmuebles deserve special mention. These property registers were established in the 1890s for voluntary registration of land titles in Lima and provincial capitals. Registration required proprietors to present proof of ownership for the previous forty years. Titles dating back to the 1850s, therefore, are copied verbatim in large indexed volumes. Subsequently, all major transactions which affected the ownership of a property, such as sales, mortgages (recorded in separate volumes), property divisions, and issues of bonds, were added. These offices are very convenient one-stop sources to document such phenomena as the concentration of landholding in one area over the last century, sources of credit, uses of capital, interest rates, exchange rates, and certain aspects of foreign investment and trade.[13]

Internal sources are not abundant until the late nineteenth and twentieth centuries. The places to find these papers have traditionally been the archives of the estates themselves and the private collections of individuals. The problem with such collections is that they have not been readily open to the investigator. One must spend valuable time establishing personal connections in order to gain access.[14]

Since 1971, a large body of internal hacienda documents have become available to serious scholars through the Centro de Documentación Agraria (CDA). This archive was created as a result of the agrarian reform (1969) to preserve privately-held hacienda papers. Immediately following the first expropriations of estates by the government, landowners began destroying internal hacienda documents. Tons of these materials were

---

13. Carlos Malpica used the Registros de Propiedad e Inmuebles to write his book, *Los dueños del Perú* (Lima, 1964), an annotated list of the families with the largest urban and rural landholdings.

14. The effect of the Public Documents Law of 1972 is opening up these archives to scholars is not known.

literally rescued from haciendas in Cuzco, the central sierra, and the north coast[15] and trucked to Lima, where they are now preserved in the CDA. The collections include a sampling of documents from many types of estates--from highland cattle ranches to modern agro-industrial complexes on the coast. Most of the account books, letters, and administrative reports date from the last quarter of the nineteenth century.

I have taken the liberty of interpreting the phrase "hacienda documents" very liberally, because I believe all these primary sources--both public and private--are useful for the study of the estate and broader aspects of agrarian life. How a scholar chooses to use these hacienda records depends on his problem, period, location, and resources, but most studies will require the use of more than one type. Most hacienda records are incomplete and fragmentary, especially for past centuries. The information lacking in one may be found in another. Comparing and verifying findings in more than one source helps correct for inherent biases, exaggerations, and outright error.

To illustrate the potential of hacienda documents and their eclectic use, let us examine the strategy I used to reconstruct the history of the estate in one region. Data from land titles, wills, court cases, and contracts were integrated and analyzed to provide a chronology of landownership and to discern patterns of concentration and fragmentation of landholding. Information in account books and administrative reports allowed me to trace the organization of production of the estates and determine periods of relative prosperity, stagnation, and decline, thus, completing an overview of the institutional and economic history of the great estates. Details garnered from thse sources and supplemented with personal data from parish registers and the *libros de cabildo* provided the basis for a collective biography of the landowners, which in turn suggested the importance of the human element in the evolution and progress of the institution. By analyzing the biographical data quantitatively, I established career patterns and documented social mobility as a means of gaining insights into the composition and stability of a local elite.[16] This represents, I think, a significant step in the

---

15. The documents from the haciendas in the Lambayeque Valley alone filled a thirteen-ton truck.

16. Susan Ramírez-Horton, "Land Tenure and the Economics of Power in Colonial Peru," (Ph.D. dissertation, University of Wisconsin, 1977). One

overall study of the function and significance of the estate in a wider societal context and suggests just one of the possible ways to use hacienda documents.

---

limitation of hacienda documents for the study of rural society in general is their over-representation of the elite and the large estate. Such groups as independent peasant agriculturalists, if mentioned at all, merit only passing comment when they affect some aspect of the hacienda's operations.

The Notarial Archives: Facts Behind the Fad
Elinor C. Burkett

Recently there has been much discussion of the importance of notarial records for historical research on colonial Peru. Especially since the publication of James Lockhart's *Spanish Peru* (Madison: University of Wisconsin Press, 1968), virtually every researcher working in this area includes consultation of these documents in her/his proposals. The notarial records are clearly significant: they provide virtually the only documentation on the common people in that society; they open up broad data on every type of business transaction; they are a primary source for wage and price studies and a fundamental basis for any social history. But while the importance is obvious, their organization, specific uses, and pitfalls are more obscure. Too often we take for granted that everyone knows how to use archival sources when, in fact, most of us learned what little we know only by experience. While the old adage about the pedagogical advantages of experience might be true, precious time can be saved if we share our knowledge with one another. This, then, is an attempt to use my experience in the notarial archives of Arequipa, 1540-1640, to contribute to this dialogue.

Each year the notaries of colonial Peru bound volumes which recorded the year's transactions. These books were then organized by notary and by year to form notarial archives. In some small cities and towns, such as Moquegua and Ayaviri, the archives are housed in the offices of contemporary notaries; in larger cities they form a separate archive or are part of a larger repository. The internal division of the volumes is chronological, usually beginning in the final days of December and continuing for one year. At times, two or more years are bound together. Some notaries, especially during the latter part of the colonial period, prepared indexes for each book. Comparatively few of the notarial volumes I consulted had such indexes, and when they did, they were often useless. Most were by name, alphabetized by the first letter of the *first* name.

More helpful were the infrequent indexes by category of document which listed the page numbers of each type of record.

There are numerous categories of documents, and a thorough discussion of each reveals some of the obvious and more hidden uses of the records.

PODERES

These simple powers of attorney comprise the majority of the documents. They specify the name of the person granting the power and the name of the person receiving it. In most cases, these documents then continue on in the formalized manner, granting general authority for business, financial, and legal negotiations. In a minority of cases, the power granted is limited: to the collection of a specified debt, the recapture of a runaway slave, appeal to the authorities for favors, etc. In my experience, their principal value is in the business connections they reveal and the social networks they reflect.

VENTAS

The second most frequent category is sales of property, slaves, produce, and goods. They list the parties to the sale, the item(s) sold with full description, the price, and the terms of sale and payment. Each type of item called for appropriate terms in the bill of sale and has special historical uses.

Urban Property:

The property is described with all buildings, huts, entrances, etc., and its location indicated by mention of the street on which it fronted and the owners of adjacent property. They are extremely useful for the study of urban history. I found no map of Arequipa for the period I was studying, but, by using older maps, descriptions of land grants, and urban property sales, I was able to draw up a rough urban plan. Then, using the bills of sale, I made up decade map overlays indicating the owner of each piece of property, property sub-divisions, and changes in land usage. This was invaluable in understanding urban development, neighborhood patterns, and systems of land usage.

Rural Property:

The description of the property is similar to that of urban property although the former tended to include slaves and tools. Mention is also made of the types of crops grown and, in some cases, the number of plants. Location is more difficult to obtain for the contemporary historian since heavy reliance was placed on topographical description. These sales indicate the major crops in areas surrounding the urban center, the relative values of these crops, the individuals involved in different types of agricultural pursuits, and changes in land utilization.

Slaves:

The slave is described in several ways: Christian name; place of origin/language group (but these are not reliable sources of ethnographic information since listings are very general--Angola, Congo, Mandingo--and not necessarily accurate; also, in many instances a slave is mentioned only as a *bozal*, meaning an African-born, non-Spanish speaking slave,(as opposed to *criollo)*; approximate age; past owners; and marital status. Distinguishing characteristics are often noted. (In several documents I consulted a slave was described as a *costal de huesos*, literally a bag of bones.) There is always a section on *tachas* (defects) which the researcher must use with great care. Owners tended to admit every conceivable defect--rebelliousness, drunkenness, thievery, lewd behavior--to avoid complaints of deception at a later date. Such defects should not be taken very seriously, especially when the document mentions that the slave is not insured/guaranteed by the seller. Statements on health are generally more believable with diseases and deformities specified. Special skills are sometimes mentioned; when they are not, the historian can often assume their existence if the price of a given slave is particularly high. These records are probably *the* primary source of information on black slaves and internal slave trade.

Produce:

Most recorded bills of sale involve only the major cash-producing and export crops. In Arequipa, this was primarily wine. Bills of sale specify quantity, bottling, type of wine, date of delivery and point of delivery. While with certain types of documents, as *poderes*, the form is so standard that one need not read them in their entirety, the varying conditions in these bills of sale make their careful perusal essential. The information is fundamental for an understanding of the economy of a given region since it shows price fluctuations, economic movements, and patterns of ownership.

In general, sales are key sources not only for the study of prices and specific commodities, but in the gathering of biographical data as well. These sources expose the activities of merchants, landowners, and middlemen, as individuals and as groups.

OBLIGACIONES

These obligations usually immediately follow the sale to which they pertain and are the IOUs of the buyer if (s)he did not make immediate payment. They mention the name of the person obligating her/himself, the person to be repaid, and the amount of the debt. Frequently they do not mention the reason for the obligation, merely stating that it is in repayment of a debt or as payment for goods bought. Thus, if the IOU is not attached to a sale, its reason for being is often obscure. They also lay out payment schedules and penalties for failure to meet these schedules. In some instances the obligation is co-signed and payment thus guaranteed by another individual, a *fiador*. In such cases, there is often a *fianza* attached between the debtor and his *fiador*. I have found the study of these relationships to be useful in analyzing economic networks since many of the debtors were common men, while most of the *fiadores* were men of social and economic importance. Apart from this I have found these IOUs to provide little information not available elsewhere.

PAGOS-RECIBOS

The business dealings initiated by sales, loans, and other kinds of promissory notes were terminated with documents certifying payment, receipt, and satisfaction. Except in instances where I had specific interest in knowing exactly when a debt was cancelled, I found these documents to be virtually useless.

ARRENDAMIENTOS

These leases usually involved the rental of urban property. They specify the name of the owner, the person renting the property, location, the use to which it would be put, special conditions, duration of the lease, and amount of rent. This information amplifies that found in urban property sales. It is particularly important since it enables the historian to ascertain property values at more frequent intervals than possible through study of sales alone. Also, the rentals shed light on commercial activity since they most involve rooms fronting on plazas or streets of merchants that were used as stores and shops. Thus, the documents reveal the identities of merchants and craftsmen and provide information on their activities.

CONCIERTOS

The contracts are difficult to describe since they vary drastically in form and content. The only standardization is in the mention of the parties to the agreement and its conditions. Just as in contemporary business contracts, these contracts carefully delineate the reason for the agreement, the rights and obligations of the parties involved, and its duration. Contracts cover hiring of skilled white workers, *fletamentos* (hauling agreements), formation of companies, etc. They are time-consuming to read since they are long, detailed, and often written in very formal legal language. They are, however, essential sources for any historian concerned with individual businessmen, economic development, and particular types of business dealings. They are basic for an understanding of the movement of capital and financing of marketing, agricultural, shipping, and mining enterprises.

ASIENTOS

These work contracts usually involve the employment of non-whites by whites since work contracts for white employees are generally found in the longer and more detailed *conciertos*. If an Indian was involved, the document was drawn up in the presence of and ratified by the *protector de naturales* or a municipal official, in order to protect the rights and interests of the Indian (or so the theory goes). This was true of all public documents involving indigenous peoples and, in some ways, reflects the legal minority of the Indians. The birthplace of the Indian is also mentioned. If a black was concerned, no such ratification or description was necessary. The name of the employer, the duration of employment (which, in the case of indigenous females, was legally limited to one year), and the salary all were specified. Payment usually included a small sum of *pesos* as well as room, board, clothing, Christian education, and medical care. Description of the duties of the employee were only rarely made; in most instances the individual contracted to do all honest work ordered by the employer. It is particularly interesting that, at least in Arequipa, there are no repeats or renewals of contracts as if an employee worked but one year and then left the labor market. Probably the contracts continued in effect without legal renewal. These work contracts reveal the names and origins of the servants, nursemaids, and fieldhands of the city and expose pay scales. Often a contract will show an unusually high salary; this indicates some special skill or personal trait of the employee that the researcher must investigate in other sources. (I generally found this to indicate that the employee was especially skilled or was an Indian noble-person.) Although most work was obviously not legally contracted for, the *asientos* nonetheless are fundamental sources of social historical data.

DOTES AND ARRAS

Dowries and marriage gifts were either incorporated into a single document or recorded in two separate ones. The former indicated who was granting the dowry, the name of the bride and groom and their parents, their places of birth, and the amount of the dowry. There was usually a listing of the items to be given as dowry, valued by identified merchants: land, slaves, household items, cash, clothing, etc. Marriage gifts were made directly by the groom to his bride and were almost always made in cash and, according to the records, in honor of the bride's virginity. The dowries are of considerably more interest than the marriage gifts. First, they are direct sources of information on women. Second, they reveal the social standing of the individuals involved by the amount of the dowry. Third, the identity of the person granting the dowry reveals a great deal about the situation of the woman and the reasons for the marriage. Fourth, they demonstrate social networks within society by showing patterns of exogamy or endogamy. Fifth, the kind of items given in dowry (moveables versus immoveables) indicate the economic power of women and the nature of class relationships. Lastly, by studying what the groom did with the money and/or goods he thus administered, the researcher can gain a deeper understanding of the meaning and function of matrimony. I consider dowries to be one of the most significant, if neglected, sources for social history.

TESTAMENTOS AND CODICILLOS

Wills and codicils are a fountain of information and are, perhaps, the most comprehensive source of information available on individuals, especially individuals who were not politically or economically important. In form, they are similar to contemporary wills. They begin by mentioning name, place of origin, and parents of the person writing the will. At times, if the will was not written in the office of the notary, they mention where it was being written. The first clauses deal with religious matters: funerals, memorial masses, charitable contributions. Small bequests are then detailed: freedom for a slave, sums of money to relatives, articles of clothing to friends. Marital status is included, and if the person was married, then some details of the financial relationship between her/him and spouse are mentioned such as the amount of dowry given or received. Debt relationships are usually set down in great detail although at times there is a simple statement that debts are listed elsewhere. (This is especially true of merchants who make reference to their account books.) A catalogue lists goods and properties owned; wealthy Spaniards usually did not make a detailed list, but Indian women, for example, noted each piece of clothing, every blanket, and pot that they owned. Executors are listed and then the major heirs mentioned. Aside from the obvious uses of the specific information, wills are revealing on other levels. Debt relationships and minor bequests are indicators of social networks; types of debts often reflect economic activity; and types of goods owned are clues to socioeconomic status.

APROBACIONES, DONACIONES, LIBERTADES, PERDONES, DECLARACIONES

There are many miscellaneous documents covering a variety of situations and needs. Approvals (*aprobaciones*) were usually made at the demand of an individual owed a sum of money and in a situation in which the wife of the debtor controlled considerable wealth. The wife than approved the debt and obliged herself in *mancomunidad* with her husband to repay it. At times a woman would also approve the sale of an item in her dowry since her husband, although administrator of the dowry, could alienate no part of it without her specific approval. Since most approvals deal with women, they are extremely important sources of data on females. But the wide range of situations they covered make them valuable sources for many different types of studies. Donations (*donaciones*) were direct grants from one individual to another, and the document usually recorded only the individuals involved and the sum, property, or item donated. In most cases, the reason given was love and service. Only rarely was a fuller explanation provided: for long service rendered, as my children, etc. Still, other information on relationships usually enables the researcher to make an educated guess: frequently a man gave money to his mistress or to an illegitimate daughter in order to help her marry. These records provide further sources of biographical data. Liberties (*libertades*) were voluntary manumissions of slaves. Fortunately, most manumissions gave some indication of the reasons: age, many years of service, kinship, etc., which help the researcher understand the bases of manumission. Also, the historical patterns of manumissions are revealed; in Arequipa the greatest concentrations of liberties followed earthquakes and volcanic eruptions that devastated the city and left the leading citizens in financial straits. These patterns contribute to our understanding of the political economy of slavery. Pardons (*perdones*) were made for a variety of reasons and are useful primarily for the insight they provide into individual personalities and the reasons for feuds and tensions. Finally, there are a variety of declarations (*declaraciones*) made about important matters. In Arequipa, most declarations were made by men who were pledging themselves not to gamble. These documents cover an extremely wide range of topics and should be perused carefully since they contribute to many different research topics.

CENSOS

I have saved this category for last since *censos* are still difficult for me to discuss. Basically, *censos* are liens placed on property, either urban or rural, by the owner. There appear to have been two major types of *censos*. The first was for charitable purposes. An individual put a lien on her/his property as a guarantee of yearly payment of a sum of money to a given church or religious institution as a charitable contribution. For example, a *censo* might specify that 250 pesos would be paid to the Convento de Santa Clara in perpetuity. Thus, whoever owned the property put up as guarantee had the *censo* obligation; the obligation stayed with the land despite sale or inheritance. Other *censos* seem to be fairly straightforward mortgages. A property owner borrowed 1,000 pesos from another individual or from an institution and pledged a piece of property as collateral for a monthly repayment of the principal plus interest. On one level the *censos* can be studied as simple business negotiations to analyze capital flows, businessmen, and institutions involved in lending and financing of new commercial and mining enterprises. But *censos* have a much larger significance that deserves considerable attention. By the eighteenth century, property owners were complaining strenuously of the burdens of the *censos* on religious institutions. Each generation made its own contributions, and as they built up over the centuries, they became oppressive to the individual and, of course, a tremendous source of revenue for the church. In certain regions, individual religious institutions appear to have gained control over entire valleys through defaults of *censos* of either a charitable or business nature. Thus, the total economic impact of the *censos*, in terms of the individuals who lost property and of the way in which property was gained and consolidated, is of great significance.

Notarial records thus can be put to many uses: drawing of urban plans, ethnic studies, economic movements and trends, and biography. But the data for these studies are not limited to the primary information in the records but can be drawn from less obvious points as well. First among these hidden aspects is the identity of the witnesses. Witnesses to documents were usually Spanish men of little political or economic importance, although at times men of position waiting in the notary's office, witnessed documents. The names of these men provide another piece in the historical picture. The records also reveal much about literacy since the individual documents were either signed by the parties involved, or if they were illiterate, by a witness. This information can help the researcher to understand educational levels of various groups in society and the positions of different individuals. The study of patterns in the writing of documents is also significant. Often, while working with the Arequipa notarial records, I had to ask myself what it meant that indigenous males made wills with much less frequency than indigenous females; that women rarely rented property; and that Indians almost never gave or received dowries. Thus, it is important not only to study the individual documents but also to analyze the overall trends and patterns in the writing of these same records.

In this general discussion of the organization and uses of these records, two other points of information come to mind. The first is that in documents sworn by women, researchers will find that often there was a permission and/or ratification of her husband included; at times a municipal official assumed this role. All women except for widows were minors before the law: they could transact no business without the permission of their husbands or guardians or, in their absence, of a municipal official.

Also, I might mention the conclusion of the documents. For the most part they are dated at the end and then certified by the notary, the witnesses named, and signatures affixed. In the corner on the bottom of the final page, the notary made a small notation which indicated his fee per page.

But while they are an exceptionally fine source of information, the notarial records nonetheless present significant problems for researchers. Some of these are specific and fairly easily dealt with. First, paleography. The intricacies of old handwriting are a problem in all research on the sixteenth through eighteenth centuries but are even more problematic in notarial records. In writing these comparatively insignificant day-to-day transactions, the notary public was considerably less careful than in taking minutes at a city council meeting or preparing letters for the central government. While language is less of a bother than in laws and court proceedings where the researcher can get lost in legal jargon, the paleographical problems can be prodigious. Thus, they demand experience and practice prior to departure if the researcher does not want to waste valuable hours.

The second specific problem is due to the number of notaries. In Arequipa there were at least three notaries recording public documents at any one time; Lima, Cuzco, and Potosí had even more, while smaller centers had but one or two. The multiplicity of scribes causes problems because of differing writing styles and formulae in documents. More difficult to deal with are problems stemming from different clientele. At first, in order to sample carefully from these records, I used one scribe per decade, but then I began to realize that the kinds of documents found in their books, and the social levels of their clients, differed considerably. I found that one scribe, perhaps the most important and socially significant of the three, handled the transactions of wealthy Spaniards and filled his books primarily with large sales, their obligations, and important business contracts. In contrast, the most insignificant notary, a man with few important contacts in the city who had recently come to Arequipa, handled the affairs of the common people and had very few major contracts or sales but many work contracts, wills of minor personages, and transfers of small pieces of land outside the town. Thus, it is extremely important for a researcher to examine the records carefully for these types of differences, both to avoid taking a skewed sample and to understand what these differing patterns mean.

But there are deeper problems inherent in notarial records that are more difficult to deal with because they are less obvious. Two examples from my own experience demonstrate this. When I began working in Arequipa, I knew that the city was a major wine producing region and hoped that sales and contracts would indicate the extent of the city's economic reliance on wine. I worked backward from 1630 on the records and was puzzled that I was finding extremely little wine mentioned. I had expected to see wine sale to merchants, contracts for bottle-making, movement of the wine, etc. I found some evidence but not enough to indicate that the city was a major wine center. As I worked backwards, however, I suddenly began to find records indicating that the production of wine was of enormous significance. I spent weeks wondering what had happened to the wine, for I had total faith in the reality of the picture reflected by these documents. Then I realized that wine production had not ceased but had reached a new level. After the earthquake of 1582 and the volcanic eruption of 1600, vineyards seem to have become more concentrated in a few hands, and wine became an even more important cash crop. This meant that the individual producers dealt directly with merchants in Potosí, Cuzco, and Lima and thus did not need to contract with middlemen: records of those sales were in the other cities. Their operations had become so much bigger that they no longer hired muleteers and bottlemakers when they needed them but developed their own mule trains and trained their slaves as bottlemakers or had regular bottlemakers in their pay. It is not that the records lied, but that in this instance, they had no reason to reflect reality.

Another case is equally interesting. Since I was interested in women, I was particularly surprised that husbands were not named as heirs by their wives nor wives by their husbands, which I felt was decidedly odd. When I began reading Spanish law on inheritance, I was startled to find that the law required a married person to leave one-half of her/his estate to her/his spouse, except for any portion entailed, or a legally stipulated portion that could be left to charities or other individuals. For a while I wondered why everyone broke the law. Then I realized that these people were not ignoring the law but that I had misinterpreted the meaning of universal heir. Everyone in that society knew how the estate had to be divided; there was no reason to mention such well-known, legally-based facts. The will only recorded the names of the heirs of the other half of the estate.

These problems exemplify some of the pitfalls of notarial research. Having such great faith in these documents, we believe the realities they reflect too easily. Thus it is especially important to be wary when using notarial records. Notation of race is another case in point. When I began reading these documents, I was pleased to find that in cases where a person mentioned was not white, the notary indicated her/his race. I kept a card file of each individual mentioned as being in Arequipa and began to find that sometimes a given woman would be mentioned as an Indian and other times, she would not. At first I doubted the accuracy of my own system, but then realized that especially where women were concerned, notarial descriptions of race were not reliable.

The difficulties do not stem solely from incomplete information in these records but also from methodological problems inherent in them. In any sizeable urban center, it is virtually impossible to read and take notes on every notarial record relevant to a study; for my period in Arequipa I estimated that it would have taken me four and one-half years of full-time work. The problem is how to get a valid sample. There are many variables: the differing clientele of the notaries, the changes caused by natural disasters, economic changes, etc. The researcher has to be extremely careful in selecting a system to ensure that the picture will not be thrown out of focus.

Secondly, it is extremely difficult to avoid getting lost in the detail. Despite their repetitive and formal nature, the documents are fascinating as a real sample of life on a day-to-day level. The minutiae they provide is intriguing, making it difficult not to drown in the information on place of origin of Indians and Spaniards, African language groups, wage and price fluctuations, names of witnesses, and literacy levels. I quickly discovered that while all this information was interesting and pertinent for urban history, I had to remind myself daily of exactly what my goals were in using the data so I did not get totally lost in detail.

All the research problems I encountered were not, however, due to the nature of the notarial records. Political hassles, archival schedules, and time limitations constantly befouled my schedule. Thus, I would like to share ten tricks of the trade that lessened these burdens for me:

(1) *Do-it-yourself microfilm*. Most provincial archives have no provisions for microfilm or photocopy, but you can do it yourself easily and cheaply. You need a standard 35mm camera with a regular or, even better, a 35mm lens. For a copy stand you can use the top part of a photographic enlarger stand (the part onto which the actual enlarger is attached) which screws into the camera back and fits onto any metal pole

(You can probably borrow this or, better yet, a complete enlarger stand, from a photographer wherever you are working.) If you can arrange to photograph outside on a patio, you need no special lights (but watch out for shadows); otherwise you will need to set some up. For film, use Kodak high-contrast copy film or H & W control film; this is sprocketed and is not microfilm, but works just fine. (The only difference is that you will be reading white writing on black pages instead of black writing on white pages.) To keep costs down, buy in bulk (100-foot roll) and roll the film yourself; ask your photo dealer for information before leaving and run a test sample to get the best exposure; set everything up and shoot one roll of film of a sample page, changing light readings. Be sure to mark down the exposure you use for each frame. Send the film to be developed; if you do it locally, make sure that the photographic studio uses the correct type of developer and the correct development time for the kind of film you are using (see the directions inside the film package). When you get it back, look at it and pick the most legible exposure. As you shoot, mark the rolls in numbered sequence and then you can easily splice the film together with tape for magnetic tape splicing and put it on a microfilm reel. Cheap and easy!

(2) *Write to the local mayor*. You will be surprised at the hospitality of local political officials to foreign historians. One researcher wrote to a mayor and received a package of local and regional histories free. I wrote to the mayor of Arequipa and four months later received a response from the councilman in charge of museums and libraries. I then had the name of the person in charge. (Do not underestimate how much time you waste trying to find out who gives the permission.) But, even more important, the imminence of my arrival sped up the process of making documents available in the library which had been buried to the public for fifty years.

(3) *Paleography*. Now that I have said my piece about the importance of preparation, I feel obligated to give some suggestions on how to do so. There is really only one way to learn to read sixteenth-century manuscripts and that is by reading. It is helpful to have someone to point out and explain basic abbreviations and numbers to you. My advisor recommended that I learn by working on one page for an hour or two daily until I could read it. You can do this by getting microfilm or photocopies of documents from manuscript collections in the United States. You will

quickly note that there are many styles of handwriting and that the script differs widely even between notaries of the same city, but once you master one, the others come with comparative ease (although there are some who might always prove impossible). The most important thing is not to get discouraged. I remember being hysterical when I first saw the documents and thought that I could never learn to read them. I have watched many others experience the same emotion, but it is a common occupational hysteria. Virtually everyone goes through a period of thinking they will never learn; but in fact, once you begin to make a little progress, it comes quickly thereafter.

(4) *Women*. Female researchers have special problems that are sticky to deal with. Whistles on the street, lecherous men, and total disdain are common and unavoidable realities. I do have one piece of advice. While in Arequipa I noticed that women who were *señora* were taken much more seriously than women who were *señorita*. It was as if the single woman was viewed as a child rather than a serious researcher. It might be dishonest and create more problems, but many women have found that calling themselves *señora* from the first was extremely helpful.

(5) *Printing*. Printing costs are very low, so take advantage of this. In working with the notarial records I found myself wasting considerable time writing down information standard in all documents of a given category. So I had forms printed that enabled me simply to fill in appropriate blanks. This made the work go much faster. Enough forms to do my entire period printed on newsprint paper cost $8.00 in Arequipa.

(6) *Your friendly resident foreigners*. The North Americans, French, and British business people and their families who live in these cities can be extremely helpful. I have found many researchers, especially students, loathe to make contact with them, but as long-term residents, the local foreign residents can aid not only in practical problems but also in research matters as well. I found an old British woman who had lived in Arequipa all her life and knew all of the important families. She had been in their homes and knew who had libraries, old maps and photographs, and family genealogies. She used her connections with this group to provide me access to these data and, further, briefed me on local political feuds, rivalries, and hatreds. I strongly suggest that you do not avoid these people.

(7) *Political fights and rivalries*. This is a sensitive, though

crucial problem. Provincial cities throughout the world are small, tight-knit places. Everyone knows about everyone else, and there are social and political rivalries having both deep roots in history and significant bases in contemporary politics. These feuds can totally destroy your research if you get caught in the middle. Be extremely careful who introduces you to the archivists. I almost made the mistake of being taken over by an arch-enemy and political rival. You might also find that the old families are anxious to know what you have found out about their ancestors. They are extremely proud and afraid that you will uncover sordid details or information that belies their family stories. At times they might encourage you to reveal negative information on rival families. You are often caught in an especially difficult situation when you need the cooperation of two feuding families. Ask your friendly foreigners for details on these matters, for once you have the information you can usually avoid the problems caused by ignorance.

(8) *Local researchers*. Local professional historians in Arequipa were helpful beyond belief: they were interested in seeing the research done and were not concerned with the nationality of the researcher. In other instances, people resent what is considered to be scientific or academic imperialism. So be discreet. Many individuals who have dedicated long years to given projects rightfully resent the intrusions of well-financed outsiders on their domain. Knowledge of the work of these people prior to arrival and the building of cooperative relations after arrival is not only essential for successful research, but common courtesy.

(9) *What to do when the archives close*. Limited hours are a constant problem for researchers, especially during the summer in Peru when most facilities close at 2:00. Often there are minor archival sources with different schedules. We sometimes ignore these since they seem insignificant or irrevelant. But when the major archives close, it is good to haunt these sources. And try private libraries; they are often marvellous.

(10) *Hidden documents*. You can also spend that time searching for the family accounts, diaries, genealogies, and rare books that are not in public places or the libraries of local intellectuals. Many of these sources are found through contacts with local elites, but in cases of downward mobility, much material originally held by important families is retained by their less important descendants. Put an advertisement in

the newspaper, asking for old books, documents, family trees, and amateur genealogists. The response will amaze you. And the archivists will be grateful for your uncovering and contribution of these valuable materials.

El Archivo General de la Nación
Guillermo Durand Flórez

ANTECEDENTES, LEGISLACION, Y ORGANIZACION

Fue creado por Decreto de 15 de mayo de 1861 durante el gobierno del President Ramón Castilla con el nombre de Archivo Nacional y su objeto era conservar los documentos históricos existentes de la colonia y recolectar y cuidar los producidos en la época republicana. Su primer director fue don Santiago Távara y posteriormente Manuel María Bravo, Ricardo Palma, Luis Benjamín Cisneros, Luis Antonio Eguiguren, y Horacio Urteaga entre los principales.

Inicialmente las disposiciones archivísticas fueron muy dispersas, y no permitían la realización de un trabajo orgánico para la protección, ordenamiento, y clasificación de los fondos documentales. Esta situación se ha subsanado mediante el Decreto Ley N°19414 de 16 de mayo de 1972 para la defensa, conservación, e incremento patrimonial de la nación. Al dictarse el Decreto Ley N°19268 ha cambiado su denominación como Archivo General de la Nación, y es un órgano de ejecución del Instituto Nacional de Cultura.

El gobierno del Archivo está a cargo de un director y un sub-director que colabora estrechamente con él.

OFICINA DE ARCHIVO HISTORICO

Con documentos, expedientes, y protocolos de 1533 cuyos fondos se describen a continuación:

La Sección Colonial tiene un volumen aproximado de 7,730 legajos y 1,500 libros.

La Sección República que consta de 1,300 legajos.

La Sección Escribanos que contiene los protocolos de escribanos de la época colonial y notarios de la república hasta 1900, consta de 3,500 protocolos ordenados por siglos y cada siglo por orden alfabético de notarios.

Sección Donaciones que consta de 200 legajos aproximadamente.

Sección Archivo Histórico de Hacienda que tiene 1,433 cajas con documentos sueltos y 4,200 con 74 libros.

LA SECCION COLONIAL

La Sección Colonial está dividida en series de la siguiente manera:

Serie Audiencia Real

De 1540 a 1820 con 2,017 legajos.

Administrativa:

En las que están clasificadas, disposiciones administrativas y correspondencia, grados de abogados, real acuerdo de justicia, libros de procuradores, y protocolos de escribanos de cámaras.

Causas Criminales y Causas Ordinarias:

Que contienen apelaciones particulares, casos de corte, capellanías, cabildos eclesiásticos, y consulado.

Juzgados Especiales:

Bienes de difuntos, censos, juzgado de cofradía, legados, y testamentos.

Tierras y Hacienda

Sentencias

Serie Cabildo

Con 1552 a 1821 con 205 legajos con subserie administrativa que contiene audiencia pública y correspondencia, gremios, justicia (causas criminales).

Serie Campesinado

Que contiene subseries: juzgado de aguas de 1577 a 1821 con 45 legajos.

Derecho Indígena que contiene de 1,552 a 1,820 con 40 legajos que contiene legislación referentes a distribución de mitas, encomiendas, empadronamiento, y visitas a pueblos de indios.

Títulos de Propiedad de Tierra de 1545 a 1825 con 44 legajos.

Tierras y Haciendas de 1693 a 1892 con 40 legajos; Tierras de Comunidad de 1545 a 1821 con 12 legajos.

Serie Real del Tribunal de Consulado

1613 a 1821 con 273 legajos, contiene documentos administrativos, aduaneros, contenciosos, y gremios de mercaderes.

Serie Real Renta de Correos

Contiene 77 legajos con documentación de funcionamiento de la administración central y provincias de virreynato.

Serie Asuntos Eclesiásticos

De 1575 a 1821 con 81 legajos relacionados con la administración de las iglesias, capellanías de coros, cédulas de provisiones, conventos y órdenes religiosas, hospitales, tribunales de la santa iglesia, libros de hacienda de parroquia, y tribunal eclesiástico.

Serie Real Hacienda

Desde 1570 a 1821 con 3,506 legajos y 1,500 libros contiene documentación de aduanas administración central, mercancías, negros, almojarifazgo, contencioso, juzgado de censo, tribunal mayor de cuentas, estancos que contiene administración general y de provincia: aguardiente, azogue, brea, naipes, papel sellado, pólvora, y tabaco.

Junta suprema de real audiencia, real casa de moneda, tributos, y recaudación eclesiastica.

Serie Superior Gobierno

Desde 1544 a 1839. Tiene 131 legajos con cédulas reales, correspondencia, ordenanzas, real acuerdo de justicia, contencioso eclesiástico, juicio de residencia, corregidores, sub-delegados intendentes tanto en lo administrativo como en lo judicial.

Serie Guerra

Desde 1681 a 1820 con 183 legajos. Contiene expediente de auditoría general, ejército, con hojas de servicio y abstecimiento y honorarios.

Serie Tribunal de Inquisición

De 1873 a 1920 con 294 legajos. Se encuentran expedientes contenciosos, secuestro de bienes, administrativo, libros de cuenta, y autos y sentencias.

Serie Jesuíta

De 1551 a 1767 con 129 legajos, contiene documentación desde que la Compañía de Jesús entró al virreynato hasta su expulsión.

Real Tribunal de Minería

De 1585 a 1823 contiene 83 legajos con datos sobre administración general, disposiciones, correspondencia, escrituras, denuncias, cuentas, disputaciones de provincias.

Serie Temporalidades

De 1777 a 1818 con 360 legajos. Este renglón tiene expediente de la junta administradora de los bienes de los Jesuitas sub-dividido en administración, capellanías, censos, colegios, contencioso, correspondencia, cuentas y dotes, fundaciones, inventarios, limosnas, procuradores, rentas, propiedades.

Serie Varios

Contiene 230 legajos con documentos distintos de correspondencia privada y comercial y negros.

LA SECCION REPUBLICA

Tiene documentación correspondiente al siglo pasado republicano, como está dicho tiene 330 legajos que están siendo clasificados conforme a su procedencia.

En trabajo de ordenamiento y clasificación se encuentran también los Archivos del Ministerio de Justicia, Culto, Instrucción y Beneficencia; así como una important colección de correos y telégrafos y colecciones particulares que han sido donadas por sus antiguos propietarios al Archivo General de la Nación.

La Sección Escribanos

Se encuentra anteriormente descrita.

La Sección Donaciones

Compuesta por entrega de documentación conservada por particulares y se mantiene la denominación del donatario. Así el Archivo Moreira, Bustamante, de la Fuente, Cisneros, etc.

La Sección Archivo Histórico de Hacienda

El Archivo Histórico y Colonial del Ministerio de Hacienda y Comercio, que funcionaba en la repartición de este nombre, ha sido incorporado como una sección del Archivo General de la Nación desde diciembre de 1970. Sus fondos pueden describirse muy sintéticamente de la siguiente manera:

Una Serie Colonial:

Que tiene de 1,254 libros manuscritos de los que corresponde 1,011 a real acuerdo, 207 al tribunal del consulado, y 57 a varios. Empieza en 1548 y llegan a 1820. En esta sección existen reales cédulas, reales órdenes, decretos autos, y reglamentos sobre asuntos militares de la época virreynal.

Una Serie Republicana:

Forma una agrupación distinta a partir de 1820 está dividida en dos subseries de documentos oficiales y de documentos particulares. Tiene una importante colección de los originales de disposiciones legales, como pueden ser decretos, resoluciones ministeriales, resoluciones supremas, resoluciones directorales, y reglamentos. También libros copiadores, comunicaciones, y correspondencia variada de este Ministerio. El total de documentación es de 1,433 cajas con documentos sueltos y 4,274 libros.

OFICINA DE ARCHIVO NOTARIAL Y JUDICIAL

Tiene los protocolos e índices de los notarios fallecidos o cesantes en sus cargos a partir de 1900 y que se incorporan por ministerio de ley al Archivo General de la Nación, y se encuentran ordenados de acuerdo al Archivo del Notario a que pertecío y está constituido por los protocolos de las escrituras originales y protocolos que contienen las minutas y los partes a los registros públicos, así como también los índices correspondientes. Este Archivo llega hasta 1973 conforme se han transferido los protocolos de los notarios de Lima y Callao que han fallecido o cesado. De igual manera existe un archivo de expedientes de escribanos fallecidos desde 1900 a 1960. En la parte judicial no se ha incorporado sino en parte.

OFICINA DE ARCHIVO ADMINISTRATIVO

Corresponde a ella la documentación procedente de la administración pública a partir de 1900 y contiene documentación de los Ministerios de Justicia, de Hacienda, de Salud, de Trabajo, y de Agricultura, y del Tribunal Mayor de Cuentas, de la Contraloría General de la República, de la Morgue Central, de la Junta Pro-desocupados, de la Prefectura de Lima.

El Archivo Administrativo se está organizando desde 1968, pues aunque los reglamentos sobre archivos disponían su formación, no se había transferido ninguna documentación y se ha ido recibiendo a partir de esa fecha, y el ordenamiento y clasificación de esta documentación se está realizando sólo desde hace dos años.

El Decreto-Ley N°19414 dispone que la documentación con antigüedad de 30 años producida por el Sector Público Nacional debe ser remitida al Archivo General de la Nación o al Archivo Departamental correspondiente. La implementación de esta sección es reciente, y en consecuencia el trabajo archivístico se viene realizando progresivamente.

ARCHIVOS DEPARTAMENTALES

Las disposiciones legales antes mencionadas permiten la creación progresiva del archivo en los departamentos, y se vienen organizando los mismos para la conservación y atención de los documentos que existen en estas circunscripciones territoriales.

Así en 1973 se creó el Archivo Departamental de Arequipa que incorporó los fondos históricos que guardaba la Universidad San Agustín a la que se han añadido documentos notariales, judiciales, y de la administración pública, y viene funcionando satisfactoriamente.

El Archivo Departamental de La Libertad se formó en 1974 y ya ha comenzado su trabajo archivístico.

El Archivo Departamental del Cuzco se ha formado recientemente en el mes de marzo del año 1975, con la transferencia de los fondos que guardaba el Archivo Histórico a cargo de la Universidad San Antonio Abad y se está iniciando la labor correspondiente.

De igual manera se están dando los primeros pasos para establecer en breve tiempo el Archivo Departamental de Tacna y Piura.

El Archivo del Fuero Agrario
Vincent G. Peloso

Initially called the Centro de Documentación Agraria (CDA), the Archivo del Fuero Agrario (or simply Archivo Agrario) in Lima forms part of the Fuero Privativo Agrario in Peru.[1] Located at Jr. Paita 429, Rimac, the Archive was established by Agrarian Organic Law No. 21022 of December 17, 1974, which placed the Archivo Agrario under the direction of a Comité Técnico. A member of the Comité, Humberto Rodríguez Pastor, is also director of the Archivo Agrario. The Comité oversees administration, cataloguing, maintenance of documents, supervision of and assistance to readers. With only a small staff, document control remains a problem.

The Archivo del Fuero Agrario is composed largely of plantation records from the coastal and highland valleys of the country. The business activities of the plantation owners during the past century are recorded in these papers. The Archivo Agrario is a product of the agrarian reform carried out in Peru after 1968. Expropriated properties were visited by social scientists to determine if records existed. Under the auspices of the Agrarian Tribunal the records were brought to Lima. Later the library of the Sociedad Nacional Agraria (SNA) was brought together with the plantation records to form the Archivo Agrario.

The SNA materials consist largely of two kinds of documents: the formal records of the activities of this organization as it represented the major agricultural interests before the government and the records of its activities as a collector and disseminator of technical agricultural information. Along with these are newspaper clippings, dailies, and agricultural journals.

Far more extensive than the SNA materials are plantation records. The organizers of the Archive grouped the materials by corporation. Over fifty of Peru's most prized properties are represented among them. And

---

1. See N. Roger Chapin, "Report on the Centro de Documentación Agraria--MUCIA Microfilm Project," Indiana University manuscript memorandum.

though no more than a dozen coastal plantations are included, their records are the most numerous in the Archive; the bulk of them are from the sugar plantations of the Lambayeque valley. A few others are from La Libertad, Ancash, and Ica, and together they stretch back to the mid-nineteenth century.

The highland materials also are concentrated in a few departments. Most heavily represented are Cerro de Pasco, Junín, Cuzco, and Puno. Scattered portions come from Huánuco and Arequipa. Despite such concentrations, the locales of these properties are some of the best areas in which to explore the character of the country's economic history. Sugar and cotton were produced in the coastal valleys, and the highland operations focused on dairy products, meat, wool, leather, foods, and tea. The materials are spotty in the early part of the twentieth century but become fuller especially after 1945.

Two general categories of materials are available: accounts and correspondence.[2] Accounts fall into two groups, those dealing with the transfer and exchange of goods and those referring to the control of labor. The correspondence parallels this material and consists of the exchange of information, advice, and commands between the owners and administrators of the properties on a regular, frequent basis.

In 1976-78 the staff of the Archivo Agrario conducted a seminar designed to encourage the presentation of research results by readers and investigators in Peruvian agrarian history and hoped to initiate an expanded seminar in 1979. The Archive also sponsors a journal, *Tierra y sociedad*, which publishes articles on agrarian history.

Despite financial and physical handicaps not unknown to archives in formation, the records of eight of the plantation-holding corporations--consisting of over a half million items--have been catalogued. The task took more than a year, and while other materials have been inventoried, cataloguing continues at a slower pace. In sum, it promises to become one of the most important repositories for the documentation of recent Latin American history.

---

2. Detailed explanation is in Centro de Documentación Agraria, *Boletín*, No. 1 (June, 1973), Lima.

The Archives of Cuzco
Donald L. Gibbs

The archives in Cuzco contain extensive and varied collections of documents accumulated during the city's last four centuries as a regional administrative, economic, and religious center. The largest and most accessible of these archives is the Archivo Histórico de la Universidad Nacional del Cuzco. Following a detailed description of this repository will be a review of church archives and other historical sources in the city. Finally, locations of manuscript materials from Cuzco now found in Lima will be noted.

First, however, potential researchers should be warned that, in spite of the amount of material available, facilities are makeshift at best. There is no heat; lighting is poor; and photocopy services remain unavailable. Only the Archivo Histórico has scheduled hours of public service and an adequate staff. Admission to the Archivo del Arzobispado or the Archivo de la Sala Capitular depends upon the judgement, free time, and good will of the priests responsible for them. Letters of introduction, especially from men who are known and respected, are helpful everywhere.

Formerly the Archivo Histórico de la Universidad Nacional del Cuzco on the city's main plaza, the Archivo Departamental del Cusco is now located at 760 Avenida de Cultura. Under the direction of Dr. Manuel Jesús Aparicio, it is open from 8 a.m. to 1 p.m. weekdays throughout the year.

The only published catalogue of the Archivo Histórico is that by Jesús M. Covarrubias Pozo. While repetitious and contradictory, this work lists, quantifies, and dates the thirty-nine sections of the archives. It does not indicate the nature of materials in those sections, only where they come from. There is also a revised two-volume catalogue available only in typescript at the Archivo. The typescript guide provides information similar to that in Covarrubias' work plus descriptions of many individual documents in some of these sections. Below is an abbreviated listing of

Archives of Cuzco 309

the institutions whose archives form the major portion of this manuscript collection. Inclusive dates and physical measurements, although based on observations and the two catalogues mentioned, must be considered estimates.

Real Audiencia del Cuzco (1754-1835)

Ten shelves of fifty-seven packets with over 2,100 documents. These are subdivided into *civil* (thirty-two packets), *penal* (eighteen packets), *administrative* (six packets), and *ecclesiastical* (one packet).

Corte Superior de Justicia (1552-1938)

About forty shelves with 25,000 documents. Most of these are nineteenth- and twentieth-century cases, increasing in number in the later years. Few cases can be found prior to 1750.

Sociedad de Beneficencia Pública (1564-1899)

Ten shelves with 2,000 manuscripts. This contains material from the archives of the Convento de San Agustín, Convento-Hospital San Juan de Dios; the hospitals of San Bartolomé, San Andrés, and Hospital de Naturales as well as the newer Sociedad de Beneficencia. The documents are primarily financial or administrative records and copies of wills, and more than half are from the nineteenth century.

Universidad Nacional de San Antonio Abad del Cuzco (1846-1927)

Eight shelves with sixty-seven volumes. This consists of eleven books of *matrículas,* eleven of *exámenes,* eighteen of *grados,* twenty-one of the *secretaría,* and six of *tesorería.*

Cabildo del Cuzco (1545-1839)

Six shelves. This is an almost complete set of the *libros de actas.*

Municipalidad & Consejo Provincial del Cuzco (1846-1899)

Six shelves with 12,000 judicial and administrative documents.

Colegio de Ciencias y Artes (1545-1878)

Six shelves with over 1,000 manuscript booklets. Besides the Colegio's own nineteenth-century records, this collection contains financial and administrative documents from the following colonial institutions: Colegio de San Bernardo, Colegio de Caciques San Francisco de Borja, Superintendencia de Temporalidades del Cuzco, Convento-Hospital Nuestra Señora de la Almudeña, the Jesuit *noviciado,* and some *cofradía* account books.

Notarial Archives (1560-1899).

160 shelves of *registros* and *protocolos* from 100 different notaries. Within this period some records exist for almost every year; from the late seventeenth century onward, there are often several volumes for each year. Included in this section are about three shelves each from the nearby towns of Sicuani (dated 1700-1896) and Urubamba (1594-1900).

Miscellaneous

The Archivo Histórico also has several small sections of printed and manuscript materials including a few decrees of Simón Bolívar and Viceroy José de la Serna, a set of *El Peruano* dated 1842-1848, and a collection of geographical monographs compiled by Jorge Cornejo

Bouroncle. Not listed in either catalogue are the records of the Caja Real del Cuzco which are unorganized, stacked high on tables in the storeroom, and not yet available to researchers.

Cuzco has two important church archives to which it is possible to gain access--the Archivo del Arzobispado and the Archivo de la Sala Capitular. A letter from the bishop would facilitate entrance into both of these. Similarly, being without the bishop's endorsement makes admittance to parish records entirely dependent on the good will of local priests. Archives of the three monasteries in Cuzco are closed to all researchers except those able to get written permission to enter from the superior of the order in Lima. Although my information on these archives is incomplete, the following paragraphs may indicate their potential utility.

The Archivo de la Venerable Curia del Arzobispado del Cuzco is now located in the Seminario de San Antonio Abad on the southern edge of the city. It is apparently the one Raúl Porras Barrenechea located in the bishop's palace. [See *Fuentes históricas peruanas* (Lima, 1963), p. 228.] This has neither a reading room nor regular hours, but the seminary's resident librarian-archivist can usually be found, and adequate arrangements for service can be made.

The Archivo del Arzobispado contains roughly sixty shelf feet of documents dating 1650 to 1930, but it consists primarily of eighteenth- and nineteenth-century material. Over half of the documents pertain to litigation over *capellanías* or annulments in the Juzgado Eclesiástico. The archivist has a two-volume typed guide to this litigation with a detailed listing of each case. The unorganized portion of this Archive should also interest researchers. It contains *cofradía* account books and membership lists, rural parish church inventories, lists of men ordained to the priesthood in the seventeenth and eighteenth centuries, and many other items.

The other major church documentary collection is the Archivo de la Sala Capitular de la Basílica Metropolitana del Cuzco. Few people are allowed to see it and then only for short periods. The part that is known is in a small meeting room in the cathedral. This contains an almost complete collection of the minutes of *cabildo eclesiástico* meetings since the early seventeenth century. These volumes and dozens of bundles of unsorted papers fill bookcases across one wall of the room. A sampling of these bundles uncovered correspondence and interior administrative records from the mid-seventeenth to the twentieth century.

It is said that the cathedral has another room full of unorganized documents in a private house, but this remains unverified.

Little information is available about the parish records in Cuzco. The cathedral parish office has several volumes of records from the earliest years of Spanish settlement. Churches in two nearby towns, Urubamba and Paucartambo, also have baptism, marriage, death, and *cofradía* records dating from the seventeenth century.

The Franciscan, Mercedarian, and Dominican monasteries still have large archives begun in early colonial years, but all are closed to the public. The Franciscans reportedly have a well organized collection of manuscripts and a good library. The other two archives were rescued from rubble after the last earthquake and have remained locked up, unused and unorganized since then. The nature of archival holdings in Cuzco's three convents remains a mystery, although many of their colonial business transactions appear in notary records available at the Archivo Histórico.

In Cuzco, many other sources of information or documentation may be of value to the historian. The files of the regional agrarian reform office hold deeds, descriptions, and a few detailed maps of haciendas in the area. Some hacienda owners also retain family archives consisting of property deeds, wills, and occasional litigation. For the art historian the Museo Virreinal in the house of Garcilaso de la Vega and the Museo de Arte Colonial in the former *palacio arzobispal* both have large collections of painting of the *cuzqueño* school as well as from other Andean regions.

In Lima at least four archives have manuscripts from Cuzco. The Rare Books and Manuscript Section of Peru's Biblioteca Nacional has a variety of legal, ecclesiastical, and financial manuscripts from Cuzco, all entered chronologically and by subject in its card catalogue. The Archivo Arzobispal has a section titled Apelaciones del Cuzco with fifty-six documents dated 1604-1813.

In the Foreign Ministry Archives at the Torre Tagle the division concerning Peru's boundary with Bolivia has a large collection of original papers collected in the Cuzco area in addition to copies of other documents from the Archivo General de Indias. The excellent typed guide to this archive lists material on taxation of Indians, missions, accounts of a bishop's inspection of parishes in the Cuzco diocese, notary records from Paucartambo and other towns, royal decrees sent to Cuzco's *cabildo*, and a variety of other manuscripts.

Finally, the Archivo General de la Nación in Lima has material from or about Cuzco in almost all its sections. Especially important, since they are not yet available in Cuzco, are the financial records in the books of the *cajas reales* housed in the Ministerio de Hacienda section. Also useful are two sections of Jesuit records: Compañía de Jesús-- *colegios* and *cuentas de haciendas*.

These few pages contain only a partial listing of the historical sources available in Cuzco. For more detailed information the reader should consult the catalogue of Jesús M. Covarrubias Pozo, *Información archivística y catálogo general del Archivo Histórico* (Cuzco: H. G. Rozas, 1964). Perhaps of greater value for its listings and copies of historical documents is the *Revista del Archivo Histórico del Cuzco,* edited by the staff of the archives and published by the Universidad Nacional del Cuzco. This journal also contains articles on material about Cuzco in other archives.

Los Archivos de Trujillo
Hernán Horna

Indudablemente que la zona norte del Perú constituye la región menos estudiada de la república por intelectuales nacionales o extranjeros. Tal sanción es particularmente aplicable a los estudios de carácter histórico a pesar de la abundancia de fuentes primarias y buenos archivos. El obstáculo primordial ha sido la carencia de guías, índices, y catálogos que faciliten la utilización de esa riqueza documental. El historiador Rafael Narváez Cardenillas de la Universidad Nacional de Trujillo acertadamente dice que hasta la fecha las investigaciones históricas en los archivos locales han sido hechas "a ojo de buen cubero." El significado de los múltiples archivos trujillanos se acrecenta debido a que durante el período colonial y de la era republicana Trujillo fue uno de los centros administrativos políticos y religiosos más importantes del país. Sin embargo la mayoría de las fuentes coloniales se concentran en el área de la antigua diócesis de Trujillo o sea aproximadamente una tercera parte de la extensión territorial del Perú actual. Todo esto es de suma importancia puesto que la región norteña a pesar de haber sido políticamente parte del Perú, cultural e históricamente desde tiempos pre-incaicos, ha sido diferente al resto del país. Los documentos coloniales incluyen materiales relacionados con las antiguas provincias de Jaén y Mainas como también el Ecuador de hoy. La importancia de los archivos no decae para el estudio del período republicano porque, no obstante la conmoción revolucionaria, se salvaron con su valioso contenido que siguió acrecentándose.

Entre los archivos más fecundos para el historiador pueden incluirse los del Palacio Arzobispal, la Municipalidad, la Beneficencia Pública, la Corte Superior de Justicia, la Universidad Nacional de Trujillo, y ocho Notarías Públicas. Casi todas éstas fuentes de estudio e investigación tienen índices de estilo cronológico y alfabético pero desafortunadamente muy incompletos.

Debido a que las Notarías Públicas han constituido una fuente de ingresos para sus administradores, ellos se han preocupado y esmerado en ordenar, catalogar, y conservar sus abundantes manuscritos para su fácil localización. Las Notarías Públicas más ricas, antiguas, y mejor organizadas son las de Toribio Amayo, Gerardo Chávez, y Julio García Flores. Las Notarías Públicas contienen algunos documentos que se remontan a los albores del período colonial, y su número aumenta en el siglo XVII. Pero los manuscritos más abundantes y accesibles son los que corresponden al período posterior a 1850. Los legajos más completos estan relacionados con la posesión de tierras, disputas entre hacendados y comunidades indígenas, conflictos sobre derechos de riego, concesiones mineras, conflictos comerciales, y en general todos los procesos civiles de la localidad. Sin lugar a dudas estos materiales ofrecen grandes oportunidades para cualquier monografía de carácter socio-económico. Dichas fuentes documentales son las más fáciles de usar no sólo por su organización sino también por la colaboración de sus administradores.

Quizás el archivo con el potencial más alto para el investigador es él del Palacio Arzobispal. En él se encuentran documentos relacionados no solo con aspectos religiosos del norte peruano sino también el resto del país, y ellos se remontan en abundancia a los primeros dias del período colonial. Dentro de esta voluminosa colección documental se encuentran cuentas de haciendas y propiedades religiosas, reportajes sobre la recaudación del tributo, censos de población, mapas, y narraciones sobre la fundación de pueblos y parroquias. Existen varios tratados y reportajes de conflictos entre la iglesia y las autoridades civiles como también las diferentes opiniones eclesiásticas relacionadas con la función de la iglesia en la sociedad peruana. El Archivo Arzobispal está en el proceso de catalogación y ordenación bajo la dirección de Patricia Netherly y con el apoyo entusiástico del Arzobispo de Trujillo, Monseñor José María Jurgens, pronto quedará accessible a los estudiosos una de las fuentes documentales más ricas del Perú.

Entre las fuentes de difícil acceso para el uso del investigador, pero de indudable importancia, tenemos los archivos de la Corte Superior de Justicia, la Municipalidad, y la Beneficencia Pública. Sin embargo en 1974, el gobierno revolucionario del General Juan Velasco Alvarado estableció un archivo departamental que eventualmente alojará y permitirá su examinación por el investigador y el público estos documentos que hasta ahora han sido raramente consultados. En el sótano de la Corte Superior de Justicia se encuentran expedientes de procesos penales y las memorias anuales de los presidentes de dicha dependencia judicial que datan desde la era colonial hasta el presente. Todos estos documentos se encuentran organizados cronológicamente. En el Archivo de la Municipalidad se encuentran ordenanzas municipales, regulaciones locales, cuentas de impuestos, actas del cabildo, permisos, y licencias que datan desde la era colonial al presente. La Beneficencia Pública contiene numerosos documentos de instituciones para-estatales. Entre ellos tenemos las cuentas de hospitales, orfanatos, reformatorios, escuelas especiales, y otras organizaciones de asistencia pública.

Finalmente en el Archivo de la Universidad Nacional de Trujillo se hallan documentos relacionados con la vida intelectual, política, y social del país. Estos manuscritos que datan desde la tercera década del siglo XIX están en proceso de organización bajo la dirección y custodia del Dr. Héctor Centurión Vallejo y están a disposición del investigador.

The Archivo Arzobispal of Trujillo
Paul B. Ganster

ORGANIZATION OF THE ARCHIVE

During a period of approximately six months in 1971, while undertaking a study of settlement patterns in the Moche Valley for the Chan Chan-Moche Valley project of Harvard University and the Peabody Museum, I was able to devote considerable time to a complete reorganization of the Archivo Arzobispal of Trujillo. When work commenced, the Archive was in a state of complete disarray. Not only had it suffered the ravages of centuries of neglect but also the earthquake of May, 1970, had damaged the room in which the Archive was located. As a result, the documents had been removed to the Seminary of San Carlos and San Marcelo in the nearby town of Moche and dumped helter-skelter in empty dormitory rooms.

Based on experience gained through two years of research using ecclesiastical documents in the Archivo Arzobispal of Lima, a system of document classification was devised for Trujillo. This system followed as closely as possible the organization of the ecclesiastical administration and courts, and the legal procedures which had originally produced the documents. By using this means of categorization, the documents fell together in a logical order by subject and content. For example, civil and criminal law cases were grouped together into the section of CAUSAS GENERALES; documentation relating to sodalities was placed in COFRADIAS; probate proceedings were filed in TESTAMENTOS; and so forth. Of course, some overlapping in the content of individual documents exists between one section and the next, but, rules were developed to attempt to eliminate potential areas of confusion. These guidelines will be discussed in a longer guide to the Archive now being completed. A letter code designation was then given to each section of documents, ranging from A through EEE.

Order within each section was established strictly on a chronological basis. Documents or *expedientes* from cases which ran for a period of years are dated for the year in which the proceedings began. Thus, the expediente for a lawsuit beginning in 1721 and concluding in 1756 would all be found in the year 1721. The documents were then grouped together into conveniently sized bundles or *legajos*. The individual expedientes within each legajo were then labelled with a code indicating section, legajo number, expediente number, and the date. The letter code indicates section, the number before the decimal point indicates legajo number, and the number after the decimal point indicates the number of the expediente within the legajo. The date of the document also serves as an identifying feature. Thus, the code designation A 1.4 1642 reveals that the document is dated 1642, is the fourth expediente in legajo 1 of Section A, or APELACIONES.

It should be noted that the last few legajos of several sections contain undated documents as well as documents that were unearthed after that section had been ordered and numbered. In addition, several sections contain thousands of short documents which have not yet been put in chronological order. The sections which include undated or unordered documents are: COMUNICACIONES ECLESIASTICAS; COMUNICACIONES CON EL GOBIERNO; DUPLICADOS: BAUTISMOS; DUPLICADOS: MATRIMONIOS; DUPLICADOS: DIFUNCIONES; DUPLICADOS: BAUTISMOS, MATRIMONIOS, DIFUNCIONES; and PAPELES VARIOS DEL SIGLO XIX Y DEL SIGLO XX.

Once the basic order of the Archive was established, heavy cardboard wrappers were obtained for each legajo. Label cards were affixed to each legajo to display the name and code letter of the section, the number of the legajo, and the dates for the expedientes contained in these. Once the Archive had been reorganized, the documents were then returned to the newly repaired room in the Palacio Arzobispal in Trujillo where they are now located. The Archbishop of Trujillo has taken considerable interest in the Archive, and it is my understanding that he has been supervising the continuing arrangement of documents by chronology and the preparation of document-by-document indices.

CONTENTS OF THE ARCHIVE

The majority of the manuscripts in the Archive date from the late seventeenth century through the middle of the nineteenth century. The following table, based on a survey of 556 legajos from the ordered and numbered sections of the Archive, illustrates this chronological distribution:

Years	Percent of Legajos
to - 1599	.5%
1600 - 1649	1.0%
1650 - 1699	5.9%
1700 - 1749	15.8%
1750 - 1799	38.9%
1800 - 1849	30.0%
1850 - 1899	5.6%
1900 -	2.3%
TOTAL	100.0%

Very few items in the Archive predate 1650. It is not until the middle or third quarter of the seventeenth century that relatively complete runs of documents in any one section begin. These more or less continuous series of manuscripts taper off or terminate during two distinct time periods. First, during the last part of the eighteenth century, documentation in some sections is greatly reduced or stops altogether as a result of royal policies restricting the scope of jurisdiction of ecclesiastical courts. Once the number of court cases in any area was reduced, the volume of papers produced declined accordingly. Second, about the middle of the nineteenth century, republican governments greatly restricted the *fueros* of the church, causing a drastic drop in the number of documents after 1850.

Space here does not permit a thorough discussion of all the contents of the Archive. Rather an attempt will be made to point out some of the more significant holdings and sections and also to suggest some possible areas for research.

The Archive contains little in the way of extraordinarily unique or valuable documents. For example, nothing remains from the early seventeenth-century idolatry *visitas*, and only a few items are to be found from the marvelous visita of Bishop Martínez Compañón in the late eighteenth century. Most of the documents the bishop left in Trujillo have disappeared.[1] The greatest strength of the Archive, then, lies in other

---

1. A microfilm copy of the Martínez Compañón visita records in the Biblioteca Nacional in Bogotá has recently been deposited in the Biblioteca Nacional in Lima.

areas. It contains a number of complete runs of documents extending over long periods of time that deal with everyday, mundane matters. These documents constitute a storehouse of valuable data for local and regional history. Important, nearly complete series of documents are to be found especially in the following sections: CAPELLANIAS (102 legajos, 1680-1880); CAUSAS GENERALES (65 legajos, 1586-1887); COMUNICACIONES ECLESIASTICAS and COMUNICACIONES CON EL GOBIERNO (approximately twenty legajos, mainly eighteenth and early nineteenth centuries); DIEZMOS (in six sections, 56 legajos, 1562-1858); HACIENDA DE UNINGAMBAL (13 legajos, 1705-1875); OBRA PIA DE SINSICAPA (8 legajos, 1587-1864); MATRIMONIOS (various sections, early seventeenth century through the twentieth century); RELIGIOSOS Y RELIGIOSAS (24 legajos, 1561-1940); TESTAMENTOS (90 legajos, 1609-1874); and SEMINARIO DE SAN CARLOS Y SAN MARCELO (40 legajos, 1641-1937).

One of the potentially rewarding areas of study in Trujillo's Archivo Arzobispal is agricultural and land tenure history. Documentation is particularly rich for the Moche and Chicama valleys, but information also exists on the entire diocese. The principal reason for the plentiful information on rural property lies in the nature of ecclesiastical finances. Endowments providing income for colleges, convents, *capellanías*, *cofradías*, ordination of priests, and so forth were based on the *censo*, or mortgage, whereby the principal was invested in urban and rural real property in return for yearly interest payments. The section of CAPELLANIAS contains a wealth of information on the censos, and consequently on rural property. Capellanías were widespread by the time that the series of documents in the Archive commences, and so most units of real property on the north coast were encumbered with one or more censos. When a new censo was established on a given piece of property for a capellanía, or for any other purpose, all previously incurred censos were listed. Thus the capellanía legajos provide an accurate picture of the debt structure of the land. Inventories of buildings, trees, crops planted, farm implements, and slaves frequently accompany these documents and indicate the assets of the properties. Furthermore, constant litigation over title to capellanías served to multiply the documentation on censos. Information in this section is particularly rich from the 1670s through the 1850s.

An even more detailed picture of land utilization is provided in the section TESTAMENTOS, which often contains *concursos de acreedores de bienes,* bankruptcy proceedings or probate proceedings. Detailed listings of all debts and assets of individual agricultural units, ranging from small farms or *chacras* to large haciendas, provide a remarkable insight into the structure and function of these landed estates.

It should be noted that the sections of CAPELLANIAS and TESTAMENTOS contain documents essential for the study of urban property in the diocese, particularly in the city of Trujillo. The detailed inventories and appraisals present vital information on urban settlement patterns, architecture, and so forth.

Additional opportunities are present in the Archive for the intensive study of the microhistory of agricultural units in northern Peru. The section HACIENDA DE UNINGAMBAL and OBRA PIA DE SINSICAPA contain very complete records from 1705 through 1875 for Uningambal and from 1587 through 1864 for Sinsicapa. Uningambal was an hacienda used mainly for grazing, and Sinsicapa was an *obraje* (cloth factory) and hacienda used for pastoral activities located in the sierra near Trujillo. Each section has records so detailed that they even include the number of animals allotted to individual *pastores*. Hence, it would be feasible to reconstruct the nature of labor utilization on these lands. These two sections offer great potential for improving our understanding of the functioning of haciendas in northern Peru.

A more global view of rural and agricultural history in the Trujillo diocese is to be found in the six sections dealing with *diezmos,* or tithes. The documentation on diezmos includes accounts that list totals and subdivisions of income and expenditures of the *caja decimal*. In addition, records are extant on the rental of the tithe collection for different *partidos,* or subdivisions, of the diocese. These documents, in the section DIEZMOS: AUTOS are very complete from the 1680s through the 1820s but are scanty for the periods 1600 to 1680 and 1830 to 1856. This section also contains many lawsuits dealing with the collection of tithes. When combined with other documentation, the accounts and lawsuits should provide concrete evidence of fluctuations in agricultural production because of natural and human causes.

The Archive also has great potential for investigating the administrative and institutional history of the diocese. The section RELIGIOSOS Y

RELIGIOSAS has valuable material on the regular clergy of the region. Although random both in terms of chronology and geography, these documents are particularly useful because of the poor preservation of archives of individual orders in northern Peru. The section of SEMINARIO DE SAN CARLOS Y SAN MARCELO consists of some forty legajos of records on that institution which nearly cover the entire eighteenth century. These legajos provide considerable data on the financial structure, daily regimen, course of studies, faculty, and students of the Seminary.

The documents in the Archive also present good opportunities for understanding the formal structure of the bureaucracy of the diocese. Information on the clerical courts and administrative posts is widely scattered throughout various sections. The sections of COMUNICACIONES ECLESIASTICAS and COMUNICACIONES CON EL GOBIERNO tell a great deal about the daily functioning of the office of *provisor y vicario general*. Intermittent documentation on the *cabildo eclesiástico* (9 legajos) is available, but it is incomplete and needs to be supplemented with material from the archive of the cabildo eclesiástico in Trujillo.

Much more documentation in the Archivo Arzobispal, however, deals with the parish priests and parishes of the region. CURATOS contains a wide variety of information on these subjects, particularly for the mid-eighteenth through the mid-nineteenth centuries. CURATOS includes data on the selection of parish priests (*concursos*), changes of benefices (*permutas*), jurisdictional conflicts between parishes, and so forth. Demographic, social, political, economic, and religious conditions in the parishes are described in the section VISITAS, PADRONES, COMUNICACIONES CON EL GOBIERNO, COMUNICACIONES ECLESIASTICAS, PAPELES VARIOS DEL SIGLO XX, and COFRADIAS.

Excellent possibilities are also present for investigating the social history of the secular clergy, particularly the parish priests. The section of ORDENES, which contains the ordination papers of priests, has ample biographical data on individual priests. CURATOS, which has the *concurso expedientes,* provides career histories as well as personal and biographical information on priests. Applications for vacant parishes frequently included statements of *méritos y servicios* that aid greatly in completing the life histories of many individuals. These documents, when unattached to other proceedings, are to be found in the section MERITOS Y SERVICIOS. Because of the *fuero eclesiástico,* many of the civil and criminal cases in which clerics were involved ended up in the church courts. As a result, the section CAUSAS GENERALES is a mine of useful information on the clergy.

The use of the Archive for research into other aspects of colonial and early republican social history would be rewarding. An obvious area in which to begin is the section MATRIMONIOS: EXPEDIENTES, which contains many expedientes concerning the dispensation from impediments to marriage as well as documents on *informaciones de soltería*. These proceedings cover the period beginning in the last quarter of the seventeenth century and ending around the mid-nineteenth century. The *informaciones*, supplying proof that both partners of a potential marriage were single and able to be married, include significant biographical data on a wide range of social classes.

The Archivo Arzobispal also has good potential for research in areas such as the ethnohistory of the Indian populations of the diocese. Material on this subject is unfortunately widely scattered throughout many sections of the Archive. Documents on the first one hundred years of Spanish occupation are extremely scarce, but a sufficient number of sources are available for the reconstruction of the history of the Indians of the region during the late colonial period.

The foregoing discussion has pointed out the principal features of the manuscript collection of the Archivo Arzobispal of Trujillo. Also, a number of the more obvious research areas for which ample documentation exists have been highlighted. Of course, many potentially fruitful areas of research have not been mentioned here. It should be clear, nonetheless, that the Archive contains a sufficient quantity and variety of manuscript materials to enable historians to improve greatly our understanding of the relatively unknown mid-to-late colonial and early national periods on the north coast of Peru.

ARCHIVO ARZOBISPAL DE TRUJILLO

Section Code	Section Name (Number of Legajos, Years)
A............	APELACIONES (27 legajos, 1643-1846)
B............	CABILDO ECLESIASTICO (9 legajos, 1680-1880)
C............	CAJA DE DEPOSITOR (2 legajos; 1724-1845)
D............	CAPELLANIAS (102 legajos, 1620-1892)
E............	CAPILLAS Y ORATORIOS (2 legajos, 1709-1927)
F............	CAUSAS GENERALES (65 legajos, 1586-1887)
G............	CAUSAS DE NEGROS (7 legajos, 1670-1839)
H............	CENSURAS (1 legajo, 1663-1843)
I............	COFRADIAS (12 legajos, 1697-1887)
J............	COLEGIOS Y ESCUELAS (2 legajos, 1787-1926)
K............	COMUNICACIONES ECLESIASTICAS (10 legajos, late 17th to early 19th c.)
L............	COMUNICACIONES CON EL GOBIERNO (10 legajos, late 17th to early 19th c.)
M............	CONFIRMACIONES (approximately 2 legajos)
N............	CONTRIBUCIONES AL GOBIERNO (9 legajos, 1703-1851)
O............	CRUZADA (approximately 1 legajo)
P............	CUENTAS DE IGLESIAS
Q............	CURATOS (35 legajos, 1642-1895)
R............	DECRETOS, EDICTOS, REGLAMENTOS, ORDENANZAS DEL OBISPO (1 legajo)
S............	DIEZMOS: AUTOS (28 legajos, 1562-1856)
T............	DIEZMOS: OFICIOS (3 legajos, 1768-1849)
U............	DIEZMOS: CAJA DECIMAL, CUENTAS (17 legajos, 1638-1827)
V............	DIEZMOS: CAJA DECIMAL, CUADERNOS PROVISIONALES DE PAGAMENTOS (3 legajos, 1800-1821)
X............	DIEZMOS: CUADRANTE Y REPARTICION GENERAL (5 legajos, 1682-1858)
Y............	DIVORCIOS (4 legajos, 1622-1917)
Z............	ESCRITURAS VARIAS (1 legajo)
AA...........	FABRICA DE IGLESIAS (9 legajos, 1631-1922)
BB...........	HACIENDA DE UNINGAMBAL (13 legajos, 1705-1875)
CC...........	HOSPITALES (2 legajos, 1649-1890)
DD...........	IDOLATRIAS (1 legajo, 1752-1831)
EE...........	INVENTARIOS DE IGELSIAS (3 legajos)
FF...........	LIBROS PARROQUIALES (8 legajos, 1665-1934)

GG............ LICENCIAS (6 legajos)
HH............ MATRIMONIOS: EXPEDIENTES (19 legajos, 17th to 19th c.)
II............ MATRIMONIOS: NULIDAD (5 legajos, 1653-1925)
JJ............ MATRIMONIOS: LITIGIOS (5 legajos, 1609-1869)
KK............ MERITOS Y SERVICIOS
LL............ MISCELANEA
MM............ MUSICOS (2 legajos, 1767-1860)
NN............ NOTARIOS (1 legajo, 1766-1854)
OO............ OBRA PIA DE SINSICAPA (8 legajos, 1587-1864)
PP............ ORDENES
QQ............ PADRONES (3 legajos, 1664-1863)
RR............ PARTIDAS DE BAUTISMO (1 legajo)
SS............ PRIMICIAS (3 legajos, 1646-1886)
TT............ REGISTROS VARIOS
UU............ RELIGIOSOS Y RELIGIOSAS (24 legajos, 1561-1940)
VV............ TESTAMENTOS (90 legajos, 1609-1874)
WW............ SEMINARIO DE SAN CARLOS Y SAN MARCELO (40 legajos, 1641-1937)
XX............ VISITAS (3 legajos, 1623-1910)
YY............ DOCUMENTOS SIN CLASIFICAR
ZZ............ ARCHIVOS DE LAS PARROQUIAS (approximately 15 legajos)
AAA........... DUPLICADOS: BAUTISMOS (18 legajos)
BBB........... DUPLICADOS: MATRIMONIOS
CCC........... DUPLICADOS: DIFUNCIONES
DDD........... DUPLICADOS: BAUTISMOS, MATRIMONIOS, DIFUNCIONES
EEE........... PAPELES VARIOS DEL SIGLO XIX Y DEL SIGLO XX

Resources for the Study of Arequipa
Fernando A. Ponce

As the most important urban area in southern Peru, Arequipa has been the setting of historically significant events since the sixteenth century. Fortunately for the investigator, the dry, temperate climate has served to keep surviving historical documentation in good condition, unlike those coastal areas where records deteriorate more rapidly. This paper constitutes a resumé of the holdings of the major archival collections and libraries located in the district of Arequipa.

ARCHIVO HISTORICO DEPARTAMENTAL DE AREQUIPA

The Departmental Historical Archive was founded in 1961 by the Universidad Nacional de San Agustín de Arequipa and was run by that institution until 1973 when this task was assumed by the Instituto Nacional de Cultura and the Archivo General de la Nación. The Archive is located in a spacious and comfortable building at 102 Calle Quesada, Yanahuara, and is under the direction of Dr. Guillermo Galdós Rodríguez. A recent publication of the Universidad Nacional, *Inédita* (1973 ff.), under the editorship of Dr. E. Ugarte y Ugarte, reprints various documents contained in the Archive, including, for example, "Las ordenanzas de Arequipa, 1539-1575," "Onomástico de los estudiantes del Seminario de San Jerónimo, 1788-1816," etc.

There are three basic groups of documents contained in the Archive: 1) notarial records, 2) prefectural records, and 3) economic and financial records. The notarial record section of the Archive is the largest and most complete of these three groups. Because the notarial records contain economic, social, and political information of all sorts, they are of special interest to the historian. The documentation is scarce for the colonial period, especially the sixteenth century, although the Registros de Escrituras Públicas or Libros de Protocolos Notariales cover the period 1549-1820. These contain considerable information on labor contracts, estates and other forms of real property, marriage, etc. The internal division of the volumes is chronological. Some are indexed alphabetically, although oftentimes this is by the individual's first name which renders it less useful to the researcher. A guide to the Libros de Protocolos for the years 1549-1820 by Fernando A. Ponce and Eusebio Quiroz Paz-Soldán, "Informe de datos bibliográfico-documentales de orden demográfico de la ciudad de Arequipa, Perú," (mimeo, 1972) is to be published by the Centro Latinamericano de Demografía (CELADE) of the United Nations. A guide to the notarial records after 1820 already exists. The second type of documentation in the notarial section consists of records of various deeds and judicial procedures.

The prefectural records of the Archive are less complete than the notarial documents and cover the period 1895-1930, those existing before and after these dates having been burned or otherwise destroyed. The documents consist primarily of the reports filed by the departmental prefects to the Ministerio del Interior and other ministries and are thus concerned primarily with political affairs. Among the more interesting data contained in them include the revolt of Nicolás de Piérola against the government of President Andrés Avelino Cáceres and information about the government of Augusto B. Leguía. Unfortunately, there is no guide or calendar of documents located in Arequipa similar to those published for the prefectural documents located in the Archivo General de la Nación in Lima.[1]

Because Arequipa has been the fiscal and administrative center of southern Peru, there are a sizeable number of documents preserved in the Departmental Archive dealing with economy and finance. Unfortunately, records for the early colonial period are absent save for the period 1800-1820. The Archive, however, possesses complete documentation for the period 1838-1890, and an inventory of these materials is present being prepared. I have utilized these sources in the writing of my dissertation (the University of Texas at Austin), which deals with the process of social change in Arequipa, 1840-1880, and have observed a reasonably good coverage for this period. These records are grouped into several volumes, the principal being the *mayor,* or the account books of the district, and the

---

1. See, for example, the *Catálogos,* No. 1 (1972) and No. 2 (1974), published by the Archivo General de la Nación, which list the prefectural documents located in that repository. Also the *Catálogo de la Sección Republicana,* 2 vols. (Lima, 1945-1946) and the journal *Publicaciones del Archivo Histórico,* 13 editions (Lima, 1960-1966).

diario (manual), which is a chronological journal of day-by-day operations of these accounts. Records of the *alcabala, provisiones, tomas de razón,* and *papel sellado y timbres* also exist for certain years. Unfortunately, most of the original documents referred to in these registers are missing, and for this reason, figures in the account books cannot be substantiated by other sources.

PARISH ARCHIVES

The city of Arequipa has two principal parishes, those of Sagrario and Santa Marta, in addition to the nearby parishes of San Antonio (district of Miraflores), Cayma (district of Cayma), and Yanahuara (district of Yanahuara). Every parish preserves certain records, and some, as in the case of Sagrario, date from 1644. During the nineteenth century many of these parish registers were lost or destroyed as was the case for the parish of Tiabaya. Many, however, still exist and include records for the several vice-parishes in each parish district. Among the documents surviving are records of visits by the bishop, inventories, information concerning *cofradías,* and the like. In Sagrario, marriage and baptismal records still exist although this is not always the case in the other parishes. Two rare censuses, one corresponding to the vice-parish of Bellavista in the El Palomar district outside of Arequipa and dated 1809, and another for that of Santa Marta about 1813 or 1816, are also preserved at the Sagrario parish. A guide to the principal parishes, indicating the materials located there, the years covered for each type of documentation, and other information is being prepared by CELADE.

CONVENT ARCHIVES

The several order convents in Arequipa contain some very good documental collections which are unknown to many researchers, a prime example being the collection of Fr. V. M. Barriga, a well-known historian of Arequipa, located in the La Merced Convent. Among the other convents are those operated by the Dominican and Franciscan orders, and the Seminario de San Jerónimo. Unfortunately, access to these collections is not always available. Unlike the Society of Jesus, expelled from the Spanish American colonies in 1767, whose documents are preserved in the Archivo General de la Nación in Lima and in other public repositories in Spain and South America, entrance to these private collections is by permission only.

ARCHIVO MUNICIPAL DE AREQUIPA

Of the several archives under the administration of the Consejo Provincial de Arequipa, the most significant is the Municipal Archive, located in the Municipal Library, which houses the records of the Cabildo de Arequipa for the years 1546 to 1791 and from 1804-1812. Among the documents located here are the books of the meetings and agreements of the Arequipa *cabildo*, and other record groups entitled *reales cédulas, provisiones, pragmáticas, instrucciones, pósito y alhóndiga, aranceles, borrador de cartas, expedientes, entradas y gastos, junta municipal de propios y arbítrios, padrones de electores* (covering two sectors of the city for the years 1813-1831), *procotolos de escribanos* (a notarial register of protocols of Alonso de Luque, 1539-1544). and *tomas de razón*. These groups vary widely both in the length and breadth of chronological coverage. A partial calendar of documents of the cabildo records and a general guide to this Archive by Alejandro Málaga Medina, Eusebio Quiroz Paz-Soldán, and Juan Alvarez Salas, eds., *Indice del libro segundo de actas de sesiones y acuerdos del cabildo de la ciudad de Arequipa, 1546-1556* (Arequipa, 1974), and the same authors' *Catálogo general del Archivo Municipal de Arequipa* (Arequipa, 1974) have also been published.

ARCHIVO DE MESA DE PARTES

This Archive contains the records of sessions of the Arequipa *cabildo* for the republican period, with the exception of those for the years 1813-1828 and 1834-1857 which have disappeared long ago. Unfortunately, these years include the important Pumacahua and Angulo revolution, the wars of independence, the creation of the Peru-Bolivian Confederation, and the turbulent period of the 1840s. Nevertheless, important documents such as the Arequipa census of 1859 and the supplement to this census for 1860, the memoirs of several mayors, records pertaining to several public works projects, and the city budgets (from 1874 onwards) are preserved in good condition. City newspapers of the period, for example, *El Registro Oficial* and the national tabloid *El Peruano*, covering almost the entire nineteenth century, are also located in the Archive.

ARCHIVO DE LA OFICINA DE ESTADISTICA Y CENSOS

The Archive of the Office of Statistics and Censuses of the city of Arequipa, which contains the vital records of the city, is also of potential value to the researcher. A good example is the nineteenth-century census records. Volume I of the three-volume census of 1862 for the city of Arequipa is missing, although volumes II and III, covering the nearby districts, still exist. The 1876 census of the entire district is preserved intact. These records were rarely used prior to 1870 but have been regularly compiled since 1936 when the government began to enforce the civil registration laws. The Catholic register is accurate for the years prior to 1936, however. Other offices within the municipal government contain miscellaneous documents dealing with a variety of subjects whose exact content is unknown.

PRIVATE ARCHIVES

While many of the commercial firms doing business in the Arequipa region during the nineteenth century, for example, the Braillard, Gibbs and Crawley, and Jack Brothers companies, did not leave records; others such as the Southern Railroad Company (presently the state-owned Empresa Nacional de Ferrocarriles, or ENAFER) have records dating from the beginning of the twentieth century, although many are incomplete. Other institutions, such as the National University, the Sociedad Pública de Beneficencia de Arequipa, the district councils, as well as the various state agencies operating in the fields of agriculture, industry, energy (for example the Electric Company of Arequipa), communications, and others, such as that operating the recent agrarian reform program, may have libraries and even document collections which can be of use to the persevering researcher.

The Genealogical Society of Utah (Church of Latter-Day Saints): A Research Resource for Andean History
Paul B. Ganster

An important research resource for Andean area specialists is the microfilm collection of the Genealogical Society of the Church of Jesus Christ of Latter-day Saints (Mormon), located in Salt Lake City, Utah. The Genealogical Society is now microfilming genealogical materials that will aid members of the church in tracing their ancestry for religious purposes. Although the Society does not function as an institution for historical research per se, serious scholars may gain access to its holdings either at the main headquarters in Salt Lake City, or at numerous branch libraries scattered around the United States and foreign countries. For additional information on both the contents of the collection and on the use of these materials, interested individuals should consult the short article by Larry R. Gerlach and Michael L. Nicholls, "The Mormon Genealogical Society and Research Opportunities in Early American History," *William and Mary Quarterly,* 32 (3d series, October, 1975):625-629. Another article on the Genealogical Society, is Roger Haigh and Frank J. Sanders, "A Report on Some Latin American Materials in the Genealogical Library of the Church of Jesus Christ of the Latter Day Saints at Salt Lake City, Utah," *Latin American Research Reivew,* 10 (Summer, 1975):193-196. An update article on the collection is C. Douglas Inglis, "The Genealogical Society of Utah and the Center for Historical Population Studies, University of Utah: Notes on Their Use for Latin Americanists," *Latin American Population Newsletter,* 1 (Fall, 1979):35-36.

Holdings of microfilmed documents for the Andean-area countries are relatively modest at the present time: 5,047 rolls for Chile, 797 rolls for Peru, 753 for Bolivia, and six for Ecuador. Camera crews, however, continue to film and add to the number of records available to investigators. Once filming does begin, an enormous amount of material is rapidly added to the collections. For example, 111,599 rolls of film are now available for Mexico, over ninety percent of the church records and seventy percent of the civil records.

As a general rule, pertinent records on film date from the conquest through 1901, or sometimes 1921. Primary emphasis is on manuscripts having a high yield of material relevant to genealogical studies. Specifically, the vital statistics contained in parish registers and civil registers have first priority, but other useful documents are also filmed. These include *censos, padrones, notariales, testamentos,* Inquisition materials, *tierras y propiedades,* civil and criminal legal cases, military records, immigration documents, municipal archives, and family archives. As a general rule, the Society concentrates on the vital statistical records, but when gaps appear in these materials, the filming crew fills in with other sources. The Society has prepared a guide to the types of documents microfilmed in Chile, *Fuentes principales de registros genealógicos en Chile* (Salt Lake City: The Genealogical Society, n.d.), 13 pp., and is in the process of preparing similar guides to its microfilmed documents on other Andean countries.

The holdings of the Genealogical Society contain a wealth of information for social history, demographic history, and other types of historical studies. Although the holdings for the Andean region are small at the present time, the ongoing filming program will rapidly increase the amount of materials available. Not only has the Genealogical Society made a large amount of information available to scholars, but also it has performed an invaluable service by assuring the preservation of copies of materials that, in many cases, are rapidly deteriorating and were inaccessible in the United States.

The Principal Archives and Libraries of Peru: Useful Names and Addresses
Tita Monzón de Davies

LIMA

Archivo General de la Nación

Palacio de Justicia - Jirón Manuel Cuadros s/n, Lima   Tel:27-5930
Director: Dr. Guillermo Durand Flórez
Assistant Director: Sr. Alberto Rosas Siles
Hours: 8 a.m. - 7:30 p.m.

Archivo Arzobispal

3ra. block, Av. Lampa, s/n   Tel:28-7289
Director: Sr. Valentín Trujillo Mena
Hours: 8 a.m. - 1 p.m.

Archivo General del Ministerio de Relaciones Exteriores

Torre Tagle Palace   Tel:27-6750
Director: Emb. Sr. Luzgardo Beleván
Hours: 8:30 a.m. - 4:45 p.m.

Archivo Histórico del Ministerio de Hacienda y Comercio

Basement of Palacio de Justicia - Jirón Manuel Cuadros s/n   Tel:40-7120
Director: Dr. Antolín Bedoya
Hours: 8 a.m. - 7:30 p.m.

Archivo del Ministerio de Economía y Finanzas

Tel:27-1012
Director: Sr. José Martínez Vegazo
Hours: 9 a.m. - 5 p.m.

Archivo de la Oficina Nacional de Estadística y Censo - ONEC

Director: Cap. G. C. Carlos Jiménez Arca
Hours: 8:30 a.m. - 4:45 p.m.

Archivo de la Beneficencia Pública de Lima

Jirón Carabaya 641   Tel:28-8070
Director: Sr. Rolando Olazo
Hours: 10:30 a.m. - 12:30 p.m.; 2 p.m. - 4 p.m.

Archivo del Ministerio de Trabajo y Asuntos Indígenas

Tel:32-2510
Director: Sr. Alberto Zevallos Corvacho
Hours: 9 a.m. - 5 p.m.

Archivo del Banco Central de Reserva del Perú

Jirón Ucayali 299 Tel:27-8076
Director: Sr. Fernando Rivarola
Hours: 9 a.m. - 4:30 p.m.

Archivo Histórico de la Biblioteca Municipalidad de Lima

Plaza de Armas s/n Tel:28-1551
Inca Garcilaso de la Vega 150
Director: Sr. Luis Málaga Bedregal
Hours: 8:30 a.m. - 4:45 p.m.

Sala de Investigaciones del Biblioteca Nacional

Av. Abancay s/n Tel:28-7690
Director: Srta. Graciela Sánchez Cerro
Hours: 9 a.m. - 8:15 p.m.

Archivo de la Cámara de Diputados

Plaza Inquisición s/n Tel:28-7980
Director: Sr. Elías Gutiérrez Cáceres
Hours: 8:30 a.m. - 4:45 p.m.

Archivo de la Universidad Nacional Mayor de San Marcos

Parque Universitario - Casona Tel:28-0052
Director: Dr. Carlos Daniel Valcárcel
Hours: 9 a.m. - 4 p.m.

Biblioteca Central de la Universidad Nacional Mayor de San Marcos

Av. República de Chile 295, Of. 508 Tel:28-4878
Director: Dr. Luis Gonzáles Mugaburu
Hours: 8 a.m. - 10 p.m.

Biblioteca de la Universidad Nacional de Ingeniería

Av. Túpac Amaru, Km. 4
Tel: 81-1070

Biblioteca del "Instituto Riva-Agüero" de la Pontífica Universidad Católica

Camaná 459 Tel:27-9275
Director: Dr. Alejandro Lastanau

Biblioteca de la Universidad Nacional Agraria (La Molina)

Tel: 35-2035

Centro de Documentación Agraria

Paita 429 (Rimac) Tel:81-2459
Director: Sr. Humberto Rodríguez
Hours: 9 a.m. - 6 p.m.

Confederación Nacional Agraria

A. Miró Quesada 327-8° piso Tel:28-8220
Exec. Co-ordinator: Sr. Elíseo Salas
Hours: 9 a.m. - 5 p.m.

Archivo del Club Nacional

Jirón de la Unión 10106, Apt. 1461 Tel:28-6060
Director: Sr. Jaime Quispe
Hours: 10 a.m. - 12 p.m.

AREQUIPA

Archivo Histórico Departmental de Arequipa

Calle Quesada 102 - Yanahuara - Arequipa Tel:21-908
Director: Dr. Guillermo Galdós Rodríguez
Hours: 8 a.m. - 3 p.m.

CUZCO

Archivo Histórico Departmental del Cuzco

Avenida de Cultura 760
Director: Dr. Manuel Aparicio Vega
Hours: 8 a.m. - 1 p.m.

Archivo de la Venerable Curia del Arzobispado del Cuzco

Universidad San Antonio Abad - Plaza de Armas - Cuzco

TRUJILLO

Archivo Departmental de Trujillo

Jirón Estete 540 - Trujillo, La Libertad
Director: Dr. Napoleón Cieza Burga
Hours: 8 a.m. - 3 p.m.

Archivo Arzobispal de Trujillo

Palacio Arzobispal

Index

ARGENTINA

Buenos Aires

    Archivo General de la Nación: 17, 86, 261
    Biblioteca Nacional: 86

Córdoba

    Archivo Histórico de Córdoba: 261

Jujuy

    Archivo de San Salvador: 261

Tucumán

    Archivo Histórico del Tucumán: 261

AUSTRIA

Vienna

    Biblioteca Imperial: 39

BOLIVIA

Cochabamba

    Archivo del Convento de San Francisco: 7n.
    Archivo del Convento de Santa Clara: 7n.
    Archivo del Convento de Santo Domingo: 7n.
    Archivo Histórico Municipal: 5-7, 46
    Palacio de Cultura: 5-6

La Paz

    Archivo de la Curia Arzobispal: 23-27
    Archivo de la Recoleta Franciscana: 27n.
    Archivo de la Universidad Mayor de San Andrés (Cota-Cota): 8-14
    Archivo del Convento de San Francisco: 27n.
    Archivo del Ministerio de Relaciones Exteriores y Culto: 4, 15-18
    Archivo del Monasterio de Concepcionistas: 27n.
    Archivo Mariscal Santa Cruz: 19-20
    Archivo Metropolitano de la Catedral: 21-23
    Biblioteca Central de la Universidad Mayor de San Andrés: 10, 12
    Biblioteca Municipal 'Mariscal Andrés Santa Cruz': 13
    Corporación Boliviana de Fomento: 9
    Corporación Minería de Bolivia (COMIBOL): 13

La Paz (continued)

    Ministerio de Defensa Nacional: 9
    Ministerio de Educación: 13
    Ministerio de Finanzas: 9
    Ministerio de Hacienda: 9
    Ministerio de Interior: 9
    Ministerio de Relaciones Exteriores: 4, 9, 15-18
    Ministerio de Salud Pública: 13
    Museo 'Casa de Murillo': 12
    Universidad Mayor de San Andrés: 8-14, 27

Oruro

    Archivo de la Corte de Justicia: 28-29
    Banco Central de Bolivia, Sucursal de Oruro: 28-29
    Biblioteca Municipal: 28
    Centro de Investigaciones Sociales, Universidad de Oruro: 29n.

Poopó (Oruro)

    Archivo Judicial: 29n.

Potosí

    Alcaldía Municipal: 35
    Archivo Arzobispal: 49
    Archivo de la Parroquia de la Concepción: 36n.
    Archivo del Convento de La Merced: 33
    Archivo del Convento de San Agustín: 33
    Archivo del Convento de San Francisco: 35n.
    Archivo del Convento de Santa Teresa: 36n.
    Archivo del Convento de Santo Domingo: 33
    Archivo del Recogimiento de Niñas Huérfanos: 33
    Archivo Diocesano: 36
    Archivo Histórico de Potosí: 30-36, 260
    Archivo Municipal: 32n.
    Museo del Arte e Historia: 30
    Sociedad Geográfica y de Historia 'Potosí': 30

Santa Cruz

    Archivo de la Catedral: 40-41
    Archivo de la Parroquia de Vallegrande: 41
    Archivo del Convento de La Merced: 41
    Archivo del Convento de San Francisco: 41
    Archivo Judicial: 41-42
    Archivo Notarial: 42-43
    Biblioteca Central de la Universidad Gabriel René Moreno: 43-44
    Biblioteca Universitaria: 43-44

Sucre

    Archivo de la Parroquia de Santo Domingo: 49
    Archivo del Cabildo Eclesiástico: 49
    Archivo del Convento de la Recoleta: 49
    Archivo del Oratorio de San Felipe Neri: 49
    Archivo Nacional de Bolivia: 13, 17, 32, 45-48, 260
    Archivo y Biblioteca Nacional de Bolivia: 3-4, 6

Sucre (continued)

    Biblioteca de la Universidad de San Francisco Xavier de la Plata: 47, 49
    Biblioteca del Convento de la Recoleta: 49
    Biblioteca Nacional de Bolivia: 46-48
    Sociedad Geográfica de Sucre: 48-49

Tarija

    Archivo de la Notaría de Hacienda: 50
    Archivo de la Parroquia Matriz: 50
    Archivo del Convento de San Francisco: 50
    Archivo Municipal: 51

CHILE

Antofagasta

    Archivo Arzobispal: 58n.

Calama

    Archivo de la Prelatura: 58n.

Chillán

    Archivo de Protocolos: 69n.

Concepción

    Archivo de Protocolos: 69n.
    Compañía de Lota: 57
    Corte de Apelaciones: 57
    Sociedad Lorenzo Arenas: 57
    Universidad de Chile: 57

Copiapó

    Archivo de Protocolos: 69

Coquimbo

    Archivo Notarial: 96

Iquique

    Archivo Notarial: 96

Punta Arenas

    Regional Research Center: 58

Santiago

    Academia Chilena de Historia: 56, 86
    Anexo de la Biblioteca del Congreso: 56, 99n., 102, 109, 133
    Archivo Claudio Gay: 55, 76n., 93-94
    Archivo de Benjamín Vicuña Mackenna: 93-94
    Archivo de Escribanos: 55, 65
    Archivo de Fondos Varios: 93-94

Index 338

Santiago (continued)
    Archivo de Jaime Eyzaguirre: 55
    Archivo de la Capitanía General: 55, 63
    Archivo de la Contaduría Mayor: 55n., 64-65, 67n., 70, 76, 79, 80-83
    Archivo de la Contratación: 67n.
    Archivo de la Intendencia de Concepción: 65
    Archivo de la Real Audiencia: 55, 63-64, 67n., 68
    Archivo de las Juntas de Beneficencias: 95
    Archivo del Cabildo de Santiago: 65
    Archivo del Departamento de Tierras y Bienes Raíces Nacionales: 95
    Archivo del Diccionario Eclesiástico: 93-94
    Archivo del Ministerio de lo Interior: 63n.
    Archivo del Ministerio de Relaciones Exteriores: 55-56
    Archivo del Museo de Medicina: 55
    Archivo del Obispado: 56, 104-105
    Archivo de los Ferrocarriles del Estado: 95
    Archivo de los Jesuitas: 55, 68-69
    Archivo del Tribunal del Consulado: 70
    Archivo del Tribunal de Minería: 55, 65, 70, 82
    Archivo Gay Morla: 69n.
    Archivo Hidrográfico Vidal Gormaz: 55
    Archivo Judicial: 68-69, 80, 82, 93-94, 96-97
    Archivo Nacional: 54-58, 61-70, 73, 76, 93-96, 103-104, 159
    Archivo Notarial: 68-70, 80, 82, 93, 95-97
    Archivo Prieto: 56
    Asociación Salitrera de Propaganda: 105
    Banco Central de Chile: 117
    Biblioteca del Congreso: 56, 60, 102, 105, 107-111, 114, 133
    Biblioteca del Estado Mayor del Ejército de Chile (BEMGE): 134
    Biblioteca Nacional: 54-57, 59, 62, 67n. 74, 92-93, 101-105, 108-114, 125, 133
    Caja de Crédito Hipotecario: 95
    Caja de la Habitación: 113
    Caja del Seguro Obligatorio: 113
    Cámara de Diputados: 99, 113
    Casa de Moneda: 78-79
    Centro Bellarmino: 116
    Centro de Historia Colonial, Universidad de Chile: 69n.
    Centro de Investigaciones de Historia Americana: 109
    Centro de Investigaciones y Acción Social: 116
    Centro Latinoamericano de Demografía (CELADE): 109, 116
    Centro para el Desarrollo Económica y Social de América Latina: 109
    Chilean Labor Archive: 119-125
    Club de la Unión: 115
    Club de Profesoras: 115
    Confederación de la Producción y el Comercio: 114
    Consejo del Estado: 78, 102
    Contraloría General de la República: 102
    Corporación de Fomento de la Producción (CORFO): 113, 117
    DESAL: 116
    Dirección de Bibliotecas, Archivos, y Museos: 54
    Dirección de Estadística y Censo: 112-113, 117
    Dirección General del Registro Electoral: 99n., 112
    Escuela Militar: 57
    Facultad Latinoamericana de Ciencias Sociales (FLASCO): 109, 116

Santiago (continued)

    General Staff Library: 134
    Instituto de Organización y Administración de Empresas: (INSORA): 116
    Instituto Latinoamericano de Investigaciones Sociales (ILDIS): 116
    Instituto Nacional de Estadística: 102
    Ministerio de Agricultura: 113
    Ministerio de Culto e Instrucción Pública: 84
    Ministerio de Defensa Nacional: 57, 134
    Ministerio de Guerra y Marina: 84, 100
    Ministerio de Hacienda: 55, 76-79, 80-84, 94, 103, 113
    Ministerio de Hacienda y Justicia: 84
    Ministerio de Industria y Obras Públicas: 94, 113, 117
    Ministerio de lo Interior: 55, 76-77, 80-82, 92, 94, 102-104, 113, 122
    Ministerio de Relaciones Exteriores: 94, 103, 114
    Ministerio de Salubridad, Previsión, y Asistencia Social: 113, 117
    Ministerio de Trabajo: 114, 121, 124
    Museo de Benjamín Vicuña Mackenna: 95
    Museo Pedagógico, Universidad de Chile: 56
    Museo Recabarren: 111
    Oficina Central de Estadística: 91, 99n., 106n., 113
    Oficina de Aduanas: 91
    Oficina de Informaciones del Senado: 102
    Seminario Matta Vial: 60
    Senado: 99, 113-114
    Servicio Nacional de Estadística: 99n.; *see also* Oficina Central de Estadística
    Sociedad Chilena de Historia y Geografía: 109
    Sociedad de Fomento Fabril: 93, 105, 114
    Sociedad Nacional de Agricultura: 93, 105, 114
    Sociedad Nacional de Minería: 93, 105, 114
    Student Federation of Chile (FECH): 115
    Superintendencia de Aduanas: 106n.
    Universidad Católica de Santiago: 86, 109, 116
    Universidad de Chile: 56, 95, 109, 116

Valdivia

    Archivo de Protocolos Notariales: 55
    Universidad Austral: 58

Valparaíso

    Archivo de Escribanos: 55
    Archivo de Protocolos: 69n.
    Archivo Notarial: 96
    Severín: 57
    Universidad Católica de Valparaíso: 57

COLOMBIA

Bogotá

    Archivo Histórico Nacional: 184
    Biblioteca Nacional: 318n.

Popayán

    Archivo de la Gobernación: 144

ECUADOR

Ambato

Archivo de la Gobernación: 202
Archivo de la Parroquia: 203
Archivo Municipal: 199-200
Biblioteca de la Casa de Montalvo: 204
Biblioteca del Colegio Bolívar: 204

Cajabamba (Chimborazo)

Archivo de la Parroquia: 203

Cotopaxi

Archivo de la Gobernación: 201
Archivo de la Parroquia de San Felipe: 203
Archivo de la Parroquia de San Sebastián: 203

Cuenca

Archivo de la Caja Real de Cuenca: 177-178
Archivo de la Curia: 179
Archivo de la Gobernación: 177-178
Archivo de la Segunda Notaría: 177-179
Archivo de la Tercera Notaría: 177-179
Archivo del Cabildo Eclesiástico: 179
Archivo del Seminario: 179
Archivo Histórico de la Municipalidad de Cuenca (AH/MC): 176-177
Archivo Nacional de Historia: Sección del Azuay (ANH/SA): 176-179, 181
Archivo y Biblioteca de la Corte Superior de Justicia del Azuay (ABCSJ/A): 179-181
Biblioteca de la Casa de la Cultura Ecuatoriana, Núcleo del Azuay: 179-180
Biblioteca del Dr. Miguel Díaz Cueva: 180
Biblioteca de Víctor Manuel Albornoz: 180
Biblioteca Municipal: 179-180
Casa de Cultura Ecuatoriana, Núcleo del Azuay: 177
Museo de las Carmelitas: 180
Museo de las Conceptas: 180
Museo Municipal: 176
Museo Municipal Remigio Crespo Toral: 180

Guayaquil

Archivo de don Pedro Robles Chambers: 196
Archivo de Escribanías: 184, 193
Archivo de la Biblioteca Carlos A. Rolando (ACAR/G): 192
Archivo de la Corte Superior (ACS/G): 193-194
Archivo de la Curia Diocesano (ACD/G): 194-195
Archivo de la Parroquia del Sagrario: 195
Archivo de la Parroquia de San Alejo: 195
Archivo de la Secretaría Municipal (ASM/G): 185-186
Archivo del Cabildo: 185
Archivo del Cementario y/o Funeraría de la Junta de Beneficencia: 195
Archivo del Convento de La Concepción: 195
Archivo del Convento de La Merced: 195
Archivo del Registro de la Propriedad (ARP/G): 192-193

Guayaquil (continued)

   Archivo Histórico de la Biblioteca Municipal (AH/BMG): 144, 182, 185-192
   Archivo Histórico del Guayas (AHG): 144, 183-184, 193-194
   Biblioteca de Autores Nacionales: Carlos A. Rolando: 183
   Biblioteca de la Casa de la Cultura Ecuatoriana: Núcleo del Guayas: 183
   Biblioteca Municipal (BMG): 182-183
   Centro de Investigaciones Históricas: 184

Latacunga

   Archivo de la Gobernación: 202
   Archivo de la Parroquia: 203
   Archivo Municipal: 198-199
   Biblioteca Municipal: 204

Patate (Tungurahua)

   Archivo de la Parroquia: 203

Pelileo

   Archivo de la Jefatura Política: 201
   Archivo Municipal: 201

Píllaro

   Archivo de la Jefatura Política: 201
   Archivo Municipal: 201

Quero

   Archivo de la Jefatura Política: 201

Quito

   Archivo Arzobispal: 157-158
   Archivo de la Auditoría Jurídica: 173
   Archivo de la Comandancia de la Fuerza Aérea: 173
   Archivo de la Comandancia del Ejército: 173
   Archivo de la Comandancia Naval: 173
   Archivo de la Pontificia Universidad Católica del Ecuador: 162-163
   Archivo de la Presidencia: 162
   Archivo de la Universidad Central: 157
   Archivo del Cabildo Eclesiástico: 158
   Archivo del Colegio Militar Eloy Alfaro: 173-174
   Archivo del Convento de San Francisco: 158-159
   Archivo del Convento de Santo Domingo: 159-160
   Archivo del Ministerio de Finanzas: 161-162
   Archivo del Ministerio de Gobierno: 160-162
   Archivo de los Hospitales Militares: 173
   Archivo de los Jesuitas: 159
   Archivo General del Ministerio de Defensa (AGMD): 172-174
   Archivo Histórico y Diplomático: 171
   Archivo Municipal: 156-157
   Archivo Nacional de Historia: 152, 160-162, 164-169
   Archivo Nacional de Relaciones Exteriores: 170-171
   Biblioteca de Carlos Manuel Larrea: 155-156

Quito (continued)

    Biblioteca de la Casa de Cultura Ecuatoriana: 154
    Biblioteca de la Universidad Católica: 155
    Biblioteca de la Universidad Central: 154-155
    Biblioteca del Banco Central: 155
    Biblioteca del Colegio Nacional Mejía: 155
    Biblioteca del Jacinto Jijón y Caamaño: 155
    Biblioteca del Poder Legislativo: 154
    Biblioteca Ecuatoriana: Aurelio Espinosa Polit: 153-154
    Biblioteca General del Ministerio de Relaciones Exteriores: 170-171
    Biblioteca Municipal: 152-153, 160
    Biblioteca Nacional: 152, 160
    Casa de Cultura Ecuatoriana: 152, 164
    Centro de Historia y Geografía Militar: 161-162, 174
    Corte Suprema de Justicia: 166-168
    Ministerio de Defensa: 172-174
    Ministerio de Finanzas: 162, 174
    Ministerio de Gobierno: 160
    Ministerio de Guerra y Marina, 178
    Ministerio de Hacienda: 161, 174, 178
    Ministerio de lo Interior: 178
    Ministerio de Relaciones Exteriores: 170-171
    Museo del Arte e Historia: 156

Riobamba

    Archivo de la Gobernación: 202
    Archivo de la Parroquia: 203
    Archivo Municipal: 200-201

Sicalpa (Tungurahua)

    Archivo de la Parroquia: 203

Tisaleo (Tungurahua)

    Archivo de la Parroquia: 203

Tungurahua

    Archivo de la Gobernación: 201
    Archivo de la Jefatura Política: 201
    Archivo de la Parroquia de San Bartolomé: 203

ENGLAND

London

    Museo Británico: 10, 39

FRANCE

Paris

    Biblioteca Nacional: 39

ITALY

Rome

    Archivo del Vaticano: 17

PERU

Arequipa

    Archivo de la Empresa Nacional de Ferrocarriles: 329
    Archivo de la Oficina de Estadística y Censos: 328-329
    Archivo de la Parroquia de Cayma (Cayma): 327
    Archivo de la Parroquia del Sagrario: 327
    Archivo de la Parroquia de San Antonio (Miraflores): 327
    Archivo de la Parroquia de Santa Marta: 327
    Archivo de la Parroquia de Yanahuara (Yanahuara): 327
    Archivo de la Sociedad Pública de Beneficencia: 329
    Archivo de la Universidad Nacional: 329
    Archivo del Convento de La Merced: 327
    Archivo del Convento de San Francisco: 327
    Archivo del Convento de Santo Domingo: 327
    Archivo del Seminario de San Jerónimo: 327
    Archivo de Mesa de Partes: 328
    Archivo Histórico Departamental: 222-223, 241, 258, 305, 325-327, 334
    Archivo Municipal: 222, 328
    Archivo Notarial: 284-299

Chiclayo

    Archivo Arzobispal: 263

Cuzco

    Archivo Arzobispal: 308, 310, 334
    Archivo de la Sala Capitular: 308, 310-311
    Archivo del Convento de La Merced: 233, 311
    Archivo del Convento de San Francisco: 311
    Archivo del Convento de Santo Domingo: 311
    Archivo Historico de la Universidad Nacional de Cuzco: 257, 308-310, 334; *see also* Archivo Histórico Departamental: 223, 257, 281, 305, 308-310, 334
    Archivo Histórico Departamental: 223, 257, 281, 305, 308-310, 334
    Museo del Arte Colonial: 311
    Museo Virreinal: 311

Huachipa

    Colección Rubén Vargas Ugarte: 226

Huancavelica

    Archivo Municipal: 223

La Libertad

    Archivo de la Cámara de Comercio, Agricultura, y Industria: 240
    Archivo Departamental: 305

Index 344

Lambayeque

    Archivo Notarial

Lima

    Archivo Arzobispal: 218, 220-221, 259, 280, 311, 332
    Archivo de la Cámara de Diputados: 333
    Archivo de la Corte Superior: 218
    Archivo de la Oficina Nacional de Estadística y Censo (ONEC): 242, 332
    Archivo de la Parroquia del Sagrario de la Iglesia Metropolitana: 221
    Archivo de la Parroquia de San Sebastián: 221
    Archivo de la Sociedad de Beneficencia de Lima: 241, 332
    Archivo del Banco Central de Reserva del Perú: 251, 333
    Archivo del Club Nacional: 249, 332
    Archivo del Fuero Agrario: 210, 231, 244-247, 251, 266, 281-283, 306-307
    Archivo del Ministerio de Economía y Finanzas: 332
    Archivo del Ministerio de Justicia, Culto, Instrucción, y Beneficencia: 303
    Archivo del Ministerio de Trabajo y Asuntos Indígenas: 261, 266-267, 304, 333
    Archivo de Manuel Bustamante de la Fuente: 266
    Archivo General de la Nación: 17, 210, 217-219, 223, 229-230, 233, 258, 262, 266, 280, 300-305, 312, 325-327, 332
    Archivo General del Ministerio de Relaciones Exteriores: 220, 311-312, 332
    Archivo Histórico de la Biblioteca Municipalidad: 333
    Archivo Histórico del Ministerio de Hacienda y Comercio: 219, 226, 232, 242, 280, 303-304, 332
    Archivo Nacional: see Archivo General de la Nación
    Biblioteca Central de la Universidad Nacional Mayor de San Marcos: 241, 251, 270, 333
    Biblioteca de Javier Prado: 250
    Biblioteca de la Universidad Nacional Agraria (La Molina): 242, 333
    Biblioteca de la Universidad Nacional de Ingeniería: 242, 333
    Biblioteca del Arq. Juan Gunther: 249
    Biblioteca del Dr. Félix Denegri Luna: 226, 242, 249
    Biblioteca del Instituto Riva Agüero de la Pontífica Universidad Católica: 242, 251, 270, 333
    Biblioteca del Ministerio de Relaciones Exteriores del Perú: 220
    Biblioteca Municipal: 222
    Biblioteca Nacional: 219-220, 222, 226, 229-230, 232, 241, 249-250, 253, 258-260, 266, 280, 311, 318n., 333
    Biblioteca Pública de la Cámara de Diputados: 241
    Casa del Pueblo (APRA): 254
    Centro de Documentación Agraria: see Archivo del Fuero Agrario
    Centro de Estudios Históricos-Militares: 253
    Confederación Nacional Agraria: 334
    Ministerio de Agricultura: 304
    Ministerio de Fomento: 266
    Ministerio de Justicia: 304
    Ministerio de Trabajo: 265
    Ministerio de Salud Pública, Trabajo, y Previsión Social: 266, 304

Piura

    Archivo Histórico Departamental: 262, 305

Tacna

    Archivo Histórico Departamental: 305

Trujillo

    Archivo Arzobispal: 210, 221, 226, 262, 280, 313-314, 316-324, 334
    Archivo de la Corte Superior de Justicia: 232, 313-314
    Archivo de la Hacienda Casa Grande: 216
    Archivo de la Sociedad de Beneficencia Pública: 313-314
    Archivo de la Universidad Nacional: 313, 315
    Archivo del Cabildo Eclesiástico: 321
    Archivo Histórico Departamental: 262, 281, 305, 334
    Archivo Municipal: 313-315
    Archivo Notarial: 313-314
    Archivo Jara: 262
    Biblioteca de la Universidad Nacional: 251

SPAIN

Madrid

    Archivo de las Cortes Españolas: 217
    Archivo Histórico Nacional: 143, 214-217
    Biblioteca de la Real Academia de la Historia: 216
    Biblioteca del Palacio Real: 216-217
    Biblioteca Nacional: 216-217

Sevilla

    Archivo General de Indias: 17, 44n., 67n., 141, 143, 181, 184, 212-215, 311

Simancas

    Archivo General de Simancas: 17, 143, 215

SWEDEN

Goteborg

    Museo de Goteborg: 39

UNITED STATES

Bloomington (Indiana)

    Lilly Library: 226

New Haven (Connecticut)

    Yale University Library: 226, 252

Ithaca (New York)

    Cornell University: 265-266

Philadelphia (Pennsylvania)

   Rosenbach Foundation: 227

Salt Lake City (Utah)

   Genealogical Society of the Church of Jesus Christ of Latter-Day Saints: 210, 330-331

Washington, D. C.

      Academy of American Franciscan History: 50
      Agencia Estadounidense para el Desarrollo Internacional (AID): 13
      Federal Records Center: 255
      Library of Congress: 222, 226, 251
      Library of the Department of Agriculture: 252
      National Archives: 255

RAYMOND H. FOGLER LIBRARY
DATE DUE

BOOKS ARE SUBJECT TO
RECALL AFTER TWO W...